T0271353

Presenteeism at Work

Coming to work sick may do more harm than staying home – for the employee, the team, and the firm. Whilst the cost of absenteeism in organizations has been widely acknowledged and extensively examined, the counter-issue of 'presenteeism' has only recently attracted scholarly attention as a phenomenon that harms employee wellbeing, disrupts team dynamism, and damages productivity. This volume brings together leading international scholars from diverse scientific backgrounds, including occupational psychology, health, and medicine, to provide a pioneering review of the subject. International in scope, the collection incorporates both Western and East Asian perspectives, making it an informative resource for multinational companies seeking to formulate human resource strategies and better manage their culturally diverse workforce. It will also appeal to scholars and graduate students researching human resource management, organization studies, organizational health, and organizational psychology.

CARY L. COOPER is 50th Anniversary Professor of Organizational Psychology and Health at Manchester Business School. He is the author/editor of over 160 books, including the *Downsizing: Is Less Still More?* (Cambridge, 2012) and *Building More Effective Organizations* (Cambridge, 2007), as well as over 100 book chapters. He has written over 400 scholarly articles for academic journals, and is a frequent contributor to national newspapers, TV, and radio. He is currently Founding Editor of the *Journal of Organizational Behavior* and Co-editor of the *Journal of Organizational Effectiveness*, and President of the British Academy of Management and the CIPD.

LUO LU is Distinguished Professor in the Department of Business Administration, National Taiwan University, Taiwan. She has been awarded the Distinguished Research Award by the Ministry of Science and Technology, Taiwan. She has published more than 180 papers in referred journals and is the series editor, author, and co-author of more than 20 books and book chapters.

CAMBRIDGE COMPANIONS TO MANAGEMENT

SERIES EDITORS:

Professor Cary L. Cooper CBE, University of Manchester
Professor Jone L. Pearce, University of California, Irvine

ADVISORY BOARD:

Professor Kim Cameron, University of Michigan
Professor Michael Hitt, Texas A&M University
Professor Peter McKiernan, University of Strathclyde
Professor James Quick, University of Texas
Professor Dean Tjosvold, Lingnan University, Hong Kong

Cambridge Companions to Management provide an essential resource for academics, graduate students and reflective business practitioners seeking cutting-edge perspectives on managing people in organizations. Each *Companion* integrates the latest academic thinking with contemporary business practice, dealing with real-world issues facing organizations and individuals in the workplace, and demonstrating how and why practice has changed over time. World-class editors and contributors write with unrivalled depth on managing people and organizations in today's global business environment, making the series a truly international resource.

TITLES PUBLISHED

Brief, *Diversity at Work*
Cappelli, *Employment Relations*
Cooper, Pandey, and Quick, *Downsizing*
Pearce, *Status in Management and Organizations*
Reb and Atkins, *Mindfulness in Organizations*
Saunders, Skinner, Dietz, Gillespie, and Lewicki, *Organizational Trust*
Sitkin, Cardinal, and Bijlsma-Frankema, *Organizational Control*
Smith, Bhattacharya, Vogel, and Levine, *Global Challenges in Responsible Business*
Sparrow, Scullion, and Tarique, *Strategic Talent Management*
Tjosvold and Wisse, *Power and Interdependence in Organizations*

Presenteeism at Work

Edited by
CARY L. COOPER
University of Manchester
LUO LU
National Taiwan University

Shaftesbury Road, Cambridge CB2 8EA, United Kingdom

One Liberty Plaza, 20th Floor, New York, NY 10006, USA

477 Williamstown Road, Port Melbourne, VIC 3207, Australia

314–321, 3rd Floor, Plot 3, Splendor Forum, Jasola District Centre, New Delhi – 110025, India

103 Penang Road, #05–06/07, Visioncrest Commercial, Singapore 238467

Cambridge University Press is part of Cambridge University Press & Assessment, a department of the University of Cambridge.

We share the University's mission to contribute to society through the pursuit of education, learning and research at the highest international levels of excellence.

www.cambridge.org
Information on this title: www.cambridge.org/9781107183780

DOI: 10.1017/9781316874868

First published 2018

A catalogue record for this publication is available from the British Library

Library of Congress Cataloging-in-Publication data
Names: Cooper, Cary L., editor. | Lu, Luo, editor.
Title: Presenteeism at work / edited by Cary L. Cooper, Luo Lu.
Description: New York : Cambridge University Press, 2018. | Series: Cambridge companions to management
Identifiers: LCCN 2018010108 | ISBN 9781107183780 (hardback)
Subjects: LCSH: Organizational behavior. | Work-life balance. | Personnel management. | BISAC: BUSINESS & ECONOMICS / Human Resources & Personnel Management.
Classification: LCC HD58.7 .P734 2018 | DDC 331.25/6–dc23
LC record available at https://lccn.loc.gov/2018010108

ISBN   978-1-107-18378-0   Hardback
ISBN   978-1-316-63515-5   Paperback

Contents

Contributors

Gunnar Aronsson, PhD

Department of Psychology, Stockholm University

GUNNAR ARONSSON is a professor of work and organizational psychology in the Department of Psychology, Stockholm University. His main research area is work organization, stress, and health. He has published a large number of scientific articles on work, stress, recovery, health, sickness presenteeism and absenteeism. He is coauthor of the book *Work Without Boundaries – Psychological Perspectives on the New Working Life* (Wiley-Blackwell 2011). Recently he has participated in two large systematic reviews and meta-analyses on Work environment and depressive symptoms (2015) and on Work environment and burnout symptoms (2017), both published in *BMC Public health*.

Caroline Biron, PhD

Management Department, Laval University

CAROLINE BIRON is an associate professor of occupational health and safety management at Laval University, Quebec, Canada. She earned a Master's degree in psychology from Laval University and a PhD from Lancaster University Management School, United Kingdom. She is actively involved in several organizations to support and evaluate implementation of interventions to reduce stress, improve well-being, and organizational performance.

Petri Böckerman, PhD

Jyväskylä University School of Business and Economics, Labour Institute for Economic Research and IZA

PETRI BÖCKERMAN is a professor of health economics at Jyväskylä University School of Business and Economics. He received his doctoral degree in economics in 2003, having been researcher at the Labour Institute for Economic Research since 1996. Böckerman is a Research

Fellow of the Institute for the Study of Labor (IZA), scientific advisor to Yrjö Jahnsson Foundation, and Docent (Adjunct Professor) of the University of Tampere. His research interests are at the intersection of empirical health and labour economics. Böckerman's research has been published in journals such as *ILR Review, Journal of Applied Econometrics*, and *Journal of the Royal Statistical Society: Series A (Statistics in Society)*, among others.

Chih-Chieh Chen, PhD
Western Business School, Southwestern University of Finance and Economics

CHIH-CHIEH CHEN, PhD, is an associate professor of human resource management in the Western Business School, Southwestern University of Finance and Economics, China. He earned his PhD from Cardiff University, UK. Previously, he worked at Academia Sinica, National Taiwan University of Science and Technology and National Chung-Hsing University, Taiwan. His research interests include human resource management, cross-cultural management and business sustainability.

Cary L. Cooper, PhD
Manchester Business School, University of Manchester

CARY L. COOPER, PhD, is the 50th Anniversary Professor of Organizational Psychology and Health at Alliance Manchester Business School, University of Manchester. He is President of the British Academy of Management, Outgoing President of RELATE, President of the Institute of Welfare Officers, and immediate Past Chair of the Academy of Social Sciences. He has published many books and scholarly articles in the areas of occupational psychology, workplace stress and well-being, and work–life balance. He was knighted by the Queen in 2014 for his contribution to the social sciences.

Hsueh-Liang Fan, PhD
Department of Business Administration, Soochow University

HSUEH-LIANG FAN is an assistant professor in the Department of Business Administration at Soochow University, Taiwan. He received his doctoral degree from the Graduate Institute of Technology, Innovation and Intellectual Property Management, National Chengchi University. His research interests include innovation management, creativity, and innovation on both individual and team levels. His papers have appeared in the *Creativity Research Journal*, the *Journal of Creative Behavior*, and *Thinking Skills and Creativity*, among others.

Aristides I. Ferreira, PhD
Instituto Universitário de Lisboa (ISCTE-IUL), Business Research Unit (BRU-IUL)
ARISTIDES I. FERREIRA is an assistant professor at ISCTE-IUL, Portugal, where he is Director of the Master program in Human Resource Management and Organizational Consulting. He is also a researcher at the Business Research Unit in the same institute. He received his PhD in Psychology from the University of Minho, Portugal. His research interests include presenteeism, leadership, and creativity. His research work has appeared in journals such as *International Journal of Project Management, Journal of Business Research, International Journal of Human Resource Management*, and *Stress and Health*.

Patricia Fosh, PhD
China Centre (Maritime), Southampton Solent University
PATRICIA FOSH, PhD, is an Honourable Research Fellow in the China Centre (Maritime), Southampton Solent University. She earned her PhD from the University of Cambridge. Previously, she was Professor at London School of Economics and Politics, and she has also held academic positions at Bristol University, Cardiff University and Imperial College. Her research interests include human resource management in China, employment law and industrial relationships.

Pierre-Sébastien Fournier, PhD
Management Department, Laval University
PIERRE-SÉBASTIEN FOURNIER is a full professor and chair of the department of management at Laval University. His research interests focus on intergenerational transmission of knowledge, workload, and psychosocial risk. He has contributed to numerous scientific journals, books, and international conferences.

Eric Gosselin, PhD
Department of Industrial Relations, University of Quebec in Outaouais
ERIC GOSSELIN, PhD, is a full professor of work and organizational psychology at the Department of Industrial Relations at the University of Quebec in Outaouais. He is also a member of the Laboratory of

Psychoneuroendocrinological Analysis of Stress and Health (LAPS^2), where he conducts studies on the relation between stress and job performance. He completed a PhD in industrial relations at the University of Montréal as well as a postdoctorate at the University of Ottawa's School of Psychology. His research interests involve psychological health and stress management, assiduity at work, career management, and the dynamics underlying conflict episodes.

Gary Johns, PhD
Concordia University, Montreal and University of British Columbia
GARY JOHNS is Professor Emeritus of Management in the John Molson School of Business, Concordia University, Montreal, and Adjunct Professor in the Sauder School of Business, University of British Columbia. He has research interests in absenteeism, presenteeism, personality, work design, research methodology, and the impact of context on organizational behavior. He has published in *Journal of Applied Psychology, Academy of Management Journal, Academy of Management Review, Organizational Behavior and Human Decision Processes, Journal of Management, Personnel Psychology*, and *Journal of Occupational Health Psychology*.

Shu-Fang Kao, PhD
Department of Applied Psychology, Hsuan Chuang University, Taiwan
SHU-FANG KAO, PhD, National Taiwan University, Taiwan, is currently a professor in the Department of Applied Psychology, Hsuan Chuang University, Taiwan. Professor Kao's research interests are: indigenous psychology, stress and adjustment, positive psychology, and other personality/social psychological topics. Professor Kao has published extensively in referred journals and is the author of several books.

Maria Karanika-Murray, MSc, PhD
Department of Psychology, Nottingham Trent University
MARIA KARANIKA-MURRAY is a work psychologist and Associate Professor at Nottingham Trent University. Her research seeks to understand how workplaces that enable healthy and productive work can be developed, with a focus on workplace design, intervention evaluation, presenteeism, and older workers. Her work has been funded by the European Agency for Safety & Health at Work, Great Britain's Health & Safety Executive, the UK Economic & Social Research Council, Heart Research UK, and the European Commission.

Mouna Knani, PhD candidate
Management Department, Laval University
MOUNA KNANI completed her doctoral thesis at Laval University, Canada. Her main research interests center on burnout, presenteeism, well-being at work, and psychosocial risks. She has received doctoral scholarships from the Fonds de Recherche du Québec – Société et Culture (FRQSC) and the Institut de Recherche en Santé et en Sécurité du Travail (IRSST). She has contributed to several scientific journals and international conferences.

Cong Liu, PhD
Professor, Hofstra University
CONG LIU, PhD, is a professor at Hofstra University. Her major research interests focus on occupational health psychology, which concerns the application of psychology to improving the quality of work life and to protecting the safety, health, and well-being of workers. She has done cross-cultural/cross-national studies examining Chinese and American employees' job stress experiences, such as conflict with a supervisor, conflict with a coworker, workplace ostracism, organizational constraints, and challenge and hindrance stressors.

Luo Lu, DPhil
Department of Business Administration, National Taiwan University, Taiwan
LUO LU, DPhil, University of Oxford, UK, is currently the Distinguished Professor in the Department of Business Administration, National Taiwan University, Taiwan. Her major research interests are: culture and self, subjective well-being, stress and adjustment, work stress and organizational health, and other personality/social/IO psychological topics. She has been awarded the Distinguished Research Award by the Ministry of Science and Technology, Taiwan. She has published more than 180 papers in referred journals and is the series editor, author, and coauthor of more than 20 books and book chapters. She has served on several editorial boards as either an editor/associate editor or a board member.

Jie Ma, MBA
Hofstra University
JIE MA is currently a doctoral student in applied organizational psychology at Hofstra University, while working as an adjunct

professor in the Department of Psychology. His major research interests place emphasis on occupational health psychology and positive organizational psychology, with specific focus on the connections between challenge/hindrance demands and engagement, and how employees can survive and thrive out of these demands. He is also interested in interpersonal dynamics in the workplace, such as workplace conflict and interpersonal empowerment.

Staffan Marklund, PhD
Division of Insurance Medicine, Department of Clinical Neuroscience, Karolinska Institute
STAFFAN MARKLUND is a professor of work and health at the Karolinska Institute, Stockholm, Sweden. He finished his doctoral degree in sociology at Umeå University in 1975. He was a visiting research fellow at Harvard University, USA in 1983, at the University of New South Wales, Australia in 1986–7 and a visiting professor at York University, Canada in 1991–2. He was a professor at the National Institute for Working Life between 1999 and 2007. His main research has been on social welfare, sickness absence, and occupational health.

Luis F. Martinez, PhD
Nova School of Business and Economics – Universidade Nova de Lisboa
LUIS F. MARTINEZ is an assistant professor at Nova School of Business and Economics – Universidade Nova de Lisboa, and holds a PhD in Social and Behavioral Sciences from Tilburg University. He held a Visiting Scholar position at the MIT Sloan School of Management. His research interests include emotion and decision-making, consumer behavior and health at work. His research work has appeared in journals such as *Decision, Harvard Business Review, Cognition and Emotion, Journal of Business Research, Journal of Economic Psychology, International Journal of Human Resource Management*, and *Stress and Health*.

Daniel P. Meltzer, PhD
Hofstra University
DANIEL P. MELTZER, is a Special Assistant Professor of Psychology at Hofstra University. His research interests include factors that influence work motivation, as well as how employees can reduce and recover from work stress.

Mariella Miraglia, PhD
University of Liverpool Management School
MARIELLA MIRAGLIA is a lecturer in organizational behavior and human resource management at the University of Liverpool Management School. Her main research interests lie in the field of organizational behaviors, human resource management, and occupational health psychology, with a special focus on absenteeism and presenteeism, performance appraisal and management, job crafting, and self-efficacy. She has published in *Journal of Vocational Behavior, Journal of Occupational Health Psychology, Human Resource Management*, and *Human Relations*.

Tânia A. M. Nunes, MSc
L'Oréal, Portugal
TÂNIA A. M. NUNES is a human resources trainee at L'Oréal Portugal, giving support to different areas such as learning for development, HR communications and employer branding. She holds a Bachelor degree in psychological sciences from the University of Coimbra and a Master degree in social and organizational psychology from ISCTE – Instituto Universitário de Lisboa.

Yanxia Wang, PhD
School of Management, Lanzhou University
YANXIA WANG, PhD, finished her postdoctoral research program in Audencia Business School in France. She also graduated from Southwestern University of Finance and Economics, China. She studied as a visiting scholar in the University at Albany, State University of New York. Her research interests include organizational health, industrial organizational psychology, and corporate social responsibility.

Liu-Qin Yang, PhD
Portland State University
LIU-QIN YANG is an associate professor of psychology at Portland State University. She received her PhD in industrial and organizational psychology from the University of South Florida. Her research interests include occupational stress, motivation, workplace mistreatment, and quantitative methodologies. Recently, she has been working on projects focused on the role of affective shift in influencing worker motivation and productivity, interventions to prevent workplace mistreatment toward healthcare workers, and reliability issues in experience sampling research.

Foreword

The *Cambridge Companions to Management* series is pleased to bring Cary Cooper and Luo Lu's path-breaking *Presenteeism at Work* to your attention. Presenteeism is the appearance of working but not working: something that is an increasing concern, not only for workers and their organizations, but for their societies. The combination of cost pressures from globalization and information technology means that more people than ever before do not have the luxury of staying away from work and resting when they become ill. For example, fully one out of every five jobs in the United States is held by a worker under contract – meaning no sick pay (National Public Radio/Marist poll). That means that every day not working results in no income for the worker on that day, so millions of people continue to work even when their health is impaired. This is heart-wrenching for those who must work under these circumstances, but it is also costly to organizations, which are not getting the work for which they are paying, and for societies, because it spreads disease and contributes to higher health care expenses as people push themselves and so become more gravely ill. Yet, presenteeism is not just a phenomenon of increased work insecurity. As Aronsson and Markland demonstrate in Chapter 6, presenteeism is a problem even in countries with extensive social supports for workers, such as Sweden. Further, as this volume demonstrates, there are cultural pressures as well: in Chapter 3, Lu and Kao report how the cultural pressures in Confucian societies foster presenteeism despite years of national and organizational policy interventions designed to limit it.

This is a book of both breadth and depth. Cooper and Lu have gathered scholars from a wide variety of disciplines and countries together to help us understand what the causes and consequences of presenteeism are. Scholars in medicine, psychology, economics, and business from Europe, Asia, and North America bring their diverse perspectives and understandings of the different contexts to enrich our understanding of presenteeism. For example, in Chapter 4, Ma,

Meltzer, Yang, and Liu document the work contexts, personal circumstances, personality traits, and motives leading to presenteeism. Chapter 8, by Miraglia and Johns, presents compelling evidence that presenteeism leads to emotional exhaustion, burnout, mental ill-health, physical ill-health, and job dissatisfaction. Further, this is the first work to move significantly beyond the study of presenteeism as an individual phenomenon with consequences for the individual and the organization to consider larger questions of team performance, organization strategy, and societal well-being.

This innovative, international, and cross-disciplinary perspective on a relatively new and increasingly important subject is a good example of why the Companions series exists. Enjoy.

Series Editor
Jone L. Pearce
University of California, Irvine

Introduction

CARY L. COOPER AND LUO LU

The cost of absenteeism in organizational functioning has been widely acknowledged and extensively examined in the management disciplines of organizational behavior, organizational theory, and strategy (Cascio & Boudreau, 2011). Yet, its alleged flip side "presenteeeism" (working while sick) has only recently attracted scholarly attention as a byproduct of organizational restructuring in the wake of the global economic recession, and subsequently as a factor in explaining worsening employee well-being, loss of productivity, strained team dynamics, hampered implementation of business strategies, and depressed organizational functioning. In the past decade, the rapid advance of digital technologies, i.e., Information and Communication Technologies (ICT), has facilitated agile working and flexibility, but also fueled the "always on" culture (McDowall & Kinman, 2017), which may be more potent in Asian societies working in harmony with the social values of diligence. Alongside this global transformation of "work taking over life, any time anywhere," presenteeism may have ceased to be *just* a work issue: cultural forces, social factors, managerial practices, employees' self-concept, values, motivations, psychological resources will all conspire to make it into a sociocultural as much as an individual personal act (of attending work given the circumstance). Unfortunately, the existing work on presenteeism is scattered across a wide range of academic disciplines and under a variety of topics, lacking the coherence and comprehensiveness to address the complexity underlying the phenomenon. This pioneering volume thus aimed to collect and update the work of early starters in this emergent yet eclectic research field of "presenteeism and organizations" to inform scholars and practitioners about the powerful role presenteeism can play in explaining individual well-being, work attitudes, productivity, team dynamics, organizational performance, and management practices.

Charting a not very long history of the field, the study of presenteeism is first championed by Cooper (1996), who construed presenteeism

1

as when people are physically present in the workplace but are functionally absent. The succinct depiction of a prevailing phenomenon in the workplace quickly captures the imagination of the popular press as well as raising the awareness of academia. A subsequent article entitled "Presenteeism: At work – but out of it" in *Harvard Business Review* helps to further bring home the message of "hidden costs" of presenteeism to organizations to the executives and human resource managers (Hemp, 2004). Mirroring the early interest in absenteeism in management studies, presenteeism is initially examined for its possible associations with loss of productivity and reduced performance. For example, the medical field approaches presenteeism as "lost productive time," and focuses also on the detrimental effects of presenteeism on health, both immediately and over a longer term (e.g., Collins et al., 2005; Turpin et al., 2004). The state-of-the-art approach to presentation in this line of research still follows the same logic of controlling absenteeism to protect productivity. In a recent HR textbook chapter entitled "the hidden costs of absenteeism," Cascio & Boudreau (2011: 72) potently introduced presenteeism as a source of low productivity due to illness that needs to be treated via human resource management tools. Yet since the earlier start by the medical and public health scholars, studies of presenteeism have gathered momentum in the management and organization field, which focus more on the individual and organizational *correlates* of presenteeism, as well as its consequences, other than financial/productivity outcomes (e.g., Johns, 2010; 2011). The first meta-analysis on studies along this line of research presented a state-of-the-art summary of empirical findings encompassing a wide range of work and personal antecedents to both presenteeism and absenteeism (Miraglia & Johns, 2016).

Presenteeism could be costly as researchers have found that when employees come to work sick, they often demonstrate lower levels of performance and productivity, feeling more depressed and exhausted (Robertson & Cooper, 2011). Although presenteeism seems to diminish immediate absenteeism and demonstrate employee perseverance, in the long term, presenteeism causes more serious problems in employees' physical and mental health, thus incurring more damage to organizational functioning (Demerouti, Blanc, Bakker, Schaufeli & Hox, 2009; Lu, Lin & Cooper, 2013).

In addition to unraveling antecedents of presenteeism at the firm level (work contexts) and the individual level (personal circumstances, personality traits), divergent motives for attending work while ill have also attracted research efforts (Lu et al., 2013, see also Chapter 4, by Ma, Meltzer, Yang & Liu, in this book). Scarce but valuable longitudinal data further corroborate the "bad presenteeism" phenomenon, that is, sickness presenteeism leads to subsequent emotional exhaustion, burnout, mental ill-health, physical ill-health, and job dissatisfaction (Demerouti et al., 2009; Lu et al., 2013; see also Chapter 8, by Miraglia and Johns, in this book). The importance of presenteeism to work adjustment and employee well-being is reflected in the academic literature, popular press, and is the foundation of organizational interventions.

Given the prevailing nature of presenteeism in modern day work settings, its central place in employee behavior and popular awareness, the recent endeavors of research on the role of presenteeism on employee well-being, employee work engagement and organizational commitment, work ethics, career management, work team management, organizational restructuring and change, multinational company strategic implementation, and cross-cultural management are timely and important. From across the wide range of organization and management topics scholars are increasingly turning to presenteeism to account for empirical findings. These scholars, all focusing on differing problems, have come to the conclusion that the act of presenteeism is an important explanation of their empirical observations.

Yet these works remain scattered across the various scientific disciplines and management and organization sub-disciplines. The diversity of subfields in which presenteeism is introduced means that scholars working in these fields focus on their specific problems. While they find that presenteeism is informative in understanding their problems, they are yet to be made more aware of one another's work, so that we may deepen our understanding of presenteeism in organizations and across diverse cultures. What is more, the extant research on presenteeism has been atheoretical, and approaching it as merely an overt behavior, the explanatory power of presenteeism may thus be underestimated (Johns, 2010). Although there have since been some theory-building efforts in the field – for example, Cooper & Lu (2016) advocated delineating the underlying psycho-social mechanisms under the overarching framework of social cognitive theory (SCT), Miraglia & Johns (2016) proposed a two-path model – testable hypotheses are yet to be derived and tested. The lack of sustained theoretical conversation about the underlying psycho-social and/or team-organizational processes of presenteeism and integrative theoretical accounts for the antecedents, consequences, and variability of presenteeism in these disciplines means that sporadically directed research efforts are in need of better coherence and consolidation for the field to stride ahead.

Though the significance of presenteeism as a fact of modern day work life has been established with large-scale surveys in the developed economies of North America and Europe, research of presenteeism in non-Western countries is almost non-existent. The only exception is Quazi (2013) reporting three Singaporean studies of presenteeism. As employees in East Asia on average work much longer hours than do North Americans and Europeans, is presenteeism more prevalent in Asian countries than in the West? If so, are Asian employees compelled by the social norm of hard work to attend work yet just doing "face time"? More importantly perhaps, does presenteeism compounded with long working hours bring more damage to the well-being of East Asian workers than their Western counterparts? Answers to these queries will be informative for multinational companies in formulating their strategies and better managing their culturally diverse workforce.

The present volume brings together leading international scholars on presenteeism in diverse scientific disciplines. Part 1 explores general theoretical and methodological issues in the study of presenteeism, while situating it on the current global stage: cultural and economic. The three chapters also provide state-of-the-art reviews of the growing literature on presenteeism from different yet complimentary perspectives. Part 2 focuses on understanding the behavior of presenteeism, its driving forces within (individual motivation), and those in the environment (organizational attendance-pressure factors, macroeconomic factors). To reflect upon the initial groundbreaking interest in the field, the intricate dynamism of assiduity at work between presenteeism and absenteeism is also explored with a fresh, more contemporary insight. Part 3 attempts to understand the consequences of presenteeism, for individual well-being, stress, and adaptation, as well as team innovation. Part 4 zooms onto presenteeism in cultural contexts, specifically collectivistic (Chinese and Latino), in contrast to individualistic culture (European and North American, where most of the existing research has been conducted).

International scholars in this volume present the state-of-the-art research from all corners of the world and diverse cultural backgrounds. Synthesizing and integrating research on presenteeism in management and organization helps to build a panoramic view of presenteeism encompassing antecedents, mechanisms, and consequences, across multiple levels (e.g., cultural, organizational, individual). This volume is the first to link presenteeism as an employee work behavior with work well-being, team process, and organization strategy. We hope that this initiative will lead to the further development of this eclectic research field, and attracting an even wider audience of scholars' attention as well as practitioners' interest to the role of presenteeism in work well-being and organizational performance.

References

Cascio, W. & Boudreau, J. (2011). *Investing in People: Financial Impact of Human Resource Initiatives*. (2nd ed.) Upper Saddle River, NJ: Pearson Education.

Collins, J. J., Baase, C. M., Sharda, C. E. et al. (2005). The assessment of chronic health conditions on work performance, absence, and total economic impact for employers. *Journal of Occupational and Environmental Medicine*, 47, 547–557.

Cooper, C. (1996). Hot under the collar. *Times Higher Education Supplement*, 21 June.

Cooper, C. L. & Lu, L. (2016). Presenteeism as a global phenomenon: Unraveling the psychosocial mechanisms from the perspective of social cognitive theory. *Cross Cultural and Strategic Management*, 23(2), 216–231.

Demerouti, E., Le Blanc, P. M., Bakker, A. B., Schaufeli, W. B. & Hox, J. (2009). Present but sick: A three-wave study on job demands, presenteeism and burnout, *Career Development International*, 14(1), 50–68.

Hemp, P. (2004). Presenteeism: At work – but out of it. *Harvard Business Review*, 82 (October), 1–9.

Johns, G. (2010). Presenteeism in the workplace: A review and research agenda. *Journal of Organizational Behavior*, 31, 519–542.

Johns, G. (2011). Attendance dynamics at work: The antecedents and correlates of presenteeism, absenteeism, and productivity loss. *Journal of Occupational Health Psychology*, 16(4), 483–500.

Lu, L., Lin, H. Y. & Cooper, C. L. (2013). Unhealthy and present: Motives and consequences of the act of presenteeism among Taiwanese employees. *Journal of Occupational Health Psychology*, 18(4), 406–416.

McDowall, A. & Kinman, G. (2017). The new nowhere land? A research and practice agenda for the "always on" culture. *Journal of Organizational Effectiveness: People and Performance*, 4(3), 256–266.

Miraglia, M. & Johns, G. (2016). Going to work ill: A meta-analysis of the correlates of presenteeism and a dual-path model. *Journal of Occupational Health Psychology*, 21(3), 261–283.

Robertson, I. & Cooper, C. L. (2011). *Well-Being: Productivity and Happiness at Work*. Hampshire, UK: Palgrave MacMillan.

Turpin, R. S., Ozminkowski, R. J., Sharda, C. E. et al. (2004). Reliability and validity of the Stanford Presenteeism Scale. *Journal of Occupational and Environmental Medicine*, 46, 1123–1133.

Quazi, H. (2013). *Presenteeism: The Invisible Cost to Organizations*. London, UK: Palgrave Macmillan.

PART I

Situating Presenteeism on the Global Stage

Theoretical and Methodological Approaches

1 Presenteeism: An Introduction to a Prevailing Global Phenomenon

MARIA KARANIKA-MURRAY AND
CARY L. COOPER

In the current economic climate and the need "to achieve more with less," many organizations strive to maintain productivity and a competitive edge. This has a substantial impact on employee health, well-being, and work outcomes. One relatively recent phenomenon that is receiving increasing attention from a range of perspectives is presenteeism. Studies abound that not only show how prevalent presenteeism is across a range of occupations and sectors (Aronsson & Gustafsson, 2005; Baker-McClearn, Greasley, Dale & Griffith, 2010; Biron, Brun & Ivers, 2006; Vézina et al., 2011) but also position it as more costly than absenteeism (CIPD, 2016). This cost can take many forms, including financial impact, performance and productivity, and individual health and well-being (Cooper & Dewe, 2008; Kivimäki, Head, Ferrie, Hemingway, Shipley & Vahtera, 2005; Stewart, Ricci, Chee, Morganstein & Lipton, 2003b). The combination of high prevalence and high cost renders a comprehensive understanding of presenteeism and its damaging but also potentially beneficial outcomes necessary.

Because of its nature and impact, presenteeism has attracted substantial research attention from a range of disciplines and perspectives, including work psychology, business and management, occupational health, public health, and economics. Research on presenteeism has exploded in the last few years. A cursory search on Google Scholar of journal papers with "presenteeism" in the title alone yielded 236 publications in the last three years, 137 in the previous three years, and 72 in the three years before that, with the first studies emerging around 1996, when Cary Cooper (1996) first introduced the term.

This chapter offers an overview of current research and thinking on presenteeism. Because of the broad scope and high volume of available research, our exposition will necessarily be selective, focusing on the major issues that sketch the field. We draw from the rich evidence to explore

9

definitions, theoretical models, antecedents, and outcomes of presenteeism, and in the process pinpoint needs for future work.

Definitional Issues

The term presenteeism is used to describe "the phenomenon of
people turning up at their jobs despite medical complaints and ill-
health that would normally require rest and absence from work"
(Aronsson, Gustafsson & Dallner, 2000: 503; also see Aronsson &
Gustafsson, 2005; Vingård, Alexanderson & Norlund, 2004;
Hemp, 2004; Johns, 2008). Cooper (1996: 15) first defined presenteeism as: "being at work when you should be at home either
because you are ill or because you are working such long hours that
you are no longer effective" – essentially describing a combination of
physical presence and functional incapacitation in the workplace.
Johns (2010) offered a more concise definition of presenteeism as
"showing up for work when one is ill."

The proliferation of definitions that have been offered reflect two
main perspectives on presenteeism (Johns, 2010). Broadly speaking,
European scholars tend to focus on presenteeism as the behavior of
attending work when one is sick and an outcome of job and occupational factors, whereas US scholars tend to be more concerned about
productivity loss due to health problems (Schultz & Edington, 2007;
Burton et al., 2004). Juxtaposed to the European perspective that
defines presenteeism as "the phenomenon of people, despite complaints
and ill health that should prompt rest and absence from work, still
turning up at their jobs" (Aronsson, Gustafsson & Dallner, 2000: 503;
also see Dew, Keefe & Small, 2005; and Johansson & Lundberg,
2004), is the definition offered by the American College of
Occupational and Environmental Medicine of presenteeism as "the
measurable extent to which health symptoms, conditions and diseases
adversely affect the productivity of individuals who choose to remain at
work" (Chapman, 2005: 2). The different approaches can be understood by looking at broader societal and economic differences. For
example, the health care system in the USA places more weight on
private health insurance, whereas in Europe there has been a historical
emphasis on social care, with governments providing health insurance,
and a focus on wellness and rehabilitation into work (e.g., Ridic,
Gleason & Ridic, 2012). The range of definitions reflects the range of

disciplinary perspectives as well as research and practice priorities. As Ashby & Mahdon (2010: 13) note, "it is important to highlight that the concept of presenteeism has been understood in different ways." A third but not popular perspective views presenteeism as "the tendency to stay at work beyond the time needed for effective performance of the job" (Simpson, 1998: S.38).

Consensus is now emerging that presenteeism describes attending work when one is unwell. Consensus in the field is important for three reasons. First, defining the behavior of presenteeism (attending work when ill) in terms of its outcomes or consequences (performance loss) risks conflating cause and effect (Johns, 2010; Karanika-Murray & Biron, under review). Association is not causation and an observed relationship between poor health and productivity loss does not imply that poor health causes productivity loss; it is possible that third factor or factors can explain this association. Such definitional ambiguities are problematic in terms of measuring productivity loss, as in most cases it is difficult to know exactly when work is not being completed and there are numerous reasons for lost productivity which cannot be attributed to health.

Second, although different perspectives can offer rich and complementary understandings in an emerging field, they also often determine the research questions and possible solutions prescribed. The risk is that without regular integration of knowledge and consensus building, this process may lead to the field splitting. It is unclear, for example, how findings from studies that use different building blocks (definitions and measures) of presenteeism can be integrated. This is also a gap that welcomes future research.

Third, definitional consensus is important for ensuing the rigor of measurement tools. Existing measures focus on the frequency of presenteeism or job productivity and also range from a single item to multiple-item scales. A popular self-report single-item measure of presenteeism, developed by Aronsson & Gustafsson (2005), asks respondents to indicate the frequency of attending work when ill within a recent time window (Hansen & Andersen, 2008; Johansson & Lundberg, 2004; Munir et al., 2009). Measures of presenteeism as the extent to which ill-health interferes with job productivity (productivity loss) reflect a number of cognitive, emotional, and behavioral aspects of accomplishing work, with reference to being ill.

Examples include the Work Limitations Questionnaire (WLQ), the Health and Work Performance Questionnaire (HPQ), the Stanford Presenteeism Scale (SPS-34 and SPS-13), the Work Productivity Short Inventory (WPSI), the Work and Health Interview (WHI), the Health and Labor Questionnaire (HLQ), and the Work Productivity and Activity Impairment Questionnaire (WPAI) (Schultz & Edington, 2007). Most popular of these are the WLQ and HPQ, both of which have strong validity and reliability and have been used in a variety of workplace settings, occupations, and health conditions (e.g., Leoppke Taitel, Haufle, Parry, Kessler & Jinnett, 2009; Schultz & Edington, 2007).

Finally, objective assessment of productivity loss has also been attempted, such as using organizational records to assess the decrease in productivity associated with health problems in a sample of telephone customer-service employees (Burton, Conti, Chen, Schultz & Edington, 1999). Although it is not our aim to review available measures of presenteeism (for a comprehensive review, see Cyr & Hagen, 2007; Schultz & Edington, 2007), it is important to note that different definitions and approaches can lead to a range of measures of presenteeism and that inconsistent measurement is not favorable to the needed integration of knowledge in the field.

Although pluralism in research is a useful and desirable way to kick-start research in any field, it can also inhibit integration of knowledge. In practical terms, agreeing a common language is essential for integrating current insights and developing solutions that can help employers and employees to address presenteeism. In the case of presenteeism, the risks that too many diverse perspectives may bring are multiplied when we consider its substantial costs for individual health and performance and for organizational efficiency and productivity.

Further Issues: Understanding Illness, Attendance and Related Decisions

The definition of presenteeism as "showing up for work when one is ill" (Johns, 2010) raises some additional considerations: (1) what does illness mean, (2) what does attending work mean, and (3) by what criteria do individuals decide whether to attend work when they are ill?

Could a deeper understanding of presenteeism, perhaps by type of illness or type of attendance, shed more light into how presenteeism is enacted? Here we explore these questions and in this way also hope to ignite further research.

Facets of Illness

The Oxford dictionary defines illness as "a disease or period of sickness affecting the body or mind." This intimates four dimensions of illness: the occurrence (a disease) of occasional or episodic illness, a temporal dimension (period of sickness) which may imply acuteness or chronicity, and two facets of illness (physical or mental). Johns (2010) distinguishes between episodic, acute, and chronic conditions, whereas Gosselin & Lauzier (2010; in Gosselin, Lemyre & Corneil, 2013) differentiate between occasional and chronic illness and between physical and psychological health. Garrow (2016) suggests that when considering the support that individuals (or their line managers) may need to manage presenteeism we should take into account the severity, duration, and frequency of a disease. "Illness", therefore, is not a unidimensional construct.

Understanding the nature of illness is essential for understanding its impact on work outcomes and the mechanisms through which presenteeism behavior can lead to different work outcomes. For example, compared to psychological or mental ill-health, physical ill-health affects functional capacity, concentration, or decision-making differently, and in this way places different demands on the individual. Aligning the nature of the illness with the job tasks can help to identify (1) the work limitations faced in each case, (2) what one can do within these limitations and how he or she can remain involved in work, (3) whether presenteeism is an appropriate attendance behavior, and (4) what support and resources one may need to continue to be at work or to facilitate return to work and recovery. In a recent study, Gosselin, Lemyre & Corneil (2013: 82) found that "the specific nature of the illness has a marked impact on the decision process leading to either presenteeism or absenteeism." Specifically, they found that some health conditions, depending on their symptoms and controllability, led to presenteeism, whereas others, more debilitating conditions, led to absenteeism. Therefore, it is important to understand what illness means (or how it is perceived and experienced by the individual) and how it is linked to presenteeism behavior.

To Attend or to Absent

The second consideration relates to attendance behavior and specifically what type of response may be appropriate for different types of illness or the type or degree of debilitation from illness. At the two extremes, we have total absence during illness and regardless of the nature of the illness. In reality, complete absence for the duration of the illness spell may be neither feasible nor advisable. For a range of reasons, individuals may decide to remain involved with work tasks during illness, i.e., engage in presenteeism behavior. Of course, some attendance in the face of illness may be more desirable than complete absence, as is implies some involvement with work, some less intensive or demanding tasks being completed, and some, albeit reduced, productivity (Karanika-Murray & Biron, under review). In reality, however, there is evidence that the costs and productivity loss associated with presenteeism are greater than those of absenteeism (Goetzel, Hawkins, Ozminkowski & Wang, 2003; Hemp, 2004; Schultz & Edington, 2007).

Despite commonality between the two behaviors, and with the exception of very few conceptual papers that examine them in tandem, "absenteeism and presenteeism have developed along parallel paths without meeting despite being tied to a single decision" (Halbesleben, Whitman & Crawford, 2014: 13). The alternative to the two extremes is well-managed attendance during illness as a way to facilitate gradual return to work. As note, Whether one attendance behavior is more appropriate than another may depend on the interaction between type of illness and job tasks (Karanika-Murray & Biron, under review). For example, if the illness affects functional capacity (e.g., a broken leg) but the job tasks are mainly of a cognitive nature, do not require physical exertion, and can be performed from home, then presenteeism can help to achieve work tasks and also support rehabilitation. If, on the other hand, the illness affects psychological or mental capacity (e.g., the flu) and the nature of the work requires decision-making or face-to-face interaction with clients, then complete absence from work or temporary adjustment of the intensity or nature work demands would be advisable. In summary, and without venturing into a discussion on the management of presenteeism, the nature of the illness and nature of work tasks may require a different attendance response. Complete absenteeism and complete presenteeism are only two options to be considered, but always in light of the health condition and the work requirements.

Discretionary or Compelled Presenteeism

The final consideration relates to the process that leads to the decision to engage in presenteeism behavior. Such an enacted decision is grounded in the individuals' consideration of his or her current circumstances, including health limitations and work tasks but also broader contextual factors. As Garrow (2016: 2) notes, "decisions on whether to 'present' or 'absent' are, however, rarely based on simple health/task information. Other factors (both organizational and personal) come into play." At the individual level, people tend to ignore ill-health symptoms, ignore doctors' orders, and self-medicate (Kivimäki et al., 2005). At the same time, even seemingly irrational or risky decisions may have adaptive purposes (Mellers, Schwartz & Cooke, 1998). Individual action cannot be viewed in isolation from broader situational and contextual influences (Morgeson & Hofmann, 1999), which is especially true in the case of presenteeism. Garrow (2016: 2) also notes that "the relative dominance of these drivers is heavily context-dependent although evidence suggests that work factors tend to be more important." Therefore, it is important to understand how an one's decision-making processes around being present or absent during illness are influenced by the broader context.

Furthermore, there is also the question of how free one is to choose between presenteeism and absenteeism. For example, punitive attendance policies and procedures (Baker-McClearn et al., 2010), or line managers' misconception and misapplication of attendance and return to work procedures, or a workplace culture that encourages attending work at all costs (Dew et al., 2005) may cultivate presenteeism, even at the point where individuals substitute presenteeism for absenteeism (Caverley et al., 2007). Viewed from the lens of volitional behavior, the range of factors leading to presenteeism can be divided into discretionary or "voluntary" (e.g., work engagement) and compelled or "involuntary" (e.g., attendance policies, job insecurity). The latter may be at least as prevalent as the former, with presenteeism cases linked to involuntary causes being as high as 54 percent (Biron, Brun & Ivers, 2006). In the same vein, Baker-McClearn et al. (2010) define two types of presenteeism: institutionally-mediated presenteeism and personally-mediated presenteeism. Therefore In short, it is important to distinguish between presenteeism behavior that is "voluntary" and based on personal choice, of course within the boundaries of illness and work, and presenteeism behavior that an individual enacts because they feel pressured to attend work even if their health may suffer.

Conceptual Work on Presenteeism

In contrast to empirical research, conceptual work on presenteeism that can helpfully explain the "how" and "why" of the phenomenon and that systematically integrates empirical research is sparse. In other words, the volume of theorizing into presenteeism to date is disproportionately small in comparison to the empirical research. Two main groups of theoretical models have been developed, one focusing on the decision process behind presenteeism and the other on the determinants of presenteeism.

The model of illness flexibility (Johansson & Lundberg, 2004) suggests that attendance requirements (the negative consequences that employees face due to absence) and adjustment latitude (modifications in the workload of sick employees) are key determinants of both sickness attendance (presenteeism) and absence. Using survey data from 4924 workers, they found partial support for the associations between adjustment latitude and attendance requirements with work behaviors, such that high attendance requirements increased the probability of attending work whilst ill (adjustment latitude was not associated with presenteeism). Aronsson & Gustafsson (2005) suggested that presenteeism is an outcome of a decision process on whether to go to work or not. They also suggested that there are two different types of attendance demands that influence sickness presenteeism: personally related factors such as one's financial situation and individual boundarylessness. Boundarylessness is linked to work factors such as control over pace of work, replaceability, sufficient resources, time pressure, and conflicting demands. Expanding on Aronsson & Gustafsson (2005), Hansen & Andersen (2008) outlined the impact of organizational and individual factors in the behavior choice process. Johns's (2010) integrated model states that a health event triggers a choice between presenteeism and absenteeism. It also identifies the factors that influence this choice and consequently the occurrence of absenteeism and presenteeism behavior as the work context (e.g., ease of replacement, absence policy, or job demands) and individual factors (e.g., personality or work attitudes). It is important here to clarify the nature of this "choice" since, as noted earlier, presenteeism can have discretionary or involuntary undertones. As an extension of this work, Miraglia & Johns (2016) proposed a more elaborate dual-path model which views job attitudes and health as the mediators of the range of personal and work-related factors that lead to presenteeism or absenteeism.

These models concur on three fronts: (1) positing presenteeism behavior as an outcome of a decision process, (2) highlighting the relational dynamics between presenteeism and absenteeism, and (3) advancing the interaction between illness, individual factors, and work-related factors as decision-making and behavior levers. The notion of adjustment latitude, whether implicit or explicit, is important here as it can help to accommodate the needs of the individual vis-à-vis the requirements of the job and the nature of the illness. In this way, adjustment latitude can help to balance the range of pressures and determinants of presenteeism in order to support individual health and performance.

In terms of determinants of presenteeism, a range of typologies have been offered. Aronsson & Gustafsson (2005) described two types of attendance demands that influence presenteeism: personal factors (e.g., financial situation and individual boundarylessness) and work factors (e.g., control over pace of work, replaceability, sufficient resources, time pressure and conflicting demands). Biron & Saksvik (2009) organized the determinants of presenteeism into work-related (e.g., difficulty in being replaced), dispositional (e.g., guilt and pressure factors), and situational (e.g., financial insecurity). Baker-McClearn et al. (2010) summarized the workplace factors that influence an individual's decision to either attend or be absent from work when ill as personal motivations (e.g., loyalty to own professional image) and workplace pressures (e.g., workplace culture). Similarly, Johns's (2010) dynamic integrated model suggests that the choice between presenteeism and absenteeism relies on evaluations of the work context (e.g., ease of replacement, absence policy, job demands) and individual factors (e.g., personality and work attitudes). Gosselin, Lemyre & Corneil (2013) proposed an integrated model of the determinants of presenteeism and absenteeism behavior, incorporating the influence of health problems, demographic characteristics, individual factors, and organizational factors. Finally, Miraglia & Johns (2016) highlighted pressure factors such as high personal or professional obligations to work, and motivational factors such as pleasure derived from work and job satisfaction.

Common in these typologies is the suggestion that there are multiple levels of determinants of presenteeism behavior and that these operate synergistically rather than in isolation. It is also worth noting that "work-related factors seem to be slightly more important than personal circumstances or attitudes in determining people's 'decision' to go ill at work (Hansen & Andersen, 2008: 956), but also that "the relatively low explanatory power of these combined factors suggests that there are still many unknowns in this field of research" (Hansen & Andersen, 2008: 956).

At the time of writing this chapter, published conceptual work on presenteeism has tended to focus predominantly on understanding the process by which a range of factors determine the behavior, but very little attention has been invested in understanding the outcomes of presenteeism. Empirical work has mirrored this, as it has tended to focus on categorizing the determinants of presenteeism, essentially viewing it as static end-behavior (Karanika-Murray, Pontes, Griffiths & Biron, 2015). As a result, we have little insight into the psychological mechanisms and psychological processes that drive presenteeism behavior (Cooper & Lu, 2016; Karanika-Murray et al., 2015) and its outcomes for individuals and organizations. Indeed, for their review, Vingård, Alexanderson & Norlund's (2004: 216) identified merely eight studies on the consequences of sickness presenteeism for the employer but failed to identify any empirical evidence focusing on its consequences for the individual, concluding that "[t]he current body of scientific literature does not provide sufficient evidence to draw conclusions on the consequences of sickness presence." This observation still holds today.

Considering how deleterious presenteeism can be to employee health (in terms of future ill-health, well-being, or sickness absence, to name a few) and costly to organizations (in terms of productivity loss, replacement costs, colleague morale, for example) and the importance of understanding its impact in order to develop ways to mitigate deleterious effects, this lack of conceptual attention on outcomes and the mechanisms that drive presenteeism is rather odd. There are two exceptions that we are aware of at the time of writing. Karanika-Murray et al. (2015) proposed that presenteeism is a combination of physical presence and psychological absence, tapping into the notion of presenteeism as working at reduced capacity. They offered empirical evidence showing that motivational states (work engagement and work addiction) fully mediate the relationship between presenteeism behavior and job attitudes (job satisfaction), viewing presenteeism as a determinant rather than end-behavior. In addition, Cooper & Lu (2016) developed the social cognitive model of presenteeism as an exploration of the possible psychosocial mechanisms that drive presenteeism behavior. They outlined how self-efficacy and outcome expectancy together impact on goal setting, which, in turn, impacts on presenteeism behavior and subsequently attainment of performance goals. In the process, their model also considers the influence of both person and contextual variables. This is one of the few dynamic models of presenteeism that can help to understand how decisions to attend work while ill are made and that also view presenteeism as one link in a longer chain of effects.

The models outlined here form a very small part of existing work on presenteeism. The field is still "markedly atheoretical" (Johns, 2010) and in need of conceptual development (Dickson, 2013). Investment in theorizing and viewing presenteeism as one part of a chain of effects is needed in order to organize the large volume of empirical studies, move beyond a singular focus on its prevalence and determinants, and enable a more comprehensive understanding of the phenomenon.

Empirical Research on the Antecedents of Presenteeism

Next, we summarize the research on possible antecedents of presenteeism behavior.

Financial pressures and job insecurity are among the most common reasons why people go to work despite being ill (Aronsson & Gustafsson, 2005; Bierla, Huver & Richard, 2013; Barnes, Buck, Williams, Webb & Aylward, 2008; Bergstrom, Bodin, Caverley, Cunningham & MacGregor, 2007; Hagberg, Lindh, Aronsson & Josephson, 2009; Prater & Smith, 2011; Widera, Chang & Chen, 2010). However, it is possible that job insecurity indicates other underlying factors associated with presenteeism including, for example, the norms and climate of the workplace. Depression has also been linked to overall work limitations and productivity loss (Burton, Pransky, Conti, Chin-Yu & Edington, 2004; McTernan, Dollard & LaMontagne, 2013). Job satisfaction is a strong predictor of the likelihood of attending work whilst ill (Aronsson & Gustafsson, 2005; Caverley et al., 2007; Krohne & Magnussen, 2011) even among those who experience chronic nonspecific musculoskeletal pain (de Vries, Brouwer, Groothoff, Geertzen & Reneman, 2011), although not all research studies have supported a positive link (Rosvold & Bjertness 2001). Work engagement too is closely associated with presenteeism (Admasachew & Dawson, 2011; Karanika-Murray et al., 2015). A number of job characteristics have also been implicated in presentee-ism, such as job control (Aronsson & Gustafsson, 2005; Alavinia, Molenaar & Burdorf, 2009; Gosselin et al., 2013). Biron, Brun, & Ivers (2006) found that lack of control was a determinant of presentee-ism but only for workers with benign health issues (for those reporting fewer than 9 days of presenteeism). Increased time pressure at work has been supported as the single most influential work-related factor in the decision to attend work when ill (Hansen & Andersen, 2008; Elstad & Vabø, 2008; Aronsson & Gustafsson, 2005). Finally, increased job demands are linked to increased likelihood of sickness presenteeism (Demerouti, Le Blanc, Bakker, Schaufeli & Hox, 2009; Kivimaki et al., 2005) and lower performance (Van den Heuvel, Geuskens, Hooftman, Koppes & Van den Bossche, 2010). Higher levels of presenteeism are associated with difficulties in staff replacement (Aronsson & Gustafsson, 2005; Biron et al., 2006; Biron & Saksvik, 2009; Dew et al., 2005; Jena, Baldwin, Daugherty, Meltzer & Arora, 2010; Widera et al., 2010) and jobs that involve higher levels of teamwork (Hansen & Andersen, 2008; Krohne & Magnussen, 2011) and specifically higher interdependence between small teams (Pauly, Nicholson, Polsky, Berger & Sharda, 2008), and an increased responsibility at work (Dellve, Hadzibajramovic & Ahlborg, 2011; Gosselin et al., 2013), which prompt employees to continue to work when unwell. Employees who attend work whilst sick often do so because their colleagues are reliant on them and because they feel an obligation towards their team (Gosselin et al., 2013; McKevitt & Morgan, 1997). Finally, there is also research into employment contract, but this seems to be inconclusive, with some showing that employees who have a permanent employment contract are more likely to come to work whilst ill than temporary staff (Aronsson, Gustafsson & Dallner, 2000) and others showing no asso-ciation between employment type and presenteeism behavior (Aronsson & Gustafsson, 2005; Hansen & Andersen, 2008).

It should be noted that drawing conclusions on an individual phe-nomenon from panel data (on which some these studies are based) may obscure some of the mechanisms of presenteeism that more fine-grained examinations can offer. Furthermore, although correla-tional research highlights the wide range of work-related factors that can influence the decision to work while ill, it also only allows to identify rather than explain causal mechanisms. For example, if pressure to attend whilst sick is a potential mechanism, some of these factors can be viewed as salutogenic for performance and health (e.g., team cohesiveness, job satisfaction, engagement). Unfolding the psychological mechanisms by which these determinants lead to presenteeism behavior can be aided by examining moderation, mediation, and reciprocal effects. For example, experience has been found to moderate the relationship between presenteeism and performance, such that more experienced nurses tend to be less affected by presenteeism as they complete their work more accurately (Martinez & Ferreira, 2012).

Strongly implicated in presenteeism are also formal organizational policies and management practices. For example, flexible work policies allow employees who are unwell to adjust their work patterns and have a more manageable workload (Krohne & Magnussen, 2011), sick pay policies allow employees paid sick days (Irvine, 2011; Chatterji & Tilley, 2002; Heymann, Rho, Schmitt & Earle, 2010), whereas better work organization or scheduling allows for work reorganization and unplanned absence (McKevitt & Morgan, 1997) during ill-health.

Research into presenteeism also differentiates between formal organizational policies and workplace culture and climate. Salient differences between occupations in the incidences of presenteeism suggest that there may be variations in workplace cultures for presenteeism (Aronsson et al., 2000). A culture for presenteeism is grounded on employees' professional values such as being responsible for vulnerable groups of people (Johns, 2010) as the work on the prevalence of presenteeism in healthcare shows (e.g., Crout, Chang & Cioffi, 2005; Dew et al., 2005; Hackett & Bycio, 1996; Karimi, Cheng, Bartram, Leggat & Sarkeshik, 2015; Martinez & Ferreira, 2012; Warren, White-Means, Wicks, Chang, Gourley & Rice, 2011; Widera et al., 2010). Workplace norms that center on responsibility, a strong work ethic, loyalty to team members, and attendance can also lead to presenteeism (McKevitt & Morgan, 1997; Baker-McClearn et al., 2010; Dew et al., 2005; Simpson, 1998). Hansson, Boström and Harms-Ringdahl (2006) found that presenteeism levels were higher in organizations that expected employees to have strong work-duty norms even when they were ill (Dew et al., 2005; Vingård et al., 2004). There is also evidence that specific groups of employees are more prone and essentially form high-risk groups for presenteeism, highlighting circumstantial determinants of presenteeism that are specific to specific work groups. For example, higher levels of presenteeism have been detected among pregnant employees, whose fear of being considered as intellectually and physically inferior to their colleagues may lead them to higher levels of presenteeism, in this way putting their health in danger (Gatrell, 2011), blue collar workers, who may be more self-conscious about their job (in)security and experience higher "pressure to attend" than white-collar workers (De Vroome, 2006), and nurses, who when enacting presenteeism may experience a related reduction in performance, increasing the number of errors and further impacting patient safety (Martinez & Ferreira, 2012; Letvak, Ruhm & Gupta, 2012). Finally, presenteeism poses challenges in small and medium sized enterprises (SMEs), where the individual and economic consequences of presenteeism may be experienced more acutely than in larger organizations (Cocker et al., 2012, 2013). These challenges are attributable primarily to the size and structure of SMEs, impacting administrative, finance and human resource responsibilities (Rauch & Frese, 2007).

Corroborating the available conceptual models, empirical research on singular antecedents shows that presenteeism behavior is linked to an array of factors located at the individual, job, or organizational levels. Because presenteeism is highly responsive to the relationship between the individual and their work environment, it is an imperative to understand the interaction among factors at these levels that influence presenteeism decisions and behavior and the factors that moderate and mediate its effects on health and performance.

Empirical Research on the Outcomes of Presenteeism

Optimal health is important for good performance and quality of working life, whereas poor health can lead to counterproductive work behaviors. Next, we outline empirical research on the range of negative as well as positive outcomes of presenteeism.

Negative Outcomes

The volume of research on the negative outcomes of presenteeism is rich. The financial costs (Centre for Mental Health, 2011; Burton, Conti, Chen, Schultz & Edington, 2002; Levin-Epstein, 2005; CIPD, 2016; Cooper & Dewe, 2008; Stewart et al., 2003a, 2003b) of presenteeism for organizations tend to be ascribed to productivity loss (Goetzel, Hawkins, Ozminkowski & Wang, 2003). The consensus is that employees who are present at work when sick can experience decline in their overall performance (Biron et al., 2006; Cooper & Dewe, 2008; Meerding, Ijzelenberg, Koopmanschap, Severens & Burdorf, 2005; Van den Heuvel, Geuskens, Hooftman, Koppes & Van den Bossche, 2010).

Despite the fact that presenteeism is viewed as a precursor to decreased performance, there is surprisingly little empirical research on the relationship between the two. The available but also inconclusive research has highlighted a weak or nonexistent relationship between presenteeism and performance (Johns, 2011; Munir, Jones, Leka & Griffiths, 2005). Miraglia & Johns (2016: 14) emphasize the role of the supervisor who may perceive presenteeism as something positive, encourage it, and consequently "reward it, assessing performance more positively, and this could nullify any negative relationship between presenteeism and rated job performance." More research on the dynamic relationship between presenteeism and performance is needed.

The relationships between presenteeism, on the one hand, and physical ill-health and absenteeism, on the other, have also received substantial attention. Presenteeism can lead to a downward spiral of future health issues (Aronsson & Gustafsson, 2005; Bergström et al., 2009; Kivimäki et al., 2005). For example, Kivimäki and his colleagues (2000) found an association of sickness presence with coronary heart disease and higher prevalence of absence leave. Furthermore, present and ill employees may spread their illness to others in the workplace, potentially leading to future sickness absenteeism among colleagues (Irvine, 2011; Widera et al., 2010). Presenteeism is also a risk factor for future poor health and sickness absence two years later, even after adjustment for possible confounders at baseline (Taloyan et al., 2012). Cross-sectional studies also link presenteeism with concurrent sickness absenteeism (Aronsson & Gustafsson, 2005; Elstad and Vabo, 2008; Hansen & Andersen, 2008; Leineweber et al., 2012). Brouwer, van Exel, Koopmanschap & Rutten (2002) showed that 35 percent of employees experienced presenteeism before or after absenteeism, a finding which has also been observed in Danish (Hansen & Andersen, 2008), Nordic (Elstad & Vabo, 2008), and Canadian employees (Caverley et al., 2007).

Prospective studies also concur that presenteeism is a predictor of future sickness absenteeism (Bergström et al., 2009; Demerouti et al.,

2009). Although working whilst sick may temporarily reduce rates of sickness absence recorded, higher future sickness absence levels are likely (De Vroome, 2006; Taloyan et al., 2012; Janssens, Clays, De Clercq, De Bacquer & Braeckman, 2013). Using a follow-up period of 1.5 years, Hansen & Andersen (2009) revealed an association of sickness presence with long-term sickness absence of at least two weeks' duration and with spells lasting at least two months. Participants who had exhibited presenteeism more than six times in the pre-baseline year had a 74 percent higher risk of sickness absence for more than two months. Although the association was consistent for various symptoms and somatic conditions, it became weaker or non-significant for specific chronic conditions. In short, regular presenteeism is strongly linked to future long-term sickness absence (Hansen & Andersen, 2009) but this may depend on the specific health condition. Adjusting for previous sick leave and work-related variables, presenteeism becomes, with certainty, a critical predictor of higher future sickness absenteeism (Bergström et al., 2009; Hansen & Andersen, 2009; Kivimaki et al., 2005). For a more meticulous examination of the relationship between presenteeism and absenteeism it is important to consider the incidence and duration of sickness absence. Janssens et al. (2013) looked at different types of future sickness absence and found that high rates of presenteeism were associated with both long and short spells of sickness absence (of one to three days), moderate rates of presenteeism (two to five instances) were associated with long spells of sickness absence only for men, whereas high rates of presenteeism and high sickness frequency (at least three sick leave episodes) was demonstrated only among women.

Presenteeism has also been linked to low mental well-being and work ability (Gustafsson & Marklund, 2011). Taloyan et al. (2012) attributed the association between presenteeism and suboptimal health largely to a higher risk of emotional exhaustion. Similarly, presenteeism has been linked to reduced job satisfaction via affective-motivational states such as work engagement and work addiction (Karanika-Murray et al., 2015). There is strong evidence that the relationship between sickness absence and presenteeism may be due to burnout incurred from individuals working beyond their physical or mental capabilities (De Vroome, 2006). Burnout increases sickness absence, which in turn increases the risk of subsequent presenteeism.

Positive Outcomes

Although there is an implicit assumption that presenteeism is implicitly "bad" and inevitably deleterious for health and performance, there are also suggestions that presenteeism may not always be taxing. Rather, there are indications that presenteeism can sometimes be beneficial for performance, well-being, and return to work, contradicting views that it is a risk factor for absenteeism (cf. Bergström et al., 2009) and health (cf. Bergström et al., 2009; Kivimäki, Head, Ferrie, Hemingway, Shipley & Vahtera, 2005). Presenteeism can be beneficial for preventing accumulation of workload, gaining esteem from colleagues and managers (Vézina et al., 2011), and achieving a sense of accomplishment, gradual recovery or citizenship behavior (Miraglia & Johns, 2016).

Presenteeism can reduce negative psychosocial effects of short or long-term absence from work. In cases where the health problem is benign, presenteeism may be used as an attempt for individuals to maintain their work performance during an illness (Demerouti et al., 2009). Employees who show up at work during illness may also feel more in control over their workload (Biron & Saksvik, 2009). Furthermore, presenteeism may yield personal motivational benefits such as a sense of accomplishment that can help individuals adjust to work and cope with demands.

In terms of performance outcomes, working on less demanding tasks or with a lowered output can prevent the accumulation of work engendered by an absence, therefore potentially making the return to work less abrupt (Johns, 2008). As such, presenteeism may be a good strategy for maintaining well-being and facilitating recovery after long-term absence due to ill-health or injury (Ashby & Mahdon, 2010). For example, Howard, Mayer and Gatchel (2009) found that the presenteeism group of chronic disabling musculoskeletal disorder patients who followed a functional restoration program were more likely to return to fulltime work one year after the treatment, compared to the absentee group, and that presentees with chronic pain reported lower levels of depressive symptoms than absentees.

Presenteeism can also indirectly benefit teams and organizations because it can indicate commitment to colleagues and the organization, in turn create camaraderie within the workplace (Dew et al., 2005), impose less burden on colleagues who may otherwise be required to cover the absentee's work (Caverley et al., 2007), and generate approval from colleagues and managers (Biron & Saksvik, 2009). In addition, presenteeism may also lead to reduced economic deprivation that would otherwise be due to absence from work (Barnes, Buck, Williams, Webb & Aylward, 2008). Nevertheless, It is unknown whether these effects are short-term; the findings do not preclude longer-term exhaustion and depersonalization (see Demerouti et al., 2009), highlighting the possibility of concurrent positive and negative outcomes.

The identified range of positive outcomes of presenteeism supports the observation that, if well managed, presenteeism can be beneficial for longer term health and for maintaining performance and other desirable work outcomes (Karanika-Murray & Biron, in preparation). As Miraglia & Johns (2016: 16) write, "going to work while ill can represent a 'sustainable' choice." Occasions when presenteeism behavior can have beneficial outcomes render the understanding of this "tipping point" (Biron & Karanika-Murray, 2011) or "trade-off" (Miraglia & Johns, 2016) a worthwhile pursuit.

Conclusions

In this chapter we have examined the prevailing phenomenon of presenteeism, with the aim to unravel and provide answers to some of the major questions and issues in the field. In need of attention are: alignment of the measurement of presenteeism with accepted definitions, examination of how types of illness and attendance options co-determine presenteeism behavior, appreciation of its complex range of outcomes and, even more importantly, its potentially beneficial outcomes for health and performance, and integration of research evidence to decipher the "how," "why," and "when" of presenteeism behavior. We hope to have inspired needed innovative and rigorous research into presenteeism.

References

Admasachew, L. & Dawson, J. (2011). The association between presenteeism and engagement of National Health Service staff. *Journal of Health Services Research and Policy*, 16(suppl 1), 29–33.

Alavinia, S. M., Molenaar, D. & Burdorf, A. (2009). Productivity loss in the workforce: associations with health, work demands, and individual characteristics. *American Journal of Industrial Medicine*, 52(1), 49–56.

Aronsson, G. & Gustafsson, K. (2005). Sickness presenteeism: Prevalence, attendance-pressure factors, and an outline of a model for research. *Journal of Occupational and Environmental Medicine*, 47(9), 958–966.

Aronsson, G., Gustafsson, K. & Dallner, M. (2000). Sick but yet at work. An empirical study of sickness presenteeism. *Journal of Epidemiology and Community Health*, 54(7), 502–509.

Ashby, K. & Mahdon, M. (2010). *Why Do Employees Come to Work When Ill: An Investigation into Sickness Presence in the Workplace.* London: The Work Foundation.

Baker-McClearn, D., Greasley, K., Dale, J. & Griffith, F. (2010). Absence management and presenteeism: The pressures on employees to attend work and the impact of attendance on performance. *Human Resource Management Journal*, 20(3), 311–328.

Barnes, M. C., Buck, R., Williams, G., Webb, K. & Aylward, M. (2008). Beliefs about common health problems and work: A qualitative study. *Social Science & Medicine*, 67(4), 657–665.

Bergström, G., Bodin, L., Hagberg, J., Aronsson, G. & Josephson, M. (2009). Sickness Presenteeism Today, Sickness Absenteeism Tomorrow? A Prospective Study on Sickness Presenteeism and Future Sickness Absenteeism. *Journal of Occupational & Environmental Medicine*, 51(6), 1–10.

Bierla, I., Huver, B. & Richard, S. (2013). New evidence on absenteeism and presenteeism. *International Journal of Human Resource Management*, 24(7), 1536–1550.

Biron, C. & Karanika-Murray, M. (2011). Presenteeism and absenteeism: Critical points on a continuum. Paper presented at the 15th conference of the European Association of Work & Organisational Psychology, 25–28 May, Maastricht.

Biron, C. & Saksvik, P. Ø. (2009). Sickness presenteeism and attendance pressure factors: Implications for practice. *International Handbook of Work and Health Psychology*, 3.

Biron, C., Brun, J.-P. & Ivers, H. (2006). At work but ill: Psychosocial work environment and wellbeing determinants of presenteeism propensity. *Journal of Public Mental Health*, 5(4), 26–37.

Brouwer, W. B., Van Exel, N., Koopmanschap, M. & Rutten, F. (2002). Productivity costs before and after absence from work: As important as common? *Health Policy*, 61(2), 173–187.

Burton, W. N., Conti, D. J., Chen, C., Schultz, A. B. & Edington, D. W. (1999). The role of health risk factors and disease on worker productivity. *Journal of Occupational and Environmental Medicine*, 41(10), 863–877.

Burton, W. N., Conti, D. J., Chen, C., Schultz, A. B. & Edington, D. W. (2002). The economic burden of lost productivity due to migraine headache: A specific worksite analysis. *Journal of Occupational and Environmental Medicine*, 44(6), 523–529.

Burton, W. N., Pransky, G., Conti, D. J., Chen, C. & Edington, D. W. (2004). The association of medical conditions and presenteeism. *Journal of Occupational and Environmental Medicine*, 46(6), S38–S45.

Caverley, N., Cunningham, J. B. & MacGregor, J. N. (2007). Sickness presenteeism, sickness absenteeism, and health following restructuring in a public service organization. *Journal of Management Studies*, 44(2), 304–319.

Centre for Mental Health, J. (2011), Managing Presenteeism: A Discussion Paper. Centre for Mental Health & Business in The Community. Retrieved from www.centreformentalhealth.org.uk/Handlers/Download.ashx?ID MF=e10f060c-4cb0-439e-9216-f80426b12d57.

Chapman, L. S. (2005). Presenteeism and its role in worksite health promotion. *American Journal of Health Promotion*, 19(4), 1–8.

Chatterji, M. & Tilley, C. J. (2002). Sickness, absenteeism, presenteeism, and sick pay. *Oxford Economic Papers*, 54(4), 669–687.

CIPD (2016). Absence management survey 2016. Available online at: www.cipd.co.uk/knowledge/fundamentals/relations/absence/absence-management-surveys

Cocker, F., Martin, A., Scott, J., Venn, A. & Sanderson, K. (2012). Psychological distress and related work attendance among small-to-medium enterprise owner/managers: Literature review and research agenda. *International Journal of Mental Health Promotion*, 14(4), 219–236.

Cocker, F., Martin, A., Scott, J., Venn, A. & Sanderson, K. (2013). Psychological distress, related work attendance, and productivity loss in small-to-medium enterprise owner/managers. *International Journal of Environmental Research and Public Health*, 10(10), 5062–5082.

Cooper, C. (1996). Hot under the Collar. *Times Higher Education Supplement*, (June), 15.

Cooper, C. & Dewe, P. (2008). Well-being–absenteeism, presenteeism, costs and challenges. *Occupational Medicine*, 58(8), 522–524.

Cooper, C. & Lu, L. (2016). Presenteeism as a global phenomenon: Unraveling the psychosocial mechanisms from the perspective of social cognitive theory. *Cross Cultural & Strategic Management*, 23(2), 216–231.

Crout, L. A., Chang, E. & Cioffi, J. (2005). Why do registered nurses work when ill?. *Journal of Nursing Administration*, 35(1), 23–28.

Cyr, A. & Hagen, S. (2007). Measurement and quantification of presenteeism. *Journal of Occupational and Environmental Medicine*, 49 (12), 1299–1300.

De Vries, H. J., Brouwer, S., Groothoff, J. W., Geertzen, J. H. & Reneman, M. F. (2011). Staying at work with chronic nonspecific musculoskeletal pain: a qualitative study of workers' experiences. *BMC Musculoskeletal Disorders*, 12(1), 126.

de Vroome, E. (2006). Prevalence of sickness absence and "presenteeism." European Foundation for the Improvement of Living and Working Conditions (Eurofound). Available online at: www.eurofound.europa.eu/ observatories/eurwork/articles/working-conditions/prevalence-of-sickness -absence-and-presenteeism.

Dellve, L., Hadzibajramovic, E. & Ahlborg Jr, G. (2011). Work attendance among healthcare workers: prevalence, incentives, and long-term consequences for health and performance. *Journal of Advanced Nursing*, 67(9), 1918–1929.

Demerouti, E., Le Blanc, P. M., Bakker, A. B., Schaufeli, W. B. & Hox, J. (2009). Present but sick: A three-wave study on job demands, presenteeism and burnout. *Career Development International*, 14(1), 50–68.

Dew, K., Keefe, V. & Small, K. (2005). Choosing to work when sick: workplace presenteeism. *Social Science and Medicine*, 60, 2273–2282.

Dickson, V. V. (2013). Presenteeism among older workers (≥ 45years) with coronary heart disease: an integrative literature review. *Ohio Public Health Journal*, 6, 31–41.

Elstad, J. I. & Vabo, M. (2008). Job stress, sickness absence and sickness presenteeism in nordic elderly care. *Scandinavian Journal of Public Health*, 36(5), 467–474.

Garrow, V. (2016). Presenteeism: A review of current thinking. Institute for Employment Studies Report 507.

Gatrell, C. J. (2011). "I'm a bad mum": Pregnant presenteeism and poor health at work. *Social Science and Medicine*, 72(4), 478–485.

Goetzel, R. Z., Hawkins, K., Ozminkowski, R. J. & Wang, S. (2003). The health and productivity cost burden of the "top 10" physical and mental health conditions affecting six large US employers in 1999. *Journal of Occupational and Environmental Medicine*, 45(1), 5–14.

Gosselin, E., Lemyre, L. & Corneil, W. (2013). Presenteeism and absenteeism: Differentiated understanding of related phenomena. *Journal of Occupational Health Psychology*, 18(1), 75–86.

Gustafsson, K. & Marklund, S. (2011). Consequences of sickness presence and sickness absence on health and work ability: A Swedish prospective cohort study. *International Journal of Occupational Medicine and Environmental Health*, 24(2), 153–165.

Hackett, R. D. & Bycio, P. (1996). An evaluation of employee absenteeism as a coping mechanism among hospital nurses. *Journal of Occupational and Organizational Psychology*, 69(4), 327–338.

Halbesleben, J. R., Whitman, M. V. & Crawford, W. S. (2014). A dialectical theory of the decision to go to work: Bringing together absenteeism and presenteeism. *Human Resource Management Review*, 24(2), 177–192.

Hansen, C. D. & Andersen, J. H. (2008). Going ill to work – What personal circumstances, attitudes and work-related factors are associated with sickness presenteeism? *Social Science & Medicine*, 67(6), 956–964.

Hansen, C. D. & Andersen, J. H. (2009). Sick at work – a risk factor for long-term sickness absence at a later date? *Journal of Epidemiology and Community Health*, 63(5), 397–402.

Hansson, M., Boström, C. & Harms-Ringdahl, K. (2006). Sickness absence and sickness attendance – what people with neck or back pain think. *Social Science and Medicine*, 62(9), 2183–2195.

Hemp, P. (2004). Presenteeism: At work – but out of it. *Harvard Business Review*, 82(10), 49–58.

Heymann, J., Rho, H. J., Schmitt, J. & Earle, A. (2010). Ensuring a healthy and productive workforce: Comparing the generosity of paid sick day and sick leave policies in 22 countries. *International Journal of Health Services*, 40(1), 1–22.

Howard, K. J., Mayer, T. G. & Gatchel, R. J. (2009). Effects of presenteeism in chronic occupational musculoskeletal disorders: Stay at work is validated. *Journal of Occupational and Environmental Medicine*, 51(6), 724–731.

Irvine, A. (2011). Fit for work? The influence of sick pay and job flexibility on sickness absence and implications for presenteeism. *Social Policy & Administration*, 45(7), 752–769.

Janssens, H., Clays, E., De Clercq, B., De Bacquer, D. & Braeckman, L. (2013). The relation between presenteeism and different types of future sickness absence. *Journal of Occupational Health*, 55(3), 132–141.

Jena, A. B., Baldwin, D. C., Daugherty, S. R., Meltzer, D. O. & Arora, V. M. (2010). Presenteeism among resident physicians. *Journal of the American Medical Association*, 304(11), 1166–1168.

Johansson, G. & Lundberg, I. (2004). Adjustment latitude and attendance requirements as determinants of sickness absence or attendance: empirical tests of the illness flexibility model. *Social Science & Medicine*, 58(10), 1857–1868.

Johns, G. (2008). Absenteeism or presenteeism? Attendance dynamics and employee well-being, in S. Cartwright & C. L. Cooper (Eds.), *The Oxford Handbook of Organizational Well-Being* (pp. 7–30). Oxford: Oxford University Press.

Johns, G. (2010). Presenteeism in the workplace: A review and research agenda. *Journal of Organizational Behavior*, 31(4), 519–542.

Johns, G. (2011). Attendance dynamics at work: The antecedents and correlates of presenteeism, absenteeism, and productivity loss. *Journal of Occupational Health Psychology*, 16(4), 483.

Karanika-Murray, M. & Biron, C. (under review). *Development of a taxonomy of presenteeism behaviour: Balancing health and performance demands*.

Karanika-Murray, M., Pontes, H. M., Griffiths, M. D. & Biron, C. (2015). Sickness presenteeism determines job satisfaction via affective-motivational states. *Social Science and Medicine*, 139, 100–106.

Karimi, L., Cheng, C., Bartram, T., Leggat, S. G. & Sarkeshik, S. (2015). The effects of emotional intelligence and stress-related presenteeism on nurses' well-being. *Asia Pacific Journal of Human Resources*, 53(3), 296–310.

Kivimäki, M., Head, J., Ferrie, J. E., et al. (2005). Working while ill as a risk factor for serious coronary events: The whitehall II study. *American Journal of Public Health*, 95(1), 98–102.

Kivimäki, M., Vahtera, J., Pentti, J. & Ferrie, J. E. (2000). Factors underlying the effect of organisational downsizing on health of employees: Longitudinal cohort study. *British Medical Journal (Clinical Research Education)*, 320(7240), 971–975.

Krohne, K. & Magnussen, L. H. (2011). Go to work or report sick? A focus group study on decisions of sickness presence among offshore catering section workers. *BMC Research Notes*, 4, 70–0500-4-70.

Leineweber, C., Westerlund, H., Hagberg, J., Svedberg, P. & Alexanderson, K. (2012). Sickness presenteeism is more than an alternative to sickness absence: Results from the population-based SLOSH study. *International Archives of Occupational and Environmental Health*, 85(8), 905–914.

Letvak, S. A., Ruhm, C. J. & Gupta, S. N. (2012). Nurses' presenteeism and its effects on self-reported quality of care and costs. *American Journal of Nursing*, 112(2), 30–38.

Levin-Epstein, J. (2005). Presenteeism and Paid Sick Days. Center for Law and Social Policy. Available online at: www.clasp.org/sites/default/files/public/resources-and-publications/publication-1/0212.pdf.

Loeppke, R., Taitel, M., Haufle, V., Parry, T., Kessler, R. C. & Jinnett, K. (2009). Health and productivity as a business strategy: A multiemployer study. *Journal of Occupational and Environmental Medicine*, 51(4), 411–428.

Martinez, L. F. & Ferreira, A. I. (2012). Sick at work: presenteeism among nurses in a Portuguese public hospital. *Stress and Health*, 28(4), 297–304.

McKevitt, C. & Morgan, M. (1997). Illness doesn't belong to us. *Journal of the Royal Society of Medicine*, 90(9), 491–495.

McTernan, W. P., Dollard, M. F. & LaMontagne, A. D. (2013). Depression in the workplace: An economic cost analysis of depression-related productivity loss attributable to job strain and bullying. *Work & Stress*, 27(4), 321–338.

Meerding, W., IJzelenberg, W., Koopmanschap, M., Severens, J. L. & Burdorf, A. (2005). Health problems lead to considerable productivity loss at work among workers with high physical load jobs. *Journal of Clinical Epidemiology*, 58(5), 517–523.

Mellers, B. A., Schwartz, A. & Cooke, A. D. J. (1998). Judgement and decision making. *Annual Review of Psychology*, 49, 447–477.

Miraglia, M. & Johns, G. (2016). Going to work ill: A meta-analysis of the correlates of presenteeism and a dual-path model. *Journal of Occupational Health Psychology*, 21(3), 261.

Morgeson, F. P. & Hofmann, D. A. (1999). The structure and function of collective constructs: Implications for multilevel research and theory development. *Academy of Management Review*, 24(2), 249–265.

Munir, F., Jones, D., Leka, S. & Griffiths, A. (2005). Work limitations and employer adjustments for employees with chronic illness. *International Journal of Rehabilitation Research*, 28(2), 111–117.

Munir, F., Yarker, J., Haslam, C. et al. (2007). Work factors related to psychological and health-related distress among employees with chronic illnesses. *Journal of Occupational Rehabilitation*, 17(2), 259–277.

Pauly, M. V., Nicholson, S., Polsky, D., Berger, M. L. & Sharda, C. (2008). Valuing reductions in on-the-job illness: "presenteeism" from managerial and economic perspectives. *Health Economics*, 17(4), 469–485.

Prater, T. & Smith, K. (2011). Underlying factors contributing to presenteeism and absenteeism. *Journal of Business & Economics Research*, 9(6), 1–14.

Rauch, A. & Frese, M. (2007). Let's put the person back into entrepreneurship research: A meta-analysis on the relationship between business owners' personality traits, business creation, and success. *European Journal of Work and Organizational Psychology*, 16(4), 353–385.

Ridic, G., Gleason, S. & Ridic, O. (2012). Comparisons of health care systems in the United States, Germany and Canada. *Materia Socio-Medica*, 24(2), 112.

Rosvold, E.O. & Bjertness, E. (2001). Physicians who do not take sick leave: hazardous heroes? *Scandinavian Journal of Public Health*, 29(1), 71–75.

Schultz, A. B. & Edington, D. W. (2007). Employee health and presenteeism: A systematic review. *Journal of Occupational Rehabilitation*, 17(3), 547–579.

Simpson, R. (1998). Presenteeism, power and organizational change: Long hours as a career barrier and the impact on the working lives of women managers. *British Journal of Management*, 9(s1), 37–50.

Stewart, W. F., Ricci, J. A., Chee, E., Hahn, S. R., & Morganstein, D. (2003a). Cost of lost productive work time among US workers with depression. *Journal of the American Medical Association*, 289(23), 3135–3144.

Stewart, W. F., Ricci, J. A., Chee, E., Morganstein, D., & Lipton, R. (2003b). Lost productive time and cost due to common pain conditions in the US workforce. *Journal of the American Medical Association*, 290(18), 2443–2454.

Taloyan, M., Aronsson, G., Leineweber, C., Hanson, L. M., Alexanderson, K. & Westerlund, H. (2012). Sickness presenteeism predicts suboptimal self-rated health and sickness absence: A nationally representative study of the Swedish working population. *PLoS One*, 7(9), e44721.

Van den Heuvel, S. G., Geuskens, G. A., Hooftman, W. E., Koppes, L. L. & Van den Bossche, S. N. (2010). Productivity loss at work; health-related and work-related factors. *Journal of Occupational Rehabilitation*, 20(3), 331–339.

Vézina, M., Cloutier, E., Stock, S. et al. (2011). *Enquête québécoise sur des conditions de travail, d'emploi et de SST (EQCOTESST) (No. R-691)*. Montréal: IRSST.

Vingård, E., Alexanderson, K. & Norlund, A. (2004). Sickness presence. *Scandinavian Journal of Public Health*, 32(63 suppl.), 216–221. Available online at: www.eurofound.europa.eu/observatories/eurwork/articles/work ing-conditions/prevalence-of-sickness-absence-and-presenteeism

Warren, C. L., White-Means, S. I., Wicks, M. N., Chang, C. F., Gourley, D. & Rice, M. (2011). Cost burden of the presenteeism health outcome: diverse workforce of nurses and pharmacists. *Journal of Occupational and Environmental Medicine*, 53(1), 90–99.

Widera, E., Chang, A. & Chen, H. L. (2010). Presenteeism: A public health hazard. *Journal of General Internal Medicine*, 25(11), 1244–1247.

2 | *Presenteeism: A Critical Review of the Literature*

MOUNA KNANI, CAROLINE BIRON, AND
PIERRE-SÉBASTIEN FOURNIER

Introduction

This chapter presents a critical review of the literature on presenteeism. The goal is to summarize and identify the main conceptual and methodological limitations of presenteeism. More specifically, we critically review the presenteeism literature with a view to suggesting future research avenues that take into account the dynamic aspects of this phenomenon. First, some of the most popular and widely used definitions of presenteeism are presented along with their limitations. Then, we consider the various measures of presenteeism and suggest some improvements. Finally, we present methodological limitations based on an overview of research and current thinking in the field. This chapter highlights the methodological importance of considering small and medium-sized enterprises (SMEs) in future research.

Definition of Presenteeism

In the academic literature, serious interest in presenteeism only emerged in the late 1990s (Johns, 2010). At its most basic, presenteeism initially referred to being at work for long hours due to job insecurity (Chapman, 2005). It is understood as the literal and natural antonym of absenteeism (Johns, 2010; Smith, 1979). This rudimentary understanding of presenteeism began to change in the early 90s, coming to refer to a particular kind of presence at work (Johns, 2010). From its initial objective definition as regular attendance, presenteeism became associated with overcommitment at work (Siegrist, 1996; Lowe, 2002; Johns, 2010). According to this view, presenteeism is a means to personal achievement and recognition characterized by overzealousness and total dedication to work. It is defined as a kind of excessive workplace presence leading to burnout (Oligny, 2009). But this interpretation failed to achieve any consensus, and it has been replaced by a new conception of presenteeism (Johns, 2010). Two schools of thought have since emerged: the first, stemming from medical research, characterizes presenteeism as attending work when sick and has been mainly used by European scholars. The second characterizes presenteeism primarily in terms of productivity loss, and is most commonly used among organizational scholars (Johns, 2010), mainly in North America.

Today, the definition that enjoys the most widespread support among researchers is that of Aronsson, Gustafsson & Dallner (2000), who wrote one of the first major articles on the subject. They define presenteeism as "the phenomenon of people who, despite complaints and ill health that should prompt rest and absence from work, are still turning up at their jobs" (Aronsson, Gustafsson & Dallner, 2000: 503).

It therefore seems overly simplistic to view presenteeism as the opposite of absenteeism, as a low level of absenteeism, or as an exaggerated level of attendance that affects worker health. To narrow matters down and arrive at a more accurate definition, it is important to distinguish presenteeism from worker laziness disengagement, or other similar phenomena (Gosselin & Lauzier, 2010; Hemp, 2004). Karanika-Murray, Pontes, Griffiths & Biron (2015) use the European definition by Aronsson (working while ill) but also specify that presenteeism implies a physical presence coupled with psychological absence. Their study suggests presenteeism is associated with affective-motivational states such as engagement, addiction, and job satisfaction. When workers show up at work with depleted physical resources due to illness, their affective and motivational states are affected; this can lead to a decrease in satisfaction due to the inability of workers to achieve expected outcomes. Psychological presence is jeopardized by illness, and workers disengage from work psychologically but feel obliged for various reasons to be present physically (Karanika-Murray et al., 2015). Current definitions of presenteeism do not take into account the differences between mental and physical processes related to presenteeism. Considering presenteeism as a physical presence and psychological absence could open avenues for research, but also raises the possibility that the exact opposite phenomenon may occur: with new ways of working such as telework, it is possible to be physically absent from work due to illness, but psychologically present and engaged via technology. This implies that the current definition of presenteeism as working through illness might be overly comprehensive and insufficiently precise to distinguish between physical and psychological presence, therefore limiting avenues both for research and for managing presenteeism more effectively in practice.

Existing research has concentrated solely on sickness presenteeism (Aronsson, Gustafsson & Dallner, 2000; Hemp, 2004; Sanderson & Cocker, 2013) while excluding a related phenomenon of equal importance and concern: nonwork-related presenteeism. Nonwork-related presenteeism was initially defined as "attending work, but not performing effectively on the job due to a lack of concentration" (Johns, 2010, 2011; Van Vegchel et al., 2001; D'Abate & Eddy, 2007). D'Abate & Eddy (2007) subsequently concluded that this lack of concentration resulted in employees attending work but engaging in personal activities. Typical examples include employees who surf the Web, reserve vacations while at the office, or chat online. This minimalist behavior can be a form of presenteeism where workers show up so as not to be accused of shirking. Few studies exist on nonwork-related presenteeism (D'Abate, 2005; D'Abate & Eddy, 2007), even though it is thought to have a much greater financial impact (productivity loss) than absenteeism or the analogous phenomenon of sickness presenteeism. A *New York Times* article, for example, reported that Super Bowl–related telephone conversations during working hours cost companies over $800 million in lost productivity (Herring, 2004, cited in D'Abate & Eddy, 2007), and the cost to companies of personal Internet use at work is pegged in the billions (D'Abate & Eddy, 2007). As we point out below, however, there are problems associated with definitions of presenteeism that refer to a "lack of concentration on the job." Indeed, such definitions imply that all types of productivity losses are considered as presenteeism, whether they are related to personal difficulties, lack of engagement or motivation problems. As shown in Table 1, most researchers define presenteeism as either working through illness or as the productivity loss that results when employees are present but not fully functional. We discuss the limits associated with current definitions of presenteeism below.

Limitations to the Definition of Presenteeism

We have identified limitations in the way presenteeism is conceptualized. One critique of presenteeism defined as working while ill is that it oversimplifies the phenomenon.

Table 1 *Definitions of Presenteeism*

Author	Definition
Collins et al. (2005).	"Presentees not working at full capacity."
Caverly et al. (2007: 305).	"Where employees are working less productively due to health or medical problems."
Aronsson & Gustafsson (2005: 958); Hansen & Andersen (2008: 957); Bergström et al. (2009: 629); Westerlund et al. (2009: 1099); Demerouti et al. (2009: 51); Johns (2010: 519); Johns (2011: 483); Sanderson et al. (2013: 172); Halbesleben et al. (2014: 177); Johansen et al. (2014: 1).	"The phenomenon that people, despite complaints and ill health that should prompt them to rest and take sick leave, go to work in any case."
Turpin et al. (2004: 1123); Prochaska et al. (2011: 736); Cancellière et al. (2011: 1); Tang et al. (2011: 337).	"Reduced productivity at work due to health." "Workers are physically present but function at less than full productivity because of illness or other health conditions."
D'Abate & Eddy (2007)	Nonwork-related presenteeism "Attending work but engaging in personal activities."

According to this definition, presenteeism only exists when someone is sick, with illness construed as the main cause of reduced performance and productivity.

A second limitation on current definitions of presenteeism is the absence of distinctions based on the severity (benign vs. severe), type (mental vs. physical), or nature (chronic or acute) of the illness involved. Working with a common cold is probably very different from working with heart disease. In the same vein, working with a chronic mental health problem such as a depression is also likely to be very different from working with a physical illness that coworkers can actually see and understand. The type of social support received is likely to differ, and the quality/quantity of work accomplished by the worker while ill may also vary. This also implies that productivity losses over time will differ substantially. By considering presenteeism as a monolithic construct without distinguishing the types of underlying health problems, current research is probably not properly capturing the dynamic nature of presenteeism in terms of determinants, consequences, and moderators (Karanika-Murray and Biron, under review).

A third limitation is that current definitions of presenteeism omit its potentially positive sides (Biron & Karanika-Murray, 2017). Miraglia & Johns (2016) introduce the idea of a positive path through which presenteeism is actually explained by a high level of engagement, satisfaction, and other positive attitudinal components. This is important because up until now, presenteeism has primarily been studied in terms of negative antecedents such as attendance pressure factors (Johns 2011) and negative consequences on health and future absence (Bergstrom, 2009; Kivimaki, 2005). As an example, suppose that two employees are affected by the same illness, but that one of them has a positive psychosocial work environment with a high level of autonomy, an active but not excessive workload, supportive colleagues, and a job that is well rewarded, both in terms of esteem from colleagues and opportunities for promotion. It is possible that the motives for presenteeism on the part of these two employees will vary; one may come to work while ill because it makes him/her feel active and provides a sense of accomplishment, whereas the other may come out of a sense of obligation or fear of negative repercussions.

Based on these three limits, we suggest that presenteeism should not be defined by its consequences on performance, but in a manner that accounts for the specificities of the illness and its potentially positive determinants and consequences. Taking into account the specificities of the underlying health problem also implies that the voluntary and involuntary aspects of presenteeism are taken into consideration.

These voluntary and involuntary aspects should not, however, be seen as characteristic of two different types of presenteeism, but rather as two dimensions of the same phenomenon. We believe that the definition of presenteeism needs to be more comprehensive, and not restricted to physical or psychological limitations. Presenteeism cannot be viewed solely as an **involuntary behavior** related to an individual's state of health. It can also be explained by other personal and/or organizational factors. The definition centered on working while ill and less productive predominates in the literature, excluding other conceptions and the fact that, for some employees, productivity losses might not occur if, for example, the work environment were favorable. We need a broader perspective on this complex phenomenon.

The first step to take in this direction is to consider the different types of presenteeism (mental/physical, chronic/acute, benign/severe) and analyze the phenomenon using a more integrated approach. Researchers are urged to take another look at presenteeism that goes beyond monolithic representations.

Toward a Positive Understanding of Presenteeism

Presenteeism is often described as a symptom of dysfunction (Zhou et al., 2016; Knani et al., under review). It is explained by organizational constraints (Miraglia & Johns, 2016; Zhou et al., 2016) such as heavy workload (Biron et al., 2006; Deery et al., 2014; Demerouti et al., 2009; Hansen & Andersen, 2008), understaffing and problems with interchangeability (Aronsson et al., 2000; Elstad & Vabo, 2008; Johansson & Lundberg, 2004; Johns, 2011), attendance policy (Grinyer & Singleton, 2000; Johns, 2010), job insecurity (Caverley et al., 2007; Hansen & Andersen, 2008; MacGregor et al., 2008; Virtanen et al., 2001), pressure from management and colleagues (Grinyer & Singleton, 2000), and downsizing (Johns, 2010).

Most studies conclude that presenteeism contributes significantly to lower employee productivity (Karlsson et al., 2010; Neftzger & Walker, 2010; Zhang et al., 2011) and deteriorating health. Presenteeism is often associated with burnout (Demerouti et al., 2009), musculoskeletal disorders (Toloyan et al., 2012), depression (Virtanen et al., 2001), risk of cardiovascular disease (Kivimaki et al., 2005), and an overall decline in general health (Bergström et al., 2009).

This behavior is conceived solely in relation to organizational and individual constraints, health issues, or loss of productivity (Chia & Chu, 2016; Zhou et al., 2016). This negative view of presenteeism, dubbed "bad presenteeism phenomenon" by Cooper and his colleagues, is overrepresented in the literature and suggests that presenteeism reflects a generalized sense of "malaise" in the work world (Cooper et al., 2015). These authors argue that seeing presenteeism as a positive behavior requires a new theoretical framework, or at least a change in existing representations (Knani et al., under review).

Presenteeism is rarely viewed as a positive behavior that is triggered by affective-motivational states (Barnes, 2016; Cocker et al., 2014; Karanika-Murray et al., 2015; Miraglia and Johns, 2016). Most research ignores the role that work-related attitudes and motivation play in presenteeism (Karanika-Murray et al., 2015). Miraglia & Johns (2016) have called for qualitative research to help us better understand the psychological factors driving the decision to show up at work when ill, especially the compromises that employees make between their health and their motivation to work while sick. Other studies point to the need to broaden our understanding of presenteeism and its field of application by examining both positive and negative trigger factors (Çetin, 2016; Chia & Chu, 2016; Giaever et al., 2016; Zhou et al., 2016).

Showing up at work when ill doesn't automatically mean one's work experience is negative (Zhou et al., 2016; Knani et al., under review). According to Chia & Chu (2016), the negative, pathogenic representation of presenteeism deserves more nuanced treatment. Recent research has shown that positive affective experiences at work (e.g., being treated fairly by one's colleagues and supervisor, feeling in harmony with one's workplace environment, feeling engaged) foster a sense of well-being at work, which manifests itself through behavior consistent with organizational citizenship, including presenteeism (Johns, 2010; Miraglia & Johns, 2016; Zhou et al., 2016). Aronsson & Gustafsson (2005) add that positive representations of presenteeism only develop in salutogenic work environments – i.e., workplaces that are stimulating, comfortable, flexible, etc. – and in situations where health issues are not serious. A salutogenic work environment fosters voluntary, "positive" presenteeism. In fact, presenteeism may be more common among dedicated and satisfied employees, as suggested by the findings of Aronsson & Gustafsson (2005), de Vries et al. (2011), and Karanika-Murray et al. (2015) showing a positive association between job satisfaction and presenteeism. However, presenteeism should not be viewed as a mechanical response to a conducive work environment; it can also be explained by the presence of positive individual motivating factors such as engagement and personal and family culture within a positive organizational context (Knani et al., under review). In this latter study, working while sick was seen by employees and owner-managers as a form of "therapy" that helped distract them from their illness, stay active, and overcome social isolation. These results suggest that presenteeism may – at least in some cases – be explained more by positive factors than negative factors or illness, hence the importance of adopting a holistic approach to better understand the phenomenon. Future research should take this line of inquiry further in order to identify the conditions in which presenteeism may be "positive" and without serious consequences for employee productivity and health (Biron & Karanika-Murray, 2017). Researchers would also do well to draw on qualitative methods to better understand how positive factors relating to a person's individual and workplace environment affect presenteeism. At the same time, future research must not overlook the fact that despite the positive factors alluded to above, sickness presenteeism remains problematic and must be managed (Knani et al., under review). It may well benefit the company and employee in the short term, but it also represents a medium- and long-term health risk that can result in more absenteeism (Bergström et al., 2009).

In keeping with this view of presenteeism as a dynamic and multidimensional construct, we review below some of the ways of measuring presenteeism and suggest ways to improve them.

Measuring Presenteeism

Unlike absenteeism, presenteeism is difficult to detect and even harder to quantify (Schultz et al., 2009; Cancellière et al., 2011; Johns, 2010, 2011). Absenteeism can be readily assessed using indicators such as absent days (Huver et al., 2012; Wang et al., 2003; Martocchio & Jimeno, 2003). Such indicators are clear and allow companies to implement concrete corrective measures to rectify the situation (Neftzger & Walker, 2010). These measures may include changes to the company absenteeism policy, stricter controls for absent employees, and stronger verification procedures (Martocchio & Jimeno, 2003). Absenteeism continues to be a valuable indicator that can shed light on employee health and workplace performance (Neftzger & Walker, 2010). Presenteeism, in contrast, is notoriously difficult to document, as numerous authors have noted (Turpin et al., 2004; Ozminkowski et al., 2004; Neftzger & Walker, 2010; Cancellière et al., 2011; Mattke et al., 2007; Zhang et al., 2011). Despite these challenges, certain measurement instruments have been developed for this purpose. We examine four of these instruments as described in the literature.

Single-Item Measures of Presenteeism

Single-item measurement uses a single generic question to measure the occurrence and frequency of presenteeism. Most studies measuring presenteeism are based on a single-item measure (Neftzger & Walker, 2010), i.e., "Did you go to work even though you should have taken sick leave during the past 12 months? If yes, how many times?" (Aronsson et al., 2000: 504; Caverley et al., 2007: 308; Aronsson & Gustafsson, 2005: 960; and MacGregor et al., 2008: 609).

Comparative Productivity, Performance, and Efficiency

A second method of measuring presenteeism consists of comparing productivity, performance, and efficiency (Mattke et al., 2007). This approach seeks to assess how an employee's performance differs from that of his or her colleagues or from normal levels. It measures an effect of presenteeism using a variety of approaches.

Estimated Lost Work Time

With this method, inspired by absenteeism measurement techniques, employees are asked to estimate lost work time. The approach was initially developed to monetize absenteeism on the basis of self-reported absent days and was subsequently extended to measure presenteeism-generated losses based on the number of hours of self-reported lost productivity. The advantages of this method are its simplicity and plausibility (Mattke et al., 2007). Its limitations derive from the difficulty of accurately converting perceived impairment or nonproductive hours into precise temporal measurements (Mattke et al., 2007). It is also important to remember that productivity losses can have multifactorial causes. Very few studies actually use this measure.

Assessment of Perceived Impairment

Another approach to measuring performance involves assessing perceived impairment by asking employees how health problems affect their ability to perform mental, physical, and interpersonal tasks and meet work demands (Ozminkowski et al., 2004; Mattke et al., 2007; Neftzger & Walker, 2010; Cancellière et al., 2011). This approach, the most common method for measuring presenteeism (Mattke et al., 2007; Aronsson & Gustafsson, 2000), draws on a variety of tools, including the following (see Table 2 for a summary):

- Worker Productivity Index (WPI) (Burton et al., 1999)
- Work Productivity and Activity Impairment Questionnaire (WPAI) (Reilly et al., 1993)
- Stanford Presenteeism Scale (SPS) (Koopman et al., 2002)
- World Health Organization Health and Work Performance Questionnaire (HPQ) (Kessler et al., 2003)
- Work Limitations Questionnaire (WLQ) (Lerner et al., 2001)

Of these five instruments, the last three are the most widely used in presenteeism research. We will briefly present the WPI and WPAI before looking in more detail at the WLQ, HPQ, and SPS.

The WPI is a general indicator of employee productivity. It takes into account absent days, disability, and actual worker performance. The WPI has been used in a number of sickness presenteeism studies. It provides a wide range of reliable information about the impact of health on productivity (Turpin et al., 2004).

The WPAI measures the effect of general health and symptom severity on work productivity (Prochaska et al., 2011; Turpin et al., 2004; Neftzger & Walker, 2010). An overall work productivity score is calculated by multiplying the hours worked by the employee's normal productivity level. The WPAI scale has primarily been tested in clinical trial settings (Prochaska et al., 2011; Turpin et al., 2004; Neftzger & Walker, 2010).

The WLQ and SPS are measurement tools used to assess presenteeism on the basis of "perceived value" (Cancellière et al., 2011). Workers are asked to estimate how much their health problems interfere with their ability to perform mental, physical, and interpersonal tasks and meet work demands (Ozminkowski et al., 2004; Turpin et al., 2004; Lerner & Henke, 2008; Neftzger & Walker, 2010; Cancellière et al., 2011).

The WLQ consists of 25 statements designed to assess the extent to which workers are limited in performing their tasks, and the decline in productivity (presenteeism) due to health problems (Ozminkowski et al., 2004; Turpin et al., 2004; Lerner & Henke, 2008; Neftzger & Walker, 2010).

The WLQ is a multidimensional tool. The 25 statements are divided into four dimensions (1) "time management" comprising five items assessing difficulties in managing time and scheduling; (2) "physical demands" comprising six items assessing ability to perform duties involving physical strength and stamina; (3) "mental and interpersonal abilities" comprising nine items assessing ability to perform cognitive and rational tasks and carry out social interactions in the workplace; and (4) "output demands" comprising five items assessing reductions in the quantity and quality of work. The WLQ has been validated for use in studies on depression (Lerner & Henke, 2008).

The SPS is a questionnaire assessing the impact of health problems on worker performance and productivity (Koopman et al., 2002). It consists of 32 items that measure cognitive, emotional, and behavioral aspects of performance when employees show up for work when ill (physical and/or psychological deterioration) (Ozminkowski et al., 2004; Turpin et al., 2004; Lerner & Henke, 2008; Neftzger & Walker, 2010).

A shorter six-item version (SPS-6) is also presented in the literature. This version can be used to establish an overall presenteeism score. A high SPS-6 score indicates a good capacity for work, despite health issues, whereas a low score indicates that even though an employee is physically present at work, he or she may "experience decreased productivity and below-normal work quality" due to health problems or personal or professional issues (Turpin et al., 2004; Brun et al., 2006).

The shorter SPS-6 also has excellent psychometric characteristics. A number of studies have shown it to be an accurate and valid scale for measuring presenteeism (Koopman et al., 2002; Turpin et al., 2004), including Turpin et al. (2004), who tested and confirmed the reliability and validity of the scale.

The HPQ was developed by Ronald C. Kessler (2003) in collaboration with the World Health Organization (WHO). This measurement instrument uses a self-reporting survey to estimate the cost of health problems as manifested in lost productivity (presenteeism), sickness absenteeism, and critical incidents, i.e., workplace successes and failures, occupational injuries, and workplace accidents (Turpin et al., 2004; Lerner and Henke, 2008; Neftzger & Walker, 2010; Prochaska et al., 2011).

In this self-reporting survey (HPQ), employees are asked to provide information on their level of absenteeism (number of hours and days), their presenteeism, and critical incidents at work. Findings by Kessler et al. (2003) attest to the usefulness of this instrument.

As a tool, the HPQ accurately assesses actual workplace performance (Turpin et al., 2004; Lerner & Henke, 2008). Results obtained with the HPQ can also be used to estimate costs in financial terms (Kessler et al., 2003). According to these authors, it is possible to determine the relationship between worker health status and workplace performance from the correlation measure. To this end, the HPQ was used in a study conducted by Wang et al. (2003) to assess the association between physical and mental health status and workplace performance (absenteeism, presenteeism, and critical incidents). The study found that depression is the only factor with a significant impact on absenteeism, presenteeism (measured as productivity loss), and critical incidents.

Limitations to Measuring Presenteeism

Measuring presenteeism is very challenging. Measurement instruments (HPQ, SPS, WPAI, WPI, etc.) have been developed to assess presenteeism, and especially the resulting loss of productivity (Johns, 2010; Schultz & Edington, 2007), but none have garnered consensual support because none of them can measure, quantify, and assess presenteeism in an accurate or, more importantly, direct manner (Schultz & Egington, 2007; Schultz et al., 2009). According to Cancellière et al. (2011), there is no agreement on the most suitable method for measuring or assessing presenteeism.

In their article "Le Stanford Presenteeism Scale (SPS-6): Destruction d'un faux semblant," Melançon et al. (2012) note that even with instruments designed to measure presenteeism, most researchers rely on "false equivalents" such as lost productive time. In doing so, they introduce bias into our understanding of the nature and consequences of the phenomenon. As for single-item measurement, use of a single generic question to measure presenteeism may spawn doubts about the internal consistency of the measurement, given the impossibility of estimating the instrument's reliability or the dimensionality of the construct of presenteeism (Johns, 2011). What is more, this measure, like the others, relies on employee self-reporting of the number of days of "forced" attendance at work (Schultz & Egington, 2007; Schultz

Table 2 *Instruments for Measuring Presenteeism*

Name of Instrument	Authors	Objectives	Composition	Health Problems Measured	Study Population	Reliability and Validity
WPAI (Work Productivity and Activity Impairment Questionnaire)	Reilly, Zbrozek, Dukes (1993)	Measure the impact of illness on productivity loss at work.	15 items: 6 items for general health issues and 9 items for specific illnesses	Impairment caused by health problems	Public sector	A valid instrument for measuring lost productivity. However, its validity with patients suffering from rheumatoid arthritis has not been established (Zhang et al., 2011)
WLQ (Work Limitation Questionnaire)	Lerner, Amick, Rogers (2001)	Measure the impact of chronic illness on work performance and productivity.	25 items divided into 4 dimensions: (1) time management; (2) physical demands; (3) mental-interpersonal demands; and (4) output demands	Chronic illness	Employees with chronic illness	Instrument validated in studies on depression (Lerner & Henke, 2008)
HPQ (World Health Organization Health and Work	Kessler, Barber, Beck et al. (2003)	Assess the workplace costs of illness as measured in decreased performance	11 statements (instrument translated into 29 languages)	Overall health and specific illnesses (cancer, migraines, fatigue,	Public sector employees	The reliability of this instrument has been demonstrated (Wang et al., 2003)

Table 2 (*cont.*)

Name of Instrument	Authors	Objectives	Composition	Health Problems Measured	Study Population	Reliability and Validity
Performance Questionnaire		(presenteeism) and critical incidents (failures, injuries, accidents)		allergies, depression, anxiety)		
SPS (Stanford Presenteeism Scale)	Koopman, Pelletier, Murray et al. (2002)	Assess the impact of chronic illness on individual productivity and performance.	Original scale with 32 items (SPS-32) or shorter scale with 6 items (SPS-6). Three dimensions: cognitive abilities, emotional abilities, and behavioral abilities.	Impact of chronic illness on performance	Employees with chronic health problems	Reliability and validity confirmed by Turpin et al. (2004).
		Measure workers' ability to concentrate and carry out their work despite illness.	SPS-6: 6 statements (2 behavioral, 2 cognitive, and 2 emotional).			Other studies have found this instrument to be invalid for measuring presenteeism (Melançon et al., 2012)
		Emphasizes health conditions	22 statements (type of work, work habits,	15 specific health conditions	Used in various	Reliability has been assessed and deemed

| WPSI (Work Productivity Short Inventory) | Ozminkowski Goetzel & Long (2003) | affecting productivity rather than type of productivity losses engendered by health problems | health status, absenteeism, presenteeism) | (allergy, respiratory infection, arthritis, asthma, anxiety, depression, bipolar disorder, stress, hypertension, migraine, cholesterol, otitis media) | sectors of activity | suitable (between 0.66 and 0.74). Viewed as a very reliable tool for estimating the prevalence of health problems affecting productivity (Ozminkowski Goetzel & Long, 2003) |

et al., 2009). For various reasons, respondents may underreport the number of days they showed up ill at work. Determining the frequency of this behavior therefore depends on the willingness of each employee to report their "on-the-job absenteeism"; this is by no means a given. Even in a best-case scenario, where employees cooperate and report presenteeism, the question remains: how frequent does this behavior need to be before it can be labeled as presenteeism? (Schultz & Egington, 2007; Schultz et al., 2009).

One thing is certain: it is difficult to determine how much time a person needs to be "less present" to be deemed a "presentee" (Melançon et al., 2012). Yet despite its limitations, the single-item assessment method is still recognized and widely used (Aronsson, Gustafsson & Dallner, 2000; Aronsson & Gustafsson, 2005; Caverley et al., 2007; MacGregor et al., 2008).

The other way to measure presenteeism is through its consequences, especially overall lost productivity (Stewart et al., 2003; Ozminkowski et al., 2004; Karlsson et al., 2010; Neftzger & Walker, 2010; Prochaska et al., 2011). This method, which is widely used in North American studies, comprises measures of absenteeism, presenteeism, and critical incidents (Neftzger & Walker, 2010; Prochaska et al., 2011). Presenteeism is measured indirectly by assessing lost productivity. Indirect measures like these are undoubtedly useful, but as with absenteeism, presenteeism must be measured by means of clear and precise indicators that directly correspond to the phenomenon being measured, and not to its ascribed effects or consequences (Johns, 2011).

In a similar vein, the definition of presenteeism comprises two dimensions, both of equal importance. The first is that workers must have health problems. The second is that they must decide to go to work despite their health problems. However, we can see that this definition doesn't hold true for all the instruments of measure. Take, for example, the SPS, which is widely used to measure presenteeism. Conceptually speaking, it defines presenteeism as "the employee's ability to focus on work without being distracted by health problems" (Koopman et al., 2002). This definition doesn't exactly match the accepted definition among scholars, i.e., "showing up for work when ill." Which leads us to ask: do the instruments used define and measure the same thing? And does this affect the results obtained?

When using productivity as a measure of presenteeism, researchers need to take into account the type of occupation and the sector of activity. For example, productivity loss is much harder to measure for knowledge-based jobs than production-based jobs (Turpin et al., 2004; Neftzger & Walker, 2010). Furthermore, it is very difficult to assign a monetary value or cost to lost productivity. Is it possible to validate these measures in relation to objective measures of productivity? Studies use a variety of methods to monetize productivity loss. For example, scores obtained with the WLQ are converted into a productivity loss percentage. Other instruments consider the hours or days of lost productivity reported by employees as the exact amount. However, these amounts vary depending on the type of job, the nature of the work (physical and/or mental) being performed when presenteeism is measured, and other factors. To refine this assessment further, researchers would be well advised to analyze presenteeism in a way that accounts for employee qualifications, employee status, and job demands.

To conclude, presenteeism is often measured as the cost of lost productivity, workplace errors, or failure to meet company production standards (Cancellière et al., 2011; Neftzger & Walker, 2010). Yet it remains difficult to assess in economic (or monetary) terms given that different studies use different measures, worker populations, and methods of converting the results (Neftzger & Walker, 2010). Johns (2010) has noted substantial variations between studies with regard to the effects and costs of presenteeism. In his view, this is no surprise given the different measures, procedures, and cost derivation techniques used (Schultz et al., 2009; Johns, 2010). In contrast, the cost differences between the study by Goetzel et al. (2004) and Collins et al. (2005) may be the result of different accounting procedures (Johns, 2010).

Looking at the literature, we note that presenteeism is sometimes also measured from a more specific angle, i.e., by assessing the impact of chronic or specific health problems (e.g., respiratory problems, heart problems, migraine, rheumatoid arthritis, back and neck pain, depression, etc.) on productivity loss (Ozminkowski et al., 2004; Karlsson et al., 2010; Neftzger & Walker, 2010).

With this type of measure, perceived impairment is assessed by asking employees how much their health problems interfere with their mental, physical, and interpersonal performance (Ozminkowski et al., 2004; Neftzger & Walker, 2010; Cancellière et al., 2011). Asking employees to self-diagnose their state of health and assess its impact on their productivity implies

Table 3 Summary Table on Presenteeism (Theory and Methodology)

Authors/ Year	Objective of the Study	Theory			Methodology						Results
		Determinants		Moderator Variables	Country	Sample size	Sectors	Research Design	Measure of Presenteeism	Statistical Method	Results
		Organizational	Individual								
Johansen et al. (2014)	Study the determinants of presenteeism	• Fear of being laid off • Can't afford to take sick leave • Nobody else available to carry out one's duties • Don't want to burden colleagues • Enjoyment of work • Going to work seen as good for health • Maintenance of social networks	• Fear of being considered unproductive or lazy • Shame at being ill • Fear of being seen as "cheating"		Norway and Sweden	2533	Private and public sectors and the self-employed	Cross-sectional	"During the last 12 months, did you go to work despite feeling so ill that you should have taken sick leave?"	Binomial logistic regression analysis	The most-reported factors causing presenteeism are (for both countries): • Unwillingness to burden colleagues (women and young employees: 43%), enjoyment of work (37%), and lack of anyone else to carry out duties (35%).
Deery et al. (2014)	Examine the association between job demands, presenteeism and absenteeism	• Job demands (+) • Understaffing • Attendance policy (+)		Age, sex, type of job	England	227	999 emergency services call centers	Cross-sectional	"During the last 12 months, did you go to work despite feeling so ill that you should have	SPSS	• High job demands (workload and attendance policy) are associated with presenteeism.

Work resources *1
- Distributive justice (-)
- Procedural justice

...taken sick leave because of your state of health?"

- (distributive justice) mediate the impact of presenteeism on absenteeism.
- Understaffing is not associated with presenteeism.
- Procedural justice is not associated with presenteeism.

Study	Aim	Variables			Controls	Country	N	Sector	Design	Measure	Analysis	Findings
Gosselin et al. (2013)	Study the dynamic between health problems, presenteeism, and absenteeism	• Control over tasks • Responsibilities at work • Work-related conflicts • Management support • Peer support • Hours spent at work and at home	• Job satisfaction • Organizational commitment • Psychological stress		Gender, marital status, age (+), Parental responsibility	Canada	3670	Public service	Cross-sectional	"Over the last six months, how many days a month did you show up for work when you felt physically ill?"	• Correlation analysis • Hierarchical regression analysis	• Greater responsibilities at work, work-related conflict, lack of control over tasks, and low support are significantly linked to presenteeism • Psychological stress is the factor with the greatest impact on presenteeism, whereas job satisfaction and organizational commitment have no effect. • Women and young managers are more prone to presenteeism

Table 3 (*cont.*)

Authors/ Year	Objective of the Study	Theory — Determinants — Organizational	Theory — Determinants — Individual	Moderator Variables	Methodology — Country	Methodology — Sample size	Methodology — Sectors	Methodology — Research Design	Measure of Presenteeism	Statistical Method	Results
Jourdain & Vézina (2014)	Assess the influence of psychosocial risks, workload, decision authority, and support on presenteeism	• Job demands: workload • Work resources: decision authority and social support	(NA)	(NA)	Quebec, Canada	1609	Private and public sectors	Cross-sectional	• "During the past 12 months, did you ever go in to work in spite of feeling that you should stay home because you were sick?" • "During the past 12 months, how many days did you go to work in this condition?"	Multiple regression analysis	Employees with high job demands, low decision authority, and low social support (job-related tension), are more prone to presenteeism. Support from supervisors attenuates the impact of the positive relationship between job demands and presenteeism.
Lu, Cooper & Yen Lin (2013)	The objective of this study is twofold: (1) delineate the motives underlying the act of presenteeism (2) examine the health consequences	(NA)	Self efficacy, neuroticism	(NA)	Taiwan	245	Service industry (44.1%); manufacturing industry (34.6%); the rest in education, health, and government organizations	Longitudinal	• "Why did you go to work while ill?" • "Have you experienced the following in the last 6 months?"	Hierarchical regression analysis	Self-efficacy and neuroticism are significantly correlated with presenteeism.

Author (year)	Aim	Factors		Variables	Country	N	Sector	Design	Measure	Analysis	Findings
	of presenteeism										
Leineweber et al. (2012)	Assess whether the positive relationship between presenteeism and absenteeism can be explained by illness, work incapacity, or work environment	• Physical work demands • Mental demands – Decision authority • Satisfaction	(NA)	Age, sex, education, income	Sweden	8304	Various sectors	Cross-sectional	"How many times and how many days the respondents had attended work during the past 12 months despite considering that their health condition should have made them report in sick" The response options were Never, 1–7; 8–30; 31–90 and 91 days and over	Logistic regression	Work environment and illness affect the relationship between presenteeism and absenteeism • Education and income have no impact on the relationship between presenteeism and absenteeism.
Robertson et al. (2012)	Study the relationship between workplace factors and presenteeism	• Resources and communication • Control and autonomy • Workplace relations • Work–family balance • Job security and change	(NA)	Sex, age, marital status, type of organization	England and other European countries	6309	Various sectors	Cross-sectional	"In the past 3 months, have you ever not felt well enough to perform your duties to your normal standard, but attended	Structural equation modeling (AMOS)	Workplace factors are predictors of presenteeism. The majority of respondents (67%) reported that presenteeism was the result of self-imposed decisions.

Table 3 (*cont.*)

Authors/ Year	Objective of the Study	Theory		Moderator Variables	Methodology						Results
		Determinants			Country	Sample size	Sectors	Research Design	Measure of Presenteeism	Statistical Method	
		Organizational	Individual								
		• Wages/benefits and working conditions							work regardless?"		
Johns (2011)	Examine the antecedents of and correlates of presenteeism, absenteeism and productivity loss due to presenteeism.	1) Work context: task interdependence, ease of replacement, adjustment latitude, • Job security, control, and legitimization of absence. 2) Work experience: equity, job security, work/family conflict, family-to-work conflict	Professional conscience, neuroticism, internal health locus of control		Canada	444	Management school	Cross-sectional	"Over the past six months I have gone to work despite feeling that I really should have taken sick leave due to my state of health." "I have continued to work when it might have been better to take sick leave."	Regression analysis	Presenteeism is positively correlated with job satisfaction, task interdependence, ease of replacement, and work-to-family conflict. It is negatively correlated with neuroticism, equity, job security, internal health locus of control, and perceived legitimacy of absence.
Leinweber et al. (2011)	Study of the relationship between presenteeism and work	• Ergonomic environment • Support from coworkers • Support from managers	(NA)	Age, sex, status, self-rated health status	Sweden	11,793	Police	Cross-sectional	"How many times during the past 12 months did you go to work even	Regression analysis	All workplace environmental factors (ergonomic environment, support from coworkers,

Author	Aim	Factors	Country	N	Setting	Study design	Measurement	Analysis	Findings
	environment factors.	• Leadership • Control • Stress					though you should have been off sick due to the state of your health?"		support from managers, leadership, control, stress) are associated with presenteeism. Low social support combined with low decision authority heightens presenteeism, especially among older people. The most significant relationship is between stress and presenteeism.
Karlsson et al. (2010)	Examine the relationship between certain psychosocial factors and productivity loss	• Job demands • Control • Leadership • Social environment • Innovation environment • Organizational commitment • Role compatibility • Role ambiguity • Coworker social support • Work mastery	Sweden	2095	Four manufacturing companies	Prospective	"How many times during the past 12 months did you go to work even though you according to your health stat should have stayed at home?"	Logistic regression	Organizational commitment, workplace social climate, job demands, control, and role compatibility are significantly correlated with presenteeism. Employee health status mediates the relationship between certain psychosocial risks and presenteeism.

Table 3 (*cont.*)

Authors/ Year	Objective of the Study	Theory				Methodology						Results
		Determinants			Moderator Variables	Country	Sample size	Sectors	Research Design	Measure of Presenteeism	Statistical Method	Results
		Organizational	Individual									
Löve et al. (2010)	Examine whether the correlation between sickness presenteeism (SP) and performance based-self esteem (PBSE) depends on workplace environmental factors	Control, psychological demands, social support, effort/ reward imbalance	PBSE • Health status • Financial or legal problems			Sweden	5582	Young adults		"How many times over the previous 12 months have you attended work/ educational activities despite feeling that you really should have time off because of your state of health?"	Logistic regression	PBSE is a predictor of SP, taking into account self-rated health, psychological and physical demands, and financial problems. There is a link between PBSE, psychosocial factors, individual factors, and presenteeism. The effect of PBSE on presenteeism is four times higher among individuals with low health status, compared to healthy individuals.

a level of "subjective" and reflexive" analysis (as is the case with the WLQ developed by Lerner et al., 2001) that can complicate the use of this assessment method (Johns, 2010).

Methodological Issues in Presenteeism Research

As illustrated in Table 3, studies have identified a series of organizational factors and individual characteristics leading to presenteeism (Johansson & Lundberg, 2004; Aronson & Gustafsson, 2005; Hansen & Andersen, 2008; Johns, 2010). The recent meta-analysis by Miraglia & Johns (2016) shows the importance of job demands, job resources, and attitudinal-motivational factors in predicting presenteeism and absenteeism choices. However, in keeping with our previous arguments on the need to break down the definitions of presenteeism, it is not clear how participants actually reach the decision that it is legitimate for them to take time off in the case of mental illness. They may continue to work while ill with mental health problems and not consider themselves as "physically present and mentally absent" (Karanika-Murray et al., 2015) because they are simply unaware that their mental health is affected. This is problematic in terms of measurement. As for the consequences of presenteeism on health, a recent systematic review by Skagen and Collins (2016) shows that presenteeism is a risk factor for future absenteeism and is associated with a decrease in future self-rated health.

Skagen and Collins (2016) also stress the need for additional theoretical and empirical work in presenteeism studies and call for qualitative and quantitative research to better our understanding of the phenomenon.

Other studies urge for more exploratory research to contribute new knowledge and understanding of presenteeism with respect to employee behavior, values, motivations, attitudes, and typical practices (Knani et al., under review). Such research would be particularly useful in the context of small and medium-sized enterprises (SMEs), which, despite their economic and social importance, are underrepresented in the research on managing and recognizing presenteeism (Knani et al., under review). Most studies in the literature have been conducted within big companies or public organizations, especially in the health and education sectors (Aronsson et al., 2000; Backer-McClearn et al., 2010; Dew et al., 2005).

Research on presenteeism has taken into account demographic variables in order to examine their direct and moderating effects on presenteeism. Among other things, studies have examined the effect of age (Gosselin et al., 2013; Hansen & Andersen, 2008), sex (Aronsson et al., 2000; Aronsson & Gustafsson, 2005), education level (Aronsson et al., 2000; Taloyan et al., 2012), family situation (Aronsson et al., 2000; Hansen & Andersen, 2008), self-rated health (Aronsson & Gustafsson, 2005; Hansen & Andersen, 2008; Kivimäki et al., 2005), and the nature of the illness (Schultz & Edington, 2007). But little research has been done on the impact of organizational characteristics, including the size of the business (SME, large corporation). Despite the role business size plays in determining working conditions (Mintzberg & Waters, 1982), it has not been analyzed in presenteeism studies and has often been overlooked in empirical research (Knani et al., under review).

It would be interesting to assess whether business size has an impact on the practice of presenteeism. It would also be interesting to determine whether the specific characteristics of the SME work environment make employees more likely to engage in presenteeism.

Despite the fact that these specific characteristics are widely recognized in the literature (Marchesnay and Julien, 1990), no studies have seriously explored their potential impact on the incidence of presenteeism. The studies reviewed here present and analyze a multitude of factors predisposing employees to presenteeism, but none of them distinguish between SMEs and big business (Knani et al., under review).

SME work environments differ from corporate work environments in a number ways. Characteristics we have noted include a scarcity of qualified workers, heightened competition, financing challenges, and constraints related to the internal organization of work, including increased workload, conflicts and ambiguous roles, and job insecurity (Chuang, 2006; De Kok, 2002; Lawrence et al., 2006). Research on employee well-being within SMEs shows that small businesses invest less in psychosocial risk prevention, exposing workers to difficult working conditions (Champoux & Brun, 2003; Chuang, 2006; De Kok, 2002; Johnson, 1995; Lawrence et al., 2006). Some studies (Johnson, 1995; Harris, 2010) have found that small business employees may be more anxious and stressed than their counterparts in large organizations. Limited financial and organizational means make it harder, and less appealing, for SMES to invest in workplace health and safety. In fact, regular financial challenges tend to relegate the issue to the back burner. Small business managers are oriented toward increasing output and growing their businesses rather than improving working conditions and risk prevention (Champoux & Brun, 2003; Chuang, 2006).

This is why it would be useful to delve deeper into this area so as to understand how SME work environments differ from corporate environments, especially with respect to presenteeism, and how organizational constraints in the SME workplace foster presenteeism. This will require working with SMEs to assess their understanding of presenteeism, their awareness of the phenomenon, their knowledge of its determinants, their concerns about its effects, and most of all, the programs put in place to prevent it (Knani et al., under review).

To conclude, despite advances in the theoretical knowledge of presenteeism, there have not been any corresponding actions taken with regard to prevention. This observation underscores the need to orient future scholarly research not only toward producing theoretical knowledge, but also to developing pragmatic tools for helping prevent and manage presenteeism. It is a shared issue requiring joint action and concrete methods.

Note

1. The positive relationship between presenteeism and absenteeism is moderated by work resources

Bibliography

Aronsson, G., Gustafsson, K. & Dallner, M. (2000). Sick but yet at work. An empirical study of sickness presenteeism. *Journal of Epidemiology & Community Health*, 54(7), 502–509.

Aronsson, G. & Gustafsson, K. (2005). Sickness presenteeism: prevalence, attendance-pressure factors, and an outline of a model for research. *Journal of Occupational and Environmental Medicine*, 47(9), 958–966.

Baker-McClearn, D., Greasley, K., Dale, J. & Griffith, F. (2010). Absence management and presenteeism: The pressures on employees to attend work and the impact of attendance on performance. *Human Resource Management Journal*, 20(3), 311–328.

Barnes, S. & Barnes, S. (2016). Presenteeism–how it can be managed and even used to the benefit of the unwell who want to work and the employer organization. *Strategic HR Review*, 15(2), 95–97.

Bergström, G., Bodin, L., Hagberg, J., Lindh, T., Aronsson, G. & Josephson, M. (2009). Does sickness presenteeism have an impact on future general health? *International archives of occupational and environmental health*, 82(10), 1179–1190.

Biron, C., Brun, J. P., Ivers, H. & Cooper, C. (2006). At work but ill: psychosocial work environment and well-being determinants of presenteeism propensity. *Journal of Public Mental Health*, 5(4), 26–37.

Biron, C. & Karanika-Murray, M. (2017). Can presenteeism be functional for health and performance? Paper presented at the Academy of management – At the interface Atlanta, USA (4–8 August).

Brun, J. P. & Lamarche, C. (2006). *Évaluation des coûts du stress au travail, Rapport de recherche, Chaire en gestion de la santé et de la sécurité du travail dans les organisations*. Québec: Université de Laval.

Burton, W. N., Conti, D. J., Chen, C. Y., Schultz, A. B. & Edington, D. W. (1999). The role of health risk factors and disease on worker productivity. *Journal of Occupational and Environmental Medicine*, 41 (10), 863–877.

Cancelliere, C., Cassidy, J. D., Ammendolia, C. & Côté, P. (2011). Are workplace health promotion programs effective at improving presenteeism in workers? A systematic review and best evidence synthesis of the literature. *BMC Public Health*, 11(1), 395.

Chapman, L. S. (2005). Presenteeism and its role in worksite health promotion. *American Journal of Health Promotion: AJHP*, 19(4), suppl-1.

Caverley, N., Cunningham, J. B. & MacGregor, J. N. (2007). Sickness presenteeism, sickness absenteeism, and health following restructuring in a public service organization. *Journal of Management Studies*, 44(2), 304–319.

Çetin, M. (2016). An exploratory study of presenteeism in Turkish context. *Emerging Markets Journal*, 6(1), 25.

Champoux, D. & Brun, J. P. (2003). Occupational health and safety management in small size enterprises: an overview of the situation and avenues for intervention and research. *Safety Science*, 41(4), 301–318.

Chia, Y. M. & Chu, M. J. (2016). Moderating effects of presenteeism on the stress–happiness relationship of hotel employees: A note. *International Journal of Hospitality Management*, 55, 52–56.

Chuang, Y. (2006). Occupational and employee stress in small businesses. *Online*: www.jimsjournal.org/4.pdf.

Cocker, F., Nicholson, J. M., Graves, N. et al. (2014). Depression in working adults: comparing the costs and health outcomes of working when ill. *PloS one*, 9(9), e105430.

Collins, J. J., Baase, C. M., Sharda, C. E. et al. (2005). The assessment of chronic health conditions on work performance, absence, and total economic impact for employers. *Journal of Occupational and Environmental Medicine*, 47(6), 547–557.

Cooper, C. L., Campbell Quick, J. & Schabracq, M. J. (eds.) (2015). *International Handbook of Work and Health Psychology*. John Wiley & Sons.

D'Abate, C. P. (2005). Working hard or hardly working: A study of individuals engaging in personal business on the job. *Human Relations*, 58(8), 1009–1032.

D'Abate, C. P. & Eddy, E. R. (2007). Engaging in personal business on the job: Extending the presenteeism construct. *Human Resource Development Quarterly*, 18(3), 361–383.

Deery, S., Walsh, J. & Zatzick, C. D. (2014). A moderated mediation analysis of job demands, presenteeism, and absenteeism. *Journal of Occupational and Organizational Psychology*, 87(2), 352–369.

De Kok, J. (2002). The impact of firm-provided training on production: testing for firm-size effects. *International Small Business Journal*, 20(3), 271–295.

Demerouti, E., Le Blanc, P. M., Bakker, A. B., Schaufeli, W. B. & Hox, J. (2009). Present but sick: a three-wave study on job demands, presenteeism and burnout. *Career Development International*, 14(1), 50–68.

Dew, K., Keefe, V. & Small, K. (2005). "Choosing" to work when sick: workplace presenteeism. *Social Science & Medicine*, 60(10), 2273–2282.

Elstad, J. I. & Vabø, M. (2008). Job stress, sickness absence and sickness presenteeism in Nordic elderly care. *Scandinavian Journal of Social Medicine*, 36(5), 467–474.

Giæver, F., Lohmann-Lafrenz, S. & Løvseth, L. T. (2016). Why hospital physicians attend work while ill? The spiralling effect of positive and negative factors. *BMC Health Services Research*, 16(1), 548.

Goetzel, R. Z., Long, S. R., Ozminkowski, R. J., Hawkins, K., Wang, S. & Lynch, W. (2004). Health, absence, disability, and presenteeism cost estimates of certain physical and mental health conditions affecting US employers. *Journal of Occupational and Environmental Medicine*, 46(4), 398–412.

Gosselin, E. & Lauzier, M. (2010). Le présentéisme. Lorsque la présence n'est pas garante de la performance. *Revue Française de Gestion*, 338, 4551.

Gosselin, E., Lemyre, L. & Corneil, W. (2013). Presenteeism and absenteeism: Differentiated understanding of related phenomena. *Journal of Occupational Health Psychology*, 18(1), 75.

Grinyer, A. & Singleton, V. (2000). Sickness absence as risk-taking behaviour: a study of organisational and cultural factors in the public sector. *Health, Risk & Society*, 2(1), 7–21.

Halbesleben, J. R., Whitman, M. V. & Crawford, W. S. (2014). A dialectical theory of the decision to go to work: Bringing together absenteeism and presenteeism. *Human Resource Management Review*, 24(2), 177–192.

Hansen, C. D. & Andersen, J. H. (2008). Going ill to work–What personal circumstances, attitudes and work-related factors are associated with sickness presenteeism? *Social Science & Medicine*, 67(6), 956–964.

Harris, E. A. (2010). *You Can Be a Successful Business Person!: Micro, Small & Medium Enterprises (MSMEs) Fundamentals*. AuthorHouse.

Hemp, P. (2004). Presenteeism: At work – but out of it. *Harvard Business Review*, 49–58.

Herring, H. B. (2004). Hey, how about that game? *New York Times*, pp. 3, 9.

Hutting, N., Engels, J. A., Heerkens, Y. F., Staal, J. B. & Nijhuis-Van der Sanden, M. W. (2014). Development and measurement properties of the Dutch version of the Stanford Presenteeism Scale (SPS-6). *Journal of Occupational Rehabilitation*, 24(2), 268–277.

Huver, B., Richard, S., Vaneecloo, N., Delclite, T. & Bierla, I. Sick but at Work. An Econometric Approach to Presenteeism. 15th IZA European Summer School in Labor Economics Buch am Ammersee, https://pdfs.semanticscholar.org/b056/2ba7d6ac60ac83a87dbbbc7f655f7a87d770.pdf.

Johansen, V., Aronsson, G. & Marklund, S. (2014). Positive and negative reasons for sickness presenteeism in Norway and Sweden: a cross-sectional survey. *BMJ Open*, 4(2), e004123.

Johansson, G. & Lundberg, I. (2004). Adjustment latitude and attendance requirements as determinants of sickness absence or attendance. Empirical tests of the illness flexibility model. *Social Science & Medicine*, 58(10), 1857–1868.

Johns, G. (2011). Attendance Dynamics at Work: The Antecedents and Correlates of Presenteeism, Absenteeism, and Productivity Loss. *Journal of Occupational Health Psychology*, 16(4), 483–500.

Johns, G. (2010). Presenteeism in the workplace: A review and research agenda. *Journal of Organizational Behavior*, 31, 519–542.

Johnson, D. (1995). Stress and stress management among owner-managers of small and medium-sized enterprises. *Employee Councelling Today*, 7(5), 14–19.

Jourdain, G. & Vézina, M. (2014). How psychological stress in the workplace influences presenteeism propensity: A test of the Demand–Control–Support model. *European Journal of Work and Organizational Psychology*, 23(4), 483–496.

Karanika-Murray, M., & Biron, C. (under review). Development of a taxonomy of presenteeism behaviour: A balancing act between health and performance demands.

Karanika-Murray, M., Pontes, H. M., Griffiths, M. D. & Biron, C. (2015). Sickness presenteeism determines job satisfaction via affective-motivational states. *Social Science & Medicine*, 139, 100–106.

Karlsson, M. L., Björklund, C. & Jensen, I. (2010). The effects of psychosocial work factors on production loss, and the mediating effect of employee health. *Journal of Occupational and Environmental Medicine*, 52(3), 310–317.

Kessler, R. C., Barber, C., Beck, A. et al. (2003). The world health organization health and work performance questionnaire (HPQ). *Journal of Occupational and Environmental Medicine*, 45(2), 156–174.

Kivimäki, M., Ferrie, J. E., Brunner, E. et al. (2005). Justice at work and reduced risk of coronary heart disease among employees: the Whitehall II Study. *Archives of Internal Medicine*, 165(19), 2245–2251.

Knani, M., Fournier, P. S. & Biron, C. (under review). Revisiting presenteeism to broaden its conceptualization: A qualitative study in SMEs.

Koopman, C., Pelletier, K. R., Murray, J. F. et al. (2002). Stanford presenteeism scale: health status and employee productivity. *Journal of Occupational and Environmental Medicine*, 44(1), 14–20.

Lawrence, S. R., Collins, E., Pavlovich, K. & Arunachalam, M. (2006). Sustainability practices of SMEs: the case of NZ. *Business Strategy and the Environment*, 15(4), 242–257.

Leineweber, C., Westerlund, H., Hagberg, J., Svedberg, P. & Alexanderson, K. (2012). Sickness presenteeism is more than an alternative to sickness absence: results from the population-based SLOSH study. *International Archives of Occupational and Environmental Health*, 85(8), 905–914.

Leineweber, C., Westerlund, H., Hagberg, J., Svedberg, P., Luokkala, M. & Alexanderson, K. (2011). Sickness presenteeism among Swedish police officers. *Journal of Occupational Rehabilitation*, 21(1), 17–22.

Lerner, D., Amick III, B. C., Rogers, W. H., Malspeis, S., Bungay, K. & Cynn, D. (2001). The work limitations questionnaire. *Medical Care*, 39(1), 72–85.

Lerner, D. & Henke, R. M. (2008). What does research tell us about depression, job performance, and work productivity?. *Journal of Occupational and Environmental Medicine*, 50(4), 401–410.

Löve, J., Grimby-Ekman, A., Eklöf, M., Hagberg, M. & Dellve, L. (2010). "Pushing oneself too hard": performance-based self-esteem as a predictor of sickness presenteeism among young adult women and men – a cohort study. *Journal of Occupational and Environmental Medicine*, 52(6), 603–609.

Lowe, G. (2002). Here in body, absent in producitivity: Presenteeism hurts output, quality of work-life and employee health. *Retrieved February*, 3, 2005.

Lu, L., Cooper, C. L. & Lin, H. Y. (2013). A cross-cultural examination of presenteeism and supervisory support. *Career Development International*, 18(5), 440–456.

MacGregor, J. N., Barton Cunningham, J. & Caverley, N. (2008). Factors in absenteeism and presenteeism: Life events and health events. *Management Research News*, 31(8), 607–615.

Marchesnay, M. & Julien, P. A. (1990). The small business: as a transaction space. *Entrepreneurship & Regional Development*, 2(3): 267–278.

Martocchio, J. J. & Jimeno, D. I. (2003). Employee absenteeism as an affective event. *Human Resource Management Review*, 13(2), 227–241.

Mattke, S., Balakrishnan, A., Bergamo, G. & Newberry, S. J. (2007). A review of methods to measure health-related productivity loss. *American Journal of Managed Care*, 13(4), 211.

Melançon, S., Lauzier, M., Gosselin, E. & Foucher, R. (2012). Le Standford Presenteeism Scale (SPS-6): déconstruction d'un faux semblant. *Affiche présentée lors du 17e Congrès de l'Association internationale de psychologie du travail de langue française (AIPTLF)*, Lyon, France.

Miraglia, M. & Johns, G. (2016). Going to work ill: A meta-analysis of the correlates of presenteeism and a dual-path model. *Journal of Occupational Health Psychology*. Advance online publication. http://dx.doi.org/10.1037/ocp0000015

Mintzberg, H. & Waters, J. A. (1982). Tracking strategy in an entrepreneurial firm. *Academy of Management Journal*, 25(3), 465–499.

Neftzger, A. L. & Walker, S. (2010). Measuring productivity loss due to health: a multi-method approach. *Journal of Occupational and Environmental Medicine*, 52(5), 486–494.

Oligny, M. (2009). Le burnout ou l'effet d'usure imputable a la regulation permanente d'incidents critiques. *Revue internationale de Psychosociologie*, 15(36), 207–228.

Ozminkowski, R. J., Goetzel, R. Z., Chang, S. & Long, S. (2004). The application of two health and productivity instruments at a large employer. *Journal of Occupational and Environmental Medicine*, 46(7), 635–648.

Ozminkowski, R. J., Goetzel, R. Z. & Long, S. R. (2003). A validity analysis of the Work Productivity Short Inventory (WPSI) instrument measuring employee health and productivity. *Journal of Occupational and Environmental Medicine*, 45(11), 1183–1195.

Prochaska, J. O., Evers, K. E., Johnson, J. L. et al. (2011). The well-being assessment for productivity: a well-being approach to presenteeism. *Journal of Occupational and Environmental Medicine*, 53(7), 735–742.

Reilly, M. C., Zbrozek, A. S. & Dukes, E. M. (1993). The validity and reproducibility of a work productivity and activity impairment instrument. *Pharmacoeconomics*, 4(5), 353–365.

Robertson, I., Leach, D., Doerner, N. & Smeed, M. (2012). Poor health but not absent: prevalence, predictors, and outcomes of presenteeism. *Journal of Occupational and Environmental Medicine*, 54(11), 1344–1349.

Sanderson, K. & Cocker, F. (2013). Presenteeism: Implications and health risks. *Australian Family Physician*, 42(4),172–175.

Schultz, A. B. & Edington, D. W. (2007). Employee health and presenteeism: a systematic review. *Journal of Occupational Rehabilitation*, 17(3), 547–579.

Schultz, A. B., Chen, C. Y. & Edington, D. W. (2009). The cost and impact of health conditions on presenteeism to employers. *Pharmacoeconomics*, 27(5), 365–378.

Siegrist, J. (1996). Adverse health effects of high effort – low reward conditions at work. *Journal of Occupational Health Psychology*, 1, 27–43.

Skagen, K. & Collins, A. M. (2016). The consequences of sickness presenteeism on health and wellbeing over time: A systematic review. *Social Science & Medicine*, 161, 169–177. doi:http://dx.doi.org/10.1016/j.socscimed.2016.06.005

Smith, D. J. (1979). Absenteeism, and presenteeism in industry. *Archives of Environmental Health*, 21, 670–677.

Stewart, W. F., Ricci, J. A., Chee, E., Morganstein, D. & Lipton, R. (2003). Lost productive time and cost due to common pain conditions in the US workforce. *Jama*, 290(18), 2443–2454.

Taloyan, M., Aronsson, G., Leineweber, C., Hanson, L. M., Alexanderson, K. & Westerlund, H. (2012). Sickness presenteeism predicts suboptimal self-rated health and sickness absence: a nationally representative study of the Swedish working population. *PloS one*, 7(9), e44721.

Tang, K., Beaton, D. E., Boonen, A., Gignac, M. A. & Bombardier, C. (2011). Measures of work disability and productivity: Rheumatoid Arthritis Specific Work Productivity Survey (WPS-RA), Workplace Activity Limitations Scale (WALS), Work Instability Scale for Rheumatoid Arthritis (RA-WIS), Work Limitations Questionnaire (WLQ), and Work Productivity and Activity Impairment Questionnaire (WPAI). *Arthritis Care & Research*, 63(S11).

Turpin, R. S., Ozminkowski, R. J., Sharda, C. E. et al. (2004). Reliability and validity of the Stanford Presenteeism Scale. *Journal of Occupational and Environmental Medicine*, 46(11), 1123–1133.

Van Vegchel, N., De Jonge, J., Meijer, T. & Hamers, J. P. (2001). Different effort constructs and effort–reward imbalance: effects on employee well-being in ancillary health care workers. *Journal of Advanced Nursing*, 34(1), 128–136.

Virtanen, M., Kivimäki, M., Elovainio, M., Vahtera, J. & Cooper, C. L. (2001). Contingent employment, health and sickness absence. *Scandinavian Journal of Work, Environment & Health*, 365–372.

de Vries, H. J., Brouwer, S., Groothoff, J. W., Geertzen, J. H. & Reneman, M. F. (2011). Staying at work with chronic nonspecific musculoskeletal pain: a qualitative study of workers' experiences. *BMC Musculoskeletal Disorders*, 12(1), 126.

Wang, P. S., Beck, A., Berglund, P. et al. (2003). Chronic medical conditions and work performance in the health and work performance questionnaire calibration surveys. *Journal of Occupational and Environmental Medicine*, 45(12), 1303–1311.

Westerlund, H., Kivimaki, M., Ferrie, J. E. et al. (2009). Does working while ill trigger serious coronary events? The Whitehall II Study. *Journal of Occupational and Environmental Medicine*, 51(9), 1099–1104.

Zhang, W., Bansback, N. & Anis, A. H. (2011). Measuring and valuing productivity loss due to poor health: a critical review. *Social Science & Medicine*, 72(2), 185–192.

Zhou, Q., Martinez, L. F., Ferreira, A. I. & Rodrigues, P. (2016). Supervisor support, role ambiguity and productivity associated with presenteeism: a longitudinal study. *Journal of Business Research*, 69(9), 3380–3387.

3 | Understanding the Excessive Availability for Work in the Confucian Asia: Interactions between Sociocultural Forces and Personal Drives

LUO LU[*] AND SHU-FANG KAO

Availability for Work: A Work Issue?

On the global stage, fierce international competition and worldwide economic recession over the years have resulted in fundamental changes in employment relationships, such as layoffs, involuntary early retirement, and temporary employment (Worrall & Cooper, 2013). Afraid of losing their job, most employees work harder than before; however, more working time leads to increased strain (Lu, 2011). The advance of Information and Communication Technologies (ICT) is also changing the nature of work, in two seemingly contradictory ways. On the one hand, ICT brings in more flexibility in terms of place and time of work, which can make work arrangements more accommodating to diverse personal needs and lifestyles. On the other hand, the widespread use of ICT easily breaches the demarcation of work and personal life. One consequence of such a blurring of the line between work and nonwork is the increasing "invisible" working hours when employees are constantly bombarded with instructions and queries sent through ICT by their employers outside the official working time. The recent move of ICT towards "CASMIT" (Cloud, Analytics, Social, Mobile, and Internet of Things) has further fueled the transformation of "work taking over life, any time, anywhere." With the vast coverage of services on smart devices in the high-tech-driven economies in East Asia such as Taiwan, Japan, and Korea, instant messages enable work-related demands from the boss to trespass on personal realms 7/24. Although governments (e.g., Taiwan) are now considering amendments to the labor law to bar such invasion by employers into workers' personal time and space, or to

69

compensate workers for these "invisible" working hours with overtime pay, implementation of such legislation will be difficult, if not impossible, given the persisting global economic state of low growth and the prevailing social values of diligence in Asia.

Long working hours in Asia, especially in the Confucian-influenced societies, is a fact of life and notorious for its alleged detrimental effects on employees and organizations. However, such excessive working hours as reported in international comparative studies or social surveys (details below) are just the tip of the iceberg. A recent news event in Taiwan may help us understand the intricate yet interwoven forces sustaining this deep-rooted work practice, which is so resistant to intervention. July 29, 2017, a strong tropical storm (typhoon NESAT) hit Taiwan with winds of over a hundred miles an hour and heavy rainfall. With flooding streets and homes, and widespread power outages, the island nation was at a standstill. All provincial government announced "no school, no work" on the day after (30th), which came to be known as the "typhoon break" over the years. Nearly 500 flight attendants of one of the largest Taiwanese airlines (Eva Air) tendered their leave of absence for the day. This collective act of staying away from work created chaotic scenes at the national airports, resulting in more than 50 flights being canceled, over ten thousand passengers affected, and an estimated 100 million per day financial loss for the company. Defying weather forecasts of local and international agencies, the day was dry and clear. With news broadcasters showing angry passengers, frustrated ground staff, apologetic managers, and the disrupted airport operation every hour in their bulletins, online debates heated up as well. The public was deeply offended by the lack of diligence and professionalism of these flight attendants (mostly young and female), and harsh criticisms describing them as selfish, immoral, and ignorant of others' welfare were aimed at them not only by those affected, but also by bystanders. It later turned out that the leave of absence was legitimate, as it is a collective bargain negotiated by the union following a similar incident resulting from the employer "forcing" staff to fly on a typhoon day the year before. Nonetheless, the legality clause did not quiet the uproar, which, if anything, was fueled by the fear of copycat protests and thus a higher probability of disruption to enterprise operations and public order in the future. In the wake of this one-sided media battering, flight attendants returned to work while shying away from cameras, avoiding damning public eyes, and offering no self-defense, as if wishing their low profile would diminish the public interest in this work issue.

What is clear from the unfolding of the above incident is that a work issue (such as attendance) in Confucian Asia is never *just* a work issue: cultural forces, social factors, managerial practices, employees' self-concept, values, motivations, psychological resources all conspire to make it into a sociocultural as much as individual-personal act. The context of a natural disaster (when nobody should be blamed for self-protection, i.e., not risking the flight) serves to highlight the unimaginably strong impetus of sociocultural forces in Asian employees' decision-making process of availability for work. In this chapter, we will attempt to understand the decision on avail-ability for work as the result of constant interactions between the Person and the Environment, taking an interactionist approach (Bandura, 1986). Figure 1 presents a general theoretical framework to guide the analysis below.

It needs to be stated upfront that the frame of reference in this exercise of cultural analysis is the Confucian tradition deeply rooted in some Asian societies, for example, Greater China, Japan, Korea, Singapore, and the ethnic Chinese communities in Malaysia, Vietnam, and Indonesia. The doctrines guiding work behaviors are generally referred to as the "Confucian Work Ethics" (Chinese

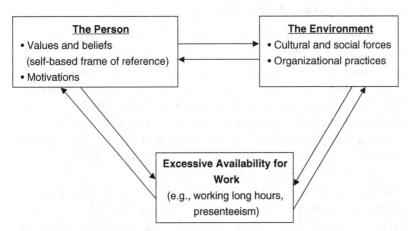

Figure 1 Reciprocal causation: A general theoretical framework for understanding the excessive availability for work

Culture Connection, 1987). It also needs to be made clear that we will address the generic issue of "excessive availability for work," including but not limited to phenomena such as working long hours, paid or unpaid overtime work, sickness presenteeism, face time, taking work home, and using ICT for work in off-time, all of which are easily observable in the work context of the above Asian societies. Championed and sanctioned by the Confucian traditional teachings, sociocultural values such as being hardworking/diligent and preserving social relatedness/interpersonal harmony, are instilled into personal motivations (approach/avoidance), functioning as push and pull factors operating in all the above work commitment-related acts for culturally Chinese employees. Thus, using a generic terminology of "excessive availability for work" will strengthen the cultural thrust, in theory developing as well as better defining the scope of empirical research. However, we may in some instances focus on behaviors of working long hours or sickness presenteeism as illustrations of the theoretical analysis as there is relatively more research on the topics. In other words, the purpose of this chapter is to situate the problem of overworking in the Chinese cultural context, while delineating diverse personal and environmental factors underlying the apparent uniform act of showing up for work.

Excessive Availability for Work and Its Backlash in Confucian Asia: A Brief History

Westerners coming to this part of the world will quickly notice two things in the East Asian work environment: extremely long working hours (including being responsive to work matters 24/7) and turning up to work when obviously ill. The latter is termed "sickness presenteeism" (SP), designating the phenomenon of people who, despite complaints and ill health that should prompt rest and absence from work, are still turning up at their jobs (Aronsson et al., 2000). We will thus focus on long working hours and SP to elucidate the facts and consequences of the excessive availability for work.

During the 1970s in Japan, there was an outbreak in cases of sudden deaths in employees due to overwork. The phrase *"Karoshi"* (or "death from overwork") began to be widely used in 1982, following the publication of the book entitled *"Karoshi"* by three physicians (Kanai, 2006). Public awareness was raised in the Japanese society, and relevant studies were published, which resulted in the accumulation of a large quantity of epidemiological evidence on the relationship between working hours and health. In recent years, numerous news reports on *karoshi* and overtime work have emerged. In 2010, the media reported at great length about the suspected *karoshi* of a 29-year-old engineer in the high-tech industry due to overtime work. This high-profile case once again solicited an intensive public debate on overwork and overtime works. According to statistics from the Dow Jones (2011) news archive, a total of 166 news reports pertaining to "overtime work" were filed between January and April 2011, which is many times higher than the isolated cases reported in the past. High-profile cases and conscious raising campaigns eventually pushed the Japanese government to legislate a 40-hour-per-week cap over a 10-year period (1988–1997). Recently (2015), the Japanese government enacted new laws to further reform the persistent culture of long working hours (e.g., overtime work), by forcing companies to ensure that their employees use up annual paid leave days.

Taiwan competes with Japan for the hardest working labor force in Asia. In the 2010 World Competitiveness Yearbook released by the International Institute for Management Development (IMD) in Switzerland, Taiwan was ranked 14 (out of 59) countries in average working hours, which amount to 2,074 hours per year. The 2009 human resources survey by the Executive Yuan Directorate-General of Budget, Accounting and Statistics (DGBAS) in Taiwan indicated that 17.6 percent of employed persons worked more than 50 hours per week. An academic survey using a national representative sample in Taiwan revealed a striking work week of 48.96 hours (Lu, 2011), while the official figure puts it at a staggering monthly 185.60 hours and on a rising trend (Council of Labor Affairs, 2010). A similar campaign to increase public awareness of the overwork problem in Taiwan harvested its achievements in recent years. The statutory working hour is now set at 84 hours in two week. The most recent high profile milestone is the cap set at 80 hours for resident doctors, effective from August 1, 2017, after many years of lobbying and negotiation. However, like the public uproar over the Eva Air flight attendants taking the typhoon break, the act of curbing working hours for the exhausting junior doctors again divided public opinion with many anxious about longer waiting time and spillover effects of manpower shortage to other health care professions.

Corroborating the observation of excessive availability for work, employees in East Asia on average do work longer hours (Taiwan: 41.6 hours per week; South Korea: 44.2; Japan: 35.4) than do North Americans (United States: 33.9; Canada: 31.7) and Europeans (Germany: 34.2; UK: 31.6) (Directorate-General of Budget, 2012). A relevant question can thus be raised: do employees in Asian countries also commit more SP than their counterparts in the West, thus compounding with long working hours bring more damage to well-being? Unfortunately, so far there have been no credible nationwide surveys on presenteeism in any Asian countries to compare the phenomenon against Western countries such as the UK (Robertson & Cooper, 2011) or the Scandinavian countries (Aronsson et al., 2000; Demerouti, Blanc, Bakker, Schaufeli & Hox, 2009). However, one study reported the scale means of 2.76 and 2.48 (four-point rating scale) for SP among Taiwanese and Mainland Chinese employees (Lu, Peng, Lin & Cooper, 2014). Another survey ($N = 640$) found that in the past six months, 78 percent of Taiwanese workers committed sickness presenteeism ("Although you feel sick, you still force yourself to go to work") (Lu & Chou, 2016). In a cultural comparative study, the same scale was used to assess SP among Taiwanese and British employees (Lu, Cooper & Lin, 2013). The prevalence of presenteeism was found to be significantly higher among the Taiwanese workers (scale mean of 2.76 vs. 2.41), who also suffered greater exhaustion and lower job satisfaction. Evidence thus supports the proposition that employees in the Confucian Asia are more available for work (excessively) than their counterparts in the West, in forms of committing longer working hours (an objective indicator) and loyal to the call of duty when ill (a more subjective judgment). A pivotal question now is: can this excessive availability for work be (at least partly) explained by cultural forces?

Cultural Impetus for the Excessive Availability for Work

As implied in the two abovementioned attendant/working hour-related incidents in Taiwan, cultural forces (i.e., values, ethics, role expectations) may function as sticks and carrots in creating and nurturing a prevailing social climate of excessive availability for work, while also sustaining it against policy interventions. However, people do not blindly subjugate themselves to cultural doctrines or passively obey societal demands; rather, the interplay between the self and the culture is a mutual construction, resulting in a constant intricate interaction between the Person and the Environment. Thus the effects of culture cannot be separately analyzed without the full appreciation of active human agency (Bandura, 1993). Adopting the most important tenet of the Social Cognitive Theory (SCT), behavioral manifestations (e.g., excessive availability for work) depend on the continuous and mutual influences among the external environment (cultural, social, and organizational), personal cognition (self views, motivations), and past behaviors. Therefore, the same behavior (e.g., long working hours, SP) will have different meanings in different locations, different cultural contexts, and for different people. In the following analysis, we will thus place the behavior of excessive availability for work within the Chinese cultural context along with the Confucian root to better understand its meaning and the relevant situational facilitators/constraints.

Why Do People Choose to Work Excessively?

The reasons why people work for long hours encompass an often complex interaction between workplace constraints, institutional regulations, incentives, working conditions, cultural values, macroeconomic climate, and personal motivations. So far, a comprehensive theory to encompass both personal and environmental factors implicated in this perplexing phenomenon is still lacking (Figart & Golden, 1998).

Porter (2004) distinguished two motivations for working long hours, pointing out that a person may work long hours because of the joy in their work. This is the behavior of a constructive, highly committed person. However, one may also be compelled to work long hours, using it as a defensive strategy to avoid repercussions such as tarnished image, or risk of being laid off in organizational downsizing. Thus, the driving forces behind long working hours can at least be dichotomized into constructive and compulsive influences.

A similar conceptual scheme can be imposed to understand the diverse motivations for committing the act of presenteeism (or the more objectively defined behavior of SP). When the term "presenteeism" was initially introduced, it implied that workers commit this act largely because of some macro-level economic factors such as recession, downsizing, merger, and acquisition (Cooper, 1996). In other words, job insecurity (fear of losing jobs) and lack of job replacement (lean operation) are among the driving forces for the act of presenteeism. Subsequent research has established that certain firm-level work contexts, personal circumstances and personality traits are correlates of presenteeism (e.g., Aronsson & Gustafsson, 2005; Johns, 2011; Löve, Grimby-Ekman, Eklöf, Hagberg & Dellve, 2010). However, contextual features need to be perceived and interpreted by employees to inform their resultant behavioral decision: to come or not to come to work when ill.

To solicit people's personal account of "why," Baker-McClearn, Greasley, Dale & Griffith (2010) conducted interviews in nine organizations and identified two triggering factors of the presenteeism act, which they termed "personal motivations" and "workplace pressures." Personal motivations include work values and beliefs such as "no one else can do the job," "loyalty to own professional image," and "obligation and commitment to colleagues, clients, and organizations." Workplace pressures refer to the organization's attendance policy, management style, and workplace culture. Situating employees' perceptions of their own circumstances and the work environment in a Chinese cultural context, Lu, Lin & Cooper (2013) delineated two distinct underlying forces: the approach and avoidance motivations. Using in-depth interviews and large-scale online surveys, they found that some employees chose to attend work while sick because they believed that they should overcome the discomfort to be loyal to their jobs, coworkers, and customers (*approach motivation*); whereas others forced themselves to work because of the fear of financial (pay) loss or the backlash of social disapproval (*avoidance motivation*). This motivational dichotomy roughly corresponds to Baker-McClearn et al.'s (2010) categorization of *personal motivations/ workplace pressures*. Lu et al. further established that the approach motivation was related to self-efficacy whereas the avoidance motivation was related to neuroticism. Though both motivations trigger the same overt behavioral manifestations of presenteeism, their different psychological (personality) predispositions suggest a dual-process mechanism in this form of excessive availability for work. We now need to map the approach/avoidance motivations to the cultural roots to understand how people subscribe meaning to their outcome expectations.

Confucian Cultural Values: The Social Contract for Excessive Work

Confucianism has a long history in East Asia, and the Greater China societies, Japan, and Korea in particular, have inherited its traditional values and abided by the essence of the "Five Cardinal Relationships" *(Wu Lun)*. The underlying doctrine states that the father–son relationship should form the foundation of all relationships, which metaphorically expands to relationship of monarch–subject, friends, brothers, and husband–wife. These are vertical intersecting relationships, which reinforce the idea that people do not exist as independent individuals but are defined through their relationships with others. People are embedded within interpersonal relationships, and thus become a part of the society. Each person has his/her own duties, and fulfilling them becomes the life goal. These cultural values are as stable as ammonites, hidden within the crevices of rock piles (Lévi-Strauss, 1955). They are gradually internalized along with participation in chartered social activities, and are naturally practiced in daily life, shaping and influencing behaviors (Hwang, 1995; Yang & Lu, 2005).

The Confucian doctrines embrace "hard work" as a virtue, which manifests as the excessive availability for work including all forms of overwork in the so-called "Confucius Circle" societies (Kanai, 2009; Lu, 2011). The widespread use of ICT (e.g., smart phones and online messaging) has helped to further create "invisible" working hours when employees are constantly bombarded with instructions and inquires sent through ICT by their employers outside official work time and even when employees take sick leave. It is thus clear that the excessive availability for work is expected of employees by their employers, tolerated and even "legitimized" by society at large. Dictated by such Confucian work ethics of being "hardworking and diligent," Chinese employees were more likely to report to work when ill (committing more SP) compared to their Western counterparts (Lu et al., 2013).

Furthermore, as loyalty and reciprocity *("bao")* are also highly valued virtues in Confucian work ethics (Lu, Siu & Lu, 2010), employees may push themselves to work when ill to convey loyalty and to reciprocate *("bao da")* the care and security (livelihood) provided by the organization. The cultural imperative for *"bao"* can explain the disparate findings pertaining to the role of supervisory support in employees' decision for committing SP. Interviewing British employees in various industries, Baker-McClearn et al. (2010) discovered that supervisory support was pivotal for employees deciding *not* to come to work when ill. In the West, an understanding supervisor presumably relieves subordinates from fear of leaving a bad impression when taking sick leaves, thus there is no need to use presenteeism as either a career-protecting or a career-promoting tactic. However, considerations in employees' decision to turn up to work while ill may be very different in a Chinese context. As *"bao"* is a highly praised Chinese virtue, the understanding supervisor would instill even stronger desire for subordinates to repay *("bao da")*, and thus invite more SP behaviors (Lin & Lu, 2013). In addition, the Chinese cultural emphasis on hard work and perseverance may drive employees to perform SP as an image management tactic, not so much for the sympathetic direct supervisor, but targeting a wider audience, including coworkers, managers of higher levels, and even customers. Such wide practice of "face time" in the Chinese work context is designed to avoid social disapproval and secure career prospects. This conjecture is confirmed in a sample of employees from diverse industries in Taiwan: 83 percent of workers committed SP, with image management as a salient consideration (Lin & Lu, 2013).

It is clear that the Confucian cultural values provide both sticks (tarnished personal image and damaged social harmony) and carrots (praise for hardworking and perseverance) in contracting employees to commit for excessive work. These culture-level leverages roughly correspond to individual-level motivations (e.g., constructive/compulsive drives in working long hours; approach/avoidance motivations in SP). However, mechanisms through which the different strands of cultural influences/forces mold individual motivations and preferences need theoretical explanation. According to the basic tenet of SCT, the transformation of environmental forces into individual motivations and the resultant behaviors is pivoted on the exercise of personal agency (manifested as a generalized belief of self-efficacy). Thus, SCT as a grand theory with a social-psychological thrust may help to explain the differential reactivity in the excessive availability for work. To reiterate, the SCT describes the triadic reciprocal determinism among the environment (e.g., cultural, social, and working condition), the individual (e.g., self-efficacy, motivations), and behavior (e.g., excessive availability for work). The SCT advocates that individuals tend to undertake behaviors that they believe will result in a "better" outcome. Defined as the belief in one's competence to cope with a broad range of stressful or challenging demands, general self-efficacy thus is a very important factor in shaping the meaning that people ascribe to situations (Bandura, 1997).

Personal Agency and the Self-System: Linking Cultural Imperatives with Individual Motivations

The basic tenet of SCT is that behavior is controlled by the person through the cognitive processes, and by the environment through facilitators and constraints in the external social situations. Specifically, to recognize the mutual, interacting influences among the persons, their behaviors, and environments, Bandura (1986) advocated the *triadic reciprocal determinism* among (a) personal attributes, such as internal cognitive and affective states and physical attributes; (b) external environment factors, such as working condition; and (c) overt behavior (as distinct from internal and physical qualities of the person). In this scheme, external environmental factors, personal attributes, and overt behavior all operate as interlocking mechanisms that affect one another bidirectionally.

Self-efficacy as a key construct in SCT, does not have only an individualistic form, nor a built-in value system. How people's belief of self-efficacy is developed, the forms it takes, the ways it is exercised, and the purposes it serves can vary cross-culturally. More specifically, there is both cultural commonality in basic agentic capacities and mechanisms of operation, and diversity in cultivating these inherent capacities. Cultural variations emerge from universalized capacities through the influence of social practices reflecting shared values and norms, incentive systems, role prescriptions, and pervasive modeling of distinctive styles of thinking and behaving (Bandura, 2012). Accordingly, we need to take into consideration the cultural influences in construing self-efficacy, as well as their mutual, dynamic interrelations to fully understand the excessive availability for work in Confucian Asia (as presented in Figure 1).

It needs to be acknowledged that researchers have examined the behavior of overworking (e.g., SP) taking into account both personal and environmental factors (e.g., Johns, 2010; Lu, Cooper & Lin, 2013); the interaction theorists, however, go further, arguing that the behavior should be considered as a co-determinant of the

Person–Environment transaction, rather than the by-product of it (cf. Bandura, 1986). In other words, the act of excessive availability for work, for example, should be seen as a part of the triadic reciprocal determinism which provides feedback to personal attributes and influences the environment subsequently. Adopting this theorem of triadic reciprocal causality, the interactions and intersections among self-efficacy, external environment, and overt behavior, in the context of excessive availability for work, can then be systematically explored.

Self-efficacy, a key construct in the SCT, is deeply rooted in the conceptions of the self. The self encompasses culture-specific ideas of the person to formulate how one sees himself/herself (Markus & Kitayama, 1998; Lu, 2003). The self is pivotal to cultivate the fundamental beliefs of the individual, including one's self-efficacy, motivations, goals, and other psychosocial mechanisms in the interaction with the environment (Bandura, 2012).

While the Western self is evolved and developed under Western cultural heritage, which is characterized by individualism and exchange relationships, Chinese self is immersed in Confucian cultural heritage, which sanctions the interpersonal relationships prototyped as the "Five cardinal dyadic relationships" *(Wu Lun)*. Such culturally decreed Chinese interpersonal bonds go far beyond the social contracts of the exchange relationships, by emphasizing the collective welfare, diligent role performance, and rigorous self-cultivation (Lu, 2012). Thus, to get a fuller understanding of the self-efficacy of Chinese people, the unique features of the Chinese self as shaped by the Confucian cultural heritage need to be unraveled.

The Self of the Contemporary Chinese People: A Bi-Cultural Hybrid in the Making

Mandated and molded by culture, the self refers to a constellation of thoughts, beliefs, feelings, and actions related to how one views himself/herself. Cultural psychologists, East and West, have exerted concerted efforts to understand the mutual construction between the culture and the self. Building on the seminal works such as Markus & Kitayama (1998), Lu proposed the theory of the "Chinese bicultural self," postulating that the self of contemporary Chinese people consists of both the individual- and social-orientated self systems (e.g., Lu, 2003, 2007, 2008). Subsequent empirical research supported the claim that the two selves not only coexist but also operate harmoniously to reflect the agentic will of the individual (Yang & Lu, 2005; Lu & Yang, 2005, 2006; Lu, 2005, 2008, 2009; Lu, Cooper, Kao, Chang, et al., 2010; Lu, Chang, Kao & Cooper, 2015).

In a nutshell, the individual-oriented self is originally conceived in the Western cultural tradition, and rooted in the Western individualistic value system, which stresses the complete realization of the true self through consistency and integration. Also, the boundary between the self and others is relatively clear and rigid, and the ultimate goal is for individuals to fully realize their self-potential and achieve self-transcendence. This self system is most evident in modern Western societies (e.g., North America and Europe), and recently implanted onto the Chinese people from the West in the processes of social changes and globalization. On the other hand, the social-oriented self has a long history in the Chinese cultural tradition, and is rooted in Confucianism. It regards the self as being embedded within interpersonal social networks, or the "Five Cardinal Relationships" (*Wu Lun*). It stresses the interdependent, relational and collective nature of interpersonal relationships, emphasizes similarities with others, and suppresses the unique self. The self that is cultivated within this context is flexible, changeable, and more focused on holistic views, which results in multifaceted external behaviors, to achieve the flexible handling of different situational demands. The boundary between the self and others is flexible and variable; individuals might even continuously pursue the expansion of the self to include others for moral growth. Such conception of the self is still widely prevalent in modern Chinese societies (e.g., Taiwan, Mainland China, Hong Kong, and Singapore), and those historically influenced by the Confucian teachings (e.g., Japan, Korea, and Vietnam).

The social practices of the self systems centered around three dimensions: self–society relations, self–group relations, and self–other relations (Lu, 2007, 2008). Regarding the self–society relations, the social-oriented self focuses on societal rules and norms, and emphasize cohesion between the self and the society. Individuals are thus compelled to display appropriate behavior in order to conform to the environment, and fulfill the roles they have been assigned in order to obtain social affirmation. In contrast, the individual-oriented self focuses on fully realizing individual potential, and emphasizes the control and domination of the self over the environment. Individuals' behaviors are thus

guided by their needs and desires, rather than by norms and requirements of the society. Self-enhancement and self-growth are viewed as
pathways to obtain self-respect and social esteem.

Regarding the self-group relations, the social-oriented self emphasizes
the integration of the individual into the group, in order to become a part
of the group, and then trying one's best to fulfill one's ascribed roles.
The goals and well-being of the group are regarded as the priority,
whereby individual interests might even be sacrificed in order to maintain the harmony and integrity of the group. In contrast, the individual-
oriented self tends to focus on maintaining the independence, rather than
integration of individuals with the group. This implies that individuals
normally give precedence to self-interests in deciding their behaviors.
Individuals are also sanctioned to rely on themselves for everything, be
self-sufficient, self-contained, and autonomous. Furthermore, individual
goals should take priority over group goals, and personal well-being
should be the most important consideration.

Finally, regarding the self-other relations, the social-oriented self
regards interdependence as the essence of human society, advocating
that humans cannot live in isolation from others. Strong emphasis is
placed on interpersonal sharing and interpersonal affect, forming
the psychological foundation for role obligations. Individuals should
display polite and reasonable behavior in order to conform to social
norms, being keenly sensitive to the evaluations and responses of
others, and regarding these as the basis of self-knowledge. In contrast,
the individual-oriented self regards social relations as exchanges, with
personal well-being at its core. Honest expression of personal preferences, feelings, and needs form the foundation of interpersonal relationships, and personal goals are achieved through fair competition
with an emphasis on rationality. Self-knowledge is mainly attained
through self-exploration, with a lesser regard for the evaluations of
others.

In summary, the self of contemporary Chinese people can be
regarded as a product of interactions and integration between these
two different orientations, which in turn determines the mental models
for interpreting the external environment. Although the influence of
Western culture is undeniable (manifesting through the operation of
the individual-oriented self), the strong imprint of the Chinese cultural
tradition still manifests itself as the dominant self-system, that is the
social-oriented self. Thus the prevalent Chinese self is different from the

prevalent Western self, in terms of its endorsed values, beliefs, cognition, affect, and social behaviors (Lu, 2012).

Accordingly, the Chinese strategies of executing human agency are also different from the Western ones. Chinese people emphasize the congruence of individual growth and social values and accept the results no matter good or bad (Lu & Gilmour, 2004a, 2004b). The pursuit of self-interest is only acceptable or legitimate after one fulfills his/her social duties in a Chinese society. In contrast, the Western cultures encourage one to pursue personal needs, rights, and talents (Geertz, 1975). The vastly different mentalities of the Chinese and Western people should be underscored, when interpreting the exercise of human agency. Specifically, exploring the uniquely Chinese version of cognitive, vicarious, self-regulatory, and self-reflective processes will enable us to unravel the action of Chinese self-efficacy in the interplay of the person and the cultural milieu in which he finds himself.

The Chinese Self-Efficacy in Action: Self-Regulatory Mechanisms in Work Commitment

Self-efficacy is concerned with people's beliefs in their capabilities to mobilize the motivation, cognitive resources, and course of action needed to exercise control over the task at hand to produce given attainments (Bandura, 1997). It should thus be defined in the context of relevant and appropriate behaviors in specific situations, which renders the cultural influences on construing and practicing of the self salient (James, 1995). Self-efficacy exerts its influence through four major processes: *cognitive, motivational, affective, and selection,* to affect the behaviors that control and construct environments. Also, the impact of most environmental influences (including cultural imperatives) on human beings is through these processes, which give meaning and valence to external events (Bandura, 1993). Thus, the action of the Chinese self-efficacy basing on the aforementioned "Chinese bicultural self" (e.g., Lu, 2003, 2005, 2008) can be analyzed along these generic processes.

First of all, *the cognitive processes* work well under the condition that human behavior, which is purposive, is regulated by forethought embodying cognized goals (Bandura, 1993). A major function of thought or forethought is to enable people to predict events and to develop ways to control those events that affect their lives. Forethoughts are construed from the observed environmental events in the world around people and the outcomes given actions produced, in short, from the interaction between external macro environment at present and the behaviors feedbacks before (Bandura, 1986). Based on the theory of bicultural self, Chinese people with a strong social orientation are more concerned about being part of the society. On the one hand, they abide by the social norm, even outperform what is expected of them. Thus, they may consider devoting to work and attaining diligent role performance as their responsibilities, realizing the value of being societal members, also as a way of exercising self-cultivation. On the other hand, even when not yet totally internalized, these societal values may still force them to "act out" devotion to work in order to avoid being excluded or sanctioned by others. Redding (1993) found that working long hours was not only highly praised as a Confucian virtue, but also tolerated as a necessary evil for raising a family, or even regarded as an insurance policy for job security and career advancement. Therefore, the cognitive processes, or more specifically, the forethoughts of Chinese people pertaining to commitment at work, both time and effort, encompass the broader self, including family, organization and society at large.

Secondly, people *motivate* themselves and guide their actions anticipatorily by the exercise of forethought as mentioned earlier. They form beliefs about what they can do, and anticipate likely outcomes of prospective actions (Bandura, 1993). The motivational processes of self-efficacy beliefs operate in three forms as casual attributions, outcome expectancies, and cognized goals of cognitive motivation.

The social orientation in the Chinese self emphasizes that people are embedded in complex relationships and sensitive to others' appraisals and responses, which are the foundation of knowing who he/she is. As such, the outcome expectations involve the imagined consequences of performing particular behaviors ("if I do this, what will others' think?"). Chinese people are expected to give precedence to others' appraisals and collective welfare rather than their individual preferences. Therefore, Chinese employees would care more for the reputation or profitability of the organization than their own welfare. Furthermore, as Chinese employees see themselves as part of the larger society and value harmonious relationships with coworkers, employers, and even stakeholders outside of the organization, they tend to act

in a way that commands appreciation by others, such as being excessively committed to work (working long hours, or working when ill).
It is important to note that Chinese employees are not *merely* using long
working hours or SP as an image management or career protection
tactic, as suggested by Western research (Baker-McClearn et al., 2010);
they genuinely value group cohesion and SP is a way of showing
solidarity and interpersonal harmony at work. Thus, for Chinese
employees, approach and avoidance motivations *jointly* drive the act
of SP. Driven by the approach motivations, Chinese employees come to
work while sick because they believe that they should fulfill their social
obligation inscribed in the job, in the "relational contract" with their
co-workers, and customers. Driven by avoidance motivations, Chinese
employees push themselves to work to avoid damning social disapproval or overburden their colleagues. The delineation of the dual-
motivation process is conceptually important, however, in reality,
they tend to be mildly correlated ($r = .25$, Lu & Chou, 2016) and jointly
trigger the SP behavior and sustain it over time (Lu et al., 2013; Lu &
Chou, 2016).

Thirdly, the *affective processes* explain how people's beliefs in their
capabilities will affect how much stress and depression they experience
in threatening or difficult situations, as well as their level of motivation
to act under such circumstances (Bandura, 1993). People who believe
they can exercise control over undesired situations do not conjure up
disturbing thought patterns; but those who believe they cannot manage
threats experience high anxiety arousal. Worse, they dwell on their
coping deficiencies, and view many aspects of their environment as
fraught with danger.

In other words, a low sense of efficacy to exercise control produces
depression as well as anxiety in stressful encounters. More specifically,
the efficacy route to depression is through a low sense of social efficacy.
This is because people who judge themselves to be socially efficacious
seek out and cultivate social relationships that provide models on how
to manage difficult situations, cushion the adverse effects of chronic
stressors, and bring satisfaction to people's lives (Bandura, 1993).
In this vein, compared with people in the West, Chinese people are
more embedded in social relations, relying more on the support from
their social networks. Furthermore, social contagion and role modeling
are more prevalent among Chinese people. On the positive side,
Chinese employees may play the role of a hardworking and perseverant

worker to gain trust from employers and coworkers, which in turn enhances their social efficacy. On the negative side, the highly praised virtues of endurance and perseverance increase the social pressure for subjugation and act as a deterrent to tardiness in a Chinese work setting.

Finally, the *selection process* points out that, by the choices people make, they cultivate different competencies, interests, and social networks that determine life courses. People choose to enter situations in which they expect success (Bandura, 1989). For Chinese people, it is beneficial to put oneself in situations conducive to the social virtues, such as ones that solicit acts of perseverance and hardworking, or those meeting others' expectations. In the work context, people with approach motivation confront challenging situations for proofs of personal strength, opportunities of showing devotion to work, expressing vigor, dedication, and absorption. In contrast, people with avoidance motivation commit presenteeism to avoid personal failure and social disapproval. While the strong social orientation still dictates excessive work availability to avoid unfavorable judgment by others, it is increasingly likely that newly nurtured individual orientation in the Chinese bicultural self seeks out mastery and growth through commitment to work. The intricate interplays among the self, self-efficacy beliefs and goals deserve more research attention, and may hold the key to understand the complex self-regulation mechanisms in the practice of human agency, when excessive availability for work is committed.

The Chinese Self-Efficacy at Work: Reinterpreting LMX

The Chinese self-practiced in the workplace within the Confucian cultural context can be observed in the subtle interactions between supervisors and subordinates. Both parties interact beyond the balanced reciprocity, and "one-to-one" relationships ascribed in Western social exchange theory. The Chinese supervisor has a fatherly concern over the life of their subordinates, and believes that it is their natural duty to care about both the work and personal lives of their subordinates. At the opposite side, the Chinese subordinates play the role of sons, internalize the idea of "reciprocity" *(bao)*, and embrace the mentality of "repaying a drop of water with a gushing stream." Therefore, they exert behaviors of dedicated service, sacrifice, obedience, and voluntary cooperation, and are willing to redouble their efforts to complete their tasks (Cheng, Chou, Wu, Huang & Farh, 2004; Lin & Cheng, 2012; Liu, 1996; Tzeng & Jiang, 2012). Both parties have exceeded the role expectations in an instrumental relationship, and have established an affective basis for their interactions in and outside of the work realm. Hence, when they experience concern, care, compassion, or kindness from the other party, they will naturally exhibit reciprocal behaviors, thereby reflecting "emotional reciprocity" in actual practice (Liu, 1996). Furthermore, subordinates' diligent and dedicated contributions to work will also earn coveted high praise from the supervisors (Cooper & Lu, 2016). Thus the culturally meaningful engagement between the Chinese supervisors and employees will enrich and broaden the quality and scope of the leader–member exchange (LMX) relationship (Dienesch & Liden, 1986).

Reinterpreting the LMX, Chinese employees are committed to excessive work availability for the following reasons. First, to embrace the spirit of facing hard times together, viewing personal sacrifice for the organization as a show of solidarity, and thus working harder out of loyalty and gratitude for the supervisors' kindness. Second, overworking in exchange for rewards of "not being fired" and social approval by their supervisors. Third, acting out of sincere love and enthusiasm for their work, and voluntarily overwork. The cultural directives will help us to understand the differential meanings and implications of excessive availability for work between Asian and Western societies.

It is worth noting that self-efficacy does create task-mastery experiences, which in turn raise self-efficacy. That is, when an individual competently accomplishes a particular task, such as persevering to complete his work regardless of hardship, such an experience can become absorbed in the overall achievement of the task (Sweetman & Luthan, 2010). Once triumphed in work accomplishments despite illness (SP resulting in good performance), employees are more likely to engage in future SP. Studies with Chinese employees reported a zero-order correlation of SP behaviors over time at .18 (measured repeatedly over 2 months, Lu et al., 2013), and .49 (measured repeatedly over 6 months, Lu & Chou, 2016). The moderately stable level of SP behavior observed over time thus provides partial support for this speculation. It is important to note that job performance was not hampered during the above study periods. The rewarding experience of excessive diligence may contribute to the persistent culture of overworking in the Confucian Asian societies.

Conclusion and Future Research Directions

Although academic interest in certain aspects of the overwork phenomenon (e.g., long working hours, presenteeism, workaholism) has been developed and evolved in the West, we still have a long way to go to uncover the culturally relevant factors and facts of this phenomenon in Asia, especially in societies under Confucian influences, such as Greater China, Japan, and Korea. Systematic research on long working hours and presenteeism in Asia is still scarce, other aspects of the excessive availability for work (e.g., face time, ICT related covert overwork) are even less rigorously examined. Most existing studies to date are descriptive of the phenomenon, and the popular view is that overworking is a by-product of the developing economies, and a social obligation of workers. Researchers have largely overlooked the Confucian cultural context, and neglected the agency of the self in exhibiting behaviors. The research on excessive availability for work, including long working hours and presenteeism can benefit from comprehensive theoretical frameworks to recognize the agentic essence of human being, the interactions and intersections among people, who are carrying their own history, and the environment they encounter at the present time. Cooper & Lu (2016) pioneered the introduction of the social cognitive theory as an overarching analytical framework to reinterpret and reorganize studies and findings pertaining to presenteeism. In their theoretical analysis, people assumed a central place, not merely as a reactive information receiver, but exercising agency in interacting with the environment. However, SCT still implies a universal and culture-free view of the Person, which needs to be remedied through rigorous culture analysis, especially the culture-informed self views that make a human being a Person. This is what we endeavored to acknowledge and incorporate in the theory-building for understanding the overwork phenomenon.

Putting theory into empirical testing is the next step in developing the field. Although contemporary interactionists acknowledge the general influence of culture in shaping values and norms, creating incentive systems and role prescriptions, and modeling of styles of thinking and behaving (Bandura, 2012), there exists no culture-sensitive measure of self-efficacy. We have presented analysis on the cultural impact in construing self views and in turn, the belief of self-efficacy. We have also applied this culturally sensitive analysis to elaborate on the role of the Chinese bi-cultural self that plays in committing to overwork (e.g., long hours and SP). The cultural level analysis enables a deeper understanding of the complicated interplay of culture at a macro level and choice of overworking behaviors at a micro level (as an individual decision). Drawing on these theoretical insights, the new self-efficacy measure for the Chinese people will encompass beliefs emanating from the *individual-oriented* self as well as those that emanate from the *social-oriented* self. The latter have never been covered in existing self-efficacy scales (e.g., Schwarzer, Bassler, Kwiatek, Schroder & Zhang, 1997; Sheier & Carver, 1982). We can adopt and modify items from these measures to assess *individual-oriented self-efficacy*, centering on the key idea of "I, as an independent individual, want to do/feel..." We can consult existing measures of the bi-cultural self-views (e.g., Lu, 2008) to develop new items to assess *social-oriented self-efficacy*, centering on the key idea of "I, as an interdependent person, want to do/feel..."

With usable measures, we can then focus on exploring the agent role of the human being by incorporating the personal and social foci within the causal structure. Situating empirical research in the current economic environment (e.g., economic slowdown, job insecurity, global competition), SCT-informed research models can be developed pivoted on the various psychological processes in producing the overworking behavior (as elaborated earlier). As depicted in Figure 1, such models will highlight people's cognitive processes in work commitment decision-making, acknowledging that people are sentient, purposive beings (Bandura, 2001). It is a fact that even when faced with mounting tasks, people act attentively to make desired things happen rather than simply succumb to demands of the situation. That is, people actively evaluate actions, set goals, and motivate themselves to perform and regulate chosen behaviors. People are not only the reactors to the environment, but also the producers. Through this agentive action, people figure out ways to adapt to social environmental constraints, redesign their behaviors, and create the situation they desire. Accordingly, the excessive availability for work can be understood in a frame of fluidity and dynamism, which reflects the Confucian cultural imperatives.

Pertaining to the practical implications for this research field, we need to focus more on employees in the "Confucian cultural circle," including those in Greater China, Japan, Korea, and Singapore, as the cultural thrust for overworking is the most salient in these societies. We cannot overstate the need to incorporate the Chinese self in the unraveling of the triadic dynamism involved in overwork (e.g., long hours and presenteeism) when Chinese employees are increasingly confronted with challenging work situations, changing values and self views. 鞠躬盡瘁，死而後已(*ju gong jin cui, si er hou yi*) is held as the highest virtue accomplishment and the utmost demonstration of work dedication, literally translated as "to bend one's back to the task until one's dying day" or "to give one's all till one's heart stops beating." Is it still attainable or desirable in a modern society? The answer will not be simple or easy for the descendants of the Confucian tradition.

Note

* Correspondence concerning this chapter should be addressed to Professor Luo Lu. The writing of this chapter was supported by grants from the Ministry of Science and Technology, Taiwan, MOST 103-2410-H-002-195-SS3 and MOST 106-2410-H-002-197-SS2.

References

Aronsson, G. & Gustafsson, K. (2005). Sickness presenteeism: Prevalence, attendance-pressure factors, and an outline of a model for research. *Journal of Occupational Environment Medicine*, 47(9), 958–966.

Aronsson, G., Gustafsson, K. & Dallner, M. (2000). Sick but yet at work. An empirical study of sickness presenteeism. *Journal of Epidemiological Community Health*, 54(7), 502–509.

Baker-McClearn, D., Greasley, K., Dale, J. & Griffith.F. (2010). Absence management and presenteeism: The pressures on employees to attend work and the impact of attendance on performance. *Human Resource Management Journal*, 20(3), 311–328.

Bandura, A. (1986). *Social Foundations of Thought and Action: A Social Cognitive Theory*. Englewood Cliffs, NJ: Prentice-Hall, Inc.

Bandura, A. (1989). Human agency in Social Cognitive Theory. *American Psychologist*, 44(9), 1175–1184.

Bandura, A. (1993). Perceived self-efficacy in cognitive development and functioning. *Educational Psychologist*, 28(2), 117–148.

Bandura, A. (1997). *Self-Efficacy: The Exercise of Control*. New York, NY: Freeman.

Bandura, A. (2001). Social cognitive theory: An agentic perspective. *Annual Review of Psychology*, 52(1), 1–26.

Bandura, A. (2012). On the functional properties of perceived self-efficacy revisited. *Journal of Management*, 38(1), 9–44.

Cheng, B. S., Chou, L. F., Wu, T. Y., Huang, M. P. & Farh, J. L. (2004) Paternalistic leadership and subordinate responses: Establishing a leadership model in Chinese organizations. *Asian Journal of Social Psychology*, 7, 89–117.

Chinese Culture Connection (1987). Chinese values and the search for culture-free dimensions of culture. *Journal of Cross-Cultural Psychology*, 18, 143–174.

Cooper, C. (1996). Hot under the collar. *Times Higher Education Supplement*, 21 June.

Cooper, C. L. & Lu, L. (2016). Presenteeism as a global phenonmenon: Unraveling the psychosocial mechanisms from the perspective of social cognitive theory. *Cross Cultural and Strategic Management*, 23(2), 216–231.

Council of Labor Affairs. (2010). *Labor Statistics*. Retrieved from: http://win .dgbas.gov.tw/dgbas04/bc5/earning/ht456.asp. Taipei, Taiwan: Executive Yuan.

Demerouti, E., Le Blanc, P. M., Bakker, A. B., Schaufeli, W. B. & Hox, J. (2009). Present but sick: a three-wave study on job demands, presenteeism and burnout. *Career Development International*, 14(1), 50–68.

Dienesch, R. M. & Liden, R. C. (1986). Leader–member exchange model of leadership: A critique and further development. *Academy of Management Review*, 11(3), 618–634.

Directorate-General of Budget (2012). *Year Book of Manpower Statistics*. Taipei, Taiwan: Executive Yuan.

Dow Jones. (2011). www.sustainability-index.com/performance.cfm [February 22, 2016].

Figart, D. M. & Golden, L. (1998). The social economics of work time: Introduction. *Review of Social Economy*, 56(4), 411–424.

Geertz, C. (1975). On the nature of anthropological understanding: Not extraordinary empathy but readily observable symbolic forms enable the anthropologist to grasp the unarticulated concepts that inform the lives and cultures of other peoples. *American Scientist*, 63(1), 47–53.

Hwang, K. K. (1995). *Knowledge and action: A social psychological interpretation of Chinese cultural tradition*. (In Chinese.) Taipei: Psychological Publication Co.

James, L. (1995). *Media, Communication, and Culture: A Global Approach*. New York, NY: Columbia University Press.

Johns, G. (2010). Presenteeism in the workplace: A review and research agenda. *Journal of Organizational Behavior*, 31, 519–542.

Johns, G. (2011). Attendance dynamics at work: The antecedents and correlates of presenteeism, absenteeism, and productivity loss. *Journal of Occupational Health Psychology*, 16(4), 483–500. doi:10.1037/a0025153

Kanai, A. (2006). Economic and employment conditions, karoshi (work to death) and the trend of studies on workaholism in Japan, in R. J. Burke (Ed.), *Research Companion to Working Time and Work Addiction*, Cheltenham, UK: Edward Elgar.

Kanai, A. (2009). "Karoshi (Work to Death)" in Japan. *Journal of Business Ethics*, 84(2), 209–216.

Lévi-Strauss, C. (1955). The structural study of myth. *The Journal of American Folklore*, 68(270), 428–444.

Lin, H. Y. & Lu, L. (2013). Presenteeism in workplace: Constructing a cross-cultural framework. *Journal of Human Resource Management*, 13(3), 29–55.

Lin, T. T. & Cheng, B. S. (2012). Life-and work-oriented considerate behaviors of leaders in Chinese organizations: The dual dimensions of benevolent leadership. *Indigenous Psychological Research in Chinese Societies*, 37, 253–302.

Liu, C. M. (1996). Affective Bao in organizations: Some preliminary points of view. *Chinese Journal of Applied Psychology*, 5, 1–34.

Löve, J., Grimby-Ekman, A., Eklöf, M., Hagberg, M. & Dellve, L. (2010). Pushing oneself too hard: Performance-based self-esteem as a predictor of sickness presenteeism among young adult women and men–a cohort study. *Journal of Environment Medicine*, 52(6), 603–609. doi:10.1097/JOM.0b013e3181dce181

Lu, L. (2003). Defining the self-other relation: The emergence of a composite self. *Indigenous Psychological Research in Chinese Societies*, 20, 139–207.

Lu, L. (2005). In pursuit of happiness: The cultural psychological study of SWB. *Chinese Journal of Psychology*, 47(2), 99–112.

Lu, L. (2007). The individual- and social-oriented self views: Conceptual analysis and empirical assessment. *US–China Education Review*, 4, 1–24.

Lu, L. (2008). The individual- and social-oriented Chinese bicultural self: Testing the theory. *Journal of Social Psychology*, 148, 347–374.

Lu, L. (2009). I or we: Family socialization values in a national probability sample in Taiwan. *Asian Journal of Social Psychology*, 12, 95–100.

Lu, L. (2011). Working hours and personal preference among Taiwanese employees. *International Journal of Workplace Health Management*, 4(3), 244–256.

Lu, L. (2012). To be or not to be? Rethinking the Chinese bicultural self. *Indigenous Psychological Research in Chinese Societies*, 37, 241–250.

Lu, L. & Chou, C. Y. (2016, July). The impact of job insecurity on the relationships between sickness presenteeism and work outcomes. Paper presented at the 31st International Congress of Psychology 2016 (ICP2016), Yokohama, Japan.

Lu, L., Cooper, C. L., Kao, S. F., Chang, T. T., Allen, T. D., et al. (2010). Cross-cultural differences in work-to-family conflict and role satisfaction: A Taiwanese–British comparison. *Human Resource Management*, 49, 67–85.

Lu, L. & Gilmour, R. (2004a). Culture and conceptions of happiness: Individual oriented and social oriented SWB. *Journal of Happiness Studies*, 5(3), 269–291.

Lu, L. & Gilmour, R. (2004b). Culture, self and ways to achieve SWB: A cross-cultural analysis. *Journal of Psychology in Chinese Societies*, 5(1), 51–79.

Lu, L., Siu, O. L. & Lu, C. Q. (2010). Does loyalty protect Chinese workers from stress? The role of affective organizational commitment in the Greater China region. *Stress & Health*, 26, 161–168.

Lu, L. & Yang, K. S. (2005). Individual- and social-oriented views of self-actualization: Conceptual analysis and preliminary empirical exploration. *Indigenous Psychological Research in Chinese Societies*, 23, 3–69.

Lu, L. & Yang, K. S. (2006). The emergence and composition of the traditional-modern bicultural self of people in contemporary Taiwanese societies. *Asian Journal of Social Psychology*, 9(3), 167–175.

Lu, L., Chang, T. T., Kao, S. F. & Cooper, C. L. (2015). Testing an integrated model of the work-family interface in Chinese employees: A longitudinal study. *Asian Journal of Social Psychology*, 18, 12–21.

Lu, L., Cooper, C. L. & Lin, H. Y. (2013). A cross-cultural examination of presenteeism and supervisory support. *Career Development International*, 18(5), 440–456.

Lu, L., Peng, S. Q., Lin, H. Y. & Cooper, C. L. (2014). Presenteeism and health among Chinese employees: The moderating role of self-efficacy. *Work & Stress*, 28(2), 165–178.

Markus, H. R. & Kitayama, S. (1998). The cultural psychology of personality. *Journal of Cross-Cultural Psychology*, 29(1), 63–87.

Porter, G. (2004). Work, work ethic, work excess. *Journal of Organizational Change Management*, 17(5), 424–439.

Redding, S. G. (1993). *The Spirit of Chinese Capitalism*. New York, NY: De Gruyter.

Robertson, I. & Cooper, C. L. (2011). *Well-being: Productivity and Happiness at Work*. Hampshire, UK: Palgrave MacMillan.

Schwarzer, R., Bassler, J., Kwiatek, P., Schroder, K. & Zhang, J. X. (1997). The assessment of optimistic self-beliefs: Comparison of the German, Spanish, and Chinese versions of the General Self-efficacy Scale. *Applied Psychology*, 46, 69–88.

Sheier, M. F. & Carver, C. S. (1982). Self-consciousness, outcome expectancy, and persistence. *Journal of Research in Personality*, 16, 409–418.

Sweetman, D. & Luthans, F. (2010). The power of positive psychology: Psychological capital and work engagement, in A. B. Bakker & M. P. Leiter (Eds.), *Work Engagement: A Handbook of Essential Theory and Research*. New York, NY: Psychology Press (pp. 54–68).

Tzeng, C. W. & Jiang, D. Y. (2012). The relationships between employee motivation and political skill: The moderating effects of *Bao*. *Research in Applied Psychology*, 53, 207–212.

Worrall, L. & Cooper, C. L. (2013). The effect of the recession on UK managers: The quality of working life 2007–2012. *Research in Applied Psychology*, 59, 23–48.

Yang, K. S. & Lu, L. (2005). Social- vs. individual-oriented self-actualizers: Conceptual analysis and empirical assessment of their psychological characteristics. *Indigenous Psychological Research in Chinese Societies*, 23, 71–143.

PART II

Understanding the Behavior of Presenteeism

4 | Motivation and Presenteeism: The Whys and Whats

JIE MA, DANIEL P. MELTZER, LIU-QIN YANG, AND CONG LIU

Motivation and Presenteeism: The Whys and Whats

Presenteeism, or "attending work while ill" (Johns, 2010: 521), is an action that can be viewed as both positive and negative. On the one hand, presenteeism indicates an employee's great commitment to work. On the other hand, it implies a potential decline in productivity, which could jeopardize personal and/or team performance. Global Corporate Challenge conducted an international study of nearly 2,000 participants (Batman & Sackett, 2016). They concluded that while employees take five absentee days a year, they reported losing more than ten times as many days in productivity by working while ill.

In this chapter, we explore the motivational antecedents of an employee's presenteeism, and the effects of the employee's presenteeism on his/her coworkers' motivation. We posit that one's motivation for presenteeism has significant implications on the outcomes of enacted presenteeism. Specifically, we focus on the proximal and distal antecedents of presenteeism through the lens of motivational theories, and suggest future studies of presenteeism to consider the underlying motivations in building up theoretical frameworks. That is to say, researchers should consider whether an employee works while ill out of passion or out of obligation. Given the limited amount of research in this area to date, we recommend avenues for potential research going forward.

Defining Presenteeism: The Deficiency in the Motivational Consideration

Presenteeism refers to the behavior of working while ill (Johns, 2010). However, this behavioral presenteeism has a definitional problem in both theory and practice. In theory, this overgeneralized definition neglects the underlying motivations, as well as the potential effects on the future motivational and behavioral outcomes of the individual and those around him/her. In practice, such a behavior-oriented definition has few implications on whether presenteeism behaviors should be encouraged or discouraged. As noted by Johns (2010), presenteeism may exacerbate illness and reduce employee effectiveness; at the same time, it is also viewed as an act of organizational citizenship behavior (OCB). The lack of insights on the motivations of presenteeism makes the link to net gain or loss unclear, and in turn, produces little guidance toward practice.

Further, it the literature is unclear on what constitutes "illness" within the context of presenteeism. This leads to disputes as to whether presenteeism has occurred, as has been noted within studies. Wang et al. (2010) proposed a relationship between depression and presenteeism; however, they found the sample limited to those with physical illness. Therefore, participants with depression or other mental illnesses at work were excluded from the final sample. To address the issue, we adjust the Johns (2010) definition of presenteeism slightly to include mental illnesses. Within this chapter, we refer to presenteeism as "working while being impaired due to physical or psychological illness." This definition is inclusive of issues such as depression and other psychological illnesses recognized by the *Diagnostic and Statistical Manual of Mental Disorders*, while still excluding subclinical symptoms such as occupational burnout. While many workers come to work regularly on days where they just feel "off," or following a relatively sleepless night, or perhaps just work when they are otherwise distracted, these would not meet the criteria for presenteeism. Presenteeism requires the employee to show up to work with a diagnosable physical or psychological illness, which impairs the capability of the employee in question.

To advance the current theoretical frameworks of presenteeism (Johns, 2010; Miraglia & Johns, 2016; Pohling, Buruck, Jungbauer & Leiter, 2016), and to add practical implications for organizations, we dedicate this chapter to exploring two areas of interest. First, what drives employees to work while they are experiencing tolerable levels of psychological or physical discomfort or/and pain that results from diagnosable illnesses? Second, how does one employee who chooses to come to work with an illness impact the motivation of other employees around them?

Motivation for Presenteeism: Why Do Employees Come to Work While Ill?

Lu, Lin & Cooper (2013) investigated the role of motivation on presenteeism, as well as the corresponding employee outcomes. They proposed and tested an approach motivation (i.e., expanding efforts due to loyalty or commitment to work) and an avoidance motivation (i.e., expanding efforts for avoiding punishment or other losses), respectively. They concluded that both types of motivation contributed to presenteeism, indicating that employees enact presenteeism for various reasons. Furthermore, these different motivations were shown to impose opposite effects on employees, with approach motivation being associated with positive work-related outcomes (e.g., better job performance), whereas avoidance motivation was associated with negative outcomes (e.g., exhaustion). These double-edged effects of presenteeism stress the role of motivation in determining the "cost and profit."

Motivation refers to an internal state describing the direction, intensity, and persistence of certain behaviors (Kanfer, 1990). Direction refers to the choice of behavior. In the domain of presenteeism, it refers to coming to work or not. Intensity refers to the amount of effort an individual exerts at work. In the domain of presenteeism, intensity could range from being sloppy to hardworking. Persistence refers to sustaining the behavior over time. In the domain of presenteeism, persistence could be indicated by the length of time working while ill. In short, motivation pivots on the reasons, rather than capabilities, in expanding one's efforts in work behaviors.

Motivation itself is unobservable, but can be inferred through the lens of need satisfaction (e.g., self-determination theory; Deci & Ryan, 2000), cognitive evaluation (e.g., self-efficacy theory; Bandura, 1977), behavioral modification (e.g., reinforcement theory; Skinner, 1969), and job design (e.g., job characteristics model; Hackman & Oldham, 1976). These four perspectives shed a light on the various sources and paradigms of motivation behind a given behavior. We incorporate these motivational factors in formulating an integrated motivational model of presenteeism (see Figure 1), in order to enlighten future research on *why* employees come to work while ill, *what* constitutes motivations of presenteeism, and *how* presenteeism associated with different motivations ends up with various consequences. Specifically, on the basis of self-determination theory – one of the most prevalent

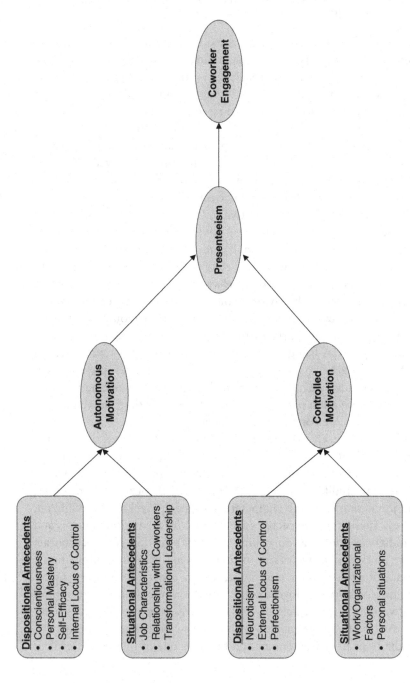

Figure 1 An integrative motivational model of presenteeism

motivational frameworks – combined with existing theoretical rationales and empirical evidences, we link specific situational and personal factors to certain types of motivation for presenteeism.

Self-Determination Theory (SDT)

SDT argues that motivation originates from fulfilling one's basic needs of autonomy, relatedness, and competence. Rather than simply answering "whether or not" the needs are satisfied, SDT further sheds a light on the degree of needs satisfaction (Gagné & Deci, 2005). It further gives rise to the concept of internalization, namely the degree to which one aligns a given behavior with one's sense of self. Specifically, if performing a certain behavior will largely satisfy one's basic needs, one will be likely to regard this behavior as an extension of oneself (i.e., high internalization) (Deci & Ryan, 2008). As an example, an employee who is allowed a flexible work schedule may see working with effort is part of oneself, because the flexibility in daily schedule satisfies his or her need for autonomy.

Inspired by the idea of internalization, SDT proposes several specific and distinctive motivations and arranges them along the motivation spectrum. Intrinsic motivation and externally regulated motivation are placed at two ends of a motivation continuum, with introjected motivation, identified motivation, and integrated motivation being arrayed in between. *Intrinsic motivation* occurs when one performs a behavior out of delight. *Integrated motivation* occurs when a person integrates the behaviors to one's self-concept. *Identified motivation* indicates that one accepts the importance or the justification of a given behavior as to attain valued personal goals. Furthermore, one could also enact a behavior to make oneself look good in the eyes of others. This reflects one's *introjected motivation*. *External motivation* occurs solely for the sake of obtaining external rewards or circumventing punishments. Since intrinsic, integrated, and identified motivation all represents the motivational states of acting out of freewill, they are all labeled as *autonomous motivation*. Introjected motivation and extrinsic motivation are classified as controlled motivation, as both capture the motivational states as being controlled by external forces (Deci & Ryan, 2008).

We adopt SDT, particularly the autonomous-controlled motivation paradigm, in formulating the motivational mechanism of presenteeism for two main reasons. Firstly, the autonomous-controlled paradigm includes discrete motivations (the specific types on the SDT continuum), which will help explain the various reasons behind presenteeism and shed a light on likely consequences associated with each discrete motivation. Secondly, SDT is often used in conjunction with other motivational theories, such as goal setting theory (Latham & Locke, 1975) or job characteristics model (Hackman & Oldham, 1976).

Applications of SDT on the Understanding of Presenteeism

The distinction between autonomous and controlled motivation is necessary to understand the antecedents of presenteeism and implications of presenteeism for employees' various outcomes. On the one hand, both types of motivation could propel employees to work while ill. On the other hand, autonomous and controlled motivation have opposite effects on employees, with autonomous motivation being related to positive consequences (e.g., better well-being and performance) and controlled motivation being associated with negative consequences (e.g., burnout) (Gagné & Deci, 2005). It is thus plausible that presentee employees with autonomous motivation should experience positive work outcomes such as engagement – being immersed in work roles – whereas those with controlled motivation may experience negative outcomes such as productivity loss and subsequent sick leave. In practice, the financial cost of reduced productivity in organizations resulting from presenteeism is estimated to be quite high (Batman & Sackett, 2016). Understanding the various motives of presenteeism is necessary for organizations to effectively manage company-wide presenteeism and their related consequences. Thus, we use the following sections to discuss possible personal and situational factors that lead to autonomous or controlled motivations for presenteeism.

Autonomous Motivation and Presenteeism

Dispositional Antecedents of Autonomous Motivation

Personality. Personality refers to stable and enduring characteristics of an individual in relation to one's emotions, cognitions, and behaviors (Costa, McCrae & Dye, 1991). Employees with certain personalities may be more self-determined to engage presenteeism than others. That is, they tend to work while sick for more autonomous reasons. In addition, personality shapes one's preferences of certain situations (Ickes, Snyder & Garcia, 1997). Thereby, for employees with certain personalities, demands to work while ill seem to be reasonable and controllable. In particular, *conscientiousness* is such a personality that could be a potential precursor of autonomous motivation for presenteeism.

People high in conscientiousness are characterized as achievement-oriented and being dependable (Costa, McCrae & Dye, 1991). A conscientious employee tends to have a stronger personal sense of competence, is inclined to keep him or herself organized and adherent to the performance standards, and is more persistent at work for achievements relative to those low in conscientiousness (Costa, McCrae & Dye, 1991). Given these characteristics, we argue that conscientiousness may facilitate autonomous motivation for presenteeism. Specifically, employees high in conscientiousness may come to work while ill, because they tend to interpret it as a reasonable action to meet work goals (i.e., identified motivation), take it as a part of their work ethics and responsibilities (i.e., integrated motivation), or do it out of their interests as to strive for achievement (i.e., intrinsic motivation). Supporting this argument, Judge & Ilies (2002) found that conscientiousness motivates employees towards higher level and more difficult work goals, and also intensified employees' beliefs on effort-performance relationship (i.e., positive expectancy) in relation to goal fulfillment. Bipp (2010) found that employees high in conscientiousness are apt to emphasize intrinsic factors of one's job (e.g., meaningfulness or responsibility), which suggests that they may want to continue working while ill. Therefore, employees high in conscientiousness are likely to autonomously exhibit presenteeism.

Motivational Traits Heggestad & Kanfer (2000) defined motivational traits as stable individual differences in relation to achieving one's goals across various situations. Like personality, motivational traits can be helpful to understand why employees engage in presenteeism. In Heggestad & Kanfer's (2000) conceptualization, motivational traits differ in two categories: approach motivation (i.e., pursuing positive stimuli, such as rewards or sense of accomplishment) and avoidance motivation (i.e., avoiding negative stimuli, such as punishment). As Elliot (2006) argued that approach motivation manifested one's tendency to act for something good, we posit that in the context of presenteeism, approach motivation engenders autonomous-oriented reasons to do so. Given this, we review three approach-oriented motivational traits, that is, personal mastery, self-efficacy, and internal locus of control, as possible dispositional antecedents for autonomous motivation of presenteeism.

Personal Mastery. Personal mastery describes one's motivational tendencies to strive for self-development, learning, and pursuing higher-level goals (Diefendorff & Mehta, 2007). Facing a challenging goal, employees high in personal mastery are more likely to expand their efforts and make breakthroughs for the sake of overcoming the challenge. Presenteeism presents a challenging situation. Employees high in personal mastery are more likely to exhibit presenteeism since they like to take challenges and strive for excellent performance through hard working and perseverance. As an example, Michael Jordan in the NBA finals playing with the flu immediately comes to mind. As can be seen, for employees with high personal mastery, presenteeism is a self-choice driven by autonomous motivation.

Self-Efficacy. Self-efficacy is one's subjective evaluation of one's capabilities to carry out an expected performance (Judge & Bono, 2001). As a motivational construct, self-efficacy fuels employees with energy to pursue valued goals (Gist & Mitchell, 1992). Employees high in self-efficacy tend to set up difficult goals (Renn & Fedor, 2001), expand higher level of effort for sake of goal accomplishment (Bandura, 1982), and are intrinsically motivated at work (McAuley, Wraith & Duncan, 1991). Research has linked self-efficacy to presenteeism in particular, and revealed that employees high in self-efficacy were prone to participate in presenteeism voluntarily (Lu, Lin & Cooper, 2013). They suggested that employees high in self-efficacy are better able to tackle job challenges and internalize presenteeism as part of their work values and professional responsibilities. By the virtue of such internalization tendencies, self-efficacy presents another source of autonomous motivation for presenteeism.

Internal Locus of Control. Locus of control reflects one's beliefs on whether the expected outcome is determined by external forces or internal powers (Johnson, Rosen, Chang & Lin, 2015). Internal locus of control refers to the mindset that the outcomes are determined by ones' own behaviors; external locus of control refers to the mindset that the outcomes are determined by other factors beyond ones' control (Ajzen, 2002). Employees high in internal locus of control believe that it is primarily their efforts that produce results. Under physical or mental illness, these employees are more likely to continue working because they see the close connections between their actions and accomplishments. In this way, they will tend to exhibit presenteeism out of autonomous motivation. Research has shown that internal locus of control represents greater sense of self-agency, which has been viewed as a predictor for intrinsic motivation (Li, Wei, Ren & Di, 2015; Ng, Sorensen & Eby, 2006). Therefore, we regard internal locus of control as a source of autonomous motivation for presenteeism.

Situational Antecedents of Autonomous Motivation

According to Morgeson & Humphrey (2006), employee autonomous motivation can be induced by a well-designed job and positive leadership, as well as by high-quality relationships with people at work. These work characteristics have motivational potential, so that employees who undertake well-designed work may have stronger autonomous motivation to expand own efforts (Humphrey et al., 2007). Positive leadership tends to enhance followers' optimal states in which the followers are more energetic and persistent. Harmonious social relationships at work, on the other hand, create a congenial environment to heighten employees' dedication to work.

Job Characteristics. Well-designed job tasks can motivate employees to outperform themselves (Gagné, Senécal & Koestner, 1997). The traditional model of job characteristics focuses on the role of autonomy, task identity, skill variety, feedback, and task significance in boosting employees' intrinsic motivation (Hackman & Olham, 1976). Given this, well-designed tasks are inherently motivating and enjoyable (Millette & Gagné, 2008). In turn, employees may feel like working, despite experiencing sickness. Taking these rationales altogether, we posit that motivating and enjoyable tasks are sources of autonomous motivation for presenteeism.

Relationship with Coworkers. As highlighted by SDT, social connectedness is a basic human need, and carries positive implications on autonomous motivation (Deci & Ryan, 2008). Furthermore, Brief & Motowidlo (1986) suggested that quality relationship with others at work escalates prosocial motives. Taking both arguments together, it is possible that employees who enjoy harmonious relationships with coworkers are more willing to work while ill, especially in a context of high task interdependence. This is because, in their eyes, presenteeism is a prosocial behavior benefiting coworkers. In short, high quality coworker relationships could be a potential antecedent of autonomous motivation for presenteeism.

Transformational Leadership. Transformational leadership is characterized by four components: idealized influence, inspirational motivation, individual consideration, and intellectual stimulation (Bass, 1990). *Idealized influence* refers to the way that leaders win followers' trust and respect through charismatic ways. *Inspirational motivation* refers to the effective communications by which that leader successfully propagates the appealing visions. *Individual consideration* captures the process by which leaders recognize each follower's own abilities, skills, and preferences, and respect and consider these individual differences in management, and mentor the followers for personal development. *Intellectual stimulation* refers to challenging status quo, and encouraging creative ways to work.

In addition to positive coworker relationships, effective leadership, especially transformational leadership, should lead to autonomous motivation for presenteeism. Tims, Bakker & Xanthopoulou (2011) found that transformational leadership boosted employee work engagement and job dedication, even at the daily level. This suggests that a transformational leader enables followers more willing to dedicate themselves at work. A substantial body of evidence further suggests that transformational leadership stimulates stronger autonomous motivation to work by satisfying employee basic psychological needs (Bono & Judge, 2003; Gilbert & Kelloway, 2014). Thus, it is reasonable to argue that transformational leadership stimulates employee self-devotion at work, making presenteeism a justifiable action to take in order to meet work goals. Therefore, transformational leadership promotes autonomous motivation to enact presenteeism.

Controlled Motivation and Presenteeism

Controlled motivation refers to a situation where one feel obligated or pushed to perform a behavior. It can result from internal reasons associated with one's ego (e.g., the desire for approval from supervisor or scruple of feeling shame), or external factors (e.g., an offer of a contingent reward or avoidance of punishment) (Ryan & Deci, 2000). The sources of controlled motivation are commonly discussed in traditional management literature in subjects like the "carrot and stick" strategy. For example, the classic theory X management style (McGregor, 1960) emphasizes the use of punishment or reward to motivate employees, which highlight its effects on generating controlled motivation on the individual. As noted earlier, both personal and situational factors can give rise to controlled motivation.

Dispositional Antecedents of Controlled Motivation

Neuroticism. Neuroticism as a personality trait describes people's dispositional tendency to experience negative internal states, such as viewing the environment more as threats than opportunities, or perceive oneself as incapable of surviving a challenge (Costa & McCrae, 1987). Research views neuroticism as a dispositional vulnerability to job stress, because employees high in neuroticism tend to restrict their attentions to those negative consequences, either to their jobs (e.g., layoff, punishment) or to their self-images (e.g., self-denial, reputation) (Lu et al., 2013). Empirical evidence shows that employees high in neuroticism were less likely to view their jobs as intrinsically motivating (Bipp, 2010), and less likely to work actively (Erez & Judge, 2001). Neuroticism was found to be a negative predictor of motivation to perform (Judge & Ilies, 2002). Liu, Lin & Cooper (2013) found neuroticism to be an antecedent for avoidance motivation for presenteeism, in that employees high in neuroticism tend to be pressured to work while ill to avoid potential punishment of absence or work delay. These theoretical suggestions and empirical evidences are suggestive that presenteeism by employees who are high in neuroticism is essentially a forced choice (i.e., resulting from controlled motivation).

External Locus of Control. Unlike those high in internal locus of control, who tend to believe in themselves as the agents of results, people high in external locus of control tend to believe external forces as agents of valued results (Judge & Bono, 2001). Perhaps due to a lack of self-agency in goal striving (Ng, Sorensen & Eby, 2006), people high in external locus of control are less proactive in expending effort in their behavior (Andrisani & Nestel, 1976). Instead, they are predisposed to feel as though they are being pushed to do so. Thus, employees high in external locus of control are likely to experience controlled motivation for presenteeism.

Perfectionism. Perfectionists are described as striving for flawlessness and being overcritical of themselves (Flett & Hewitt, 2002). Perfectionism has three forms: self-oriented (i.e., holding oneself to high standards), other-oriented (i.e., holding others to high standards), and socially prescribed (i.e., perception that perfection is expected by others) (Hewitt & Flett, 1991). As presenteeism is a self-directed behavior, self-oriented and socially prescribed perfectionism are more relevant.

Socially prescribed perfectionism could be a potential precursor of controlled motivation for presenteeism. Employees high in socially prescribed perfectionism are overly concerned with other people's opinions, and thus try to project a perfect image of themselves in the eyes of others. This reflects a controlled motivation, specifically in the form of introjected motivation. In addition, empirical evidence has supported a positive link between socially prescribed perfectionism and extrinsic motivation (Stoeber, Feast, Jennifer & Hayward, 2009). When the situation requires it, employees high in socially prescribed perfectionism may choose presenteeism in order to make themselves look good in front of others. This implies controlled motivation as the intervening mechanism.

With regard to self-oriented perfectionism, we believe it overlaps with both controlled motivation and autonomous motivation. If one perceives presenteeism as a behavioral manifestation of the perfect self, the motivation may be more autonomous. In contrast, if one considers presenteeism as a means to produce the perfect self, controlled motivation is more salient. The empirical findings on this point are currently inconsistent. Stoeber et al. (2009) found that self-oriented perfectionism was positively related to both identified and intrinsic motivation. However, Mills & Blankstein (2000) found that self-oriented perfectionism had a positive relationship with extrinsic motivation, but not with autonomous motivation. Accordingly, we propose that self-oriented perfectionism can be an antecedent of both types of motivation for presenteeism.

Situational Antecedents of Controlled Motivation

Work- and Organization-Related Factors. Under this umbrella, we will describe four factors most relevant to presenteeism: time pressure, organizational policies and resources, job insecurity, and transactional leadership. *Time pressure* refers to the extent to which employees feel the time constraints to complete tasks, which intensifies the urge to work faster or overtime (Baer & Oldham, 2006). Under time pressure, employees have to allocate all possible efforts to get work done, including attending work while ill (Johns, 2010). Time pressure represents itself as a situational control with little sense of autonomy (e.g., time autonomy). Therefore, presenteeism in the context of time pressure is more likely to be a choice following controlled motives.

Organizational Policies and Resources. Organizations may enact a series of policies to restrict sick leaves, such as attendance bonus, or punishment for a certain amount of sick leave. These administrative practices essentially provide an external reinforcement cue to push presenteeism to occur. At times, organizations have no alternative but to expect presenteeism as a way to cope with particular situational constraints, such as understaffing (Deery, Walsh & Zatzick, 2014; Johns, 2010). As suggested by Caverley et al. (2007). Understaffing is one of the most common factors resulting in presenteeism, as employees have to regulate their behavior to fulfill these requirements and avoid negative consequences under such a directive environment. In short, attendance-related organizational policies and lack of organizational resources contribute to controlled motivation for presenteeism.

Job Insecurity. Job insecurity describes one's anticipated threats to future job existence, such as worrying about the working environment or career prospects (Sverke, Hellgren & Näswall, 2002). Economic up and down swings and increasingly competitive work environments make job insecurity a prevalent work stressor in modern society. Confronting job insecurity, one may have to demonstrate a dedication to the employer by means of presenteeism in order to increase job security. But one may not do the same thing in another situation where their employment and job prospects are better ensured. Furthermore, job insecurity represents a sense of threat, uncertainty and uncontrollability that is opposite to the sense of autonomy, relatedness, and competence (Vander Elst, Van den Broeck, De Witte & De Cuyper, 2012). Thus, job insecurity bolsters controlled motivation for presenteeism.

Transactional Leadership. Transactional leaders are those who set clear performance expectations to followers and control employees through rational or economic strategies (Bass, 1990). By definition, transactional leadership evokes controlled motivation to work, for it emphasizes the exchange between task performance and rewards (Tyssen, Wald & Heidenreich, 2014). Some specific strategies used by transactional leader may include, but are not limited to, contingent rewards and oversights (Charbonneau, Barling & Kelloway, 2001). Transactional leaders may demand employees to continue working while ill by using contingent rewards (e.g., pay for attendance), which highlights controlled motivation as the key. Transactional leaders are also accustomed to disapproving of those who failed to perform at the expected level. Employees may therefore see it necessary to continue working while ill in order to maintain the expected level of performance and productivity, and avoid supervisor's blame or criticism. In other words, under transactional leadership presenteeism is regulated by external forces rather than internal will. We thus propose transactional leadership is a precursor of employees' controlled motivation for presenteeism.

Situational Factors in One's Personal Domain. Besides the aforementioned factors, two particular situational factors in one's personal life domain are also relevant to controlled motivation of presenteeism. First, when one faces *financial constraints*, monetary incentives available at work should have strong effects on regulating one's behaviors, such as presenteeism. As an example, an employee is likely to continue working while ill to earn the paycheck for paying bills. Previous studies regarded financial difficulties as a direct source of presenteeism, which emphasizes the fact that for those who are undergoing financial problems, they *have to* exhibit presenteeism (Hansen & Anderson, 2008; Johns & Miraglia, 2015). Therefore, under financial constraints presenteeism would be more of a pressured choice than an autonomous option. Accordingly, we posit financial constraints as precursors of controlled motivation for presenteeism.

Additionally, *poor family relationship* might also account for controlled motivation of presenteeism. Hansen & Andersen (2008) found that a taxing home life would push a person to use presenteeism as an official excuse to escape from a stressful family environment. In a similar vein, Yaniv (2011) showed that marital estrangement predicts one's desire to work overtime, as working longer hours would enable one to stay away from an unpleasant home situation. Attending work while ill in this situation represents an act aimed at buffering the family complications, with little sense of autonomous dedication to one's work. Therefore, we propose poor family relationship as a precursor of controlled motivation for presenteeism.

Other Possible Antecedents of Autonomous/Controlled Motivation

Exhausting the list of possible antecedents for each type of motivations goes beyond the scope of this chapter. Nevertheless, we will briefly review a few more personal and situational factors that are potentially responsible for autonomous and controlled motivations leading employees to work while ill. *Psychological ownership* is "the state in which individuals feel ownership of a certain target or that a piece of that target is theirs" (i.e., "It is mine") (Pierce, Kostova, & Dirks, 2003: 86). Psychological ownership is characterized by a sense of efficacy, immersion of the self with work, and accountability (Avey, Luthans & Jensen, 2009). As psychological ownership indicates a strong identity with one's job, we propose that it contributes to autonomous motivation for presenteeism.

Anxiety complex describes one's trait-like failure-avoidance motives in enacting a behavior (e.g., withdraw, mitigate risks), for the purposes to move away from negative consequences or simply acts out of anxiety about potential failure (Heggested & Kanfer, 2000). Applied to presenteeism, anxiety complex can potentially give rise to controlled motivation as it comes with a habitual tendency to fear imagined failure and loss. Employees high in anxiety complex may ruminate about the potential punishments for missing a deadline or failing to complete a task due to sick leave. Thus, we consider anxiety complex as another dispositional antecedent of controlled motivation.

Compulsory social expectation signifies a pushing force to enact *compulsory citizenship behavior (CCB)* that is described as involuntary organizational citizenship behaviors (OCBs), or extra-role behaviors out of social pressure (Vigoda-Gadot, 2007). The external pressure to participate in these behaviors turns these prosocial behaviors from voluntary (i.e., autonomously motivated) to compulsory (i.e., resulting from controlled motivation). Presenteeism may be viewed as a form of CCB in that employees may feel compelled to work while ill. In this way, the act of presenteeism may be a function of controlled motivation, specifically being controlled externally by the social expectation.

To summarize, the essence of our motivational model of presenteeism is to elaborate the underlying psychological forces leading employee to continue working while ill. Namely, do individuals work while ill because they want to, or because they feel pressured to? The motivation of presenteeism has not received adequate attention within the literature, and the antecedents of autonomous and controlled motivations have only been studied in a preliminary fashion. However, the mediation model of autonomous motivation and controlled motivation for presenteeism not only elaborates *why* people extend working efforts while ill, but also aggregates a variety of personal and situational factors into the framework for a systematic consideration on *what* contributes to each motivation. For example, to what extent will autonomous motivation mediate the relationship between transformational leadership and presenteeism? As another example, to what extent will controlled motivation mediate the relationship between perfectionism and presenteeism? Although we conceptually summarized numerous personal attributes and situational factors for this model, empirical investigations of these potential mediation mechanisms are urgently needed.

Presenteeism: Implications for Coworker Motivation

In the prior sections, we have discussed plausible reasons that employees may choose to come to work while physically or psychologically ill, as well as potential personal and work environmental factors which may account for employee autonomous or controlled motivation leading to such a choice. Naturally, one may ask what would happen to the employees themselves and those around them after focal employees come to work while ill. Considering the existing body of literature on personal and organizational consequences of presenteeism (for a review, see Johns, 2010), we will examine the potential implications of presenteeism as an important indicator of overall work motivation (work engagement) among the presentee's coworkers – an understudied consequence. We focus on motivational consequences of presenteeism, in an effort to address one of the key limitations in the presenteeism literature – lack of understanding of motivational processes underlying the relations of presenteeism with commonly studied outcomes (e.g., personal health, work productivity loss, Miraglia & Johns, 2016). Indeed, "... the vast majority of research on sickness presenteeism has focused predominantly on its prevalence, determinants, and financial costs, while omitting research that evaluates potential motivational and attitudinal consequences" (Karanika-Murray et al., 2015: 100). In the following sections, we discuss the potential consequences of presenteeism for coworker work motivation – specifically work engagement – at both individual and group level. In particular, we focus on work engagement – a positive, fulfilling state of mind at work as indicated by vigor, dedication and absorption (Schaufeli et al., 2002) – as the indicator of work motivation that may be influenced by the presenteeism behavior, because work engagement has been shown to be a reliable antecedent of various employee performance outcomes like task performance and organizational citizenship behavior (for a review, see Christian, Garza, & Slaughter, 2011).

Presenteeism and Coworker Work Engagement

The primary focus of past research on presenteeism was on factors and outcomes related to focal employees who exhibit presenteeism, such as low performance ratings (see reviews, Johns, 2010; Miraglia & Johns, 2016), and as a result little is known about the consequence of focal employees' presenteeism for other organizational members, especially coworkers in the same work group. To the best of our knowledge, there exists one study that examined presenteeism from the perspectives of coworkers (Luksyte, Avery & Yeo, 2015). Specifically, Luksyte and colleagues found that teammates' presenteeism – as conceptualized by either a specific teammate's presenteeism or average presenteeism from all team members' self-reports except for the focal employee's – significantly predicted the focal employee's lower emotional engagement (e.g., feeling energetic at the task) and behavioral engagement (i.e., allocation of effort toward one's tasks or work roles) at work. In short, individual employees' presenteeism behavior could have important implications for other coworkers in the same work group.

We argue that individual employees' presenteeism can negatively affect their coworkers' or entire work group's engagement levels, for two important reasons. First, because presenteeism represents physical presence and insufficient psychological presence, presentees cannot be fully engaged in interactions with coworkers in collaboration, which could hurt the engagement levels of specific coworkers and further decrease the overall engagement levels of the work groups. The consequence of focal employees' presenteeism for coworker and work group engagement can occur especially in cases where a low psychological presence of focal employees hurts work-related interactions or presenteeism spreads within the work group or organization. Additionally, presenteeism reflects reduced capacity for task completion, which not only hurts presentees' capacity to fulfil their individual work roles but also accounts for their less-than-optimal contribution to shared work tasks in a work group, resulting in reduced quality of completion of interdependent tasks and increased process losses during collaborations. Accordingly, the engagement levels of coworkers in collaboration with the presentee(s) or the overall engagement of the entire work group may decrease, which could further contribute to reduced productivity of these coworkers and the entire work group (Christian et al., 2011).

At a different level, we also argue for the existence of group-level presenteeism and its potential influence on work group engagement levels. Considering the typical 17 to 55 percent rate of prevalence of presenteeism among individual employees (based on large-scale studies; Aronsson et al., 2000; Kivimäki et al., 2005), we contend that there may be group-level presenteeism when a vast majority of members in the group enact the presenteeism behavior. Specifically, if many members of the same work group exhibit presenteeism, there may be a shared understanding that coming to work sick is a common and acceptable practice. The phenomenon of group-level presenteeism emerges, partially because group members may adopt presenteeism through social learning processes such as modeling such a behavior from more senior group members (Bandura, 1971). Similar to the construct of group-level organizational citizenship behaviors like helping coworkers (Podsakoff, Whiting, Podsakoff & Blume, 2009), we argue that an average frequency or extent of the presenteeism behavior across members of a work group will affect the group-level effectiveness including engagement levels. Specifically using the rationale described earlier regarding the nature of individual-level presenteeism (limited psychological presence and compromised work-related capacity), we argue that group-level presenteeism (operationalized as an average frequency/extent of presenteeism behavior across all group members during a specific time period) would negatively affect group-level work engagement (Costa, Passos & Bakker, 2014; Metiu & Rothbard, 2013). For example, in cases that multiple members of a work group come to work sick, interdependent or complex work tasks that require the full attention and capacities of those sick members will probably be completed neither on time nor at a high quality.

Such a process loss in teamwork due to group-level presenteeism is partially supported by the evidence that teammates' presenteeism leads to withheld work efforts from the healthy teammates, because presenteeism poses a threat to the well-being of the healthy teammates and could make them feel upset and unwilling to compensate for any deficiencies resulting from coworkers' illness (Luksyte et al., 2015).

In summary, consistent with existing empirical evidence (albeit limited) and a wealth of theoretical evidence, we posit that the presenteeism behavior can influence presentees' coworkers' work engagement levels, as well as the overall group engagement levels. Future research is warranted to examine the nature and prevalence of group-level presenteeism, and the processes underlying its development.

Conclusions

In this chapter, we dedicated attention to the motivational mechanisms underlying presenteeism, which is a necessary but understudied line of research for describing why employees go to work while ill. As previous studies suggested, presenteeism may be driven by different motives (e.g., Lu et al., 2013). Based on a comprehensive motivational model of SDT, we propose that motivation for presenteeism lies on a spectrum along which various subtypes of motivation can be conceptually identified and examined (Ryan & Deci, 2000). Specifically, we focused on the autonomous and controlled motivations of presenteeism, and reviewed various personal attributes and diverse types of situational factors responsible for these two types of motivation for presenteeism. Importantly, we extend our understanding of presenteeism to a reasonably integrated model where the antecedents, motivational process, and differential consequences of presenteeism could be better aligned.

With regard to the consequences of presenteeism, we particularly focused on the motivation contagion effect of presenteeism (Dik & Aarts, 2007). Presenteeism is driven by one's own motivation, but exerts negative influences on coworkers' work motivation. As we noted above, coworkers will feel the pressure and consequentially become less engaged when seeing close work partners exhibit presenteeism. In addition to the individual-level effects, we also consider the prevalence of presenteeism and its motivational contagion effects at the group level, in line with the idea of presenteeism culture proposed by Johns (2010). Presenteeism at group level may manifest itself as a social norm that amplifies the threats to employees' well-being. This is of particular concern to organizational management, given the numerous negative consequences of presenteeism (e.g., Karanika-Murray, Pontes, Griffiths & Biron, 2015).

We recommend future research to examine the antecedents and consequences of presenteeism on the basis of current motivational model. First, the effects of autonomous and controlled motivations should be further tested using rigorous research designs and diversified samples. It would be particularly interesting to examine if the two types of motivation account for similar magnitude of effects on presenteeism. Since autonomous motivation and controlled motivations exert opposite influence on individuals' well-being (Deci & Ryan, 2000, 2008), comparing the effect size of each motivation on presenteeism would further clarify when and how presenteeism serves as gains or losses for employees, especially among different cultures and occupations. Second, we recommend future research to consider boundary conditions under which dispositional characteristics and situational factors may exert stronger or weaker influence on autonomous motivation and controlled motivation for presenteeism (London, 1983). For example, we argued that time pressure is an antecedent for controlled motivation. However, it is possible that employees with sufficient job resources do not view themselves as being pressured, but rather enjoy such a fast work pace as it accelerates task completion, reflecting autonomous motivation (Schaufeli & Bakker, 2004). Our final recommendation is to extend the model by empirically investigating the differential effects of presenteeism driven by autonomous motivation and controlled motivation on employee consequences. This line of research is highly intriguing as it could reveal the advantages and disadvantages of presenteeism by investigating the various effects it has on employees through different motivational channels. Additionally, the differential consequences of presenteeism driven by different motivations will further verify the value and validity of this motivational model.

References

Ajzen, I. (2002). Perceived behavioral control, self-efficacy, locus of control, and the theory of planned Behavior1. *Journal of Applied Social Psychology*, 32, 665–683.

Andrisani, P. J. & Nestel, G. (1976). Internal–external control as contributor to and outcome of work experience. *Journal of Applied Psychology*, 61, 156–165.

Aronsson, G., Gustafsson, K. & Dallner, M. (2000). Sick but yet at work. An empirical study of sickness presenteeism. *Journal of Epidemiology and Community Health*, 54, 502–509.

Avey, J. B., Luthans, F. & Jensen, S. M. (2009). Psychological capital: A positive resource for combating employee stress and turnover. *Human Resource Management*, 48, 677–693. https://doi.org/10.1002/hrm.20294

Baer, M. & Oldham, G. R. (2006). The curvilinear relation between experienced creative time pressure and creativity: moderating effects of openness to experience and support for creativity. *Journal of Applied Psychology*, 91, 963–970.

Bandura, A. (1971). *Social Learning Theory*. New York, NY: General Learning Press.

Bandura, A. (1977). Self-efficacy: toward a unifying theory of behavioral change. *Psychological Review*, 84, 191–215.

Bandura, A. (1982). Self-efficacy mechanism in human agency. *American Psychologist*, 37, 122–147.

Bass, B. M. (1990). From transactional to transformational leadership: Learning to share the vision. *Organizational Dynamics*, 18, 19–31.

Batman, D. & Sackett, O. (2016) Clocking on and checking out: Why your employees may no be working at optimal levels and what you can do about it (White Paper) (May 2016). Global Corporate Challenge: GCC Insights.

Bipp, T. (2010). What do people want from their Jobs? The Big Five, core self-evaluations and work motivation. *International Journal of Selection and Assessment*, 18, 28–39.

Bono, J. E. & Judge, T. A. (2003). Self-concordance at work: Toward understanding the motivational effects of transformational leaders. *Academy of Management Journal*, 46, 554–571.

Brief, A. P. & Motowidlo, S. J. (1986). Prosocial organizational behaviors. *Academy of Management Review*, 11, 710–725.

Caverley, N., Cunningham, J. B. & MacGregor, J. N. (2007). Sickness presenteeism, sickness absenteeism, and health following restructuring in a public service organization. *Journal of Management Studies*, 44, 304–319.

Charbonneau, D., Barling, J. & Kelloway, E. K. (2001). Transformational leadership and sports performance: The mediating role of intrinsic motivation. *Journal of Applied Social Psychology*, 31, 1521–1534.

Christian, M. S., Garza, A. S. & Slaughter, J. E. (2011). Work engagement: A quantitative review and test of its relations with task and contextual performance. *Personnel Psychology*, 64, 89–136.

Costa, P. T. & McCrae, R. R. (1987). Neuroticism, somatic complaints, and disease: is the bark worse than the bite? *Journal of Personality*, 55, 299–316.

Costa, P. T., McCrae, R. R. & Dye, D. A. (1991). Facet scales for agreeableness and conscientiousness: A revision of the NEO Personality Inventory. *Personality and Individual Differences*, 12, 887–898.

Costa, P. L., Passos, A. M. & Bakker, A. B. (2014). Team work engagement: A model of emergence. *Journal of Occupational and Organizational Psychology*, 87, 414–436. https://doi.org/10.1111/joop.12057.

Deci, E. L. & Ryan, R. M. (2000). The "what" and "why" of goal pursuits: Human needs and the self-determination of behavior. *Psychological Inquiry*, 11, 227–268.

Deci, E. L. & Ryan, R. M. (2008). Self-determination theory: A macrotheory of human motivation, development, and health. *Canadian Psychology/Psychologie Canadienne*, 49, 182.

Deery, S., Walsh, J. & Zatzick, C. D. (2014). A moderated mediation analysis of job demands, presenteeism, and absenteeism. *Journal of Occupational and Organizational Psychology*, 87, 352–369.

Diefendorff, J. M. & Mehta, K. (2007). The relations of motivational traits with workplace deviance. *Journal of Applied Psychology*, 92, 967.

Dik, G. & Aarts, H. (2007). Behavioral cues to others' motivation and goal pursuits: The perception of effort facilitates goal inference and contagion. *Journal of Experimental Social Psychology*, 43, 727–737.

Erez, A. & Judge, T. A. (2001). Relationship of core self-evaluations to goal setting, motivation, and performance. *Journal of Applied Psychology*, 86, 1270–1279.

Elliot, A. J. (2006). The hierarchical model of approach-avoidance motivation. *Motivation and Emotion*, 30, 111–116.

Fernet, C., Gagné, M. & Austin, S. (2010). When does quality of relationships with coworkers predict burnout over time? The moderating role of work motivation. *Journal of Organizational Behavior*, 31, 1163–1180.

Flett, G. L. & Hewitt, P. L. (2002). Perfectionism and maladjustment: An overview of theoretical, definitional, and treatment issues, in G. L. Flett, P. L. Hewitt, G. L. Flett & P. L. Hewitt (Eds.), *Perfectionism: Theory, Research, and Treatment* (pp. 5–31). Washington, DC: American Psychological Association. doi:10.1037/10458-001.

Fredrickson, B. L. (2004). The broaden-and-build theory of positive emotions. *Philosophical Transactions of the Royal Society of London. Series B, Biological Sciences*, 359, 1367–1377.

Gagné, M. & Deci, E. L. (2005). Self-determination theory and work motivation. *Journal of Organizational Behavior*, 26, 331–362.

Gagné, M., Senecal, C. B. & Koestner, R. (1997). Proximal job characteristics, feelings of empowerment, and intrinsic motivation: A multidimensional model. *Journal of Applied Social Psychology*, 27, 1222–1240.

Gilbert, S. & Kevin Kelloway, E. (2014). Using single items to measure job stressors. *International Journal of Workplace Health Management*, 7, 186–199.

Gist, M. E. & Mitchell, T. R. (1992). Self-efficacy: A theoretical analysis of its determinants and malleability. *Academy of Management Review*, 17, 183–211.

Hackman, J. R. & Oldham, G. R. (1976). Motivation through the design of work: Test of a theory. *Organizational Behavior and Human Performance*, 16, 250–279.

Hansen, C. D. & Andersen, J. H. (2008). Going ill to work – What personal circumstances, attitudes and work-related factors are associated with sickness presenteeism? *Social Science & Medicine*, 67, 956–964.

Heggestad, E. D. & Kanfer, R. (2000). Individual differences in trait motivation: Development of the Motivational Trait Questionnaire. *International Journal of Educational Research*, 33, 751–776.

Hewitt, P. L. & Flett, G. L. (1991). Perfectionism in the self and social contexts: Conceptualization, assessment, and association with psychopathology. *Journal of Personality and Social Psychology*, 60, 456–470.

Humphrey, S. E., Nahrgang, J. D. & Morgeson, F. P. (2007). Integrating motivational, social, and contextual work design features: A meta-analytic summary and theoretical extension of the work design literature. *Journal of Applied Psychology*, 92, 1332–1356. doi:10.1037/0021-9010.92.5.1332

Ickes, W., Snyder, M. & Garcia, S. (1997). Personality influences on the choice of situations, in R. Hogan, J. A. Johnson & S. R. Briggs (Eds.), *Handbook of personality psychology* (pp. 165–195). San Diego, CA: Academic Press. doi:10.1016/B978-012134645-4/50008-1

Johns, G. (2010). Presenteeism in the workplace: A review and research agenda. *Journal of Organizational Behavior*, 31, 519–542.

Johns, G. & Miraglia, M. (2015). The reliability, validity, and accuracy of self-reported absenteeism from work: A meta-analysis. *Journal of Occupational Health Psychology*, 20, 1–14.

Johnson, R. E., Rosen, C. C., Chang, C. H. D. & Lin, S. H. J. (2015). Getting to the core of locus of control: Is it an evaluation of the self or the environment?. *Journal of Applied Psychology*, 100, 1568–1578.

Judge, T. A. & Bono, J. E. (2001). Relationship of core self-evaluations traits – self-esteem, generalized self-efficacy, locus of control, and emotional stability – with job satisfaction and job performance: A meta-analysis. *Journal of Applied Psychology*, 86, 80–92.

Judge, T. A. & Ilies, R. (2002). Relationship of personality to performance motivation: a meta-analytic review. *Journal of Applied Psychology*, 87, 797–807.

Kanfer, R. (1990). Motivation theory and industrial and organizational psychology, in M. D. Dunnette, L. M. Hough, M. D. Dunnette & L. M. Hough (Eds.), *Handbook of industrial and organizational psychology, Vol. 1, 2nd ed* (pp. 75–170). Palo Alto, CA: Consulting Psychologists Press.

Karanika-Murray, M., Pontes, H. M., Griffiths, M. D. & Biron, C. (2015). Sickness presenteeism determines job satisfaction via affective-motivational states. *Social Science & Medicine*, 139, 100–106.

Kivimäki, M., Head, J., Ferrie, J. E., et al. (2005). Working while ill as a risk factor for serious coronary events: the Whitehall II study. *American Journal of Public Health*, 95, 98–102.

Latham, G. P. & Locke, E. A. (1975). Increasing productivity and decreasing time limits: A field replication of Parkinson's law. *Journal of Applied Psychology*, 60, 524.

Li, Y., Wei, F., Ren, S. & Di, Y. (2015). Locus of control, psychological empowerment and intrinsic motivation relation to performance. *Journal of Managerial Psychology*, 30, 422–438.

London, M. (1983). Toward a theory of career motivation. *Academy of Management Review*, 8, 620–630.

Lu, L., Lin, H. Y. & Cooper, C. L. (2013). Unhealthy and present: motives and consequences of the act of presenteeism among Taiwanese employees. *Journal of Occupational Health Psychology*, 18, 406–416.

Luksyte, A., Avery, D. R. & Yeo, G. (2015). It is worse when you do it: Examining the interactive effects of coworker presenteeism and demographic similarity. *Journal of Applied Psychology*, 100, 1107–1123. https://doi.org/10.1037/a0038755

McAuley, E., Wraith, S. & Duncan, T. E. (1991). Self-Efficacy, Perceptions of Success, and Intrinsic Motivation for Exercise1. *Journal of Applied Social Psychology*, 21, 139–155.

McGregor, D. (1960). *The Human Side of Enterprise.* New York, NY: McGraw-Hill.

Metiu, A. & Rothbard, N. P. (2013). Task Bubbles, Artifacts, Shared Emotion, and Mutual Focus of Attention: A Comparative Study of the Microprocesses of Group Engagement. *Organization Science,* 24, 455–475. https://doi.org/10.1287/orsc.1120.0738

Millette, V. & Gagné, M. (2008). Designing volunteers' tasks to maximize motivation, satisfaction and performance: The impact of job characteristics on volunteer engagement. *Motivation and Emotion,* 32, 11–22.

Mills, J. S. & Blankstein, K. R. (2000). Perfectionism, intrinsic vs extrinsic motivation, and motivated strategies for learning: A multidimensional analysis of university students. *Personality and Individual Differences,* 29, 1191–1204.

Miraglia, M. & Johns, G. (2016). Going to work ill: A meta-analysis of the correlates of presenteeism and a dual-path model. *Journal of Occupational Health Psychology,* 21, 261–283.

Morgeson, F. P. & Humphrey, S. E. (2006). The Work Design Questionnaire (WDQ): developing and validating a comprehensive measure for assessing job design and the nature of work. *Journal of Applied Psychology,* 91, 1321–1339.

Ng, T. W., Sorensen, K. L. & Eby, L. T. (2006). Locus of control at work: a meta-analysis. *Journal of Organizational Behavior,* 27, 1057–1087.

Podsakoff, N. P., Whiting, S. W., Podsakoff, P. M. & Blume, B. D. (2009). Individual- and organizational-level consequences of organizational citizenship behaviors: A meta-analysis. *Journal of Applied Psychology,* 94, 122–141.

Pohling, R., Buruck, G., Jungbauer, K. L. & Leiter, M. P. (2016). Work-related factors of presenteeism: The mediating role of mental and physical health. *Journal of Occupational Health Psychology,* 21, 220–234.

Pierce, J. L., Kostova, T. & Dirks, K. T. (2003). The state of psychological ownership: Integrating and extending a century of research. *Review of General Psychology,* 7, 84–107.

Renn, R. W. & Fedor, D. B. (2001). Development and field test of a feedback seeking, self-efficacy, and goal setting model of work performance. *Journal of Management,* 27, 563–583.

Ryan, R. M. & Deci, E. L. (2000). Self-determination theory and the facilitation of intrinsic motivation, social development, and well-being. *American Psychologist,* 55, 68–78.

Schaufeli, W. B. & Bakker, A. B. (2004). Job demands, job resources, and their relationship with burnout and engagement: A multi-sample study. *Journal of Organizational Behavior*, 25, 293–315.

Schaufeli, W. B., Salanova, M., González-Romá, V. & Bakker, A. B. (2002). The measurement of engagement and burnout: A two sample confirmatory factor analytic approach. *Journal of Happiness Studies*, 3, 71–92.

Skinner, B. F. (1969). *Contingencies of reinforcement*. East Norwalk, CT: Appleton-Century-Crofts.

Stoeber, J., Feast, A. R. & Hayward, J. A. (2009). Self-oriented and socially prescribed perfectionism: Differential relationships with intrinsic and extrinsic motivation and test anxiety. *Personality and Individual Differences*, 47, 423–428.

Sverke, M., Hellgren, J. & Näswall, K. (2002). No security: a meta-analysis and review of job insecurity and its consequences. *Journal of Occupational Health Psychology*, 7, 242–264.

Tims, M., Bakker, A. B. & Xanthopoulou, D. (2011). Do transformational leaders enhance their followers' daily work engagement?. *The Leadership Quarterly*, 22, 121–131.

Tyssen, A. K., Wald, A. & Heidenreich, S. (2014). Leadership in the context of temporary organizations: A study on the effects of transactional and transformational leadership on followers' commitment in projects. *Journal of Leadership & Organizational Studies*, 21, 376–393.

Vander Elst, T., Van den Broeck, A., De Witte, H. & De Cuyper, N. (2012). The mediating role of frustration of psychological needs in the relationship between job insecurity and work-related well-being. *Work & Stress*, 26, 252–271.

Vigoda-Gadot, E. (2007). Redrawing the boundaries of OCB? An empirical examination of compulsory extra-role behavior in the workplace. *Journal of Business and Psychology*, 21, 377–405.

Wang, J., Schmitz, N., Smailes, E., Sareen, J. & Patten, S. (2010). Workplace characteristics, depression, and health-related presenteeism in a general population sample. *Journal of Occupational and Environmental Medicine*, 52, 836–842.

Yaniv, G. (2011). Workaholism and marital estrangement: A rational-choice perspective. *Mathematical Social Sciences*, 61, 104–108.

5 | The Dynamic of Assiduity at Work: Presenteeism and Absenteeism

ERIC GOSSELIN

Introduction

Although the root of interest in presenteeism and absenteeism goes back a long way, there is reason to believe that the study of these organizational phenomena cannot be easily separated and that it would be beneficial to consider them as behavioral variants originating from concurrent realities (Johns, 2010). While absenteeism was an undeniable organizational concern in the 1980s, a concern reflected in researchers' clarification efforts, presenteeism, however, was not brought to our attention until recently (Deery, Walsh & Zatzick, 2014; Lu, Lin & Cooper, 2013). Also, roughly 20 years have passed since the first modern writings on this concept (Miraglia & Johns, 2016), writings initially triggered by the Scandinavian studies, namely those by Aronsson, Gustafsson & Dallner (2000), which shed light on an as-yet-unknown aspect of assiduity at work.

The literature on absenteeism accumulated to date usually considers the phenomenon as a singular behavior. Until recently, absenteeism at work was depicted as a dichotomous reality: a worker was either present or absent. Some subtleties, of course, are given regarding certain aspects of that behavior (cf. voluntary vs. involuntary), but the fact remains that less absenteeism was almost always expressed as the desired situation. This reflected the saying which states that *absents are always in the wrong* and conveyed the idea that presence ensured performance (Martinez & Ferreira, 2012). As such, beyond the issues with assessing the phenomenon, research efforts were primarily directed towards exploring the determinants of absenteeism for the purpose of identifying the mechanisms making it possible to curtail this behavior.

A similar strategy was initially implemented to demystify presenteeism behavior. Thus, like absenteeism, presenteeism was originally considered a separate reality for which the whys and wherefores remained to be identified. Therefore, the first explanatory attempts sought to delimit the corollaries of this behavior that, until then, had been unobserved. To do so, two strategies were established that reflected the two complementary perspectives put into operation by the efforts of European and North American researchers (Skagen & Collins, 2016). On the one hand, the aim was more to identify the factors responsible for this behavior, whereas, on the other hand, its impact on productivity was central to the investigations (Johns, 2010).

Despite a tradition, admittedly still quite young, the recent work on presenteeism, while continuing that dual quest, is now directed more towards a holistic view of assiduity at work. As expressed by Johns (2010), the efforts to understand both presenteeism and absenteeism must take an integrated approach to these behaviors rather than focus on increasing knowledge that is specific to each one. Thus, it can be stated that it is definitely no longer about updating specialized knowledge on these behaviors, but about developing combined knowledge.

This chapter attempts to take stock of the knowledge acquired to date regarding the interface structuring the behaviors of presenteeism and absenteeism. After a short review of the parameters delimiting these concepts, advances in unified models of the dynamic of assiduity at work will then be discussed. That will ultimately involve issuing some recommendations for developing an overall analytical framework of assiduity at work. Those suggestions will help glimpse an integrated research strategy for putting together the many pieces of the puzzle underlying the behaviors of presenteeism and absenteeism at work.

The Two Tales of Assiduity at Work

Simply said, assiduity is a person's desire and ability to go to a location where he/she is expected to be. When applied to the work environment, that concept traditionally involved a worker appearing at his/her workstation according to the schedule set for him/her. However, that view of assiduity at work aligned with the belief that presence ensured performance, which today, as is widely agreed, proves to be more a wishful thinking than a reality. In that context, it is appropriate to consider that the concept of assiduity necessarily involves a normative aspect, meaning that it comes with expectations that dictate, objectively or subjectively, the location where the worker is supposed to be. That assumes that sound management of assiduity at work would not force presence at all costs, but rather the worker's presence or absence when the parameters of the situation call for it. Thus, it would be desirable for a worker to be absent at certain times and present at others, with assiduity at work therefore covering both absence and presence. There is merit in revising the concept of assiduity at work in order to encompass the desire to appear at work regularly in keeping with the established rules, but also the option of being away when it is beneficial for the individual and the organization. Therefore, it is now possible to consider that assiduity at work hinges on absenteeism behaviors as well as on those that can be associated with presenteeism.

Presenteeism Many definitions of presenteeism have been proposed to date (Johns, 2010; Monneuse, 2013). From when originally conceived up until its modern conception, various moments have occurred during which the evolution can be identified when presenteeism initially went from mere presence at work to an overly intensive occupational commitment (over-engagement) to turning up at work even when ill (Gosselin & Lauzier, 2011). Even so, despite this definition-related struggle, consensus is currently arising around the view expressed by Aronsson, Gustafsson & Dallner (2000: 503) that identifies presenteeism as "the phenomenon of people who, despite complaints and ill health that should prompt rest and absence from work, are still turning up at their jobs." This definition currently resonates with most authors, with a few exceptions (e.g., Chern Wan, Downey & Stough, 2014; D'Abate & Eddy, 2007), who may well follow suit, given that presenteeism underlies the existence of two minimal conditions: the worker having an health problem and still being present at work despite that condition. However, it must be recognized that this definition overlooks an aspect of the literature on the subject associated with the North American tradition of research into presenteeism. The latter focuses more on relative nonproductivity during episodes of presenteeism, thereby implying that some degree of quantitative and/or qualitative nonproductivity is necessarily inherent in episodes of presenteeism.

Consistent with that approach, like others (e.g., Prater & Smith, 2011; Yamamoto, Loerbrooks & Terris, 2009) and for reconciling the European and North American views, we believe it is relevant to consider a partial reframing of the definition of presenteeism. Using the definition developed by Gosselin and Lauzier (2011) as a starting point, it is now appropriate to describe presenteeism as the behavior of a worker who, despite physical and/or psychological health problems requiring him/her to be away, insists on turning up at work and who, at that time, shows a relative decrease in productivity that can be directly attributed to his/her health problems. Expanding the definition this way then includes three conditions that become essential for considering a worker's behavior as presenteeism; the latter must: 1) be ill 2) be at work and 3) exhibit decreased productivity, either quantitative or qualitative, caused by his/her health problem.

This redefining of the phenomenon has the advantage, beyond introducing the concept of relative nonproductivity, of highlighting the asymmetry between a specific health problem and performance of job content. Thus, poor health means nonproductivity only based on the specific type of tasks performed by a worker. As for presenteeism, it requires there to be an observable decrease in performance and, in this respect, health problems are far from identical. Although it is useful, as shown by Hemp (2004), to estimate average nonproductivity attributable to presenteeism, it remains highly reductionist. As such, a back ache will not have the same impact for a clerical worker as it does for a construction worker. In both cases, there will likely be a decline in performance, but definitely to a much different degree, based on the nature of the tasks. Likewise for a specific health problem affecting a worker, with depression causing much different nonproductivity compared to, for example, an arthritis problem. This differential view of health problems based on occupational groups seeks to inventory illnesses and jobs most at risk and, thereby, more susceptible to the negative impacts of presenteeism behavior.

It should also be mentioned that, as was once the case for absenteeism, many considers less presenteeism to be the desired situation and that measures for eliminating this behavior to be welcome. However, it is far from being that simple. In fact, the negative impacts of presenteeism are far from identical, even leading some authors (e.g., Miraglia & Johns, 2016) to believe that it could, in some instances, be beneficial for both the employee and the organization. As such, it is appropriate to

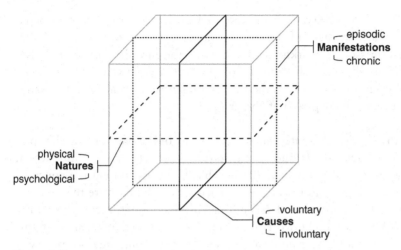

Figure 1 Presenteeism cube
Source: Translate from Gosselin and Lauzier (2011; 21)

consider that there are different types of presenteeism and that the phenomenon cannot be depicted in a one-sided manner. Further, some are calling for clarification of the situation, believing that the current positions on presenteeism are ambiguous because "employees coming despite ill health is simultaneously presented as a problem and an aspiration" (Irvine, 2011: 755).

Therefore, an effort to categorize the types of presenteeism is needed for separating what is normal from what is, or could become, problematic for workers and the organization (Monneuse, 2013). Some characteristics (e.g., task/role; episodic, acute or chronic conditions) have been identified in this connection (Garrow, 2016; Johns, 2010). Specifically, Gosselin and Lauzier (2011) suggest a classification of presenteeism behaviors based on their nature (physical vs. psychological), their manifestation (episodic vs. chronic), and their cause (voluntary vs. involuntary). This triptych is illustrated by the presenteeism cube (Figure 1). Breaking down presenteeism behaviors this way has the advantage of better delineating the phenomenon in the organization and thereby being better equipped to understand the whys and wherefores. This also helps show that presenteeism behaviors do not all involve the same things. Although a distinction involving the nature and causes of this behavior is important, it is especially its manifestations (i.e., recurrence) that are currently drawing researchers. As such, the recent observations indicate that presenteeism can be considered a warning sign of future absenteeism (Bergström et al., 2009; Gustafsson & Marklund, 2011). Thus, the chronicity of presenteeism reportedly has a dual impact on productivity, based on the worker's drop in performance at the time of presenteeism behaviors and, later, during a likely period of absenteeism.

Absenteeism Absenteeism at work is one of the oldest research topics in occupational and organizational psychology (Halbesleben, Whitman & Crawford, 2014). That longevity among the concerns of managers and researchers has led to a vast literature that make it possible to understand the multiple dimensions of this complex reality (Johns, 2003). However, it would be incorrect to claim that this concept no longer holds any secrets, but it should be acknowledged that many studies delimiting absenteeism, and its various consequences, have been conducted and that there are now multiple answers to the initial questions. Although the heyday of this research topic is definitely behind us, the significance of this organizational problem is still current. Changes in contexts, values or even forms of work organization are constantly renewing this challenge. Thus, with changing socio-organizational issues, interest in the phenomenon remains and continues to be fully relevant (Shrivastava, Shrivastava & Ramasamy, 2015).

There is general agreement on defining absenteeism at work as "a lack of physical presence at a behavior setting when and where one is expected to be" (Harrison & Price, 2003: 204). The concept of expectation is therefore central to the distinction between a situation being absenteeism and one that should be considered as merely absence from work. Thus, some absences like vacation or statutory holidays will not be considered absenteeism because the worker does not have to turn up at work on those occasions. Although there is no consensus, some people state that absenteeism differs from merely absence from work due to its impromptu, unplanned nature (Kampkötter & Marggraf, 2015), while some even go so far as to limit the concept of absenteeism to only absences caused by health problems (Holden, Scuffham, Hilton, Vecchio & Whiteford, 2010).

Beyond that subtlety, the volitional nature of the behavioral choice is not a criterion to consider for ruling on the nature of work absences.

Thus, it is theoretically possible to categorize all of a worker's acts of absenteeism as voluntary or involuntary. Voluntary absenteeism reflects a situation where the worker's absence is a deliberate choice; the worker may be capable of going to work, but decides for personal reasons (cf. recreation, personal activities, etc.) to act otherwise. On those occasions, the worker cannot provide legitimate reasons, by organizational standards, for his/her behavior (Brummelhuis, Johns, Lyon & Hoeven, 2016).

Conversely, involuntary absenteeism originates from an uncontrollable situation, usually relating to the worker's health. On those occasions, the worker is unable to go to work and adequately perform the duties for which he/she is responsible. The reasons behind this particular type of absenteeism, often referred to as sickness absenteeism, are usually standardized by organizational policies that set out a justification procedure (short- vs. long-term). However, there is still a grey area between these two types of absenteeism (Johns, 2008) and that it is still difficult to assess the fully legitimate nature of an absence. This, of course, limits the ability to accurately identify the determinants of these types of absenteeism (Brummelhuis et al., 2016). That being said, it is nevertheless possible to differentiate relatively distinct sets of determinants for the occurrence of voluntary absenteeism and involuntary absenteeism.

This split between the voluntary and involuntary nature of absenteeism is a source of discussion on optimal measuring of the phenomenon. Discussions arguing against estimating the frequency or length of the absences, with the first being considered more an indicator of the voluntary nature compared to the second (Allisey, Rodwell & Noblet, 2016; Johns & Hajj, 2016). In addition to that are other challenges regarding the measuring of absenteeism that involve the reliability of organizational records or even the validity of self-reported absences (Johns & Miraglia, 2015).

Interface Between Presenteeism and Absenteeism

To date, many explanatory models have been put forth for explaining the whys and wherefores of absenteeism and presenteeism (Johns, 1997; Laaksonen, Pitläniemi, Tahkonen & Lahelma, 2010). Although atheoretical to a large extent, on both sides (Johns, 2010; Halbesleben, Whitman & Crawford, 2014), these comprehensive frameworks look mostly at each of these behaviors in isolation, thereby seeking to determine a unique set of variables associated with absenteeism or with presenteeism.

From this perspective, it is usually considered that absenteeism originates from five specific sources that can be associated with socio-demographic indicators, personality, work setting, social context and decision-making process leading to the adoption of this behavior (Gosselin, Lemyre & Corneil, 2013). However, despite the significant impact of each of those factors, the predictive capability of absenteeism models is still limited (Harrison & Martocchio, 1998), since a large part of the root of this behavior remains unknown. As for presenteeism, the explanatory models are more generic, owing to a more recent research tradition. Thus, it is generally agreed that this behavior originates from multiple variables to which various labels are applied, but which can mainly be categorized as personal, organizational and social factors (Hansen & Andersen, 2008; Sheridan, 2004), factors that interact for structuring a selection decision: turning up at work despite health problems.

It must be recognized that the common denominator of these two behaviors is poor health, which will result in either presenteeism or absenteeism. Since illness is an inevitable aspect of being human (Niven & Ciborowska, 2015), the worker, during episodes of illness, has no choice but to make a decision about the nature of his/her assiduity. As such, the decision-making process leading to either assiduity behavior is unique (Hansen & Andersen, 2008). It is during a single decision-making moment that the worker chooses to turn up at or be away from his/her job. In simple terms, think of a worker who wakes up one morning and realizes that he/she is sick. Within the next few minutes, he/she will have to decide whether to go to work or be away from his/her job. At that point, the study of assiduity at work must focus on the factors driving this decision-making process and tilting the scale towards choosing the assiduity behavior that proves most appropriate.

That was the proposal made by Johns (2010: 534) who encouraged researchers to reconcile the presenteeism clarification efforts with those for absenteeism in order to develop a holistic view of assiduity at work. In that connection, he said, "extant research on presenteeism has made very scant use of existing and well-developed theory on absenteeism, a curious omission indeed." By doing so, Johns (2010) felt that, beyond the specific variables that may individually result in the behaviors of presenteeism or absenteeism, an integrated view needed to be established for a unified understanding of these behaviors pertaining to assiduity at work. It now seems appropriate to give priority to a combined theoretical and conceptual development of assiduity behaviors (presenteeism and absenteeism) within a single reference framework (Halbesleben, Whitman & Crawford, 2014).

Relational Dynamic Between the Assiduity Behaviors Although presenteeism and absenteeism definitely are behaviors that can be explained through separate sets of variables (Aronsson & Gustafsson, 2005), it appears that they are still inherently related phenomena. Further, this behavioral arrangement was acknowledged right from the start with the expression of two competing hypotheses: the complementarity effect and the substitution effect (Gosselin, Lemyre & Corneil, 2013; Johns, 2011).

The complementarity effect suggests that both behaviors are positively connected, in that the occurrence of one determines the appearance of the other. Thus, according to that hypothesis, a worker exhibiting presenteeism will, in parallel, adopt absenteeism behaviors, and vice versa. Recent studies on the time-related impact of presenteeism on absenteeism partially support that hypothesis. As observed by Hansen & Andersen (2008), Gustafsson and Markund (2011), Tayolan et al. (2012), or even Skagen & Collins (2016), presenteeism today can be considered a warning sign of future absenteeism. In general, it is reportedly the chronicity or worsening of the health condition that is behind the complementarity effect (Bergström et al., 2009; Gustafsson & Marklund, 2011), with the first forcing presenteeism behavior to be adopted and the second leading to absenteeism.

The substitution effect, however, shows an opposite relationship. Thus, consistent with that approach, adopting one of those behaviors presupposes that the other will not be engaged in. With a dual decision-making logic, choosing to turn up at work necessarily involves the one of not being away. Thus, the substitution effect suggests that a negative relationship exists between these two behaviors. The direction of the substitution effect is usually shown as unidirectional, with absenteeism behavior replaced by presenteeism behavior. Although it can be likened to the "good soldier syndrome," which leads a worker to turn up under any circumstance (Miraglia & Johns, 2016) or to a feeling of "irreplaceability" (Monneuse, 2013), one of the main drivers of this choice is reportedly insecurity at work, where the worker turns up for fear of the negative consequences that may result from absence.

Research that have looked at the statistical connections between absenteeism and presenteeism usually show a positive, though moderate, link between these behaviors (Caverley et al., 2007; Gosselin, Lemyre & Corneil, 2013; Johns, 2011; Hansen & Andersen, 2008; MacGregor et al., 2008; Miraglia & Johns, 2016; Munir et al., 2007). Specifically, the studies observe correlations usually wavering between r = .14 and r = .24 (Johns, 2010). These results argue in favor of acknowledging that the most plausible hypothesis for a relational dynamic between these behaviors is the one involving complementarity. Even so, prudence is called for, and the weakness of the correlations observed does not entirely invalidate the substitution hypothesis, which also has its advocates (Aronsson, Astvik & Gustafsson, 2013; Aronsson, Gustafsson & Mellner, 2011; Robertson, Leach, Doerner & Smeed, 2012). Also, other hypotheses may be considered and can be found, here and there, in the recent literature on the subject, thus raising the view of multiple relational profiles between absenteeism and presenteeism (cf. Garrow, 2016; Monneuse, 2013).

Modeling Assiduity at Work Although research seeking to clarify the phenomena of absenteeism and presenteeism individually is still welcome, it appears that future efforts must also take a holistic view of assiduity behaviors. Increasingly more authors are hearing that call and are now seeking to understand the dual dynamic of assiduity at work. Consistent with that approach, absenteeism and presenteeism are no longer seen as merely other sides of the same coin (Leineweber et al., 2012), but more as related rather than opposite behaviors (Gosselin, Lemyre & Corneil, 2013). Those contributions have a particular focus on joint modeling of the assiduity-at-work behaviors, where the cornerstone is the hinge in the decision process leading to one or the other behavior.

Some integrated models of absenteeism and presenteeism have been developed in recent years. For example, there are those by Aronsson & Gustafsson (2005), Gosselin & Lauzier (2011), and Deery, Walsh & Zatzick (2014). Despite some distinct aspects, these models of

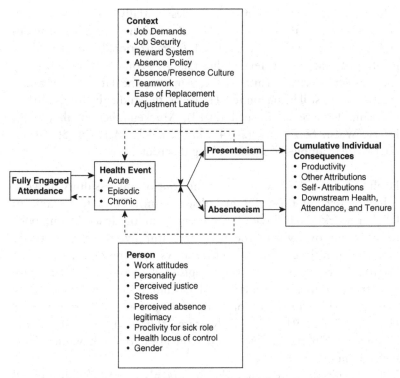

Figure 2 Johns' dynamic model of presenteeism and absenteeism
Source: Johns (2010: 532)

assiduity at work are structured along the same lines. Thus, starting with poor health, they set out various categories of factors that potentially enter into the decision-making process leading to the choice of turning up at or being away from work. Although sometimes explicitly shown (e.g., Gosselin & Lauzier, 2011), the decision-making process is usually an implicit variable in these models. The various factors entering into the decision-making process can be broadly categorized as personal determinants and organizational determinants, which are considered the two bases of assiduity-related decisions.

The model put forth by Johns (2010), in addition to being one of the most tested (e.g., Johns, 2011; Martinez & Ferreira, 2012), is a good illustration of the few integrated models of assiduity at work (Figure 2). That model assumes that the worker's choice is structured based on a hierarchical organization of variables: initially poor health; then decision-making attractors specific to individual factors (personal) and those that are context-related (organizational). It should be mentioned that, as yet, few studies take this route of simultaneously explaining presenteeism and absenteeism, with the data involving integrated models still being limited. However, the studies by Johns (2011), Gosselin, Lemyre & Corneil (2013), Muckenhuber et al. (2013), Deery, Walsh & Zatzick (2014), and Krpalek, Meredith & Ziviani (2014) are examples of studies taking this route.

Health Status is the key aspect at the root of any assiduity-at-work behavior (except for voluntary absenteeism). Thus, to be able to label a worker's behavior as presenteeism or absenteeism, poor health must overwhelm the person. Naturally, there are various types of health conditions (physical vs. psychological) and the occurrence can vary (e.g., acute, episodic, chronic). Severity, too, is a strong contributing factor in determining the behavioral choice (Irvine, 2011). In that connection, Leineweber, Westerlund & Hagberg (2012: 912) relevantly state, "Often the severity of the illness may tip the scales if a person goes to work while ill or, instead choose sick leave."

It was initially determined that a person's overall health affected his/her assiduity behaviors. As such, overall health is a predictor of both absenteeism and presenteeism (Johns, 2011), clearly showing that health is the keystone of assiduity at work. Several studies looked at both the nature and severity of the health condition by attempting to identify a differentiated record of illnesses underlying absenteeism or presenteeism.

Although it is still not possible to identified a specific list of illnesses predisposing a person to absenteeism versus presenteeism, it is now possible to derive several differential findings. For example, some conditions, such as rheumatism, migraines, gastritis, insomnia, allergies or depression, seem susceptible to presenteeism. As for absenteeism, asthma, blood pressure problem and thyroid trouble seem to be health problems behind this behavior (Hansen & Andersen, 2008; Gosselin, Lemyre & Corneil, 2013). Within that framework, it is possible to generally consider that the health problem's debilitating nature and recurrence act as decision-making mechanisms leading the worker to turn up or be away (Halbesleben, Whitman & Crawford, 2014).

As pointed out by Gosselin, Lemyre & Corneil (2013: 82), "it is reasonable to assume that the specific nature of the illness has a marked impact on the decision process leading to either presenteeism or absenteeism."

Personal Factors are a group of variables that include psychological characteristics and sociodemographic indicators. Most of the suggested factors in that group of variables, which largely cut across the models, derive a large part of their rationale from previous empirical studies that looked at absenteeism or presenteeism separately. As such, there are few theoretical bases to go along with these factors and, to date, we have little information on the real differential impact (absenteeism vs. presenteeism) of those variables.

Even so, it is already possible to state that a diverse set of individual factors can result in an inclination of the behavioral choice in a health problem situation, and that inclination is not always bilateral, i.e., that the etiology of absenteeism and presenteeism is not the same. Thus, based on the few results seen to date, it should be considered that the impact of the individual variables can be either parallel, inverse or differentiated.

Most of the indicators relating to the individual impact presenteeism and absenteeism in a *parallel* way (Miraglia & Johns, 2016). This, among other things, is what is seen with occupational stress (Gosselin, Lemyre & Corneil, 2013) and optimism (Miraglia & Johns, 2016), where these characteristics drive a complementarity plan, i.e., these two variables affect presenteeism and absenteeism in a coordinated way. With a substitution logic, *opposite* relationships can also be seen. For example, satisfaction at work increases presenteeism, but reduces absenteeism (Miraglia & Johns, 2016), while perceived legitimization of absence acts in the opposite direction (Johns, 2011). Therefore, it is possible to claim that these variables drive a kind of *for better or for worse effect*. Lastly, *differentiated* impact of some indicators are also reported. Among them, organizational commitment reduces absenteeism, but has no impact on presenteeism in the study by Gosselin, Lemyre & Corneil (2013); whereas neuroticism negatively affects presenteeism, but has no effect on absenteeism, according to the observations by Johns (2011).

Contextual Factors, which some refer to as organizational factors, with connections analogous to those seen with the personal ones may be reported. First, some contextual variables show a *parallel* effect on presenteeism and absenteeism. This is true of jobs that involve social isolation (Karlsson, Bjorklund & Jensen, 2010), workload or control over the work (Miraglia & Johns, 2016). *Opposite* effects are also seen. Among them, job insecurity (Miraglia & Johns, 2016), responsibilities (Gosselin, Lemyre & Corneil, 2013) and task interdependencies (Johns, 2011) can reportedly reduce absenteeism, but at the expense of presenteeism. So, this mirror effect reportedly exists with the impact of colleague support and the work-to-family conflict, which reportedly have the opposite impact (Johns, 2011; Miraglia & Johns, 2016). Lastly, some *differentiated* links can be identified in the literature. In particular, the feeling of equity (Johns, 2011) and the number of hours worked (Gosselin, Lemyre & Corneil, 2013), which reduce presenteeism, while having no impact on absenteeism. Or even ease of replacement, which has no connection with absenteeism, but is an aspect that facilitates presenteeism (Johns, 2011).

All in all, it can be said that, with equivalent health problems, personal factors are responsible for inter-individual variability, whereas contextual factors are reportedly more connected with inter-organizational variability of assiduity among workers. That being said, the fact remains that the various integrated models tested usually manage to be better predictors of presenteeism than absenteeism. From the findings of the only meta-analysis conducted on the subject to date, Miraglia & Johns (2016: 16) state that "although many variables were related to both attendance behaviors, the magnitude of the links was systematically greater for presenteeism than absenteeism." However, it must be recognized that we are still in the exploratory phase and that theoretical advances are needed to establish the relevance of the determinants of the assiduity-at-work behaviors. Also, like some (e.g., Deery, Walsh & Zatzick, 2014; Krpalek, Meredith & Ziviani, 2014), effort will have to be made to confirm the indirect impacts (cf. moderators and mediators). However, it is already possible to state that the parameters leading to presenteeism show some specific aspects that are not merely the simple reflection of those leading to absenteeism (Böckerman & Laullanen, 2010).

The Missing Part of the Puzzle

Despite the various explanations about the phenomenon of assiduity at work that are rooted, implicitly or explicitly, in the logic of the decision process, there is no view that incorporates the concept of attitude specifically connected with assiduity at work. Even though some call for considering the impact of generic attitudes at work (cf. satisfaction, organizational commitment, loyalty), use of the concept of attitude in choosing between absenteeism or presenteeism is still instrumental, i.e., along the line of a group of personal variables among many others. Some suggest incorporating attitudes into the conceptual framework (e.g., Krane et al., 2014), sometimes in connection with presenteeism (Rebmann, Turner & Kunerth, 2016; Richard, Skagen, Pedersen & Hover, 2017), sometimes with absenteeism (Haccoun & Jeanrie, 1995; Usta, Ugurlu & Simsek, 2016), but few place the concept of attitude as a mediator between the determinants and the mechanics leading to the behavioral choice; a role usually attributed to the concept of attitude (Kim & Hunter, 1993; Michelik, 2008). Drawn from integrated models proposed to date regarding the behaviors of absenteeism and presenteeism at work, and centred around the concept of attitude towards assiduity, Figure 3 shows a general model of assiduity at work.

A long research tradition links attitude with the adoption of a behavior (Ajzen & Fishbein, 2005; Brief, 1998), a concept often depicted as a personal cognitive construct that has the purpose of preparing for action (Gosselin, Dolan & Morin, 2017). Although it must be paired with the intention to act (Sheeran, 2002), attitude towards a goal is still a definite predictor in the adopting of a behavior. One might conclude that attitude towards assiduity at work would be particularly obvious in determining behavior. Since a worker who is ill

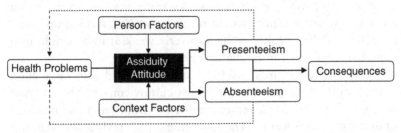

Figure 3 A general model of assiduity at work

must necessarily act, i.e., either turn up at or be away from his/her job, he/she is faced with a forced choice, where the link between attitude and behavior is a close one because it is a behavior "involving an action directed at a target, performed in a given context, at a certain point in time" (Azjen & Fishbein, 2005: 182). Although strength, stability and accessibility must be considered (Schleicher, Hansen & Fox, 2011), attitude towards assiduity at work should potentially be specific, which, according to the principle of compatibility, more directly associates with behavior (Ajzen, 1988; Siegel et al., 2014). As wisely stated by Bainbridge Frymier and Keeshan Nadler (2017: 46): "a specific attitude predicts a specific behavior"; it is right into this plan that attitude towards assiduity at work falls.

As such, we feel it is wise to incorporate into general modeling of absenteeism and presenteeism the concept of assiduity attitude; a concept that would make it easier to differentiate expected behavior from what one seeks to eradicate. It must be recognized that workers cannot in all instances refrain from presenteeism or avoid absenteeism. At certain times, presenteeism is the desired behavior and, at others, absenteeism is the preferable action. Identifying an assiduity-related attitude would help delimit the boundaries of "normal" by attempting to understand the factors creating the required balance leading the worker to turn up when he/she can and be away when he/she must.

Measuring the affective, cognitive and behavioral aspects underlying an assiduity attitude in workers would help gain a better grasp on the behavioral orientation and factors behind the inclination of that attitude. It would thereby be possible to understand the relative weight of the various personal and organizational factors in the structuration of that attitude. Assessing workers' attitude towards assiduity at work would help identify their overall propensity towards turning up at or being away from work. It would thereby be possible to determine the state of an organizational situation, knowing that an overly strong attitude towards assiduity would result in workers turning up more, regardless of their health, while an overly weak attitude would lead them to being away for the slightest health problem.

That attitude towards assiduity at work would also be a good indicator of the essence of the assiduity culture conveyed by an organization. Organizational values are often identified as a major source of excessive presenteeism. The same thing was previously said about the impact of culture on absenteeism (Allen & Higgins, 1979).

As mentioned by Gosselin, Lemyre & Corneil (2013), in the matter of assiduity management, more is not always better, and that grey area between good and better could be firmed up by measuring an attitude towards assiduity at work. To wit, beyond a culture of absenteeism or presenteeism, the fact remains that the best guarantee of balanced assiduity at work is a "culture of health" (Quelch & Boudreau, 2016).

Conclusion

It is not our intent to look critically at past or future scientific contributions. Every contribution to the subject of assiduity at work, or individually to presenteeism or absenteeism, is essential and helps with better understanding the complex dynamic of the behaviors leading a worker to be at the top of his/her ability to perform his/her work every day. However, the fact remains that an overall view now needs to be developed to look more at the forest than the trees.

Thus, the scientific contributions on assiduity at work must be included within a broader project seeking to better understand the mechanisms of well-being as well as with the optimal conditions enabling every worker, based on specific competencies and contexts, to contribute to the organization's success. Although attempts of this kind have arisen, they are still too infrequent. It is not to an organization's advantage to severely suppress absenteeism at work or tolerate excessive presenteeism; a healthy assiduity-at-work balance should be favored to ensure that workers are where they need to be. However, the underlying parameters of that healthy balance are still to be discovered, and then put to use in the workplace.

References

Ajzen, I. (1988). *Attitudes, Personality, and Behavior*. Chicago, IL: Dorsey.

Ajzen, I. & Fishbein, M. (2005). The influence of attitudes on behavior, in D. Albarracín, B. T. Johnson & M. P. Zanna (Eds.), *The Handbook of Attitudes*. Mahwah, NJ: Erlbaum: 173–221.

Allen, R. F. & Higgins, M. (1979). The absenteeism culture: becoming attendance oriented. *Personnel, 56*, 30–39.

Allisey, A., Rodwell, J. & Noblet, A. (2016). An application of an extended effort-reward imbalance model to police absenteeism behaviour. *Personnel Review, 45*, 663–680.

Aronsson, G., Gustafsson, K. & Dallner, M. (2000). Sick but yet at work: An empirical study of sickness presenteeism, *Journal of Epidemiology Community Health*, 54, 502–509.

Aronsson, G. & Gustafsson, K. (2005). Sickness presenteeism: Prevalence, attendance-pressure factors, and an outline of a model for research. *Journal of Occupational Environmental Medicine*, 47, 958–966.

Aronsson, G., Astvik, W. & Gustafsson, K. (2013). Work conditions, recovery and health: A study among workers within pre-school, home care and social work. *British Journal of Social Work*, 4, 1–19.

Aronsson, G., Gustafsson, K. & Mellner, C. (2011). Sickness presence, sickness absence, and self-reported health and symptoms. *International Journal of Workplace Health Management*, 4, 228–243.

Bainbridge Frymier, A. & Keeshan Nadler, M. (2017). *Persuasion: Integrating Theory, Research, and Practice*. New York, NY: Kendall/ Hunt Publishing Company.

Bergström, G., Bodin, L., Hagberg, J., Aronsson, G. & Josephson, M. (2009). Sickness presenteeism today, sickness absenteeism tomorrow? A prospective study on sickness presenteeism and future sickness absenteeism. *Journal of Occupational and Environmental Medicine*, 51, 629–638.

Böckerman, P. & Laukkanen, E. (2010). Predictors of sickness absence and presenteeism: Does the pattern differ by a respondent's health? *Journal of Occupational and Environmental Medicine*, 52, 332–335.

Brief, A. P. (1998). *Attitudes In and Around Organizations*. Thousand Oaks, CA: Sage.

Brummelhuis, L. L., Johns, G., Lyons, B. J. & Hoevent, C. L. (2016). Why and when do employees imitate the absenteeism of co-worker? *Organizational Behavior and Human Decision Processes*, 134, 16–30.

Caverley, N., Cunningham, J. B. & MacGregor, J. N. (2007). Sickness presenteeism, sickness absenteeism, and health following restructuring in a public service organization. *Journal of Management Studies*, 44, 304–319.

Chern Wan, H., Downey, L. A. & Stough, C. (2014). Understanding non-work presenteeism: Relationship between emotional intelligence, boredom, procrastination and job stress. *Personality and Individual Differences*, 65, 86–90.

D'Abate, C. R. & Eddy, E. R. (2007). Engaging in personal business on the job: Extending the presenteeism construct. *Human Resource Development Quarterly*, 18, 361–383.

Deery, S., Walsh, J. & Zatzick, C. D. (2014). A moderated mediation analysis of job demands, presenteeism, and absenteeism. *Journal of Occupational and Organizational Psychology*, 87, 252–260.

Garrow, V. (2016). *Presenteeism: A Review of Current Thinking* (IES Report). Brighton: Institute for Employment Studies, 84 pp.

Gosselin, E. & Lauzier, M. (2011). Le présentéisme: Lorsque la présence n'est pas garante de la performance. *Revue Française de gestion*, 211, 15–27.

Gosselin, E., Lemyre, L. & Corneil, W. (2013). Presenteeism and absenteeism: Differentiated understanding of related phenomena. *Journal of Occupational Health Psychology*, 18, 75–86.

Gosselin, E., Dolan, S. & Morin, D. (2017). *Aspects humains des organisations: Psychologie du travail et comportement organisationel*. Montreal: Chenelière Éducation.

Gustafsson, K. & Marklund, S. (2011). Consequences of sickness presence and sickness absence on health and work ability: A Swedish prospective cohort study. *International Journal of Occupational Medicine and Environmental Health*, 24, 153–165.

Haccoun, R. R., & Jeanrie, C. (1995). Self-reports of work absences as a function of personal attitudes towards absence, and perception of the organisation, *Applied Psychology*, 44, 155–170.

Halbesleben, J. R. B., Whitman, M. V. & Crawford, W. S. (2014). A dialectical theory of the decision to go to work: Bringing together absenteeism and presenteeism. *Human Resource Management Review*, 24, 177–192.

Hansen, C. D. & Andersen, J. H. (2008). Going ill to work – What personal circumstances, attitudes and work-related factors are associated with sickness presenteeism? *Social Science and Medicine*, 67, 956–964.

Harrison, D. A. & Martocchio, J. J. (1998). Time for absenteeism: A 20-year review of origins, offshoots, and outcomes. *Journal of Management*, 24, 305–350.

Harrison, D. A. & Price, K. H. (2003). Context of consistency in absenteeism: Studying social and dispositional influences across multiple settings. *Human Resource Management Review*, 13, 203–225.

Hemp, P. (2004). Presenteeism: At work – but out of it. *Harvard Business Review*, October. 49–58.

Holden, L., Scuffham, P. A., Hilton, M. F., Vecchio, N. & Whiteford, H. A. (2010). Work performance decrements are associated with Australian working condition particularly the demand to work long hours. *Journal of Occupational & Environmental Medicine*, 52, 281–290.

Irvine, A. (2011). Fit for work? The influence of sick pay and job flexibility on sickness absence and implications for presenteeism. *Social Policy & Administration*, 45, 752–769.

Johns, G. (2011). Attendance dynamics at work: The antecedents and correlates of presenteeism, absenteeism, and productivity loss. *Journal of Occupational Health Psychology*, 16, 483–500.

Johns, G. & Miraglia, M. (2015). The reliability, validity, and accuracy of self-reported absenteeism from work: A meta-analysis. *Journal of Occupational Health Psychology*, 20, 1–14.

Johns, G. (1997). Contempory research on absence from work: Correlates, causes, and consequences, in C. L. Cooper & L. T. Robertson (Eds.), *International Review of Industrial and Organizational Psychology*. New York, NY: Wiley, 115–173.

Johns, G. (2010). Presenteeism in the work place: A review and research agenda. *Journal of Organizational Behavior*, 31, 519–542.

Johns, G. (2008). Absenteeism and presenteeism: Not at work or not working well, in C. L. Cooper & J. Barlinf (Eds.), *The Sage Handbook of Organizational Behavior* (pp. 160–177). London: Sage.

Johns, G. & Hajj, R. A. (2016). Frequency versus time lost measures of absenteeism: Is the voluntariness distinction an urban legend? *Journal of Organizational Behavior*, 37, 456–479.

Johns, G. (2003). How methodological diversity has improved our understanding of absenteeism from work. *Human Resource Management Review*, 13, 157–184.

Kampkötter, P. & Marggraf, K. (2015). Do employees reciprocate to intra-firm training? An analysis of absenteeism and turnover rates. *International Journal of Human Resource Management*, 26, 2888–2907.

Karlsson, M. L., Björklund, C. & Jensen, I. (2010). The effects of psychosocial work factors on production loss, and the mediating effect of employee health. *Journal of Occupational and Environmental Medicine*, 52, 310–317.

Kim, M. & Hunter, J. (1993). Relationships between attitudes, intentions, and behavior. *Communication Research*, 20, 331–364.

Krane, L., Larsen, E. L., Nielsen, C. V., Stapelfeldt, C. M., Johnsen, R. & Risor, M. B. (2014). Attitudes towards sickness absence and sickness presenteeism in health care sectors in Norway and Denmark: A qualitative study. *Public Health*, 14, 1–13.

Krpalek, D., Meredith, P. & Ziviani, J. (2014). Investigating mediated pathways between adult attachment patterns and reported rates of absenteeism and presenteeism. *Journal of Workplace Behavioral Health*, 29, 259–280.

Laaksonen, M., Pitläniemi, J., Rahkonen, O. & Lahelma, E. (2010). Work arrangements, physical working conditions, and psychosocial working conditions as risk factors for sickness absence: Bayesian analysis of prospective data. *Annals of Epidemiology*, 20, 332–338.

Leineweber, C., Westerlund, H., Hagberg, J., Svedberg, P. & Alexanderson, K. (2012). Sickness presenteeism is more than an alternative to sickness absence: Results from the population-based SLOSH study. *International Archives of Occupational Environmental Health*, 85, 905–914.

Lu, L., Lin, H. Y. & Cooper, C.L. (2013). Unhealthy and present: Motives and consequences of the act of presenteeism among Taiwanese employees. *Journal of Occupational Health Psychology*, 18, 406–416.

MacGregor, J. N., Cunningham, J. B. & Caverley, N. (2008). Factors in absenteeism and presenteeism: Life events and health events. *Management Research News*, 31, 607–615.

Martinez, L. F. & Ferreira, A. I. (2012). Sick at work: Presenteeism among nurses in a Portuguese public hospital. *Stress and Health*, 28, 297–304.

Michelik, F. (2008). La relation attitude-comportement: un état des lieux. *Éthique et Économique*, 6, 1–11.

Miraglia, M. & Johns, G. (2016). Going work ill: A meta-analysis of the correlates of presenteeism and a dual-path model. *Journal of Occupational Health Psychology*, 21, 261–283.

Monneuse, D. (2013). *Le surprésentéisme: travailler malgré la maladie.* Paris: De Boeck.

Muckenhuber, J., Burkert, N., Dorner, T. E., Grobschädl, F. & Freild, W. (2013). The impact of the HDI on the association of psychosocial work demands with sickness absence and presenteeism. *European Journal of Public Health*, 24, 856–861.

Munir, F., Yarker, J., Haslam, C. et al. (2007). Work factors related to psychological and health-related distress among employees with chronic illnesses. *Journal of Occupational Rehabilitation*, 17, 259–277.

Niven, K. & Ciborowska, N. (2015). The hidden dangers of attending work while unwell: A survey study of presenteeism among pharmacists. *International Journal of Stress Management*, 22, 207–221.

Prater, T. & Smith, K. (2011). Underlying factors contributing to presenteeism and absenteeism. *Journal of Business & Economic Research*, 9, 1–14.

Quelch, J. A. & Boudreau, E. C. (2016). *Building a Culture of Health: A New Imperative for Business*. Springer International Publishing.

Rebmann, T., Turner, J. A. & Kunerth, A. K. (2016). Presenteeism attitudes and behavior among Missouri kindergarden to twelfth grade (K-12) school nurses. *Journal of School Nursing*, 32, 407–415.

Richard, S., Skagen, K., Pedersen, K. M. & Hover, B. (2017). Assessing the propensity for presenteeism with sickness absence data. COHERE discussion paper, University of Southern Denmark, 1–37.

Robertson, I., Leach, D., Doerner, N. & Smeed, M. (2012). Poor health but not absent: Prevalence, predictors, and outcomes of presenteeism. *Journal of Occupational and Environmental Medicine*, 54, 1344–1349.

Schleicher, D. J., Hansen, S. D. & Fox, K. E. (2011). Job attitude and work values, in S. Zedeck (Ed.). *APA Handbook of Industrial and Organizational Psychology* (Volume 3, pp. 137–189), Washington, DC: American Psychological Association.

Sheridan, A. (2004). Chronic presenteeism: The multiple dimensions to men's absence from part-time work. *Gender, Work and organization*, 11, 207–225.

Shrivastava, S. R., Shrivastava, P. S. & Ramasamy, R. J. (2015). A comprehensive approach to reduce sickness absenteeism. *Journal of Injury and Violence Research*, 7, 43–44.

Siegel, J. T., Navarro, M. A., Tan, C. N. & Hyde, M. K. (2014). Attitude–Behavior Consistency, the Principle of Compatibility, and Organ Donation: A Classic Innovation. *Health Psychology*, 33, 1084–1091.

Sheeran, P. (2002). Intention-behavior relations: A conceptual and empirical review. *European Review of Social Psychology*, 12, 1–36.

Skagen, K. & Collins, A. M. (2016). The consequence of sickness presenteeism on health and wellbeing over time: A systematic review. *Social Science and Medicine*, 16, 169–177.

Taloyan, M., Aronsson, G., Leineweber, C., Magnusson Hansson, L., Alexandersson, K. & Westerlund, H. (2012). Sickness presenteeism predicts suboptimal self-rated health and sickness absence: A nationally representative study of the Swedish working population. *PLoS ONE*, 7, 1–8.

Usta, H. G., Ugurlu, C. T. & Simsek, A. S. (2016). Absenteeism attitude of university students: Logistic prediction between variables. *International Journal of Social Science*, 50, 169–182.

Yamamoto, S., Loerbrooks, A. & Terris, D. D. (2009). Measuring the effect of workplace health promotion interventions on presenteeism: A potential role for biomarkers. *Preventive Medicine*, 48, 471–472.

Sickness Presenteeism and Attendance-Pressure Factors

GUNNAR ARONSSON AND STAFFAN MARKLUND

Introduction

What does a working Swede think and do when he or she wakes up in the morning with an aching body and a fever? Conclude that it is not possible to go to work, pick up the phone, call in sick and go back to bed? Sometimes it can be that simple, but at other times it can be a much more complicated decision.

For Iris, a bus driver who barely makes ends meet, it is a trade-off between wage-loss during sick leave and the turmoil and stress of sitting all day at the wheel with all the responsibility that entails and not being physically or mentally on top of things.

For Hans, a teacher in a primary school, his thoughts concern what will happen in the school, and with the children, if he calls in sick. Maybe I can teach, but might I completely lose focus and concentration after a few lessons? Not so good. Can a substitute be brought in at short notice? How will it affect the other teachers and students? What about the examination that was planned for today?

Our third person, the social scientist Nils is writing an article on sick leave with a deadline next Friday. He does not have to meet a single person in order to finish the article, so he decides not to call in sick but to stay at home and work on his home computer, owned by the university. No one else can take over his job and if he did not finish it now, there would be a lot of stress and many problems later on.

Karin, 27, who finally got a temporary job at the preschool and had a few tough weeks when she felt sluggish and tired, has still gone to work thinking that she has little alternative. If I continue like this I will never become healthy and energetic again. Being sick and temporarily employed is not a good life. But on the other hand – sick leave is no good if I'm away when I should be evaluated and considered for the permanent job that I absolutely need. So, what should I do?

These examples show that the decisions about going to work or not can be simple but also very complex. The decisions are dependent on a range of different factors and the factors may differ between different employment situations and job conditions. These examples are from a Swedish context where the social security system is relatively well developed and therefore the financial loss during sickness absence is limited. A large proportion of the workforce has also permanent employment so the risk for them of being fired because of illness is formally nonexistent. Different factors have different weights in different countries depending on the social welfare system and employment security.

Obviously, sickness presence (i.e., working while ill) is in many cases not a decision just about health. Many other factors are considered when people make decisions about sick leave or sickness presence. The basis for sick leave is reduced ability to work due to illness. Disease or capacity loss may be acute (e.g., gastroenteritis), episodic (e.g., migraine), or chronic (e.g., onset of diabetes). The individual must make a decision about how they will relate to their illness or loss of capacity with respect to work attendance.

Sick leave may sometimes be the only option, but in some cases an individual can choose sickness presence. In that way sickness absence and sickness presence can be seen as mutually exclusive courses of action in case of illness or loss of capacity.

Given a certain degree of ill health and loss of capacity a number of additional factors affect the likelihood of sickness presence or absence. The initial exemplification illustrated a number of attendance requirements, coherent organization of work and the individual's specific work situation. If the individual chooses sickness presence or sickness absence may be a function of a number of factors associated with the expected outcome in different aspects. This is the overall picture and we will now make a more detailed review of the research on sickness absence.

Sickness presence has generally been defined as going to work even when you are so ill that, in view of your state of health, you should take sick leave (Aronsson et al., 2000). Sickness presence research was initially focused on identifying conditions which predicted going to work when ill (Aronsson et al., 2000). Prevalence of sickness presence in different professions and in relation to working conditions were in focus. Not unexpectedly, the most important determinant of sickness presence was the individual's state of health and work ability. Those with poorer health exhibited more sickness presence. Gradually more and more determinants were identified and often classified into work-related factors and personal life-related (contextual) factors.

Other basic research questions concerned to what extent sickness presenteeism should be considered harmful, neutral, or even positive and the relation between sickness absence and sickness presence. These questions are treated in other chapters in this book.

In the quantitative research on the determinants or attendance factors, there are sometimes conflicting results within as well as between studies. Qualitative studies of individual persons or profiles have contributed with knowledge about the complex decisions an individual has to handle in the choice between sickness presence and sickness absence. Such decisions include different consequences for the individual but also for colleagues and other people such as clients, patients, children, customers, and other groups. A frequent answer in interviews about why individuals practice sickness presence is that they have an interesting job that contributes to pleasure. A sense of commitment toward the organization is also an important reason individuals give for presenteeism.

After ten years of empirical sickness presenteeism research there was a clear need for scientific models that could organize and summarize the diverse and even conflicting research findings concerning determinants for sickness presence. We will therefore start with a description and result from two studies, one large qualitative study and one meta-analytic study which summarize research into general models. After this presentation we will continue with a more detailed description of the different attendance factors.

A Model of Absence Management and Presenteeism

This model was based on qualitative data and constructed in a large multi method intervention case study for increased health and well-being at the workplace (Baker-McClearn et al., 2010). Semi structured interviews were conducted with 123 people from 9 public and private organizations in the UK. Many different personnel categories were represented as well as managers, human resource staff, and occupational health personnel. Policy documents were studied and observational notes were made to supplement the interviews.

The study and the interviews revealed a wide range of causes of sickness presence in the different workplaces. Based on the empirical material and on the previous research literature the conclusion was that presenteeism could be seen as institutionally or individually mediated. Institutional mediation was related to the organizational context and pressure from the organization. Important institutionally mediating work attendance pressure factors were sickness absence policies, such as trigger points for withdrawal of sick pay, threat of disciplinary action, and other forms of pressure. On the institutional reward side there were bonuses, incentives, and promotion prospects with the intention to press down sickness absence. These types of tools for reducing sickness absence were much more common in the private sector than in the public sector organizations. Regarding institutions the employees viewed the HR departments as being actors in the implementation of absence management, while occupational health services could act for the benefit of the employee.

The individual mediation reflected the individuals' internal drivers, such as their "moral" concern on not letting their colleagues, clients, and the organization down or how they perceived that absence might impact their own career prospects (Baker-McClearn et al., 2010: 322). Individual mediation was much more frequent in the public sector, where employees experienced greater conflicting emotions than in the private sector.

A main conclusion from this qualitative study was that sickness presence or presenteeism is a complex and multidimensional phenomena. On the individual level a number of mediating factors operate in a dynamic manner, promoting or discouraging presenteeism in different contexts and an individual may have varying thresholds for presenteeism. The level of the threshold can be raised because of higher work pressures or internal pressures and then be lowered when individual pressure is over or when the organizational pressure is low.

A Dual Path Model Based on Meta-Analysis

The most recent and comprehensive model is based on a meta-analysis of 109 samples (n = 175,965) and performed by Miraglia & Johns (2016). The focus of the model was based on different aspects of job design and organizational policies. The demand–control–support model was the main job design frame of reference for the analysis. For several decades that model has been dominating in studies of the relationship between psychosocial working conditions and health (Karasek, 1979; Karasek & Theorell, 1990; Johnson & Hall, 1988). In addition to the demand–control–support model Miraglia & Johns (2016) also analyzed the role of different organizational policies, which constrain the opportunity to be absent and consequently foster presenteeism.

In the meta-analytic study the researchers tested and received support for a double path from work to presenteeism (Miraglia & Johns, 2016). Firstly, and not surprisingly, there is a health impairment path from work conditions to sickness presence via stress and ill health.

Secondly, sickness presence can also stem from work conditions but via job attitudes. High work satisfaction raises work engagement and affective commitment to the organization. It motivates employees to spend more time and energy at work, and work more intensively. Work satisfaction may therefore act as a trigger for people to work when ill.

The mediation model resolves some paradoxical results in earlier studies. The reason for the paradoxes was to find in the dual nature of presenteeism, i.e., sickness presenteeism are related to attractive (work autonomy) as well as to bad job characteristics (time pressure).

Thus, *job demands* can be related to sickness presenteeism through both pathways. Job demands, high workload, understaffing, time pressure create a pressure for being at the workplace also when ill. Heavy workload can harm health and indirectly increase the tendency to work when sick through the health impairment path. Job demands such as challenging tasks may prompt sickness presence by engagement and high motivation to attend.

Also studies of *job control* and presenteeism have produced contradictory results. Negative as well as non-significant and positive correlations between have been reported. The mediated dual pathway model seems to reconcile the mixed evidence. Job control is an important resource in work and can indirectly reduce presenteeism, because of its positive effect on health and well-being (i.e., reduce the need to work when sick). On the other side, as job control is positively associated with job satisfaction, there is a motivational link to increased sickness presenteeism and decreased absenteeism.

Collegial and supervisor support is directly and negatively related to sickness presenteeism. Helpful colleagues, a trusting relationship with the supervisor and a supportive organization may reduce the feeling that absence may be unjustified. A supportive environment may also facilitate the possibility of being replaced in case of sickness. A supporting environment can also be a buffer against strain, and other work-related health problems, which lower the presenteeism risk. Individuals who can benefit from workplace support report higher job satisfaction as well as better health, which may explain that social support may have both a positive and negative relation to sickness presence.

Constraints for absenteeism may be a reason for sickness presenteeism. Organizational policies, job insecurity, personal financial difficulties, and acceptance of a few absence days without medical certificate are examples of such constraints. Constraints may be formal or informal. Constraints on absenteeism may result in substitution, i.e., if there are restrictions for sick leave, the likelihood of sickness presence will increase and absence is substituted by presenteeism.

In the following section we will go more into a detailed description of different types of constraints, job design factors, and personal and background factors.

Constraints and Job Design Factors Affecting Presenteeism and Absenteeism

Somewhat different concepts and terms are used in the two models but the concrete variables are rather similar. We will start in what Miraglia & Johns (2016) conceptualize as constraints, which closely correspond to what Baker-McClearn and collaborators (2010) call institutional mediators.

Constraints or Institutional Mediators

Job insecurity, reductions in the organization, replaceability, regulations of absence, presence cultures are potential constraints for sickness absence. Some of these constraints are linked to specific occupations and sectors of the labor market and some have different effects on presenteeism in specific national contexts.

Job Insecurity and Staff Reductions

Job security is one aspect of an organization's policy but also of the labor legislation in a country. There are a number of studies which have analyzed the relation between job insecurity and sickness presenteeism

(Caverly et al., 2007; Böckerman & Laukkanen, 2009; Kim et al., 2016; d'Errico et al., 2016). The general hypothesis is that job insecurity – for example, having temporary employment or work in an organization where there are staff reductions – makes people more likely to go to work despite ill health (Aronsson & Gustafsson, 2005). Several cross-sectional studies have pointed in that direction (Heponiemi et al., 2010; Arnold, 2016; d'Errico et al., 2016; Kim et al., 2016), but there are also studies that go in the opposite direction or found no relationship between job insecurity and sickness presence (Claes, 2011). Particularly interesting is a Finnish prospective study in which researchers followed the hospital employees who were transferred from a temporary to a permanent contract (Virtanen et al., 2003). The results showed a significant increase in absenteeism, which almost doubled with the experience of increased stability of employment. The researchers interpret this as the insecurity of temporary employment generating a high level of sickness presence.

Sickness presence during periods of staff reductions has also been studied and the results are not entirely conclusive since there are forces working for both sickness absence and sickness presence (Caverley et al., 2007). Staff reductions followed by increased time pressure and feelings of a broken psychological contract, as well as experience of injustice, are stressors that are likely to result in increased sick leave, but at the same time there are forces that can promote increased sickness presenteeism, due to fear of losing the job and more competition about jobs.

Absence Policies and Presence Culture

Absence policy is about corporate responses to absence. Some companies have a formal policy on how repeated absence of an individual is treated. If some forms of sanctions are associated with absenteeism, it may result in avoidance of occasional episodes of sick leave or an individual returning to work earlier than he or she should (Grinyer & Singleton, 2000). A company's absenteeism policy or insurance system regulations around the repeated absence will be particularly relevant for people with chronic illness (Nyberg et al., 2008; Roelen & Groothoff, 2010).

In the research literature, the concept of absence cultures varies as it may include formal rules as well as informal structures (Taylor et al.,

2010; Roelen & Groothoff, 2010). Aronsson and Gustafsson (2000) found that one reason for the high frequency of sickness absence among employees in education, health and care was a professional ethic and a culture of helping and assisting individuals who are at some form of disadvantage. Several studies in similar occupations have reached the same interpretation. A British medical study observed that the high sickness presence was an expression of doctors' professional identity, which included a resistance to accepting the patient role (McKevitt et al., 1997; McKevitt & Morgan, 1997). In-depth interviews with physicians who themselves had experienced a period of relatively long sickness found strong cultural barriers to accepting sick leave. "It is something that our patients need – not us." These attitudinal barriers were reinforced by an organizational design by which absence meant additional workload for their colleagues.

A concept of interest in this context is "competitive presenteeism" (Johns, 2010). The type of culture seems mainly found in male senior manager environments. Younger men seem to have a weak resistance to the kind of presence culture while women offer more resistance (Simpson, 1998).

Replaceability

Replaceability is another attendance requirement that can be considered both from a policy perspective and from a job design perspective. Low replaceability may arise in different ways.

It can be a consequence of the nature of a person's work. It may be that the work tasks themselves are such that it is difficult for someone else to carry them out. The position may have a high and specific knowledge content and no other person can directly step in and take over the work. Low replaceability can also be affected by a company's management strategy, as can be witnessed in the fact that many companies that have undergone organizational slimming have a policy of not taking in extra workers.

Given that the labor market seems to be going in the direction of having more and more of the types of jobs and work tasks where employees cannot readily be replaced if they go on sick leave, it is important that efforts are made to investigate the situations and conditions of the individuals who are affected by this (Aronsson et al., 2011). The result is that the work will not be done without piling up for those who are away from work. This increases the likelihood of sickness presence, and replaceability has been found as a significant determinant for sickness presence in a few studies (Aronsson, Gustafsson & Dallner, 2000; Aronsson & Gustafsson, 2005). A Canadian study of downsizing in a public authority found that the lack of backup in case of absence was a common cause of sickness presenteeism (Caverley et al., 2007).

Job Design Attendance Factors

The job demand–control–support model was the theoretical frame of reference in the meta-analytic study as well as a job design perspective (Miraglia & Johns, 2016). As was reported above, all these three concepts were connected in a complex manner to sickness presence both by the health path and the job satisfaction path. Therefore we will not go into the mediating issues for these concepts again but focus more on methodological and conceptual questions.

Job Control

A number of studies have found that good job control or high decision latitude are related to increased levels of presenteeism (Leineweber et al., 2011; Dhaini et al., 2015; Chang et al., 2015; d'Errico et al., 2016; Arnold, 2016). On the other hand, some studies have shown no significant association between job control and presenteeism (Jourdain & Vezina, 2014; Jassens et al., 2016). In addition to the dual nature of the job control concept the diverging results may have to do with differences in the composition of occupations in separate studies or with other methodological differences.

Contradictory results may also be related to how job-control is defined in different occupational settings. In general, job-control includes the employees' ability to adjust working pace and the choice of tasks, but it may in some occupations only refer to a low degree of supervisory authority or control. Thus, some professional groups may report a high degree of job control while their working days are circumscribed by demands from clients or customers.

A Swedish study by Johansson & Lundberg (2004) shows that adaptability of job tasks to the individual's health status is essential to future subjective health and to reduce absenteeism but does not affect presenteeism. A follow up, based on different data, showed that high adjustment latitude decreased the risk of experienced presenteeism (Johansson et al., 2014). This may be an indicator that adjustment latitude is a mediator that improves health.

Job Demands and Workload

A number of studies based on mixed occupational groups have shown that high workload increased presenteeism (Bakker et al., 2009; Jourdain & Vezina, 2014; Mandiracioglu et al., 2015; Jassens et al., 2016; Pohling et al., 2015; Arnold, 2016). On the other hand, high demands in some occupations stimulate low absenteeism due to selection into jobs with high demands of individuals who often have high standards for their own performance (Johns, 2009). Some studies of employed in health and social services seem to show weak correlations between high workload and presenteeism (Dhaini et al., 2015), while other studies show strong correlations (Elstad & Vabo, 2008). Interestingly, in this context, and possibly a piece of the puzzle, which may help to explain the differences in the various studies, is a longitudinal study from the Netherlands, which showed that high demands were associated not only with sickness presence but also with burnout (Demerouti, 2009). Sickness presence could in that case be regarded as a risky kind of behavior. In a large Danish cross-sectional study, time pressure with several requirements variables was clearly correlated with high risk of sickness presenteeism (Hansen & Andersen, 2008). The results of a Swedish study of police officers goes in the same direction: high stress and low social support increases the likelihood of sickness presenteeism (Leineweber et al., 2011).

Personal Factors Affecting Presenteeism

Gender

Studies based on mixed occupational categories have generally not detected strong differences or been able to determine whether gender differences in sickness absence is primarily associated with the sexual division of labor, or whether it is individually related. In many studies the researchers control statistically for gender because gender is often relevant for absenteeism.

A large study that focused on managerial leadership showed only marginal differences between women and men concerning how differences in leadership styles affected sickness presenteeism (Nyberg et al., 2008). A Finnish study found that women – but not men – increased their sickness presenteeism when they worked in permanent full-time positions as compared to working part-time or in temporary employment. However, this effect may partly be caused by differences between men and women in the distribution of occupations and sectors (Böckerman & Laukkanen, 2009).

Two studies based on more homogeneous occupational groups have reported gender differences. A Swedish study of general practitioners found that female physicians reported sickness presenteeism more often than male physicians (Gustafsson-Sendén et al., 2016). Furthermore, experienced work–family conflict mediated the association as the women who reported a work–family conflict also more often experienced a work–family conflict. Another gender related result comes from a Danish study of ambulance workers (Hansen et al., 2011). The researchers found a correlation between masculinity, measured by a scale indicating male norms, and presenteeism. Men with high values of masculinity had higher sickness absence and lower absenteeism than men with lower values. Scientists push the question if it's masculine to come to work even if you are sick and reflect on whether such behavior may explain part of the difference between men's and women's sickness absence.

The strong gender difference in sickness presence emanates from the gender-related division of work. In Sweden, as in many other countries, women are highly overrepresented in occupational groups, where everyday tasks are to provide care or welfare services, or teach or instruct, i.e., occupations where relationships with other persons play an important part in work outcome. In a Swedish study of a representative sample (Aronsson & Gustafsson, 2000), this groups had a substantially increased risk of sickness presence compared with member in groups working with things or symbols. This risk was especially accentuated for those who worked with sick, young and small children, and elderly people – that is, the most dependent and vulnerable "client groups." In that way women are much more exposed to conditions, which may involve moral obligations for attendance. In addition to the moral obligation, that type of work is relatively poorly paid. For a large group of women this means they are exposed for two rather strong attendance factors (Aronsson & Gustafsson, 2000, 2005).

Personality

There are hardly any studies examining the relationship between sickness presence and personality dispositions. Aronsson & Gustafsson (2005) found that individual boundarylessness, as measured by the degree of agreement with the statement, "I find it hard to say no to others' wishes and expectations," was related to increased risk of sickness presence. Such a disposition is usually seen as an aspect of performance-based self-esteem. This characteristic was found to predict sickness presence in a cohort study of a group of young adults (Love et al., 2010).

Johns (2010) discusses in his review article possible personality traits and cites as low self-esteem, conscientiousness, "workaholism," strong work ethics, internal "health locus of control" and "hardiness" as possible characteristics that can increase the likelihood of sickness presenteeism. In the meta-analytic study (Miraglia & Johns, 2016) it was possible to test two such personality variables – optimism and conscientiousness – which was seen as personal resources and supposed to correlate positively with sickness attendance. Conscientious people could be expected to make the extra effort to show up in the face of health limitations, and optimistic people was thought to be more dedicated in their job which was supposed to promote attendance even not in perfect health. The result was that conscientiousness and presenteeism were unrelated, while optimism were negatively related to both absence and presence via health but associated with higher presenteeism but lower absenteeism via the job satisfaction path.

Personal Financial Situation and Sick Pay

Personal financial situation can be measured by income level and by an individual's perceptions of his or her personal financial difficulties and cash margins. In the meta-analyses (Miraglia & Johns, 2016) pure income was only weakly related to presenteeism, but the estimate for personal financial difficulties was more substantial. This is in line with a Swedish study where individuals with a small so-called cash margin were shown to have a significantly higher risk of presenteeism (Aronsson & Gustafsson, 2005).

Concerning compensation, Lovell (2004) found, not surprisingly, that low or no sick pay contributed to presenteeism. The results here are likely to vary with the design of the compensation system, both in terms of size of compensation for any qualifying days, and of who is the payer of the compensation (insurance agency or employer). In Sweden, as in many other countries, all of these compensation parameters have varied considerably over the past 20 years. However, as far as we know, there are no studies that have used this variation for quasi-experimental studies of sickness presence.

How Employees Explain their Presenteeism

Most knowledge about motives for sickness presenteeism emanates from quantitative studies, where groups with different work conditions have been compared and the relationship between work conditions and sickness presenteeism has been statistically tested (Caverley et al., 2007; Hansen & Andersen, 2008; Taylor et al., 2010; Lu et al., 2013; Johansen et al., 2014; Szymczak et al., 2015). These studies are using preformulated response alternatives to analyze the connection to sickness presence. Qualitative studies have shown rather similar results, but more specific questions can be studied and analyzed and new determinants are easier to discover (Baker-McClearn et al., 2010; Szymczak et al., 2015).

It seems that a feeling of a moral obligation to work and interpersonal relations and consideration about consequences for other people often emerge and are prominent themes in studies where employees explain their own presenteeism.

A study of Canadian public service organizations found that concern about colleagues and supervisors was the main reason for presenteeism (Caverley et al., 2007). A Danish study of employees' attitudes towards sickness absence found that those with a conservative attitude to absence were most likely to turn up ill at work, but that attitudes were generally less important than working conditions (Hansen & Andersen, 2008). Similar questions were used in a study of Taiwanese employees (Lu et al., 2013). Both motives related to loyalty with colleagues or work tasks and motives related to worries about losing the job or that work mates or supervisor might react negatively predicted sickness presenteeism.

Using a more specific design, Szymczak and collaborators (2015) studied reasons why medical staff attended work while experiencing different symptoms of sickness. The most frequent reasons were related to not wanting to let colleagues or patients down but even in these occupations fear of negative views from colleagues were prevalent.

However, the motives were not always altruistic. Fears of negative views from colleagues and supervisor have also been prominently reported as reasons for presenteeism. As mentioned, Baker-McClearn and collaborators (2010) reported differences between public sector and private sector employees in personal motives behind presenteeism. Those employed in the public sector more often expressed commitment to colleagues and clients, whereas private sector employees were more often concerned with not wanting to be seen as poor performers.

Based on survey data from Norway and Sweden of 2500 sick-listed workers, reasons for sickness presenteeism were scrutinized (Johansen et al., 2014; Marklund et al., 2015). The participants had to agree or disagree to statements as positive aspects as "I enjoy work," as well as negative as "I am worried about being laid off."

The results with this self-declarative method were similar to results from other studies based on correlation analyses. Almost half of the respondents reported going to work while ill because they did not want to burden colleagues with their sick leave, and about a third report that nobody else could carry out their responsibilities. However, another large share reported that they did not want to be considered lazy or unproductive (Johansen et al., 2014).

In accordance with results in other studies, the Norwegian–Swedish study also found distinct differences between occupational groups in terms of the reasons the respondents gave for sickness presenteeism (Marklund et al., 2015). Self-employees, managers and highly educated persons more often report that they practice sickness presenteeism because nobody else is able to carry out their responsibilities. Less educated persons and those with no management responsibilities more often report that they cannot afford to take sick leave.

A much higher proportion of Swedish respondents claimed that they practiced sickness presenteeism because they could not afford to be on sick leave (Johansson et al., 2015). One reason for this is probably related to differences in generosity in the sickness insurance compensation. Sickness benefits in Norway are more generous than in Sweden. A sick-listed person in Norway receives full compensation for the loss of income from the first day, while in Sweden the employees themselves pay for the starting day and receive about 80 percent of the loss of income. Individuals with lower income will suffer more from the loss of income than individuals with higher income. This interpretation is in line with former studies, which have pointed out that the economic consequences of sickness absence can contribute to sickness presenteeism (Caverley et al., 2007; Roelen & Groothoff, 2010).

Experience of Attendance as a Health-Promoting Factor

Research on sickness presence has had its focus on negative motives and constraint against absence as attendance motives. More rarely, positive or health motives for sickness presenteeism, expressed by the individual, have been investigated. The Norwegian–Swedish study (Johansen et al., 2014) gave an opportunity to study and compare such motives. The somewhat surprising result was that a considerably larger share in Norway than in Sweden reported that the main reason for sickness presence was that they enjoyed their work, or that their pride depended on not taking sick leave, or that going to work was beneficial for their health.

The reason for the higher ranking of positive motives in Norwegian workplaces may depend on what the authors have called disease tolerance (Aronsson et al., 2015). A higher disease tolerance level allows individual to take advantage of certain positive effects of being at work and avoid some negative sides of being at work when ill.

Further empirical analyses showed that the advantages were mainly about stimulation of being at work, adjusted workload, and an understanding supervisor and supportive colleagues. Such circumstances allowed the worker to adapt the job to his or her actual work capacity. The value of adaptability in the work situation was described in connection to job control. This concept has also been emphasized in relation to work rehabilitation. Chances for successful work rehabilitation and return to work after a longer period of sickness absence increases significantly when a person with reduced work capacity can customize workload and job demands to her health (Johansson & Lundberg, 2004).

The opportunity for creating such disease-tolerant workplaces may be associated with a range of conditions such as the company's finances, staffing, culture in the workplace, type of work, technology, and technical aids, etc. However, there is a lack of research and knowledge on the importance of such contextual conditions.

Summary and Conclusions

The complexity of causes behind sickness presenteeism can be summarized as the existence of a lot of mediating factors that operate in a dynamic manner, promoting or discouraging presenteeism in different contexts.

Although ill-health and lost work capacity both are by definition important, there is also a complex pattern of organizational and personal reasons for sickness absence and presence or presenteeism. The decisions for sickness presence are dependent on a range of different factors which may differ between different individuals, their employment situations, and job conditions. Sickness presence is obviously in many cases not a decision just about the severity of ill-health or the degree of work capacity. Quantitative as well as qualitative studies have shown that several other factors are considered when people make decisions on sick absence or presence. Different factors have different weight in different countries depending on the social welfare system, constraints for absence, and employment security.

The initial exemplification with our four actors illustrated a number of attendance factors, positive as well as negative, and also the influences from an individual's specific work situation and actual context. What decision an individual chooses may be a function of the weight he or she assigns a number of factors associated with the expected outcome.

A further aspect of the complexity is that an individual might have varying intra-individual thresholds for presenteeism. The threshold level can be raised because of higher work demands or internal pressures, and then lowered when pressure is over or when pressure is low.

From a theoretical as well as from a practical perspective sickness presenteeism research emerges as an important and necessary complement to sickness absenteeism research in relationship to work and health. For certain groups sickness absence is an insufficient and downright misleading measure, because there are other circumstances than health that determines the presence at work during illness. Thus, workers in certain types of work conditions have probably poorer health than measures of sickness absence indicates. This is especially the case when various external circumstances are forcing individuals to choose sickness presence rather than sickness absence when ill. Lack of reasonable protection against loss of income when sick may be one such external circumstance, but strong attendance cultures at work may be another. Absenteeism measures are therefore not neutral in relation to certain work conditions and occupational groups (Aronsson et al., 2011).

There are also practical conclusions to be drawn from the presenteeism research. Many studies of sickness absence and ill health do not measure sickness presence. The same applies to practical occupational safety activities. Different types of interventions for reduction of absence, also those with positive rewards, may increase the problems with presenteeism. Therefore, it should always be a routine to measure sickness presence and reasons for presence in research as well as in practical contexts. The use of presenteeism measures allows for an evaluation of the efficiency of the interventions and organizational policies for reducing absenteeism without creating increased presenteeism.

The work environment factors that operate in relation to sickness are well known from years of work in environment research. Ordinary occupational safety and healthy activities for a better balance between control and job demands and support from colleagues and supervisors will therefore reduce the illness risks in the job and therefore also in many cases reduce the risk for harmful sickness presence. There are, however, exceptions. Workers with low income and workers who are difficult to replace are two groups where these problems are obvious. In theoretical terms it can be described as sickness absence being substituted by sickness presence.

Sickness presence is not always easy to discover. Too-high motivation and commitment can act as attendance driving factors, resulting in high levels of presenteeism with disease risks in the long run. It may be difficult for supervisors or the occupational health and safety experts to discover and understand that such highly positive behavior can lead to sickness presence, which is harmful for the employees' health as well as for the productivity of the company.

Employees with low income may try to compensate by working when ill. Economic pressure, fear of losing one's job and one's income and low compensation when sick and absent may force an employee even to hide his or her health problems and lowered productivity. It may therefore be difficult for a supervisor or employer to handle this problem on the individual level, but for safety and productivity reasons, employers and employers' organizations may have an interest in taking collective measures which may reduce constraints for paid sick leave and other forces that foster harmful sickness presence.

References

Arnold, D. (2016). Determinants of the annual duration of sickness presenteeism, empirical evidence from European data. *Labour*, 30:198–212.

Aronsson, G. & Gustafsson, K. (2005). Sickness presenteeism: Prevalence, attendance-pressure factors, and an outline of a model for research. *Journal of Occupational and Environmental Medicine*, 47:958–966.

Aronsson, G., Gustafsson, K. & Dallner, M. (2000). Sick but yet at work. An empirical study of sickness presenteeism. *Journal of Epidemiology and Community Health*, 54:502–509.

Aronsson, G., Gustafsson, K. & Mellner, C. (2011). Sickness presence, sickness absence, and self-reported health and symptoms. *International Journal of Workplace Health Management*, 4:228–243.

Aronsson, G., Johansen, V., Marklund, S., Rönning, R. & Solheim, L. (2015). Sjukfrånvarons dimensioner – svensk-norska jämförelser och analyser. *Liber förlag* (Swedish).

Baker-McClearn, D., Greasley, K., Dale, J. & Griffith, F. (2010). Absence management and presenteeism. *Human Resource Management Journal*. 20:311–328.

Bakker, A. B., Schaufeli, W. B. & Hox, J. (2009). Present but sick, a three-wave study of job demands, presenteeism and burnout. *Career Development International*, 14:50–68.

Böckerman, P. & Laukkanen, E. (2009). Presenteeism in Finland. Determinants by gender and the sector of economy. *Ege Akademic Review*, 9:1007–1016.

Caverley, N., Cunningham, J. B. & MacGregor, J. N. (2007). Sickness presenteeism, sickness absenteeism, and health following restructuring in a public service organization. *Journal of Management Studies*, 44:304–319.

Chang, Y.-T., Su, C.-T., Chen, R., Yeh, C.-Y., Huang, P.-T., Chen, C.-J. & Chu, M. (2015). Association between organization culture, health status and presenteeism. *Journal of Occupational and Environmental Medicine*, 57:765–771.

Claes, R. (2011). Employee correlates of sickness presence, a study across four European countries. *Work & Stress*, 25:224–242.

D'Errico, A., Ardito, C. & Leombruni, R. (2016). Work organization, exposure to workplace hazards and sickness presenteeism in the European employed population. *American Journal of Industrial Medicine*, 59:57–72.

Demerouti, E., Le Blanc, P. M., Bakker, A. B., Schaufeli, W. B. & Hox, J. (2009). Present but sick: a three-wave study on job demands, presenteeism and burnout. *Career Development International*, 14:50–68.

Dhaini, S., Zuniga, F., Ausserhofer, D., Simon, M., Kunz, R., de Geest, S. & Schwendimann, R. (2015). Absenteeism and presenteeism among care workers in Swiss nursing homes and their association with psychosocial work environment. *Gerontology*, 62:386–395.

Elstad, J. I. & Vabo, M. (2008). Job stress, sickness absence and sickness presenteeism in Nordic elderly care. *Scandinavian Journal of Public Health*, 36:467–474.

Grinyer, A. & Singleton, V. (2000). Sickness absence as risk-taking behaviour: A study of organizational and cultural factors in the public sector. *Health, Risk & Society*, 2:7–21.

Gustavsson Sendén, M., Schenck-Gustafsson, K. & Fridner, A. (2016). Gender differences in reasons for sickness presenteeism – a study among GPs in a Swedish health care organization. *Annals of Occupational and Environmental Medicine*, 28:50, doi 10.1186/s40577-016-0136-x.

Hansen, C. D. & Andersen, J. H. (2008). Going ill to work. What personal circumstances, attitudes and work-related factors are associated with sickness presenteeism? *Social Science & Medicine*, 67:956–964.

Hansen, C. D., Lund T. & Labriola, M. (2011). Is it masculine to turn up ill at work? A study of the association between traditional male role norms and sickness presenteeism amongst Danish ambulance workers. *European Journal of Public Health*, 21, Suppl 1.

Heponiemi, T., Elovainio, M., Pentti, J. et al. (2010). Association of contractual and subjective job insecurity with sickness presenteeism among public sector employees. *Journal of Occupational and Environmental Medicine*, 52:830–835.

Jassens, H., Clays, E., de Clerco, B. et al. (2016). Association between psychosocial characteristics of work and presenteeeism. *International Journal of Occupational Medicine and Environmental Health*, 29:331–344.

Johansen, V., Aronsson, G. & Marklund, S. (2014). Positive and negative reasons for sickness presenteeism in Norway and Sweden. *BMJ Open*, 2014;4, Feb 13, e0044123.doi:10.1136.

Johansson, G. & Lundberg, I. (2004). Adjustment latitude and attendance requirements as determinants of sickness absence or attendance. *Social Science & Medicine*, 58:1857–1868.

Johansson, G., Gustafsson, K. & Marklund, S. (2015). The association between adjustment latitude and sickness presence – a panel study of

Swedish employees. *International Journal of Occupational and Environmental Health*, Online publ., doi.org/1013075/ijomeh.1896 .00318.

Johns, G. (2009). Absenteeism or presenteeism? Attendance dynamics and employee well-being, in Cartwright, S. & Cooper, C. L. (Eds.), *The Oxford Handbook of Organizational Well-Being (7–30)*. Oxford: Oxford University Press.

Johns, G. (2010). Presenteeism in the workplace: A review and research agenda. *Journal of Organizational Behavior*, 31:519–542.

Johnson, J. V. & Hall, E. M. (1988). Job strain, work place social support, and cardiovascular disease: a cross-sectional study of a random sample of the Swedish working population. *American Journal of Public Health*, 78(10), 1336–1342.

Jourdain, G. & Vezina, M. (2014). How psychological stress in the workplace influences presenteeism propensity. *European Journal of Work and Organizational Psychology*, 23:483–496.

Karasek, R. A. (1979). Job demands, job decision latitude and mental strain. *Administrative Science Quarterly*, 24:285–308.

Karasek, R. A. & Theorell, T. (1990) *Healthy Work: Stress, Productivity, and the Reconstruction of Working Life*, New York, NY: Basic Books.

Kim, J. Y., Lee, J., Mutaner, C. & Kim, S. S. (2016). Who is working while ill? Nonstandard employment and its association with absenteeism and presenteeism in South Korea. *International Archives of Occupational and Environmental Health*, 89:1095–1101.

Leineweber, C., Westerlund, H., Hagberg, J., Svedberg, P., Luokkala, M. & Alexanderson, K. (2011). Sickness Presenteeism among Swedish Police Officers. *Journal of Occupational Rehabilitation*, 21:17–22.

Lu, L., Lin, H. Y. & Cooper, C. L. (2013). Unhealthy and present – motives and consequences of the act of presenteeism among Taiwanese employees. *Journal of Occupational Health Psychology*, 18:406–416.

Love, J., Grimby-Ekman, A., Eklof, M., Hagberg, M. & Dellve, L. (2010). "Pushing oneself too hard": Performance-based self-esteem as a predictor of sickness presenteeism among young adult women and men. *Journal of Occupational and Environmental Medicine*, 52:603–609.

Lovell, V. (2004). *No time to be sick: Why everyone suffers when workers don't have paid sick leave.* Washington, DC: Institute for Women's Policy Research. Publication No 242.

Mandiracioglu, A., Bolukbas, O., Demirel, M. & Gumeli, F. (2015). Factors related to presenteeism among employees of the private sector. *International Journal of Occupational Safety and Ergonomics*, 21:80–85.

Marklund, S., Aronsson, G., Johansen, V. & Solheim, L. J. (2015). Previous sickness presence among long-term sick-listed in Norway and Sweden – a retrospective study of prevalence and self-reported reasons. *International Journal of Social Welfare*, 24:376–387.

McKevitt, C. & Morgan, M. (1997). Illness doesn't belong to us. *Journal of the Royal Society of Medicine*, 90:491–495.

McKevitt, C., Morgan, M., Dundas, R. & Holland, W. W. (1997). Sickness absence and 'working through' illness: A comparison of two professional groups. *Journal of Public Health Medicine*, 19:295–300.

Miraglia, M. & Johns, G. (2016). Going to work ill, a meta-analysis of the correlates of presenteeism and a dual-path model. *Journal of Occupational Health Psychology*, 21:261–283.

Nyberg, A., Westerlund, H., Magnusson Hansson, L. & Theorell, T. (2008). Managerial leadership is associated with self-reported sickness absence and sickness presenteeism among Swedish men and women. *Scandinavian Journal of Public Health*, 36:803–811.

Pohling, R., Buruck, G. & Jungbauer, K.-L. (2015). Work-related factors of presenteeism – the mediating role of mental and physical health. *Journal of Occupational Health Psychology*, 21:232–234.

Roelen, C. A. M. & Groothoff, J. W. (2010). Rigorous management of sickness absence provokes sickness presenteeism. *Occupational Medicine*, 60:244–246.

Szymczak, J., Smathers, S., Hoegg, R. N., Klieger, S., Coffin, S. & Simmons, J. S. (2015). Reasons why physicians and advanced practice clinicians work while sick. *Journal of the American Medical Association, JAMA, Pediatrics*, 169:815–821.

Taylor, P., Cunningham, I., Newsome, K. & Scholarios, D. (2010). Too scared to go sick – reformulating the research agenda on sickness absence. *Industrial Relations Journal*, 41:270–288.

Virtanen, M., Kivimäki, M., Elovainio, J., Vahtera, J. & Ferrie, J. E. (2003). From insecure to secure employment: Changes in work, health, health related behaviours, and sickness absence. *Occupational and Environmental Medicine*, 60:948–953.

7 | Presenteeism in Economic Research*

PETRI BÖCKERMAN

Introduction

Change is a constant ingredient of modern work life. Thus, job demands and the complexity of job tasks that workers are required to accomplish and perform in everyday work are increasing in organizations and firms. Increasing job demands and incessant changes may be stressful, at least for certain employees, and cause significant and long-lasting health effects as well. Most individuals spend a substantial portion of their total time at work. Thus, work-related behaviors have significant spillover effects on other aspects of life. For these reasons, work-related sickness is also a particularly important aspect of employee well-being from the broader economic perspective.

Theoretical considerations in economic research have put special emphasis on the determination of the optimal amount of work-related sickness behavior. An important feature of formal economic models is the asymmetric information that prevails between employees and employers. This underlying structure implies that employers cannot directly observe employees' health endowment and/or health status, which are the key determinants of work-related sickness behavior. This implication makes it challenging for firms to design optimal policy responses to work-related sickness.

There are two equally important and widespread aspects of work-related sickness behavior. These aspects are absenteeism ("absent from work because of sickness") and presenteeism ("present at work despite sickness"). There is a large theoretical and empirical body of literature in economics regarding the determinants and consequences of absenteeism (Treble & Barmy, 2011). This research has evaluated the optimal compensation rate of sick leave and substantially broadened the understanding of the determinants of absenteeism, for example, by examining the effect of business cycle fluctuations on sickness absence. However, only very recently has theoretical and empirical research in economics more deeply examined the underlying causes and implications of presenteeism. Thus, studies from other disciplines such as organizational and health psychology, and management have examined presenteeism from different angles, well before economics.

Presenteeism has significant implications for multiple aspects of work life. Presenteeism costs individual workers, firms, and society as a whole. For example, there is a substantial amount of empirical evidence showing that working while sick leads to worse health outcomes in the long run (Skagen & Collins, 2016). Thus, working while sick may contribute to the incidence of disability pension over the long observation period. These costs are carried by the society as a whole. Ultimately, presenteeism may considerably contribute to workers' ill health and firms' costs. Therefore, it is crucial to have a greater knowledge of the economic determinants of both sickness absenteeism and presenteeism, which constitute the two important work-related sickness categories.

The objective of this chapter is to provide a condensed overview of both theoretical and empirical work in economic research on presenteeism. For brevity, the discussion is focused on the most important aspects in the emerging literature in economics on presenteeism. Because the chapter focuses solely on research in economics, the number of approaches and studies that are described is very limited.

The chapter is structured as follows. First, we describe the formal theoretical considerations that additionally elucidate the optimal amount of presenteeism. The models consider that employers and employees strive to maximize profits and the perceived utility. We then highlight the key empirical patterns from the sparse empirical literature in economics on presenteeism. The last section of the chapter concludes by stating certain important gaps and challenges in the current theoretical and empirical knowledge of presenteeism from the economics perspective. The concluding section also discusses the specific topics that the literature should put more emphasis on to provide more practical implications that would benefit firms in the design of policies to minimize the costs associated with presenteeism and absenteeism. These lessons could be implemented in organizations and firms to achieve the optimum amount of absenteeism and presenteeism.

Theoretical Considerations

Employers and employees are the relevant agents who determinate the rate of absenteeism and presenteeism in organizations and firms. Employers and employees respond to the financial incentives and constraints that are established by sickness insurance systems. Economic theory assumes that both employers and employees make rational choices subject to constraints.

The optimal amount of absenteeism in organizations and firms is clearly not zero for a number of reasons. An important reason for this is that sick workers cause output losses in firms, as discussed in detail below. This feature is arguably particularly important in the context of increasingly popular teamwork where the total output of the team is often dependent on the performance of the weakest link in the team. Conversely, self-management teams may consist of workers who are multi-skilled, which makes them relatively easy to substitute for each other.

Sickness insurance has significant effects on the financial incentives to work while sick or to be absent. Sickness insurance is an important element of social insurance in nearly all industrialized countries. Workers are entitled to compensation when they are absent from work due to a certified sickness. Compensation is nearly always proportional to the wage level. Details of the sickness insurance systems, such as the maximum amount of compensation, vary from country to country. Importantly, there is a moral hazard related to compensation that is provided by sickness insurance because higher compensation levels tend to lead to longer sickness absence spells, all else being equal (Ziebarth & Karlsson, 2014).

An important cost component related to work-related sickness is caused for firms by the fact that absenteeism often leads to the use of replacement workers. Other workers may also have to work paid overtime to compensate for the lost labor input of those who are absent. Importantly, an increase in paid overtime causes substantial costs to firms because firms must pay an overtime premium. Collective labor agreements typically stipulate the amount of overtime premium; in addition, there is a maximum amount of overtime that a worker can perform during a certain time period. Binding collective labor agreements are particularly relevant in the context of blue-collar occupations. For white-collar workers, in most settings, it is very difficult to measure the output of a single worker in an organization. This statement implies that it is challenging to evaluate the amount of work needed to cover absent white-collar workers in terms of the required overtime. Therefore, his/her lost input due to absence may be covered by coworkers' unpaid overtime if the lost labor input is needed to achieve the binding production requirements.

Economic incentives also determinate the optimal rate of presenteeism. From the employer's perspective, the standard neoclassical model of firm is based on the notion that a firm combines a set of inputs to produce output. The most common production inputs in the standard model are labor and capital. The fact that certain employees work while sick is a potentially important determinant of output because effective labor input has two components: hours of work and productivity (output per hours of work). A worker's current health status and working capacity are the key determinants of output per hours of work. Maximum output per hours of work is possible to achieve only if workers are completely healthy at work and thus contribute fully to the production of output. Importantly, working while sick may also increase the rate of serious work-related accidents at work, which has significant negative consequences on other workers at the workplace. Therefore, working while sick implies that the output per hours of work is lower than the maximum because of the reduced effort and/ or mistakes that working while sick causes in organizations and firms, all else being equal. This finding leads to losses in firm's output and causes substantial costs for firms.

From the employee's perspective, the standard neoclassical textbook model in economics assumes that individuals only consider their personal, individual-specific costs and benefits while making work-related decisions such as whether to work while sick or not. Workers work while they are sick if their personal utility level is higher than their utility level while absent from work, all else being equal. This finding is arguably a very limited view.

Importantly, the existence of externalities is a decisive aspect of presenteeism. Externality is the cost or benefit that has an influence on an agent who did not choose to incur that cost or benefit. Importantly, returning prematurely to work from sick leave causes potentially significant negative externalities to coworkers in the workplace. The negative externalities are particularly important in the context of contagious diseases (Pichler & Ziebarth, 2017). This pattern is caused by the observation that working while sick will increase the prevalence of absenteeism in the organization as a whole, which increases a firm's costs and leads to the reduction of output. Therefore, the evaluation of the existence of negative externalities on coworkers is essential to determinate the optimal length of sickness absence.

In addition to negative externalities that are inflicted on coworkers in the workplace, there are also potentially important negative externalities that impact firm's customers and other relevant agents. For example, in hospitals and other healthcare settings, those who work while sick may cause substantial harm to patients by spreading contagious diseases and may prolong the patients' recovery from the illness for which they were originally admitted to hospital. Thus, if they are relevant negative externalities inflicted on the firm's customers, these effects should be fully considered in the determination of the optimal rate of absenteeism. In other contexts, negative externalities arguably have only relatively small, second-order effects that can be ignored in the economic analysis. For example, certain white-collar occupations such as the work of a reporter are very independent, and they do not require day-to-day interaction with coworkers, which would cause substantial negative externalities.

Considering the negative externalities leads to longer optimal sickness absence spells than the standard model, which is solely based on the individual's utility. However, it is also important to note that the role of negative externalities is not identical for all diseases. The negative externalities are particularly important for contagious diseases such as seasonal infectious diseases, while the negative externalities caused by chronic conditions such as back pain are most likely minor in practical workplace contexts. This finding complicates the considerations regarding the optimal sickness leave scheme because the compensation rate of sickness insurance cannot be conditioned on the exact nature of an illness. Ultimately, the negative externalities to coworkers should be fully considered in the firm's optimal policy regarding work-related sickness.

There are only three formal theoretical models of presenteeism that have been presented in the economic literature. The early theoretical models include those by Chatterji & Tilley (2002) and Brown & Sessions

(2004). These models are based on the notion that employers can fully regulate the optimal amount of presenteeism by setting the wage level and/or specific details of sick pay scheme for the affected workers.

Chatterji & Tilley (2002) argue that there is a particularly strong incentive for employers to offer higher compensation than the statutory sick pay set by sickness insurance legislation. These additional payments are able to prevent ill workers with reduced job performance from being at work because workers respond strongly to financial incentives. Thus, increased sick pay implies that employees remain off work longer. Hence, by using additional payments, firms can avoid the output losses that are caused by those who work while sick. Consequently, in the (long-run) equilibrium of the model, there is no presenteeism because firms can fully and freely optimize the amount of output that they produce in the market. Thus, the most important implication of the model is fundamentally in conflict with the empirical evidence on presenteeism.

Based on the augmented efficiency wage model, Brown & Sessions (2004) argue that, by taking advantage of the eligibility criterion for firm-financed sick pay, employers can cause workers to either engage in absenteeism or presenteeism. A firm's ultimate goal is to reduce the costs associated with presenteeism. Importantly, the model presented by Brown & Sessions (2004) does not allow for the simultaneous occurrence of absenteeism and presenteeism. Additionally, the model assumes that firms have full command over the specific compensation rules of sickness insurance. This statement is clearly not the appropriate characterization of the sickness insurance system in the countries that have statutory sickness insurance. Firms only rarely provide firm-specific insurance policies for workers in Europe. Most European countries have compulsory sickness insurance set by legislation that covers the population. In contrast, in the United States, most firms are directly involved in the design of sickness insurance schemes because insurance policies are provided by employers as part of the compensation package for workers. Taken together, the model by Brown & Sessions (2004) is not able to provide a universal explanation for the existence of presenteeism that has been reported for all industrialized countries because it focuses on firm-specific aspects of sickness insurance schemes. Thus, the key empirical implications of the theoretical models by Chatterji & Tilley (2002) and Brown & Sessions (2004) are not consistent with the empirical observations that have been convincingly documented in the literature.

Hirsch et al. (2017) present the first complete economic model of work attendance that incorporates both work-related sickness categories (i.e., absenteeism and presenteeism). In the model, presenteeism is interpreted as the outcome of the optimizing behavior of both employers and employees. An important aspect of the model is that there is asymmetric information between employees and employers. Employees know their underlying productivity and health status, but this information is not directly observable to employers. Thus, health status is employees' private information. The assumption is reasonable.

In the model by Hirsch et al. (2017), workers choose their workplace presence depending on their disutility associated with workplace attendance; this is unobservable to their employer. The disutility depends on workers' health status. The disutility is larger for those who have poor health statuses. To simplify the theoretical analysis, workers are assumed to be risk neutral in the models on employment relations. Workers are usually assumed to be risk averse in the theoretical models because they have only limited opportunities to obtain comprehensive insurance against fluctuations in wages and salaries. Attendance at work is costly for a worker because attendance reduces worker's utility owing to the lower level of leisure time. Therefore, workers naturally attempt to minimize attendance at work.

However, workers encounter a trade-off. Attendance at work has a counterbalancing effect because attendance decreases the probability that the worker is dismissed from the job. For a worker, dismissal causes a substantial amount of disutility because the search for a new job is costly for the affected worker. Thus, the fear of unemployment (i.e., perception of job insecurity) may increase the prevalence of presenteeism in organizations and firms. There is also earlier evidence according to which sickness absenteeism is at a higher level when the aggregate unemployment rate is lower (Askildsen et al., 2005). Thus, both categories of work-related sickness behavior may respond significantly to macroeconomic conditions.

To make the model tractable and generate predictions that are consistent with the stylized empirical facts of presenteeism, there are two types of workers in the model by Hirsch et al. (2017). Some workers have low disutility from the work, and other workers have high disutility. Those workers who work while sick show inefficiently high effort. In contrast, those who are absent show inefficiently low effort. Because of the asymmetric information between employers and employees, employers are forced to use only the wage level to financially incentivize workers. Thus, the wage level is the relevant decision variable for a firm.

The presence of asymmetric information implies that employers are forced to set wages to incentivize the "average" worker in the firm. In the absence of asymmetric information, workers would obtain an optimal person-specific wage set by firm. Therefore, in the equilibrium, employers provide overly strong incentives for sick workers and overly weak incentives for healthy workers to attend work. This fundamental feature of the model implies that some sick workers attend work, and other healthy workers are absent from work. Thus, there is a suboptimal allocation and mixture of labor input in the firm that has a negative impact on a firm's output and economic performance. Consequently, there are both presenteeism and absenteeism in the model equilibrium; this is the key novel feature of the model compared with earlier theoretical considerations.

The theoretical model presented by Hirsch et al. (2017) has three important implications that can be tested with suitable empirical data. First, the model implies that workers differ notably in terms of their presenteeism behavior. This implication reflects the underlying fundamental differences in the disutility from workplace attendance among workers. In particular, workers who have poor health statuses and/or encounter significant work-related stressors such as adverse working conditions in their working environments and/or poor management practices that expose them to work-related disamenities should have a significantly higher incidence of presenteeism. Second, workers with longer tenure (i.e., work experience in the current firm) who typically have stronger *de facto* dismissal protection should have less presenteeism because the probability of dismissal has an effect on the incentives of workers to attend while sick. A higher probability of dismissal implies that a worker is more likely to attend while sick, all else being equal. The probability of dismissal may be related to an employee's age. In Sweden, there is an explicit last-in-first-out rule according to which those who have the longest tenure also have the strongest job protection against dismissals. Third, presenteeism should be more relevant for high-skilled workers whose productivity is higher. It is arguably more difficult to find a suitable replacement for a high-skilled worker than for a low-skilled worker who only has a general set of skills.

The level of formal educational attainment can be used to measure the skill level of workers in empirical research.

Empirical Applications

There are only a very limited number of empirical studies on the issues directly related to presenteeism in economics. As in other disciplines that have examined the determinants and consequences of presenteeism, the existing empirical studies are based on survey data that contain self-reported information on presenteeism and employee characteristics such as educational attainment and self-assessed health. Survey data also contain certain information on firm characteristics such as firm size that may be relevant to better understand the determinants of presenteeism. Surveys are usually cross-sectional; thus, they do not allow researchers to follow the same employers and workers over time. There are empirical studies that strive to quantify the specific costs associated with presenteeism. Importantly, the comprehensive and accurate measurement of costs associated with presenteeism has substantial practical value for organizations and firms that strive to minimize the negative consequences of presenteeism on financial performance.

Most notably, Pauly et al. (2008) provide comprehensive empirical evidence on manager perceptions regarding the costs associated with presenteeism. The objective of the study is to cover various types of jobs that have very different actual content. The data cover 804 middle-level managers from the United States. The sample size is very limited to derive conclusions that would be nationally representative. The data contain detailed questions about the costs of work-related illness and the consequences of working while sick. Pauly et al. (2008) document that jobs with a particularly high incidence of team production, high requirements for timely delivered output, and high difficulties of substitution for absent workers have significantly higher costs for both absenteeism and presenteeism.

Interestingly, Pauly et al. (2008) conclude that substitution opportunities are a somewhat less important factor for presenteeism than absenteeism. Poor substitution is a particularly relevant feature from the economic perspective because, when substitution between workers is not possible, after he or she returns to work, a (white-collar) worker must accomplish all those tasks that were not done during his or her absence from work. This work significantly increases the incentives to work while sick, but may cause substantial negative externalities to coworkers, as described earlier.

Kigozi et al. (2017) provide a comprehensive summary of the empirical literature that has evaluated the costs that are associated with presenteeism in firms. The systematic review covers 28 studies. One main conclusion of the summary is that the costs associated with presenteeism are only rarely included in economic evaluations.

Kigozi et al. (2017) state that the literature has used two methods to estimate the losses associated with presenteeism. The first method is the direct approach. The method involves relevant respondents to estimate the extra hours that would be needed to compensate for inefficient hours that were caused by working while sick. The second method that has been used in the literature also uses self-reported information to provide a perceived overall estimate of how much illness has reduced performance at work. This approach has been the most popular method in the literature.

The most important problem with self-reported information is that it may contain a substantial amount of systematic measurement error. For example, personality traits may have an influence on the manner in which respondents answer the questions, and the same characteristics of persons may also affect their work-related sickness behavior such as presenteeism. This observation makes it difficult to derive well-grounded conclusions for policy design.

Hirsch et al. (2017) evaluate the empirical implications of their theoretical model using German survey data. The researchers find that presenteeism is typically at the higher level for those workers who have worse health, all else being equal. Health status is measured using self-assessed health. Hirsch et al. (2017) also find that adverse working conditions increase the prevalence of presenteeism. These empirical findings are consistent with the predictions of the theoretical model because the formal model states that a higher (health-related) disutility derived from attendance at work is associated with a higher incidence of presenteeism. However, the association between worker's tenure and presenteeism is quantitatively weak. Therefore, tenure is not a practically important determinant of presenteeism, at least not according to the German survey data. It is important to note that the effects may be notably different in other institutional contexts. Furthermore, Hirsch et al. (2017) find that the relationship between employees' educational attainment and presenteeism is also not as clear as the theoretical model implies.

Conclusions

There are two important work-related sickness categories that have been examined in the literature. There is a large body of theoretical and empirical literature in economics regarding the determinants and consequences of absenteeism (Treble & Barmy, 2011). However, economic research has only recently begun to examine more deeply both the determinants and consequences of presenteeism. There are several relevant challenges in future theoretical and empirical studies on presenteeism in economics. The challenges related to empirical research are also highly relevant for investigations that are conducted in other disciplines such as organization and management studies.

There are important issues related to the existing theoretical models. First, theoretical models that are based on the optimizing behavior of firms and workers should incorporate more relevant aspects of institutions because they are important determinants of the prevalence of presenteeism. For example, the financial incentives of sickness insurance schemes are directly relevant for the decision whether to work while sick or not. Second, theoretical models should more fully consider that workers have different preferences towards working while sick. Preferences may also be related to noneconomic determinants of presenteeism such as peer pressure from coworkers to attend work while sick. Peer pressure may be particularly strong in small, self-managed teams that are currently common in organizations and firms. The integration of economic and noneconomic determinants of presenteeism would open new possibilities to understand the underlying motives of presenteeism more deeply. Third, there should be more theoretical modeling that fully considers the empirical fact that absenteeism and presenteeism prevail simultaneously in many organizations and firms. There is also a positive correlation between the prevalence of absenteeism and presenteeism at the individual level (Böckerman & Laukkanen, 2010). Currently, there is only one theoretical framework in economics (Hirsch et al., 2017) that can explain one of the basic stylized facts of the empirical literature (i.e., the simultaneous existence of both absenteeism and presenteeism). Fourth, theoretical models should consider the negative effects of working while sick on employees' health status; this may cause an increase in the amount of absence for sickness in the long run. These long-term effects have been ignored in the theoretical models, but they are nevertheless important for the complete evaluation of the costs related to presenteeism.

There are also equally important challenges related to the empirical perspective of the research on presenteeism. First, research should be based on nationally representative data that are available for many countries. Most of the empirical literature focuses on a narrow set of industries and firms. A key problem is that both the motives and consequences of presenteeism are most probably significantly heterogeneous across organizations. Thus, the specific organizations that have garnered researchers' focus may be those where the effects are anticipated and/or are according to prior theoretical considerations. This supposition makes it particularly difficult to extrapolate from these results to the population as a whole. This hindrance is an important issue because there is earlier evidence supporting the notion that the determinants and consequences of presenteeism are heterogenous across industries and firms. Nationally representative data are also needed to derive policy conclusions that can be implemented in a broad range of firms. Thus, this apparent heterogeneity calls for more studies. It would also be particularly important to consider this heterogeneity in the design of management policies to reduce the prevalence of both absenteeism and presenteeism because different groups of workers clearly respond differently to economic and noneconomic incentives. Therefore, the average effects on which the literature has greatly focused on provide us with an incomplete picture of the determinants of absenteeism and presenteeism compared to a more nuanced setting that would allow for the heterogeneity of the effects.

Second, workers are clearly not randomly assigned to firms. This statement implies that the correlations that are calculated using observational data (e.g., the correlations between employee characteristics such as educational attainment and presenteeism) do not reveal causal effects about the underlying determinants of presenteeism. Thus, the most important difficulty in interpreting the cross-sectional correlations is establishing whether the relationships between background characteristics and presenteeism are causal or not. Therefore, the sorting of workers into workplaces and job tasks within firms cannot be ignored. In particular, if jobs that have a higher incidence of various stressors also attract more able and healthier employees, or those who are mentally and physically more resilient towards stressors, the cross-sectional correlations between individual characteristics and the measures of work-related sickness behavior will be biased, at least to a degree. The size of this bias is not known. One tractable approach with linked survey and register data is to use information on employees' wage and work histories. Therefore, to alleviate this problem, it is useful to condition based on employees' work and earnings histories, which are most likely highly correlated with unobserved worker traits, thus reducing the potential for omitted variables bias. A key challenge for empirical studies is that the use of work and earnings histories requires the use of linked survey and register data in which work and earnings histories are derived from comprehensive register-based data. Linking survey data to register-based information on employees' work and wage histories is possible in Nordic countries by utilizing person-specific identification codes (Böckerman et al., 2012, 2013).

Third, most of the empirical research on presenteeism uses cross-sectional data. The use of panel data would allow researchers to fully control for person-specific fixed effects such as time-invariant personality traits that are potentially important determinants of both absenteeism and presenteeism. Fully considering personality traits and other time-invariant characteristics would allow researchers to more precisely identify the independent effects of the economic determinants of presenteeism. This identification would provide valuable information to design policies to reduce presenteeism and the negative externalities that it causes in organizations and firms.

Fourth, there are important gaps in the literature regarding more specific issues. One neglected aspect of research has been the effect of new management initiatives on work-related sickness. High involvement management practices have become an increasingly popular element of contemporary human resource management. These practices contain several different aspects such as self-managed teams, problem-solving groups, information sharing, incentive pay and supportive practices such as employer-provided training and associated recruitment methods. There is also most likely a substantial amount of heterogeneity in the effects of new management initiatives on presenteeism by gender, age groups and type of employer. Future research should focus more on the potential role of high involvement management practices in the determination of presenteeism.

Fifth, economic research on the determinants and consequences of presenteeism would benefit greatly from the use of linked survey and register data. The measures of presenteeism and employee characteristics are nearly always based solely on survey information. However, by linking comprehensive register-based information from employees and firms, it is possible to broaden the potential determinants of presenteeism and provide additional valuable lessons for policymakers.

Note

* Work related to this chapter has been financially supported by the Strategic Research Council funding for the project *Work, Inequality and Public Policy* (293120). I am grateful to Markku Jokisaari and Terhi Maczulskij for useful comments regarding the earlier version of this text. The usual disclaimer applies.

References

Askildsen, J. E., Bratberg, E. & Nilsen, Ø. A. (2005). Unemployment, labor force composition and sickness absence: a panel data study. *Health Economics*, 14(11), 1087–1101.

Brown, S. & Sessions, J. G. (2004). Absenteeism, presenteeism, and shirking. *Economic Issues*, 9(1), 15–23.

Böckerman, P. & Laukkanen, E. (2010). What makes you work while you are sick? Evidence from a survey of workers. *The European Journal of Public Health*, 20(1), 43–46.

Böckerman, P., Bryson, A. & Ilmakunnas, P. (2012). Does high involvement management improve worker wellbeing? *Journal of Economic Behavior and Organization*, 84(2), 660–680.

Böckerman, P., Bryson, A. & Ilmakunnas, P. (2013). Does high involvement management lead to higher pay? *Journal of the Royal Statistical Society: Series A (Statistics in Society)*, 176(4), 861–885.

Chatterji, M. & Tilley, C. J. (2002). Sickness, absenteeism, presenteeism, and sick pay. *Oxford Economic Papers*, 54(4), 669–687.

Hirsch, B., Lechmann, D. S. & Schnabel, C. (2017). Coming to work while sick: An economic theory of presenteeism with an application to German data. *Oxford Economic Papers*, 69(4), 1010–1031.

Kigozi, J., Jowett, S., Lewis, M., Barton, P. & Coast, J. (2017). The estimation and inclusion of presenteeism costs in applied economic evaluation: a systematic review. *Value in Health*, 20(3), 496–506.

Pauly, M. V., Nicholson, S., Polsky, D., Berger, M. L. & Sharda, C. (2008). Valuing reductions in on-the-job illness: "presenteeism" from managerial and economic perspectives. *Health Economics*, 17(4), 469–486.

Pichler, S. & Ziebarth, N. R. (2017). The pros and cons of sick pay schemes: Testing for contagious presenteeism and noncontagious absenteeism behavior. *Journal of Public Economics*, 156, 14–33.

Skagen, K. & Collins, A. M. (2016). The consequences of sickness presenteeism on health and wellbeing over time: A systematic review. *Social Science and Medicine*, 161, 169–177.

Treble, J. & Barmby, T. (2011). *Worker Absenteeism and Sick Pay*. Cambridge University Press.

Ziebarth, N. R. & Karlsson, M. (2014). The effects of expanding the generosity of the statutory sickness insurance system. *Journal of Applied Econometrics*, 29(2), 208–230.

PART III

Understanding the Consequences of Presenteeism

8 | *Presenteeism and Well-Being at Work*

MARIELLA MIRAGLIA AND GARY JOHNS

Introduction

People have always worked while sick for a wide range of reasons, such as losing pay while absent, fear of job dismissal, enjoyment of the job, and feelings of obligation to their employer or team. Nonetheless, scholarly interest in the causes of presenteeism and its implications for employees and organizations only emerged in the late 1990s but is increasing rapidly. As an example, a search of the Web of Science shows that the number of mentions of the term *presenteeism* in the title or topic of journal articles rose from 187 in 2006 to 2753 in 2016.

Interest in presenteeism has also been increasing among organizations in light of its scale and costs for individuals and businesses. Presenteeism has been repeatedly found to be more costly than absenteeism (e.g., Collins et al., 2005; Hemp, 2004), with estimates ranging from 1.8 to 10 times that of absence (Sainsbury Centre for Mental Health, 2007). This interest is also related to the consequences of working while ill for individual health, given the greater attention that organizations are paying to employee health and well-being. Health and well-being at work, in fact, are among the key elements in the Europe 2020 strategy for growth, competitiveness, and sustainable development (European Commission, 2010). Employers are recognizing the implications of these factors for workforce performance and are investing in well-being programs as part of their human resources strategies (Chartered Institute of Personnel and Development, 2016).

In this light, the purpose of this chapter is to examine the relationship between presenteeism, defined as going to work when ill (Aronsson, Gustafsson & Dallner, 2000; Johns, 2010), and well-being at work. The chapter will look at the components of well-being both as antecedents and outcomes of working when ill. Considering the broad literature on both themes of the chapter, we first clarify what we mean by presenteeism and specify the framework used in relation to employee well-being. We then focus on how well-being can influence working when sick and under which conditions the latter can harm or enhance well-being.

What is Presenteeism?

According to the preliminary findings of the Sixth European Working Conditions Survey (EWCS; Eurofound, 2016), which interviewed almost 44,000 workers across 35 European countries, 43 percent of those surveyed responded positively to the question, "Over the past 12 months, did you work when you were sick?" Another survey conducted by the Chartered Institute of Personnel and Development (CIPD) among 600 British organizations across various sectors and sizes found that 72 percent of employers reported employees working while sick (CIPD, 2015). Perhaps even more worrying, almost a third of the organizations reported an *increase* in people turning up at their job when ill (CIPD, 2015).

Interest in presenteeism is thus increasing on all fronts. But what exactly is presenteeism? To define it, we need to look at the multiple and diverse streams of research that have investigated the topic. Johns (2010) identifies two main traditions, linked to two distinct geographical areas. The first one includes British and European scholars in management and organizational behavior, but also in occupational health and epidemiology, who have especially focused on job insecurity and on the job or occupational characteristics that might stimulate presenteeism (e.g., Simpson, 1998; Virtanen, Kivimäki, Elovainio, Vahtera & Ferrie, 2003; Worrall, Cooper & Campbell, 2000). The second tradition is more common among American scholars, who have been more interested in the consequences for productivity at work associated with health impairment. To this aim, medical, epidemiological, and occupational health researchers and consultants have aimed at quantifying and monetizing the impact of general illness or of specific medical conditions (e.g., asthma, headache) on work productivity as well as identifying pharmaceutical and medical interventions to reduce productivity loss (e.g., Goetzel et al., 2004; Koopman et al., 2002; Zhang, Gignac, Beaton, Tang & Anis, 2010).

The two traditions have led to two main conceptualizations (and thus operationalizations) of presenteeism. The first perspective defines presenteeism as working while ill, referring to specific behavior (Aronsson et al., 2000; Johns, 2010). Hence, presentees are people who continue to work when they should have taken sick leave because of their state of health (Aronsson et al., 2000). The second definition refers to productivity loss associated to working while ill (e.g., Turpin et al., 2004). This means that employees are presentees when they are on the job but not performing up to their full capabilities due to illness. For a more complete discussion of the multitude of presenteeism definitions that can be found in the literature, we refer the reader to Johns (2010, 2012) and Wężyk & Merecz (2013).

Although an estimation of the consequences of working while ill for productivity is of utter importance for organizations and the economy in general, the logic and utility of the second definition of presenteeism as productivity loss has been questioned (Johns, 2010). Indeed, since it incorporates the outcomes of going to work ill (i.e., a reduction in performance), it conflates the cause with a particular consequence. This may preempt the investigation of the various antecedents of the act of going to work ill as well as the various implications of this behavior. Therefore, this chapter adopts the first definition, referring to presenteeism as the act of going to work when ill. This framing does not ascribe motives or consequences to presenteeism (Johns, 2010), allowing for the understanding of how well-being both affects and is affected by working while unwell. Additionally, by not emphasizing productivity loss, this conceptualization does not imply that presenteeism is necessarily negative, but opens the way to explore both positive and negative repercussions of the behavior on well-being.

What is Well-Being?

Well-being refers to "optimal psychological functioning and experience" (Ryan & Deci, 2001: 142). As with presenteeism, the precise conceptualization and operationalization of the concept, that clearly define what well-being is and what its principal dimensions are, are still the subject of debate. However, research has converged on two general viewpoints which assign somewhat different meaning to the construct and arise from distinct philosophical backgrounds (Ryan & Deci, 2001). We refer to the hedonic and eudaimonic perspectives on well-being.

The hedonic tradition conceptualizes well-being as happiness. Aristippus, a Greek philosopher from the fourth century BC, identified the achievement and maximization of pleasure as the main purpose in life, and happiness as a collection of pleasant experiences. Some centuries later, the hedonic perspective was used in psychology to describe well-being in terms of pleasure versus pain, and maximizing human happiness became the principal aim of hedonic psychology (Kaheneman, Diener & Schwarz, 1999). Such hedonic experiences have been assessed via the construct of *subjective well-being* (Diener & Lucas, 1999; Lucas, Diener & Suh, 1996), which includes both affective and cognitive indicators of happiness. Subjective well-being consists of three components, the presence of positive affect (e.g., joy, contentment), the absence of negative affect (e.g., sadness, fear, anxiety), and life satisfaction (i.e., the cognitive constituent). Well-being thus stems from a balance between positive and negative affect as well as from the positive assessment of one's life. Therefore, the hedonic definition captures both the individual assessment of short-term life experiences (i.e., positive and negative emotions, feelings, and states) and the cognitive long-term assessment of the experience of life.

Having its roots in philosophers such as Aristotele and Fromm, the eudaimonic perspective sees well-being as something more than mere happiness, more than the simple pursuit of pleasure and avoidance of pain. Rather, it pertains to the achievement of one's full potential, finding meaning in life, and human flourishing. These can only occur when people feel authentic and alive, when they are engaged with meaningful challenge in life, and when their activities and goals correspond to their values (Ryff, 1995). The eudaimonic tradition focuses on *psychological well-being*, which depicts an individual's positive functioning and development and comprises six dimensions: autonomy, personal growth, self-acceptance, life purpose, environmental mastery, and positive relations with others (Ryff, 1989; Ryff & Keyes, 1995).

Although the hedonic and eudaimonic perspectives emerged and developed separately, evidence from a number of studies has indicated connections between the two (Keyes, Shmotkin & Ryff, 2002; O'Donnell, Deaton, Durand, Halpern & Layard, 2014). Particularly, Keys et al. (2002) tested the factor structure underlying the two dimensions on a sample of 3,032 Americans aged 25–74 years old. The analysis showed two correlated latent factors, suggesting that the subjective and psychological dimensions are related but distinct conceptions of well-being.

To conclude, well-being is a multidimensional concept, inclusive of aspects of both the hedonic and eudaimonic perspectives and consequently indicative of a happy and a meaningful life. Relying on this dual approach, this chapter investigates the interplay of positive and negative affect, life satisfaction, and the multiple aspects of eudaimonia with working while sick.

The Interplay Between Well-Being and Presenteeism

Presenteeism is a complexly determined behavior reflecting a wide range of individual and contextual factors. These include work demands and pressure, job insecurity, and organizational policies relating to sickness absenteeism, as well as individual differences in health condition and personality (Miraglia & Johns, 2016). With regard to the consequences of presenteeism, studies have especially focused on the costs related to the behavior, in terms of reduced productivity, and much less on the effects on employee health and well-being.

This chapter examines the reciprocal associations between presenteeism and well-being. Such relationships may be more complicated and controversial than expected. First, a lack of subjective well-being, indexed by decreased physical or mental health or increased strain, may trigger working while ill. Similarly, positive attitudes and striving to achieve meaning in life (eudemonia) may induce presenteeism. However, they may also decrease presenteeism by supporting health and buffering stress at work. As for the consequences for well-being, working despite physical and mental impairment may preclude the possibility for recovery, exacerbate health conditions, and eventually further damage employee health and well-being. Once again, however, the opposite may be true under certain conditions. That is, there may be some positive value in working while ill, when the illness in question is neither contagious nor over-debilitating. In other words, in some cases presenteeism may be a sustainable and positive determinant of employee well-being.

The following sections will first treat well-being as a cause of the behavior of working while ill. We will explain how the lack of subjective well-being, described as poor mental and physical health and high stress, elicits presenteeism. We will then explore the more variable associations of satisfaction (with life and work) and psychological well-being (autonomy, environmental mastery, self-acceptance, positive relationships with others) with working when sick. We will illustrate how these associations can be positive or negative, depending on the processes and mechanisms that the well-being dimensions activate, and we will discuss the underlying models, theories, and constructs that can explain this. Finally, we will look at the hindering and fostering consequences of presenteeism for subjective and psychological well-being.

Well-Being as Determinant of Working While Ill

Physical and Mental Health

Well-being is a driver of both emotional and physical health (Ryff & Singer, 1998). The six dimensions of psychological well-being are related to health promotion and immunological functioning through their impact on specific physiological systems (Keyes et al., 2002).

A first mechanism through which well-being may influence presenteeism behavior is, thus, health promotion. As with sickness absenteeism, health impairment is a prerequisite of working while ill, as it is only after a health event (episodic, acute, or chronic; Johns, 2010) that individuals are faced with the decision to go to work despite their poor medical condition or to call in sick. A recent meta-analysis reports a corrected population correlation between general health status and presenteeism of –.31 ($K = 67$, $N = 125,345$; Miraglia & Johns, 2016). This not only indicates that poor general health is associated with higher presenteeism, but it also reinforces the basis for the validity of presenteeism as a construct. Correspondingly, those exhibiting elevated presenteeism also exhibit elevated absenteeism ($\rho = .35$; Miraglia & Johns, 2016).

Studies have investigated the specific medical conditions associated with presenteeism. A systematic review of the literature showed that presentees suffer from specific health conditions, such as allergies and arthritis, and that they are also carriers of higher health risks, such as lack of physical activity and elevated body weight (Schultz, Chen & Edington, 2009). The harmful effects of health habits are confirmed by a survey on about 20,000 employees from three companies in various economic sectors conducted by the Health Enhancement Research Organization (HERO, 2013). The data reflects higher odds of presenteeism for smokers (28 percent more), people who do not eat healthily (66 percent more), and those who do not exercise regularly (50 percent more). The HERO survey also examined the specific health risk factors that increase the likelihood of working while sick. In order, such risks are pain related to musculoskeletal disorders (knee/leg and neck/back pain), asthma, and chronic conditions such as diabetes, high cholesterol, high blood pressure, and obesity. Moreover, chronic depression dramatically increased the odds of reporting high presenteeism by 131 percent (HERO, 2013; see also Munir et al., 2009). Likewise, significant relationships have been found between presenteeism and higher levels of anxiety and lower levels of psychological well-being (Ashby & Mahdon, 2010).

The role of mental health and psychological problems is of particular interest, since such conditions may induce employees to turn up at work more frequently when compared to others suffering from physical ailments. Mental ill health is often viewed as an inadequate reason for absenteeism (Johns & Xie, 1998), it is more difficult to disclose in the workplace due to associated stigma (Corrigan, 2005; Hinshaw, 2007), and it can be viewed as a sign of weakness and lack of self-control (Johns & Xie, 1998). These factors stimulate self-protective motives that consequently provoke presenteeism (Johns, 2010).

The investigation of the medical conditions underlying presenteeism has been a preoccupation of the research stream centered on productivity loss. Using multiple measures, procedures, and cost estimation methods, numerous studies have focused on the main drivers of such loss and calculated the related costs (Kigozi, Jowett, Lewis, Barton & Coast, 2017; Schultz & Edington, 2007). Consistent with the findings described above, the strongest health hazards for productivity loss are depression (Burton, Pransky, Conti, Chen & Edington, 2004; Collins et al., 2005; Goetzel et al., 2004; Lerner et al., 2004; Munir et al., 2009), migraine (Collins et al., 2005; Goetzel et al., 2004; Schwartz, Stewart & Lipton, 1997), asthma and respiratory problems (Collins et al., 2005; Goetzel et al., 2004), severity of pain – especially related to allergies, musculoskeletal disorders, and mental problems (Allen, Hubbard & Sullivan, 2005) – and further chronic conditions such as diabetes and arthritis (Burton et al., 2004; Goetzel et al., 2004).

To conclude this section, a few words must be spent on the distinction between objectively diagnosed medical conditions and an individual's perception of these conditions. Johns (1997, 2009, 2010) illustrated the relevance of personal attributions and interpretations in explaining absenteeism. The decision to be present at work while sick may be influenced by the employee's self-assessment of the ailment, definition of minor and major health problems, propensity to adopt a sick role, and tendency to disclose illness in the workplace (Johns, 2009). In other words, given a somatic condition, psychological factors ultimately influence the decision between absenteeism and presentee-ism. An example of the consequent distinctions among being sick, feeling sick, and enacting a sick role comes from the medical field. Doctors and nurses are at a particularly high risk of presenteeism (Garrow, 2016), and a study of UK doctors found that over 80 percent had continued to work with illnesses for which they would have pre-scribed sick leave for their patients (McKevitt, Morgan, Dundas & Holland, 1997). Precisely the same percentage was found in a study among Norwegian physicians (Rosvold & Bjertness, 2001). This is caused by professional norms that stress responsibility toward patients, self-treatment practices, and difficulty assuming a sick role (Christie & Ingstad, 1996; Gustafsson Sendén, Løvseth, Schenck-Gustafsson & Fridner, 2013; McKevitt et al., 1997). Moreover, presenteeism is encouraged by an anti-sickness culture that frames illness as a sign of weakness and promotes a low sense of self-care (Crout, Chang & Cioffi, 2005). A study among British prison officers reported similar findings (Kinman, Clements & Hart, 2016).

Stress and Stressors

According to a recent survey among over 1,000 UK HR professionals, stress is the number one cause of long-term absence and the second most common cause of short-term absence after minor illness (CIPD, 2016). The same survey lists workload, family or nonwork relation-ships, and management style as the main triggers of stress. However, tempering such opinions, meta-analysis has indicated a negative, but modest, correlation between work stress and absence ($\rho = .145$; Darr & Johns, 2008). The modest association might suggest a link between stress and presenteeism, since stress is often viewed as an illegitimate reason to be absent (Johns & Xie, 1998). Moreover, stress is highly associated with migraine and psychological problems (Johns, 2009), close correlates of presenteeism. In this regard, an Australian study estimated that workplace stress can result in a loss of 2.14 working days per employee per year due to presenteeism, meaning a total annual cost of $533 per individual (Medibank Private, Econtech, 2008).

Job stressors have been positioned as job demands within the Job Demands–Resources (JD–R) theory (Bakker & Demerouti, 2014).

Demands capture the organizational, social, and physical aspects of the job requiring physiological and psychological effort and costs for the individual. Therefore, they include aspects of the job that might be appraised as stressful, such as role ambiguity and conflict, onerous physical or psychological requirements, heavy workload, time pressure, overtime work, and long working hours. Although it may appear counterintuitive, job demands have been shown to relate positively to presenteeism. Miraglia and Johns (2016) reported an average population correlation of .16 between working while ill and overall job demands, assessed as a global measure or as omnibus work pressure. The job features most highly related to the behavior were elevated workload ($\rho = .28$), understaffing ($\rho = .25$), time pressure ($\rho = .16$), and overtime work ($\rho = .15$). Multiple reasons suggest why employees already taxed by excessive workload, tight deadlines, and long work hours continue to put in physical and mental effort while ill, when a sick day off could offer them a break from such a tiring, adverse situation, facilitating recovery. First, these stressful demands may require physical presence to deal with a high volume of work or meet a tight schedule, compelling attendance (Böckerman & Laukkanen, 2010). Second, consistent with conservation of resources theory (Hobfoll, 2001), an individual facing excessive job requests may compensate any possible losses in resources or productivity by capitalizing on all the available resources, including continuing to work through illness. Thus, presenteeism can be used as a compensation strategy (Demerouti, Le Blanc, Bakker, Schaufeli & Hox, 2009). Third, heavy workload, understaffing, and time pressure have been associated with health impairment (Bowling & Kirkendall, 2012; Ng & Feldman, 2008; Pohling, Buruck, Jungbauer & Leiter, 2016), subsequently exposing individuals to the risk of presenteeism (Miraglia & Johns, 2016). A similar positive association exists for strain and burnout (Bakker & Demerouti, 2014; Crawford, LePine & Rich, 2010; Schaufeli & Taris, 2014), two factors that can also prompt presenteeism. In support of this, a study conducted among 545 Norwegian university physicians demonstrates that emotional exhaustion, one of the three components of burnout, mediates the relationship between role conflict (i.e., job demands) and presenteeism (Thun & Løvseth, 2016). Finally, not all demands are appraised by the individual as stressful, and some of them can be positively valued and perceived as opportunities to promote future gain and personal growth. Hence, they may turn into challenges, thus stimulating engagement and motivation (Crawford et al., 2010; LePine, Podsakoff & LePine, 2005). These are the so-called challenge demands, such as high levels of responsibility for innovation or time pressure, which can induce presenteeism via engagement and positive motivation to attend.

Among stressors, a particularly relevant variable for attendance behavior and for individual well-being is job insecurity, especially in the light of the recent series of financial crises affecting the Western economy. Even if sick, people in insecure jobs may substitute presence for absence to avoid any negative consequences that can be associated with absenteeism (Hansen & Anderson, 2008). Absenteeism has been repeatedly found to be negatively associated with the unemployment rate (Shoss & Penney, 2012), suggesting that presenteeism might increase with job threat, and in fact meta-analytic results show that people experiencing job insecurity and personal financial problems report a higher number of sickness presence days (Miraglia & Johns, 2016).

Regarding job stressors, we can mention the results of the meta-analytic model presented by Miraglia & Johns (2016). The empirical model uncovered two distinct paths to presenteeism, an attitudinal-motivational path and a health impairment one. These paths mediate the relationship between work features and working while ill. Job insecurity, personal financial difficulties, and elevated job demands were found to lead to presenteeism by damaging health (i.e., via the health impairment path). However, they were also found to be negatively and indirectly related to working while ill through the attitudinal-motivational path, since they decreased job satisfaction.

With regard to the physiological, psychological, and behavioral consequences of stressors, burnout and strain provoke an intensification in physical and mental symptoms (Darr & Johns, 2008), which can consequently increase the tendency to work when sick (Miraglia & Johns, 2016; Thun & Løvseth, 2016). In a longitudinal study of nurses, Demerouti et al. (2009) uncovered a positive and reciprocal relationship between emotional exhaustion and presenteeism. By preventing recovery, continuing to work when unwell caused feelings of exhaustion, which in turn led to work accumulation and damaged coping strategies in a negative loop that escalated presenteeism.

Finally, it is interesting to note a study by Gilbreath & Karimi (2012) investigating job-stress-related presenteeism and its association with management behaviors. In a sample of Australian hospital nurses, psychological strain and presenteeism were found to be positively related, especially in situations characterized by negative supervisor behaviors, such as nonparticipative decision-making, incapacity to manage group dynamics, uninterest in employees' ideas, and a closed communication style. The study speaks to the relevance of simultaneously investigating work features and individual appraisals (e.g., felt stress) to understand and tackle presenteeism in the workplace.

Life Satisfaction

Although some studies have reported that life dissatisfaction is associated with increased presenteeism conceptualized as impaired productivity (Burton et al., 2005; Musich, Hook, Baaner & Edington, 2006; Musich, Hook, Baaner, Spooner & Edington, 2006), no research has investigated the link between overall satisfaction with life and the act of working while ill.

However, an important indicator of life satisfaction is positive equilibrium between the work and nonwork spheres, including family commitment and leisure activities. Such balance entails relationships with the individual's broader environment, which can influence attendance dynamics and ultimately the decision to attend work or not when sick. Interference between work and family has been shown to relate positively to presenteeism (Miraglia & Johns, 2016). Indeed, work to family conflict may represent a symptom of excessive workload or long work hours (Mostert, 2009; van der Heijden, Demerouti, Bakker & The NEXT Study Group, 2008), which may simultaneously cause conflict at home, as employees may need to take work home and so reduce family time, and force attendance at work even when sick. Moreover, dissatisfaction with one's family life has been described as a "double risk factor" (Hansen & Andersen, 2008), suggesting that it can both increase the likelihood of opting for presence over absence and decrease individual health, consequently occasioning presenteeism.

Surprisingly, family to work conflict is also positively correlated with working when ill (Miraglia & Johns, 2016). One might assume that employees with high family responsibilities, which interfere with work duties, would be disinclined to engage in presenteeism because these individuals may actually use sick days to deal with family problems

(Kossek & Ozeki, 1999). In addition, heavy work demands have been found to decrease work motivation (ten Brummelhuis, Ter Hoeven, De Jong & Peper, 2013), which should decrease presence at work. However, the positive correlation might reflect dissatisfaction with family life or difficult home circumstances that, as aforementioned, represent a "double risk factor" responsible for presenteeism (Hansen & Andersen, 2008). Furthermore, it is plausible that when family life is overtaxing (as a high level of family to work interference may denote) individuals may get more satisfaction from investing time in the job rather than dealing with home obligations, consequently preferring to go to work when ill. This recalls what Hochschild (1997) describes as the "home becoming work" effect. To sum up, a lack of balance between work and nonwork life may contribute to presenteeism.

Finally, if we direct our focus to the workplace, we cannot exclude from our analysis the role of attitudes such as job satisfaction. Satisfaction with the job is associated with elevated presenteeism (Miraglia & Johns, 2016). Along with strong feelings of affective attachment to the organization or elevated levels of work engagement, job satisfaction represents a positive motive to attend that can push people to invest greater effort and energy at work, to "go to the extra mile," increasing the time spent on the job even when in suboptimal medical condition (Christian, Garza & Slaughter, 2011; Macey & Schneider, 2008; Pfeffer, 1998). Some qualitative studies report that individuals continue to work when sick because of interest in the job and the feeling of pleasure and satisfaction derived from it (Biron, Brun, Ivers & Cooper, 2006; Krohne & Magnussen, 2011), and a sense of commitment toward the organization (Falco, Girardi & Parmiani, 2013; Taylor, Cunningham, Newsome & Scholarios, 2010) or to the job per se (Caverley, Cunningham & MacGregor, 2007; McKevitt et al., 1997; Quazi, 2013). In other words, people continue to work while ill because they want to, because of the sense of satisfaction or feeling of belonging obtained from their work. This is also in line with the withdrawal model of absenteeism (Johns, 1997) that assumes that people use absence days to withdraw temporarily from unpleasant circumstances. The model describes an empirically verified continuum of withdrawal behaviors from work, starting with the withdrawal of citizenship behavior and continuing with lateness, absence, and turnover (Berry, Lelchook & Clark, 2012; Harrison, Newman & Roth, 2006). On the contrary, positive job attitudes, such as being satisfied with the job, affectively committed to the organization, work-engaged, and feeling justly treated, foster organizational citizenship behavior (OCB; Dalal, Baysinger, Brummel & LeBreton, 2012; Hoffman, Blair, Meriac & Woehr, 2007) and good attendance at work. Presenteeism can be seen as an example of OCB (Johns, 2010), further explaining the positive association between positive attitudes and working when sick.

On a final note, and speaking to the contradictory etiology of presenteeism behaviors, a negative relationship between job attitudes and presenteeism cannot be excluded. This would operate via a health enhancement mechanism. In fact, job satisfaction, work engagement, and feelings of justice tend to foster good health (e.g., Ford & Huang, 2014; Meyer, Maltin & Thai, 2012; Robbins, Ford & Tetrick, 2012; Schaufeli & Taris, 2014), which in turn may decrease the occasions of making a decision between absence or presence in the case of illness symptoms.

Psychological Well-Being

Autonomy. A strong sense of personal determination and authority contribute to an individual's psychological well-being (Ryff & Keyes, 1995). With regard to the relationship between control at work and presenteeism, research reports a decided mix of positive, negative, and non-significant associations (e.g., Aronsson & Gustafsson, 2005; Deery, Iverson & Walsh, 2012; Gustafsson & Marklund, 2011), resulting in a negative but very small meta-analytic correlation ($\rho = -.03$, Miraglia & Johns, 2016). Conceptually, a negative relationship would reflect the ability of job control to counterbalance job demands and decrease strain and burnout, consequently lowering presenteeism. However, a dual-path model linking control over the job to presenteeism via health-impairment and motivational/attitudinal mechanisms (Miraglia & Johns, 2016) can better reconcile the inconsistent findings in the literature. Indeed, job control can discourage presenteeism via the health path, since it reduces health ailments and thus the necessity for working while ill. At the same time, control over the job may elicit presenteeism by increasing the levels of satisfaction and engagement with the job (i.e., via the motivational/attitudinal path).

To clarify the consequences of the ability to influence what happens on the job, Johansson and Lundberg (2004) introduced the concept of adjustment latitude, referring to employees' opportunity to reduce their performance output and alter work procedures and tasks in response to sickness. Following this logic, adjustment latitude is suggested to relate positively to attending work while ill, since an individual is able to adjust the work pace and activities according to his or her health condition. For example, a person could decrease cognitive effort, avoid meetings, take longer breaks, or skip heavy physical activity, and this could favor presence at work despite illness. However, more research is needed on the construct, as only a very weak positive association was found between adjustment latitude and presenteeism (Johansson & Lundberg, 2004), perhaps a reflection of single-item measurement.

Environmental Mastery. This dimension of psychological well-being refers to the capacity to shape the environment to meet personal needs and desires. Environmental mastery is conceptually related to the construct of self-efficacy, a pillar of social-cognitive theory (Bandura, 1986). Self-efficacy refers to an individual's beliefs in his or her own ability to control the environment, act upon it, and influence life events (Bandura, 1997). With regard to presenteeism, a two-wave study conducted in Taiwan showed a positive relationship between self-efficacy and working while ill (Lu, Peng, Lin & Cooper, 2014). More precisely, self-efficacy beliefs were predictors of approach motives inducing presenteeism, reflecting ethical reasons prizing loyalty and diligence toward the profession and the organization and values celebrating self-resilience. The positive association can be explained by looking at the specific characteristics of highly self-efficacious employees. They set difficult goals for themselves, frame obstacles as challenges, put in great effort to meet objectives and standards, and adopt active coping strategies to face external demands (Bandura, 1997). Thus, they put great emphasis on self-resiliency and self-accomplishment, and this may induce them to show up at work when sick to achieve their goals and maintain performance standards. However, self-efficacy also represents a personal resource, which can reduce experienced stress and support health (Xanthopoulou, Bakker, Demerouti & Schaufeli, 2009), thus diminishing the probability of working in presence of medical complaints. Once again, this indirect, negative relationship would be explained via a health enhancement mechanism.

Self-Acceptance. How good people feel about themselves and how easily they accept their own limits contribute to their psychological well-being. In the context of presenteeism, a study of Swedish young adults (Löve, Grimby-Ekman, Eklöf, Hagberg & Dellve, 2010) investigated the consequences for working while sick of performance-based self-esteem (PBSE), which refers to the extent to which an individual's self-esteem depends on his or her performance. The study showed a positive relationship between PBSE and presenteeism. Not surprisingly, those people who based they self-worth on their work and define themselves according to it are more likely to invest more in the job, pushing themselves to work hard, contribute overtime, and show up when ill.

Positive Relationships with Others. The development and maintenance of positive and trusting interpersonal relationships is a further component of psychological well-being that holds relevant implications for presenteeism. The impact of social dynamics on absenteeism has been well documented in the literature, where absence has been shown to be related to normative control and social integration (e.g., Dello Russo, Miraglia, Borgogni & Johns, 2013; Diestel, Wegge & Schmidt, 2014; Johns, 1997, 2008, 2009; ten Brummelhuis, Johns, Lyons & ter Hoeven, 2016). One of the core findings is that high team cohesion and strong social integration are predictive of lower levels of absence. A similar logic could be applied to presenteeism. High social integration could stimulate extra effort to turn up at work when ill. Indeed, harmonious and trusting relationships with colleagues are associated with a higher number of presenteeism days (Biron et al., 2006; Caverley et al., 2007; Hansen & Anderson, 2008). The reason for this is that team membership may activate an obligation to attend to fulfil social expectations and induce a fear of causing burden for colleagues by increasing their workload (Grinyer & Singleton, 2000). A clear example comes from the care, welfare, and education sectors. Helping professionals are responsible for the well-being of other individuals, and are exposed to high emotional demands and to a professional culture that emphasizes role meaningfulness, irreplaceability, and responsibility for others. Doctors, for instance, can consider it unfair to their colleagues to stay at home even if sick when they have already a day fully booked with patient appointments (McKevitt et al., 1997). Similar findings were found among prison officers, who would not skip a shift if unwell to avoid letting colleagues down (Kinman et al., 2016).

However, teams can develop norms that support self-care and health maintenance and improvement, consequently discouraging working while ill. In this regard, a recent multilevel study found a negative relationship between team health climate and presenteeism (Schulz, Zacher & Lippke, 2017). When team members are concerned, care and talk about health problems, they are less likely to work when ill.

Mixed findings have been reported for the association of presenteeism with collegial and supervisory support (Baker-McClearn, Greasley, Dale & Griffith, 2010; Biron et al., 2006; Caverley et al., 2007), with meta-analytic analyses showing negative, albeit weak, correlations (Miraglia & Johns, 2016). The underlying explanation is that a supportive workplace may act as a job resource for those who are ill. This may boost health, thus reducing subsequent presenteeism. Also, it may provide employees with the confidence needed to disclose illness in the workplace and avail themselves of time off from work to recover from sickness (Munir, Leka & Griffiths, 2005). Supportive colleagues and supervisors, in addition, can facilitate provisions for adjustment and backup, decreasing attendance pressure (Aronsson et al., 2000; Johns, 2011).

Well-Being as an Outcome of Working While Ill

Many studies have focused on the financial costs of presenteeism for organizations and the economy in general, attributable to the reduction in individual productivity that working while ill occasions. Some US and Australian studies have attempted to monetarize the value of presenteeism and to estimate the costs in terms of loss in productivity associated with various physical and mental ailments (for a review see Garrow, 2016). However, very few studies have assessed the consequences of presenteeism for employee well-being. Below we summarize the extant literature on the implications of presenteeism for health and well-being, trying to address a crucial question: Is presenteeism bad or good for individual well-being?

Can Presenteeism Harm Well-Being?

By precluding the possibility of recovery, it is likely that showing up at work when ill jeopardizes downstream physical and mental health and well-being. Some preliminary evidence for a positive relationship between presenteeism and an increased risk of future illness (and subsequent absenteeism) comes from a review of 12 longitudinal studies which evaluated the effects of sickness presenteeism on subsequent physical and mental health (Skagen & Collins, 2016). Working while ill was found to predict future poor self-rated general health (Bergström et al., 2009; Dellve, Hadzibajramovic & Ahlborg, 2011; Gustafsson & Marklund, 2011) and this increased with the frequency of the behavior, in a dose–response association (Bergström et al., 2009; Gustafsson & Marklund, 2011). However, the findings were less clear when specific measures of physical health were included. For instance, Gustafsson & Marklund (2011, 2014) reported that both presenteeism and absenteeism predicted future physical complaints, such us musculoskeletal pain. In a sample of male civil servants, Kivimäki and colleagues (2005) showed that unhealthy individuals taking no sick leave were twice as likely to experience serious coronary episodes as opposed to individuals using sickness absence. In a Chinese sample, presenteeism at baseline was associated with physical health measured two months later (Lu, Lin & Cooper, 2013), but the effect disappeared at a three-month follow-up (Lu et al., 2014). With regard to mental well-being, working while ill portends an increased risk of depression (Conway et al., 2014) and decreased mental health, including anxiety, low energy, and negative affect (Gustafsson & Marklund, 2011; Lu et al., 2013). Presenteeism has also been linked to burnout (Dellve et al., 2011; Demerouti et al., 2009; Lu et al., 2013), eliciting feelings of emotional exhaustion, depersonalization, and detachment from the job role over time, possibly in an attempt to recover from the emotional demands of the job, both among nurses and prison officers (Demerouti et al., 2009; Kinman et al., 2016). Moreover, as aforementioned, Demerouti and colleagues (2009) showed a positive reciprocal relationship between presenteeism and emotional exhaustion, indicating that working while sick increases such exhaustion that, in turn, raises the likelihood of presenteeism. However, Lu et al. (2014) failed to find a significant association between presenteeism and mental health at a three-month follow-up. These mixed findings signal some lack of consensus in terms of the consequences of presenteeism for physical and mental health. Skagen & Collins (2016) attribute this to the wide variety of approaches and methods used in the literature with regard to presenteeism definitions, recall periods, measures, and statistical techniques.

Taken together, these findings seem to confirm that presenteeism may constitute a hazard for the individual's quality of life. However, clear research on the consequences of the behavior for attitudinal, affective, and motivational processes is sparse.

With regard to overall quality of life, we might presume that presenteeism may push the employees to neglect family responsibilities or leisure activities, since being at work when sick may limit the full recovery process after illness and then it may force them to use spare time and home time to restore physical and mental energy (Demerouti, Bakker & Bulters, 2004; Geurts, Kompier, Roxburgh & Houtman, 2003). This can harm work–life balance, exacerbate work–family conflict, and eventually decrease life satisfaction.

Furthermore, presenteeism may reduce employee satisfaction with the job over time via its influence on affective-motivational states. Indeed, working through medical discomfort was found to diminish work engagement while increasing individual propensity to addiction to work (i.e., work addition) among 158 office workers. The final outcome was a worse personal evaluation of the job (Karanika-Murray, Pontes, Griffiths & Biron, 2015). The data also indicated that although presentees may be dependent on work in an unhealthy manner, their engagement may still maintain their satisfaction with that work. Further research is needed to understand the effects of presenteeism for subjective and psychological well-being as well as for motivational impairment.

Little research has been conducted on the consequences of presenteeism for the well-being of others, such as colleagues and customers. Decreased performance due to working while ill might be one problem, especially for highly interdependent teams. The risks of working during contagious illness are obvious, as presentees threaten the health of coworkers and members of the public. This could be even more alarming considering the food industry or the health sector, where many physicians and nurses continue to work when sick and have even shown up with infectious diseases (McKevitt et al., 1997; Rosvold & Bjertness, 2001; Widera, Chang & Chen, 2010). This action is ironic in light of the fact that coworkers are inclined to treat virulent peers with disdain (Luksyte, Avery & Yeo, 2015).

A recent case reported in the popular press exemplifies the danger of working under virulent conditions (Addady, 2016; Rhodan, 2016). A successful US restaurant chain went through two norovirus outbreaks which affected numerous customers and caused a loss of $750 million in few days, as investors exited the company (Fickenscher, 2016). The outbreaks were apparently caused by employees turning up at work with the virus. Unfortunately, there is very little hard research on such events except for qualitative accounts of how workers in such industries feel pressured to show up sick (Hopkins, 2014).

In the short term, continuing to work while sick may be desirable for the organization, since the individual is still on the job and some productivity is better than zero productivity, but this must be carefully evaluated in relation to the evident risks for health and safety, especially for certain professions. Working under unhealthy conditions harms the quality and quantity of work (Hemp, 2004), causing slips and lapses of judgement, which can lead to involuntary violation of health and safety standards. Thus, a study of 1,205 UK pharmacists found that presentees tended to make errors more frequently, such as giving a patient the wrong medication or prescribing the wrong dosage. Presentee pharmacists also experienced higher levels of depression and anxiety than their absentee counterparts (Niven & Ciborowska, 2015). Working while unwell requires more effort to maintain the expected level of performance, as employees need to increase concentration and cognitive labor to overcome the distracting symptoms of illness such as pain. Hence, the capability to monitor and respond promptly to environmental demands is constrained, therefore increasing the likelihood of errors and accidents. The risks for professions with rigorous health and safety targets, such as physicians or pilots, are self-evident.

Can Presenteeism Foster Well-Being?

The positive motives associated with presenteeism and the attitudinal/motivational path leading to it (Miraglia & Johns, 2016) corroborate the idea that, under certain circumstances, presenteeism may be a "sustainable" choice for the individual. Of course, this would depend on numerous factors. Primarily, the nature of illness must not be contagious or overly debilitating. This view is supported by a recent report by the UK Institute for Employment Studies (Garrow, 2016) that introduced the idea of "positive presenteeism." In an attempt to recognize and distinguish between positive and negative presenteeism, the report calls for attendance policies aimed at reducing unnecessary or prolonged absenteeism and transforming this in positive presenteeism by offering adequate and well-structured return-to-work programs and organizational support. This could be the case for people recovering from long-term sickness, where an "assisted" form of presenteeism can facilitate their reintegration of the single into work and into society in general. The expression positive presenteeism also depicts those workers suffering from chronic or long-term health conditions, such as migraine or depression, who can be encouraged to remain on the job with appropriate support and workload and schedule adjustments that correspond to their work ability (Garrow, 2016). In particular in the US, notions of reasonable workplace accommodation often approximate positive presenteeism.

Two principal pillars underlie the possibility that presenteeism can be beneficial for people's mental health and well-being. First, work can be a medicine, a cure, as it can contribute to positive functioning and facilitate the adoption of a more active view of the sick role (Roe & van Diepen, 2011). Performing a task and being committed to a work role may stimulate the cognitive functions, focus concentration on the work activity, turn attention away from illness and negative states, and generate positive feedback and feelings of appreciation and worth. In this light, working with a medical condition can be self-affirming for the person, promoting self-esteem. Therefore, it can outweigh the costs of presenteeism. The therapeutic effect of work is the basis of vocational rehabilitation interventions and occupational therapies (Kendall, Burton, Lunt, Mellor & Daniels, 2015).

The second pillar is that presenteeism can be constructive only when presentees have the right kind of support and control over their jobs. Collegial and supervisory support is essential to sustain reintegration into work, promote a positive self-image, and provide practical help on the job. Line manager support is of utter importance, especially in the light of the recent trend of the devolvement of the HR function to line managers (CIPD, 2016). To make sure that they are able to fulfill these expectations, it is important to equip them with knowledge of the diverse illness conditions, their consequences for performance, and the work factors that can exacerbate or reduce such conditions. It is also essential to provide them with the skills necessary to approach employees regarding sensitive issues, and the power and tools to take action. For example, line managers should be able to adjust workload or offer flexible solutions, such as part-time work, working from home, or flexible or shorter working hours. Therefore, training and awareness should be promoted among organizational management, especially in relation to working with "invisible" problems, such as mental health related. Indeed, managerial understating and support may reduce the stigma associated with psychological issues (e.g., depression), and encourage employees to disclosure these, facilitating better integration at work (Center for Mental Health, 2011; Malachowski, Boydell, Sawchuk & Kirsh, 2016). There might, however, be some obstacles. For example, this presumes that managers have access to the individual's health information. Due to confidentiality policies in some companies, this may not be allowed, disenabling managers to adopt opportune practices (Malachowski et al., 2016).

Moreover, managers must be ready and open to recognize and accept that presentees can work only at a lower productivity or pace, avoiding putting excessive pressure and expectations on them. Careful attention should be devoted to job design in order to redesign job activities and scheduling around the presentee's health condition, needs, and work ability. Working time and methods should be modified in a non-harmful way that ensures recovery and rehabilitation, and ergonomic adjustments should be made when necessary. All of this said, in cases of employees suffering from chronic health conditions, a prerequisite of positive presenteeism is that the individual not only is keen to stay at work but also values being at work as helpful for the rehabilitation and recovery process or as beneficial for positive functioning and well-being (Roe & van Diepen, 2011).

Some evidence has supported the benefits of positive or sustainable presenteeism for reintegration and rehabilitation purposes. For instance, a study conducted by Howard and colleagues (2009) among 2,000 individuals affected by chronic occupational musculoskeletal disorders demonstrated that employees who were designated as presentees were more likely to complete a functional restorative treatment program and return to work fulltime than those who took more sick leave. The medical literature offers examples of people under medical treatment who benefited from an equilibrium between work and absence (Kendal et al., 2015). Moreover, it presents best practices for return to work schemes and occupational health tool boxes to monitor the psychological well-being of returnees or to limit the impact of common health problems in the workplace, such as musculoskeletal, mental health, and stress complaints (Kendal et al., 2015; Munir et al., 2008).

One of the challenges for future research is to understand the implications of presenteeism for those people who are ill but not present at primary care or not included in rehabilitation or return to work programs. It remains a question to understand how absence and presence can be balanced. In this regard, health promotion interventions in the workplace can help, by enhancing the well-being and productivity of employees working when ill. Cancelliere and colleagues (Cancelliere, Cassidy, Ammendolia & Côté, 2011) systematically reviewed the literature on workplace health promotion strategies and their effectiveness in promoting presentees' performance. Although the authors call for caution in interpreting the results in the light of the scarce rigorous research conducted in the area, the review showed some preliminary support for the effect of such programs. Successful ventures offered organizational leadership, health risk screening, individually tailored programs, and a supportive workplace culture (Cancelliere et al., 2011).

Conclusions

The relationship between presenteeism and well-being in the workplace is not as straightforward as it may appear. By discussing and systematizing some of the evidence in the literature, this chapter intended to propose presenteeism as both an outcome and a determinant of employee health and well-being.

To begin, the absence of subjective well-being is likely to prompt the individual to work when sick. Physical and mental health problems, particularly depression and high stress, inclusive of both job stressors and strain reactions (e.g., burnout), escalate presenteeism behavior. However, the pattern of relationships is more complex when examining the role of life satisfaction, a component of subjective and psychological well-being. If the influence of overall life satisfaction on presenteeism has not been uncovered yet, attitudes toward the job, such as job satisfaction, show a dual-direction association with the behavior. On the one hand, positive job attitudes encourage attendance despite illness since they boost motivation and enhance feelings of pleasure deriving from work. On the other hand, they sustain people's health, consequently decreasing presenteeism occasions. Similarly, the dimensions of psychological well-being (i.e., autonomy, environmental mastery, self-acceptance, positive relationships) can relate to presenteeism either positively and negatively, depending on the activated mechanism, as illustrated in the previous sections.

Matters are also complicated when looking at presenteeism as a determinant of subjective and psychological well-being. Working while ill is certainly detrimental for productivity (Hemp, 2004; Niven & Ciborowska, 2015) and physical and mental health (Skagen & Collins, 2016), with negative repercussions on quality of life. However, our chapter illustrates how presenteeism can also provide a sustainable, functional alternative to absence under some specific circumstances, such as noncontagious illness or chronic medical conditions. Clearly, this positive perspective is valid only when the individual is willing continue to work even if unwell, when the design of the job can be adjusted to his or her needs, and when adequate organizational, supervisory, and collegial support is provided. We emphasize, however, that such support on the whole tends to discourage presenteeism (Miraglia & Johns, 2016).

While research is flourishing with regard to the causes and correlates of presenteeism, more studies are necessary to investigate its effects for the employee and for other people who might be affected, such as colleagues and clients. Both managers and scholars need to better understand the potential positive outcomes and the conditions that can foster them. These moderating conditions pertain to several elements: First, they regard the individual and his or her specific medical ailments, stage of recovery, and personal traits and states (e.g., personality, psychological capital). Second, they are related to the job, including characteristics such as demands, resources (e.g., support), and control, as well as the possibility to adjust them to one's needs. In this regard, more research on constructs such as adjustment latitude (Johansson & Lundberg, 2004) and job crafting (Tim & Bakker, 2010; Wrzesniewski & Dutton, 2001) is desirable. Third, the organization plays an important role, and the influence of occupational and group norms and organizational culture should be explored.

Moreover, as noted by Johns (2009: 21), "presenteeism is a black hole when it comes to organizational policies." And it still is. Perhaps the most worrying aspect in the abovementioned CIPD survey (2015) is that 56 percent of employers admitted that they did not take any actions to manage presenteeism. Hence, despite rising awareness of the problem of presenteeism, specific policies to tackle it or actions to prevent it are still missing (Hemp, 2004; Johns, 2009, 2011).

Attendance policies are almost universal for absenteeism, even if they are often observed in the breach. Many companies carefully monitor employee absence, but they rarely if ever record the number of days that employees go to work ill. Organizations may adopt severe absenteeism policies, such as little or no paid sick leave or strict trigger points for disciplinary actions. Such policies can effectively limit absenteeism (Farrell & Stamm, 1988; Johns, 2008) but often at the increased cost of presenteeism (Miraglia & Johns, 2016). This is in line with the substitution hypothesis proposed by Caverley and colleagues (2007), suggesting that when employee are constrained from taking a day off they will substitute presence for absence. Thus, attendance policies should be carefully formulated. Formal rules could be created, clarifying, for example, that ill employees are not expected to be at work, especially when this would further damage their health or infect colleagues or customers (Johns, 2009). Attendance policies should also allow a margin of flexibility and empower line managers to pursue a balance between absence and presence at work. For instance, flexible or remote work may be encouraged in some cases, depending on the nature of both the illness and work activities.

This implies that managers should understand these policies, have ownership and control of them, and be educated about presenteeism and its consequences for productivity, health, and well-being (Ashby & Mahdon, 2010; Hemp, 2004). Managers should be able to talk to employees about sensitive issues such as health and to recognize the signs of reduced well-being and high levels of stress so as to offer support and possible solutions (Ashby & Mahdon, 2010). Managers also act as role models for attendance behavior (Kristensen et al., 2006; Markham & McKee, 1995), and they are important models of the organizational culture. By showing the way, they can promote the emergence of a culture that discourages working when ill while endorsing healthy habits, self-care, and disclosure of illness. Such a culture should demystify the negative and risky consequences of absenteeism (Johns & Miraglia, 2015) and oppose viewing absence as a sign of weakness (Ramsey, 2006; Simpson, 1998) while reframing it as a legitimate behavior when a person is genuinely ill. Presenteeism culture requires further attention, and more studies are necessary to continue to pursue what little is in the literature (e.g., Dew, Keefe & Small, 2005; Johns, 2010; Ramsey, 2006; Simpson, 1998). This is especially true in the light of the existence and pervasive impact of absence culture and underlying norms (e.g., Nicholson & Johns, 1985; Johns, 1997, 2001, 2002, 2008, 2009; Rentsch & Steel, 2003).

To conclude, a challenge for practitioners and academics alike remains to seek an equilibrium between absenteeism and presenteeism and to understand when the latter can contribute positively to individual well-being, or when, contrarily, it should be discouraged.

References

Addady, M. (2016). Chipotle's being accused of trying to cover up its norovirus outbreak. *Fortune*, January 21. Retrieved from http://fortune .com/2016/01/21/chipotle-accused-norovirus-cover-up/.

Allen, H., Hubbard, D. & Sullivan, S. (2005). The burden of pain on employee health and productivity at a major provider of business services. *Journal of Occupational and Environmental Medicine*, 47, 658–670.

Aronsson, G. & Gustafsson, K. (2005). Sickness presenteeism: prevalence, attendance-pressure factors, and an outline of a model for research. *Journal of Occupational and Environmental Medicine*, 47, 958–966.

Aronsson, G., Gustafsson, K. & Dallner, M. (2000). Sick but yet at work. An empirical study of sickness presenteeism. *Journal of Epidemiology and Community Health*, 54, 502–509.

Ashby, K. & Mahdon, M. (2010). *Why Do Employees Come to Work When Ill? An Investigation into Sickness Presence in the Workplace*, London: The Work Foundation.

Baker-McClearn, D., Greasley, K., Dale, J. & Griffith, F. (2010). Absence management and presenteeism: The pressures on employees to attend work and the impact of attendance on performance. *Human Resource Management Journal*, 20, 311–328.

Bakker, A. B. & Demerouti, E. (2014). Job Demands–Resources Theory, in P. Y. Chen & C. L. Cooper (Eds.), *Work and Wellbeing: Wellbeing: A Complete Reference Guide* (Vol. III). Hoboken, NJ: John Wiley & Sons, Inc.

Bandura, A. (1986). *Social Foundations of Thought and Action*. Englewood Cliffs, NJ: Prentice Hall.

Bandura, A. (1997). *Self-Efficacy: The Exercise of Control*. New York, NY: Freeman.

Bergström, G., Bodin, L., Hagberg, J., Lindh, T., Aronsson, G. & Josephson, M. (2009). Does sickness presenteeism have an impact on future general health? *International Archives of Occupational and Environmental Health*, 82, 1179–1190.

Berry, C. M., Lelchook, A. M. & Clark, M. A. (2012). A meta-analysis of the interrelationships between employee lateness, absenteeism, and turnover: Implications for models of withdrawal behavior. *Journal of Organizational Behavior*, 33, 678–699.

Biron, C., Brun, J., Ivers, H. & Cooper, C. L. (2006). At work but ill: Psychological work environment and well-being determinants of presenteeism propensity. *Journal of Public Mental Health*, 5, 26–37.

Böckerman, P. & Laukkanen, E. (2010). What makes you work while you are sick? Evidence from a survey of workers. *European Journal of Public Health*, 20, 43–46.

Bowling, N. A. & Kirkendall, C. (2012). Workload: A review of causes, consequences, and potential interventions, in J. Houdmont, S. Leka & R. R. Sinclair (Eds.), *Contemporary Occupational Health Psychology: Global Perspectives on Research and Practice* (Vol. 2, pp. 221–238). Chichester, UK: Wiley-Blackwell.

Burton, W. N., Chen, C. Y., Conti, D. J., Schultz, A. B., Pransky, G. & Edington D. (2005). The association of health risks with on-the-job productivity. *Journal of Occupational and Environmental Medicine*, 47, 769–777.

Burton, W. N., Pransky, G., Conti, D. J., Chen, C. & Edington, D. W. (2004). The association of medical conditions and presenteeism, *Journal of Occupational and Environmental Medicine*, 46, S38–S45.

Cancelliere, J., Cassidy, D., Ammendolia, C. & Côté, P. (2011). Are workplace health promotion programs effective at improving presenteeism in workers? A systematic review and best evidence synthesis of the literature, *BMC Public Health*, 11, 395–406.

Caverley, N., Cunningham, J. B. & MacGregor, J. N. (2007). Sickness presenteeism, sickness absenteeism, service organization. *Journal of Management Studies*, 44, 304–319.

Center for Mental Health (2011). Managing Presenteeism: A Discussion Paper. Retrieved from: www.centreformentalhealth.org.uk/managing-presenteeism

Chartered Institute of Personnel and Development, CIPD (2015). *Absence Management: Annual Survey Report*. London: CIPD.

Chartered Institute of Personnel and Development, CIPD (2016). *Absence Management: Annual Survey Report*. London: CIPD.

Christian, M. S., Garza, A. S. & Slaughter, J. E. (2011). Work engagement: A quantitative review and test of its relations with task and contextual performance. *Personnel Psychology*, 64, 89–136.

Christie, V. M. & Ingstad, B. (1996). Reluctant to be perceived as ill – The case of the physician, in O. Larsen (Ed.), *The Shaping of a Profession*.

Norwegian Physicians Past and Present (pp. 491–499). Canton, MA: Science History Publications.

Collins, J. J., Baase, C. M., Sharda, C. E. et al. (2005). The assessment of chronic health conditions on work performance, absence, and total economic impact for employers. *Journal of Occupational and Environmental Medicine, 47, 547–557.*

Conway, P. M., Hogh, A., Rugulies, R. & Hansen, A. M. (2014). Is sickness presenteeism a risk factor for depression? A Danish 2-year follow-up study. *Journal of Occupational and Environmental Medicine, 56, 595–603.*

Corrigan, P. W. (Ed.). (2005). *On the Stigma of Mental Illness: Practical Strategies for Research and Social Change.* Washington, DC: American Psychological Association.

Crawford, E. R., LePine, J. A. & Rich, B. L. (2010). Linking job demands and resources to employee engagement and burnout: A theoretical extension and meta-analytic test. *Journal of Applied Psychology, 95, 834–848.*

Crout, L. A., Chang, E. & Cioffi, J. (2005). Why do registered nurses work when ill? *The Journal of Nursing Administration, 35, 23–28.*

Dalal, R. S., Baysinger, M., Brummel, B. J. & LeBreton, J. M. (2012). The relative importance of employee engagement, other job attitudes, and trait affect as predictors of job performance. *Journal of Applied Social Psychology, 42, E295–E325.*

Deery, S., Iverson, R. D. & Walsh, J. (2012). Why do employees work when ill? A study of the antecedents and outcomes of presenteeism. Paper presented at the Academy of Management annual meeting (August), Boston, MA.

Dello Russo, S., Miraglia, M., Borgogni, L. & Johns, G. (2013). How time and perceptions of social context shape employee absenteeism trajectories. *Journal of Vocational Behavior, 83, 209–217.*

Dellve, L., Hadzibajramovic, E. & Ahlborg, G. (2011). Work attendance among healthcare workers: prevalence, incentives, and long-term consequences for health and performance. *Journal of Advanced Nursing, 67, 1918–1929.*

Demerouti, E., Bakker, A. B. & Bulters, A. J. (2004). The loss spiral of work pressure, work-home interference and exhaustion: Reciprocal relations in a three-wave study. *Journal of Vocational Behavior, 64, 131–149.*

Demerouti, E., Le Blanc, P. M., Bakker, A. B., Schaufeli, W. B. & Hox, J. (2009). Present but sick: A three-wave study on job demands, presenteeism and burnout. *Career Development International, 14, 50–68.*

Dew, K., Keefe, V. & Small, K. (2005). Choosing to work when sick: workplace presenteeism. *Social Science and Medicine, 60, 2273–2282.*

Diener, E. & Lucas, R. E. (1999). Personality and subjective well-being, in D. Kahneman, E. Diener & N. Schwarz (Eds.), *Well-Being: The Foundations of Hedonic Psychology* (pp. 213–229). New York, NY: Russell Sage Foundation.

Diestel, S., Wegge, J. & Schmidt, K-H. (2014). The impact of social context on the relationship between individual job satisfaction and absenteeism: The roles of different foci of job satisfaction and work-unit absenteeism. *Academy of Mangement Journal, 57,* 353–382.

Eurofound (2016). *First findings: Sixth European Working Conditions Survey.* Retrieved from www.eurofound.europa.eu/publications/resume/2015/working-conditions/first-findings-sixth-european-working-conditions-survey-resume

European Commission (2010). *EUROPE 2020. A European Strategy for Smart, Sustainable and Inclusive Growth.* Brussels: European Commission.

Falco, A., Girardi, D. & Parmiani, G. (2013). Presenteismo e salute dei lavoratori: Effetti di mediazione sullo strain psico-fisico in un'indagine longitudinale. *Giornale Italiano di Medicina del Lavoro ed Ergonomia, 35,* 138–150.

Farrell, D. & Stamm, C. L. (1988). Meta-analysis of the correlates of employee absence. *Human Relations, 41,* 211–227.

Fickenscher, L. (2016) Latest norovirus appearance costs Chipotle $750 M. *New York Post* (March 16). Retrieved from http://nypost.com/2016/03/16/latest-norovirus-appearance-costs-chipotle-750m/

Ford, M. T. & Huang, J. (2014). The health consequences of organizational injustice: Why do they exist and what can be done? in S. Leka & R.R. Sinclair (Eds.), *Contemporary Occupational Health Psychology: Global Perspectives on Research and Practice* (Vol. 3, pp. 35–50). Chichester, UK: Wiley-Blackwell.

Garrow, V. (2016). *Presenteeism. A Review of Current Thinking.* Brighton: Institute of Employment Studies.

Geurts, S. A. E., Kompier, M. A. J., Roxburgh, S. & Houtman, I. L. D. (2003). Does work-home interference mediate the relationship between workload and well-being? *Journal of Vocational Behavior, 63,* 532–559.

Gilbreath, B. & Karimi, L. (2012). Supervisor behaviour and employee presenteeism. *International Journal of Leadership Studies, 7,* 114–131.

Goetzel, R. Z., Long, S. R., Ozminkowski, R. J., Hawkins, K., Wang, S. & Lynch, W. (2004). Health, absence, disability, and presenteeism cost estimates of certain physical and mental health conditions affecting US employers. *Journal of Occupational Environmental Medicine, 46,* 398–412.

Grynier, A. & Singleton, V. (2000). Sickness absence as risk-taking behaviour: A study of organisational and cultural factors in the public sector. *Health, Risk, & Society*, 2, 7–21.

Gustafsson, K. & Marklund, S. (2011). Consequences of sickness presence and sickness absence on health and work ability: A Swedish prospective cohort study. *International Journal of Occupational Medicine and Environmental Health*, 24, 153–165.

Gustafsson, K. & Marklund, S. (2014). Associations between health and combinations of sickness presence and absence. *Occupational Medicine*, 64(1), 49–55.

Gustafsson Sendén, M., Løvseth, L. T., Schenck-Gustafsson, K. & Fridner, A. (2013). What makes physicians go to work while sick: a comparative study of sickness presenteeism in four European countries (HOUPE). *Swiss Medical Weekly*, 14, 1–6.

Hansen, C. D. & Andersen, J. H. (2008). Going ill to work–what personal circumstances, attitudes and work-related factors are associated with sickness presenteeism? *Social Science & Medicine*, 67, 956–964.

Harrison, D. A., Newman, D. A. & Roth, P. L. (2006). How important are job attitudes? Meta-analytic comparisons of integrative behavioral outcomes and time sequences. *Academy of Management Journal*, 49, 305–325.

Hemp, P. (2004, October). Presenteeism: At work – but out of it. *Harvard Business Review*, 49–58.

HERO (2013). New findings and realistic solutions to employee presenteeism: A white paper from the Health Enhancement Research Organization. Retrieved from http://hero-health.org/research-studies/

Hinshaw, S. P. (2007). *The Mark of Shame: Stigma of Mental Illness and an Agenda for Change*. New York, NY: Oxford University Press.

Hobfoll, S. E. (2001). The influence of culture, community, and the nested-self in the stress process: Advancing conservation of resources theory. *Applied Psychology: An International Review*, 50, 337–421.

Hochschild, A. (1997). *The Time Bind. When Work Becomes Home and Home Becomes Work*. New York, NY: Metropolitan Books.

Hoffman, B. J., Blair, C. A., Meriac, J. P. & Woehr, D. J. (2007). Expanding the criterion domain? A quantitative review of the OCB literature. *Journal of Applied Psychology*, 92, 555–566.

Hopkins, B. (2014). Explaining variations in absence rates: Temporary and agency workers in the food manufacturing sector. *Human Resource Management Journal*, 24, 227–240.

Howard, K. J., Mayer, T. G. & Gatchel, R. J. (2009). Effects of presenteeism in chronic occupational musculoskeletal disorders: stay at work is validated. *Journal of Occupational and Environmental Medicine*, 51, 724–731.

Johansson, G. & Lundberg, I. (2004). Adjustment latitude and attendance requirements as determinants of sickness absence or attendance. Empirical tests of the illness flexibility model. *Social Science & Medicine (1982)*, 58, 1857–1868.

Johns, G. (1997). Contemporary research on absence from work: Correlates, causes, and consequences. *International Review of Industrial and Organizational Psychology*, 12, 115–174.

Johns, G. (2001). The psychology of lateness, absenteeism, and turnover, in N. Anderson, D. S. Ones, J. K. Sinangil & C. Viswesvaran (Eds.), *Handbook of Industrial, Work and Organizational Psychology* (Vol. 2, pp. 232–252). London: Sage.

Johns, G. (2002). Absenteeism and mental health, in J. C. Thomas & M. Hersen (Eds.), *Handbook of Mental Health in the Workplace* (pp. 437–455). Thousand Oaks, CA: Sage.

Johns, G. (2008). Absenteeism and presenteeism: Not at work or not working well, in C. L. Cooper & J. Barling (Eds.), *The Sage Handbook of Organizational Behavior* (Vol. 1, pp. 160–177). London: Sage.

Johns, G. (2009). Absenteeism or presenteeism? Attendance dynamics and employee well-being, in S. Cartwright & C. L. Cooper (Eds.), *The Oxford Handbook of Organizational Well-Being* (pp. 7–30). Oxford: Oxford University Press.

Johns, G. (2010). Presenteeism in the workplace: A review and research agenda. *Journal of Organizational Behavior*, 31, 519–542.

Johns, G. (2011). Attendance dynamics at work: The antecedents and correlates of presenteeism, absenteeism, and productivity loss. *Journal of Occupational Health Psychology*, 16, 483–500.

Johns, G. (2012). Presenteeism: A short history and a cautionary tale, in J. Houdmont, S. Leka & R. R. Sinclair (Eds.), *Contemporary Occupational Health Psychology: Global Perspectives on Research and Practice* (Vol. 2, pp. 204–220). Chichester, UK: Wiley-Blackwell.

Johns, G. & Miraglia, M. (2015). The reliability, validity, and accuracy of self-reported absenteeism from work: A meta-analysis. *Journal of Occupational Health Psychology*, 20, 1–14.

Johns, G. & Xie, J. L. (1998). Perceptions of absence from work: People's Republic of China versus Canada. *Journal of Applied Psychology*, 83, 515–530.

Kahneman, D., Diener, E. & Schwarz, N. (Eds.) (1999). *Well-Being: The Foundations of Hedonic Psychology.* New York, NY: Russell Sage Foundation.

Karanika-Murray, M., Pontes, H. M., Griffiths, M. D. & Biron, C. (2015). Sickness presenteeism determines job satisfaction via affective-motivational states. *Social Science and Medicine*, 139, 100–106.

Kendall, N., Burton, K., Lunt, J., Mellor, N. & Daniels, K. (2015). Developing an intervention toolbox for common health problems in the workplace. Retrieved from HSE www.hse.gov.uk/research/rrpdf/rr1053 .pdf

Keyes, C. L. M., Shmotkin, D. & Ryff, C. L. (2002). Optimizing well-being: the empirical encounter of two traditions. *Journal of Personality and Social Psychology*, 82, 1007–1022.

Kigozi, J., Jowett, S., Lewis, M., Barton, P. M. & Coast, J. (2017). The estimation and inclusion of presenteeism costs in applied economic evaluation: a systematic review. *Value in Health*. Advance online publication. http://dx.doi.org/10.1016/j.jval.2016.12.006

Kinman, G., Clements, A. & Hart, J. (2016). Struggling on regardless: Presenteeism in UK prison officers. *Proceedings of the BPS Division of Occupational Psychology Conference*, Nottingham, 141–145.

Kivimäki, M., Head, J., Ferrie, J. E. et al. (2005). Working while ill as a risk factor for serious coronary events: The Whitehall II study. *American Journal of Public Health*, 95, 98–102.

Koopman, C., Pelletier, K. R., Murray, J. F. et al. (2002). Stanford presenteeism scale: health status and employee productivity. *Journal of Occupational and Environmental Medicine*, 44, 14–20.

Kossek, E. E. & Ozeki, C. (1999). Bridging the work-family policy and productivity gap: A literature review. *Community, Work & Family*, 2, 7–32.

Kristensen, K., Juhl, H. J., Eskildsen, J., Nielsen, J., Frederiksen, N. & Bisgaard, C. (2006). Determinants of absenteeism in a large Danish bank. *International Journal of Human Resource Management*, 17(9), 1645–1658.

Krohne, K. & Magnussen, L. H. (2011). Go to work or report sick? A focus group study on decisions of sickness presence among offshore catering section workers. *BMC Research Notes*, 4, 70–77.

LePine, J. A., Podsakoff, N. P. & LePine, M. A. (2005). A meta-analytic test of the challenge stressor – hindrance stressor framework: An explanation for inconsistent relationships among stressors and performance. *Academy of Management Journal*, 48, 764–775.

Lerner, D., Adler, D. A., Chang, H. et al. (2004). The clinical and occupational correlates of work productivity loss among employed patients with depression. *Journal of Occupational and Environmental Medicine*, 46, S46–S55.

Löve, J., Grimby-Ekman, A., Eklöf, M., Hagberg, M. & Dellve, L. (2010). "Pushing oneself too hard": Performance-based self-esteem as a predictor of sickness presenteeism among young adult women and men–a cohort study. *Journal of Occupational and Environmental Medicine*, 52, 603–609.

Lu, L., Lin, H. Y. & Cooper, C. L. (2013). Unhealthy and present: Motives and consequences of the act of presenteeism among Taiwanese employees. *Journal of Occupational Health Psychology*, 18, 406–416.

Lu, L., Peng, S.-Q., Lin, H. Y. & Cooper, C. L. (2014). Presenteeism and health over time among Chinese employees: The moderating role of self-efficacy. *Work and Stress*, 28, 165–178.

Lucas, R. E., Diener, E. & Suh, E. (1996). Discriminant validity of well-being measures. *Journal of Personality and Social Psychology*, 71, 616–628.

Luksyte, A., Avery, D. R. & Yeo, G. (2015). It is worse when you do it: Examining the interactive effects of coworker presenteeism and demographic similarity. *Journal of Applied Psychology*, 100(4), 1107–1123.

Macey, W. & Schneider, B. (2008). The meaning of employee engagement. *Industrial and Organizational Psychology*, 1, 3–30.

Malachowski, C. K., Boydell, K., Sawchuk, P. & Kirsh, B. (2016). The "work" of workplace mental health: An institutional ethnography. *Society and Mental Health*, 6, 207–222.

Markham, S. E. & McKee, G. H. (1995). Group absence behavior and standards: a multilevel analysis. *Academy of Management Journal*, 38, 1174–1190.

McKevitt, C., Morgan, M., Dundas, R. & Holland, W. W. (1997). Sickness absence and "working through" illness: A comparison of two professional groups. *Journal of Public Health Medicine*, 19, 295–300.

Medibank Private, Econtech (2008). Economic impact of workplace stress in Australia. Retrieved from www.medibank.com.au/client/documents/pdfs/the-cost-of-workplace-stress.pdf

Meyer, J. P., Maltin, E. R. & Thai, S. (2012). Employee commitment and well-being, in J. Houdmont, S. Leka & R. R. Sinclair (Eds.), *Contemporary Occupational Health Psychology: Global Perspectives on Research and Practice* (Vol. 2, pp. 19–35). Chichester, UK: Wiley-Blackwell.

Miraglia, M. & Johns, G. (2016). Going to work ill: A meta-analysis of the correlates of presenteeism and a dual-path model. *Journal of Occupational Health Psychology*, 21, 261–283.

Mostert, K. (2009). The balance between work and home: The relationship between work and home demands and ill health of employed females. *South African Journal of Industrial Psychology*, 35, 1–8.

Munir, F., Leka, S. & Griffiths, A. (2005). Dealing with self-management of chronic illness at work: Predictors for self-disclosure. *Social Science & Medicine*, 60, 1397–1407.

Munir, F., Mackay, C., Yarker, J., Haslam, C., Kazi, A. & Cooper, L. (2009). Back, but not better: ongoing mental health hampers return to work outcomes. *Occupational Health at Work*, 5, 17–20.

Munir, F., Yarker, J. & Haslam, C. (2008). Sickness absence management: Encouraging attendance or "risk-taking" presenteeism in employees with chronic illness? *Disability & Rehabilitation*, 30, 1461–1472.

Musich, S., Hook, D., Baaner, S. & Edington, D. W. (2006). The association of two productivity measures with health risks and medical conditions in an Australian employee population. *American Journal of Health Promotion*, 20(5), 353–363. http://doi.org/10.4278/0890-1171-20.5.353

Ng, T. W. H. & Feldman, D. C. (2008). Long work hours: A social identity perspective on meta-analysis data. *Journal of Organizational Behavior*, 29, 853–880.

Nicholson, N. & Johns, G. (1985). The absence culture and the psychological contract: Who's in control of absence? *Academy of Management Review*, 10, 397–407.

Niven, K. & Ciborowska, N. (2015). The hidden dangers of attending work while unwell: A survey study of presenteeism among pharmacists. *International Journal of Stress Management*, 22, 207–221.

O'Donnell, G., Deaton, A., Durand, M., Halpern, D. & Layard, R. (2014). *Wellbeing and Policy*. London: Legatum Institute.

Pfeffer, J. (1998). *The Human Equation: Building Profits by Putting People First*. Boston, MA: Harvard Business School Press.

Pohling, R., Buruck, G., Jungbauer, K.-L. & Leiter, M. P. (2016). Work-related factors of presenteeism: The mediating role of mental and physical health. *Journal of Occupational Health Psychology*, 21, 220–234.

Quazi, H. A. (2013). *Presenteeism. The Invisible Cost to Organizations*. Basingstoke, UK: Palgrave Macmillan.

Ramsey, R. (2006). "Presenteeism" a new problem in the workplace. *Supervision*, 67(8), 14–17.

Rentsch, J. R. & Steel, R. P. (2003). What does unit-level absence mean? Issues for future unit-level absence research. *Human Resource Management Review*, 13, 185–202.

Rhodan, M. (2016, February 8). Chipotle blames sick employees for norovirus outbreak. *Time*. Retrieved from http://time.com/4212692/chipotle-closed-stores-norovirus-burrito/

Robbins, J. M., Ford, M. T. & Tetrick, L. E. (2012). Perceived unfairness and employee health: A meta-analytic integration. *Journal of Applied Psychology*, 97, 235–272.

Roe, R. A. & van Diepen, B. (2011). Employee health and presenteeism: The challenge for human resource management, in A-S. Antoniou & C. Cooper (Eds.), *New Directions in Organizational Psychology and Behavioral Medicine* (pp. 239–258). Farnham, UK: Gower.

Rosvold, E. O. & Bjertness, E. (2001). Physicians who do not take sick leave: Hazardous heroes? *Scandinavian Journal of Public Health*, 29, 71–75.

Ryan, R. M. & Deci, E. L. (2001). On happiness and human potentials: A review of research on hedonic and eudaimonic well-being. *Annual Review of Psychology*, 52, 141–166.

Ryff, C. D. (1989). Happiness is everything, or is it? Explorations on the meaning of psychological well-being. *Journal of Personality and Social Psychology*, 57, 1069–1081.

Ryff, C. D. (1995). Psychological well-being in adult life. *Current Directions in Psychological Scence*, 4, 99–104.

Ryff, C. D. & Keyes, C. L. M. (1995). The structure of psychological well-being revisited. *Journal of Personality and Social Psychology*, 69, 719–727.

Ryff, C. D. & Singer, B. (1998). The contours of positive human health. *Psychol. Inq. 9*, 1–28.

Sainsbury Centre for Mental Health (2007). *Mental Health at Work: Developing the Business Case*. Policy Paper 8. London: Sainsbury Institute for Mental Health.

Schaufeli, W. & Taris, T. (2014). A critical review of the job demands-resources model: Implications for improving work and health, in G. Bauer & O. Hämmig (Eds.), *Bridging Ooccupational, Organizational and Public Health* (pp. 43–68). Dordrecht: Springer.

Schultz, A. B., Chen, C. & Edington, D. W. (2009). The cost and impact of health conditions on presenteeism to employers: a review of the literature. *Pharmacoeconomics*, 27, 365–378.

Schultz, A. B. & Edington, D. W. (2007). Employee health and presenteeism: A systematic review. *Journal of Occupational Rehabilitation*, 17, 547–579.

Schulz, H., Zacher, H. & Lippke, S. (2017). The importance of team health climate for health-related outcomes of white-collar workers. *Frontiers in Psychology*, 8, 74.

Schwartz, B. S., Stewart, W. F. & Lipton, R. B. (1997). Lost work days and decreased work effectiveness associated with headache in the workplace. *Journal of Occupational and Environmental Medicine*, 39, 320–337.

Shoss, M. K. & Penney, L. M. (2012). The economy and absenteeism: A macro-level study. *Journal of Applied Psychology*, 97, 881–889.

Simpson, R. (1998). Presenteeism, power and organizational change: Long hours as a career barrier and the impact on the working lives of women managers. *British Journal of Management*, 9, 37–50.

Skagen, K. & Collins, A. M. (2016). The consequences of sickness presenteeism on health and wellbeing over time: A systematic review. *Social Science & Medicine*, 161, 169–177.

Taylor, P., Cunningham, I., Newsome, K. & Scholarios, D. (2010). "Too scared to go sick"—Reformulating the research agenda on sickness absence. *Industrial Relations Journal*, 41, 270–288.

ten Brummelhuis, L. L., Johns, G., Lyons, B. J. & ter Hoeven, C. L. (2016). Why and when do employees imitate the absenteeism of co-workers? *Organizational Behavior and Human Decision Processes*, 134, 16–30.

ten Brummelhuis, L. L., Ter Hoeven, C. L., De Jong, M. D. T. & Peper, B. (2013). Exploring the linkage between the home domain and absence from work: Health, motivation, or both? *Journal of Organizational Behavior*, 34, 273–290.

Thun, S. & Løvseth, L. T. (2016). A health impairment process of sickness presenteeism in Norwegian physicians: The mediating role of exhaustion. *Health*, 8, 846–856.

Tims, M. & Bakker, A. B. (2010). Job crafting: Toward a new model of individual job redesign. *SA Journal of Industrial Psychology/SA Tydkrif Vir Bedryfsielkunde*, 36, 1–9.

Turpin, R. S., Ozminkowski, R. J., Sharda, C. E. et al. (2004). Reliability and validity of the Stanford Presenteeism Scale. *Journal of Occupational and Environmental Medicine*, 46, 1123–1133.

van der Heijden, B. I. J. M., Demerouti, E., Bakker, A. B. & The NEXT Study Group coordinated by Hasselhorn, H. M. (2008). Work–home interference among nurses: Reciprocal relationships with job demands and health. *Journal of Advanced Nursing*, 62, 572–584.

Virtanen, M., Kivimäki, M., Elovainio, J., Vahtera, J. & Ferrie, J. E. (2003). From insecure to secure employment: changes in work, health, health related behaviours, and sickness absence. *Occupational and Environmental Medicine*, 60, 948–953.

Wężyk, A. & Merecz, D. (2013). Prezentyzm – (nie) nowe zjawisko w środowisku pracy. *Medycyny Pracy*, 64, 847–861.

Widera, E., Chang, A. & Chen, H. L. (2010). Presenteeism: A public health hazard. *Journal of General Internal Medicine*, 25, 1244–1247.

Worrall, L., Cooper, C. & Campbell, F. (2000). The new reality for UK managers: perpetual change and employment instability. *Work, Employment & Society*, 14, 647–668.

Wrzesniewski, A. & Dutton, J. E. (2001). Crafting a job: Revisioning employees as active crafters of their work. *Academy of Management Review*, 26, 179–201.

Xanthopoulou, D., Bakker, A. B., Demerouti, E. & Schaufeli, W. B. (2009). Work engagement and financial returns: A diary study on the role of job and personal resources. *Journal of Occupational and Organizational Psychology*, 82, 183–200.

Zhang, W., Gignac, M. A., Beaton, D., Tang, K. & Anis, A. H. (2010). Productivity loss due to presenteeism among patients with arthritis: Estimates from 4 instruments. *Journal of Rheumatology*, 37(9), 1805–1814.

9 Presenteeism, Burnout, and Health

ARISTIDES I. FERREIRA

Introduction

Organizational and occupational literature considers stress as a modern pandemic with high costs for people's lives and well-being, as well for organizations and the economy in general (Shirom, 2005). Job stress has direct and indirect impact on organizational behavior and job design. A study conducted by the American Institute for Stress (Stambor, 2006), shows that the prevalence of stress costs more than $300 billion annually to the US economy. To account for these costs, researchers considered missed work and stress reduction treatment (Stambor, 2006). However, these studies did not consider the time that people go to work despite having stress and how this disease affects individuals' productivity. This behavior constitutes presenteeism and is a relatively new concept that is a prevalent phenomenon in organizational psychology research (Lu, Lin & Cooper, 2013). By definition, presenteeism refers to the behavior of going to work while one is ill (Aronsson, Gustafsson & Dallner, 2000). It has important implications for theory and organizational practice, however, and unlike the concept of absenteeism, it has been much less studied and is more difficult to measure. Studies conducted in Australia revealed that the direct costs of presenteeism have been estimated to be 2.7 percent of the GDP, which is the equivalent to $34.1 billion of the Australian GDP in 2009/ 10 (Econtech, 2011).

In the twenty-first century, great economic challenges have arisen, and many organizations have been either downsizing their employees, or going out of business. In this difficult labor context, presenteeism tends to increase due to job insecurity and reduced resources (Lu et al., 2013). Concomitantly, companies tend to reduce important benefits, flexitime and paid time off (Bockerman & Laukkanen, 2010). As a result, companies have been creating more presenteeism cultures by stimulating competition, productivity and organizational restructuring (Simpson, 1998). According to Johns (2010), it is important to understand the antecedents of presenteeism, as well as the reasons behind why individual employees continue to go to work despite having a physical or psychological health problem. Presenteeism may aggravate clinical symptoms and reduce quality of life, as well as adversely affect individuals' productivity. In fact, the literature has shown how presenteeism can be related to psychological problems, such as job stress and burnout (Boles, Pelletier & Lynch, 2004; Demerouti, Le Blanc, Bakker, Schaufelli & Hox, 2009; Ferreira & Martinez, 2012). Research has also shown that high demanding tasks tend to be associated with high levels of presenteeism (Demerouti et al., 2009). The variations of work engagement for instance, can also be affected by systematic variations in outcomes, such as stressful and demanding tasks (Bakker, Schaufeli, Leiter & Taris, 2008) and can be explained by specific experiences and events (Kühnel, Sonnentag & Bledow, 2012). The intervening variables of job burnout and well-being in the relationship between presenteeism antecedents are also not well known (Neto, Ferreira, Martinez & Ferreira, 2017). Hence, and because previous studies have focused only on identifying the antecedents of presenteeism (Johns, 2010), I intend to propose an integrated model considering work, nonwork and biological antecedents of presenteeism, and to explore possible intervening variables of job burnout and well-being.

In sum, this chapter aims to contribute to the existing literature and provide interesting guidelines for practice by firstly exploring how burnout influences the frequency of presenteeism, considering work, and nonwork antecedents of burnout. Secondly, this research also aims to explore how well-being mediates the effects of burnout and acts of presenteeism, as well the productivity loss due to presenteeism. Accordingly, I present an integrated model (Figure 1) supported by the literature that may help researchers develop hypotheses for future research. Moreover, I provide interesting intervention proposals to reduce employees' burnout and consequently, their reduced health/well-being and presenteeism.

Presenteeism and its Antecedents

Presenteeism was defined in the early literature as going to work while one is ill, rather than identifying causes and the effect/consequence it has on productivity loss (Cooper, 1996). As mentioned by Johns (2010: 522), "presenteeism is the grey area that exists between no productivity (i.e., absenteeism) and full work engagement." Other authors have considered the concept of nonwork related presenteeism as attending work while one is engaged in personal activities (D'Abate & Eddy, 2007; Wan, Downey & Stough, 2014). According to Lu et al. (2013), the behavioral perspective of presenteeism must be considered, as well as possible psychosocial and organizational factors as possible antecedents of presenteeism. As suggested by Hemp (2004), individuals experience presenteeism when they are at work, but with low productivity due to limited physical and psychological capabilities. Hemp mentions that the inherent losses of productivity are independent of the workers' will to work. Moreover, the symptoms associated with health problems (e.g., attention problems, motor difficulties, cognitive problems, burnout or negative effects) are mostly responsible for a significant and unquestionable reduction of job performance.

Krohne & Magnussen (2011) concluded that an individual's decision to attend work despite being ill is mainly based on the severity of the health complaint. Specifically, some health symptoms may be considered tolerable and noninterfering with performance, while others may be unbearable. Additionally, perceptions of health problems may vary from person to person. Thus, while some health symptoms may be considered bearable by some, they may be unbearable to others. Aronsson & Gustafsson (2005) argued that for any given health status, the factors behind the decision to go to work sick are both personal and work-related. While personal factors are linked to financial demands and individuals' difficulty in saying no, work-related factors are due to difficulties in staff replacement, time pressure, conflicting demands and insufficient resources. In addition, there is evidence that people who work in high demanding physical, cognitive and social contexts are inclined to be present at work even though they are ill in order to maintain the usual high levels of performance (Demerouti et al., 2009).

For Johns (2010), presenteeism may be related to other factors such as "positive feelings towards work" and "moral obligations." The author proposed the Dynamic Model for Presenteeism and Absenteeism, based on the idea that the behaviors of presenteeism and absenteeism have the same antecedents. In terms of contextual antecedents, presenteeism is associated with physical and psychological demands, adjustment latitude (the possibility of adapting the work to the state of health), ease of replacement and teamwork. Concerning the latter, an obsession with team members' work and attendance frequently emerges with regards to the importance of achieving common goals (Johns, 2010). As for the individual antecedents of presenteeism, Johns (2010) emphasizes that workers with "conscientious" personalities, positive work attitudes and perceptions, as well as workaholics, tend to exhibit more presenteeism. A recent meta-analysis with 109 samples (Miraglia & Johns, 2016) shows that the frequency of presenteeism is directly correlated with job insecurity, job demands, optimism, job control, collegial and supervisor support and personal financial difficulties.

Both job demands and job resources play an important role to explaining presenteeism behavior (Admasachew & Dawson, 2011). According to the Job Demands–Resources model (JD–R; Bakker & Demerouti, 2007), people with high demanding tasks tend to develop mental fatigue, which is a response to the reduction in resources due to task performance (Bakker, Demerouti & Verbeke, 2004). High levels of workload require a mobilization of extra energy, however the level of energy is diminished (due to the task demands), which may lead to chronic health problems and loss of well-being and consequent acts of presenteeism and reduced productivity. Job demands promote health disruption (due to the high levels of effort), leading to a depletion of energy from which the employee is not able to recover adequately (Meijman & Mulder, 1998), thus increasing the probability of health problems such as burnout.

Presenteeism and Burnout: The Maslach Perspective

Burnout is considered a critical issue for organizations since it has an important impact on productivity (Kahn, Schneider, Jenkins-Henkelman & Moyle, 2006), and tends to adversely affect organizational outcomes, such as absenteeism and turnover (Maslach, Schaufeli & Leiter, 2001). Job stressors reduce the employees' capacity to exert control over their work environment, which in turn, affect their capacity to perform tasks in an efficient way (Bakker et al., 2004). One of the most recognized models of burnout (Maslach, 1998) conceptualizes a multidimensional construct constituted with three dimensions: emotional exhaustion, depersonalization (or cynicism), and accomplishment (or personal efficacy).

Emotional exhaustion can be defined as an intense form of fatigue which appears as a consequence of prolonged intense physical and psychological (affective, cognitive) strain caused by prolonged exposure to specific work conditions. In other words, emotional exhaustion can be defined as the feeling of being affectively drained. *Depersonalization* is characterized by emotional indifference towards others (colleagues and supervisors) and detachment from reality and the self. It represents the act of being cynical and detached from others. Depersonalization is also an attempt to put distance between oneself and others. In other words, people develop an indifferent or cynical attitude when they are exhausted or discouraged. Lastly, personal *accomplishment* expresses a decrease in feelings of competence and pleasure associated with a professional activity. Accomplishment refers to the perception that the individual has no capacity to accomplish all of the required tasks/goals. In other words, due to stress, people perceive a sense of incompetence.

Golembiewski (1986) developed a different perspective of burnout stating that the burnout process develops a sequence which starts on depersonalization, to lower levels of personal accomplishment and then to emotional exhaustion. Employees detach from their functions and this process leads to depersonalization, which interferes with individual performance. The perception that their goals are not achieved culminates in emotional exhaustion problems. The sequence conceptualized by Maslach (1982) mentions that employees facing a problem experience emotional fatigue/exhaustion when their stress reaches high levels. As a coping strategy, employees start depersonalizing their relationships adopting a cynical posture, which might be considered an emotional buffer (Cordes, Dougherty & Blum, 1997). People spend less time with interactions and as a consequence, receive less support from their supervisor and coworkers, thus diminishing their capacity to accomplish tasks. Through structural equation modeling, Cordes et al. (1997) found empirical evidence to support the emotional exhaustion–depersonalization–personal accomplishment sequence initially suggested by Maslach (1982).

Burnout was initially thought of as being associated with specific jobs (e.g., physicians, nurses, lawyers, and teachers), but studies have shown that it extends to all professional activities (Schaufeli, Leiter, Maslach & Jackson, 1996), as well as students (Maroco & Tecedeiro, 2009). Ferreira & Martinez (2012), for instance, found a positive correlation between presenteeism and emotional exhaustion among elementary school teachers. Rössler (2012) argued that the risk of burnout is still significantly higher in certain occupations such as health care workers. Specifically, besides the effects of an extensive workload, long working hours and night shifts, these professionals have specific stressors since they work in demanding environments with patients, families and other medical staff. The professional staff in human service institutions is often required to spend considerable time with other people, and the interaction is frequently around the clients' current problems. For those employees who work continuously with people who have serious problems such as chronic stress, anger, fear and despair, their job can be emotionally draining and pose a risk of burnout (Maslach & Leiter, 2008). Additionally, a meta-analysis conducted with 66 studies and 71 independent samples (Park, Jacob, Wagner & Baiden, 2014) showed that job control is an important variable, predicting burnout, however this relationship is stronger with professionals from human services (professionals such as health professionals and educators) (Maslach, 1982).

A longitudinal study conducted with Dutch nurses showed that presenteeism increases depersonalization and emotional exhaustion (Demerouti et al., 2009). However, the relationship between presenteeism and emotional exhaustion was reciprocal, in the sense that employees experience emotional exhaustion and in turn, develop coping strategies (e.g., reduced productivity, avoidance behaviors, and difficulties to accomplish tasks/goals) which in turn, increase their levels of emotional exhaustion.

Taking into account a cross cultural perspective, the relationship between job burnout and control is higher in countries with low power distance because they have less autonomy and there is no tolerance of low job control (Park et al., 2014). Another meta-analysis with 141 studies (Fila, Purl & Griffeth, 2017), showed that the perception of job demands is higher in individualistic countries. The existence of positive resources spirals seems to be more prominent in higher power distance countries. In countries with accepting unequal power distribution and authority, employees are more likely to positively affect the perceptions of others (Fila et al., 2017).

Presenteeism and Burnout: The Recovery and COR Perspectives

According to the Recovery Theory (Meijman & Mulder, 1998), people need time to recover and recharge from physical and psychological efforts due to job demands. Employees need to switch off from work to prevent an ongoing deterioration in mood and productivity. Basically, individuals need to develop internal strategies (i.e., to rest after efforts at work) to return to their pre-stress levels. For example, there is evidence that spending time on weekend activities (i.e., low effort activities such as watching TV and social/physical activities) explain subsequent lower levels of burnout (Ragsdale & Beehr, 2016). The authors found that this relationship is mediated by the effect of weekend recovery experiences of psychological detachment, relaxation, master and control. When it is not possible to recover and gain the required energy to cope with more demands, health conditions worsen. The presence at work despite being with health problems (presenteeism) does not allow people to recover and to have time to acquire the needed resources. In other words, "continuous attention to work while ill deprives people of opportunities to recuperate from illness" (Lu et al., 2014: 167), worsening health conditions and increasing the levels of emotional exhaustion (Demerouti et al., 2009).

The Conservation of Resources model (COR; Hobfoll, 1988) proposes that burnout appears when employees feel that they might lose important resources in the future, the actual loss of a resource (e.g., objects, individual characteristics, or other conditions that are highly valued) or the incapacity to achieve additional resources following significant investments of resources (e.g., inability to achieve a higher position in their career after having invested in their job). According to this theory, people develop strategies to maintain and protect their valued resources (Halbesleten, 2006). This model explains that employees tend to accept the loss or failure of resources to gain additional benefits in the future (Hobfoll & Freedy, 1993). This situation happens because people develop efforts to minimize losses as a strategy to reduce perceptions of discomfort or job stress. If resources are scarce, people tend to feel strain. People tend to value several resources such as material objects (e.g., car, house), personal characteristics (e.g., respect, self-esteem), professional aspects (e.g., development, career progression), social aspects (e.g., family, colleagues), and energy (e.g., vigor). Individuals aim to protect and defend these resources and even spend some amount of energy maintaining and developing these resources (Park et al., 2014). The Hobfoll COR explains how the loss of resources due to health impairment processes may result in loss spirals. In anticipating the possibility of losing resources, employees must develop strategies to use other available resources (Hobfoll, 1988). According to Hakanen, Schaufeli & Ahola (2008), burnout increases future depression symptoms, which, in turn, increase future burnout and lead to sickness presence.

Burnout and Well-Being

Research has shown that reduced psychological well-being has an impact on employees' life influencing productivity at work, essentially when one is ill (Cooper & Dewe, 2008). These findings were supported by the Conservation of Resources theory (Hobfoll, 2001) which emphasizes that emotionally exhausted employees perceiving that they have reduced resources, tend to be more tired and consequently, perceive less well-being. Furthermore, negative work-related events (with high demands) predict decreasing perceptions of well-being, predicting physical and psychological problems (e.g., sleeping problems), which in turn, affect employees' productivity (Elovainio, Raaska, Sinkkonen, Makipaa & Lapinleimu, 2015).

According to Hakanen et al. (2008), home (e.g., quantitative home demands, emotional home demands and negative spillover from family to work) and job demands (e.g., quantitative workload, work contents and physical work environment) are indirectly related with depression (via burnout). Burnout at T1 has a significant positive correlation with depressive symptoms on time 2 ($r = .16$, $p < .001$). The motivational and health impairment process was supported through a two-wave three-year cross-lagged panel design, supporting the JDR model. This study revealed that burnout predicts depression and not the opposite. Job demands appear as the main promoter of health impairment processes (Hakanen et al., 2008) and consequently, reduced well-being and sickness presence.

Moreover, Miraglia & Johns (2016) found that health plays an important mediating role to explain presenteeism and that the direct relationship of health with presenteeism is higher (-.31) than with absenteeism (-.27). This evidence suggests that the perception of a reduced health status (e.g., due to burnout) leads to a reduced perception of well-being, which, in turn, affects presenteeism behavior and productivity due to sickness presence (Neto et al., 2017).

An Integrated Model

As mentioned above, due to the emerging economical challenges of recent decades, presenteeism behavior has increased, essentially due to proliferation of pressure, competitiveness and fear of losing jobs. However, few studies have emphasized the potential of intervening variables (mediators) that reduce the effect of work and individual predictors of presenteeism behavior and productivity loss due to presenteeism.

Work-Related Variables

The literature has shown that high straining jobs with high workload and low control (Hagberg, Vilhemsson, Tornqvist & Toomingas, 2007) are associated with lost productivity. The influence of work related factors on presenteeism variables (frequency and productivity loss) was mediated by health indicators of well-being and musculoskeletal complaints (Pohling, Buruck, Jungbauer & Leiter, 2016). Moreover, there is evidence that workload (i.e., to know if the person has control over what he or she does), fairness (i.e., evaluate if resources are allocated fairly), and values (i.e., a match between one's own values and the values of the organization) influenced presenteeism productivity losses (Pohling et al., 2016). The authors showed a correlation between presenteeism behavior and health-related productivity loss, as well as with mental well-being. Similar studies were found by other researchers (e.g., Adler, McLaughlin, Rogers, Chang, Lapitsky & Lerner, 2006; Gucer, Oliver, Parrish & McDiarmid, 2009). The internal experience of burnout mediates the relationship between work environment variables and the outcomes of presenteeism frequency and productivity losses due to presenteeism (Darr & Johns, 2008; Pohling et al., 2016). Taking into account that health-related productivity loss and presenteeism behavior share the same antecedents with minor differences considering intervening variables (Pohling et al., 2016), I present the same outcomes in Figure 1: presenteeism behavior and productivity loss.

Individual Variables

Burnout tends to be associated with negative attitudes towards the workplace environment, which increase turnover intention (Lee & Ashforth, 1996), reflecting low productivity (Taris, 2006) and higher absenteeism due to sickness problems (Maslach et al., 2001). In this sense, individual characteristics also play an important role to explain burnout (Alarcon, Eschleman & Bowling, 2009). For example, personality is also an important predictor of burnout with core self-evaluation explaining the variance associated with burnout (Alarcon et al., 2009). Core self-evaluation can be defined has the belief that each individual has about their own capacities and comprises four constructs: self-esteem, self-efficacy, emotional stability and internal locus of control. Core self-evaluation traits together predict 26 percent of the variance in emotional exhaustion, 17 percent in depersonalization, and 30 percent in personal accomplishment (Alarcon et al., 2009). As for the Five-Factors model (i.e., emotional stability, agreeableness, conscientiousness, extraversion and openness to experience), all together explain 29 percent of the emotional exhaustion variance, 26 percent of depersonalization, and 23 percent of personal accomplishment. As expected, emotional stability ($\beta = -.45$, $p < .01$) is the trait that explains more emotional exhaustion. As for the depersonalization, emotional exhaustion ($\beta = -.29$, $p < .01$) and agreeableness ($\beta = -.22$, $p < .01$) were the most important traits. Finally, extraversion ($\beta = .21$, $p < .01$), conscientiousness ($\beta = .17$, $p < .01$), and emotional stability ($\beta = .15$, $p < .01$) were the traits with more influence in personal accomplishment (Alarcon et al., 2009).

Intervening Variables and Moderators

When investigating presenteeism, several intervening variables should be taken into account (Neto et al., 2017). Firstly, overall health plays an important role, since the decision of engaging in presenteeism depends on the severity of the health problems and associated symptoms (Johns, 2010; Krohne & Magnussen, 2011). For example, burnout reflects high risks for cardiovascular disease (Melamed, Shirom, Toker, Berliner & Shapira, 2006), more occupational injuries (Nahrgan, Morgeson & Hofmann, 2011) and mental health problems (Maslach et al., 2001). This evidence suggested in Model 1 that burnout leads to physical and psychological diseases (health problems). Employees will perceive high levels of emotional exhaustion and, depending on their psychological, physical and genetic propensities, they might develop physical and psychological problems (e.g., sleeping problems), affecting their well-being and in turn, their productivity (Elovainio et al., 2015). Secondly, as Brown & Sessions (2004) recognized, presenteeism does not seem to affect everyone in the same way in terms of productivity loss. Employees perceive their health problems in different ways (Krohne & Magnussen, 2011), while for some individuals a health problem may be considered unbearable, for others the same problem may not interfere with performance. Thirdly, different health problems have a different impact on different occupations (Burton, Pransky, Gonti, Chen & Edington, 2004). On this topic, Pransky & Dempsey (2004) have also argued that different health problems might have a different impact on the execution of particular work competencies or skills. It seems that presenteeism behavior at time 1 does not affect mental and physical health at time 2 (Lu, Peng, Lin & Cooper, 2014). Only individuals with low self-efficacy and high levels of initial presenteeism behavior tend to decrease their mental and physical health status at time 2. There was an absence of significant correlations between presenteeism frequency at time 1 and health at time 2. Individual characteristics of self-efficacy moderated this relationship, explaining that the relationship between presenteeism and health depends on the individual characteristics of self-efficacy (Lu et al., 2014). In fact, according to the authors, self-efficacy seemed to attenuate and mitigate the negative effects of presenteeism on health status.

Moreover, there is evidence that health problems decrease employees' perceptions of well-being (Elovainio et al., 2015). The existence of health problems due to burnout symptoms, such as depression (Shirom, 2005) and cardiovascular disease (Melamed et al., 2006) will allocate resources to deal with the problems (Hobfoll, 2001), which in turn, may influence individuals' productivity at work (Cooper & Dewe, 2008). Job demands are variables that require physical and psychological efforts with subsequent implications for individuals' lives in terms of psychological and physiological costs, reflecting job burnout. Job resources are related with work engagement, which in turn, reflects positive outcomes such as organizational commitment (Schaufeli & Bakker, 2004). Health impairment and loss of well-being appear as a consequence of the reduced energy promoted by job demands and is mediated by job burnout (Schaufeli & Bakker, 2004). Additional job demands require physical and psychological efforts and reflect physical and psychological costs (e.g., work pressure, poor environmental conditions, emotional demands, physical/psychological demands, time constraints, role overload, role ambiguity, etc.).

People will need to allocate more resources to reduce job demands, allowing people to achieve their goals and to stimulate their individual goals. Examples of job resources are social support, coworkers support, supervisor support, salary, and job security. We can classify the origin of job resources from four different sources: organizational, social, organization of work, and task/job characteristics. As for the organizational sources, we can include variables such as wage, career opportunities, training, and job security. Social relations integrate variables such as team climate, peers, and supervisor support. Organization of work includes variables such as role clarity or perceptions in decision-making. Finally, job task characteristics includes the well-known five dimensions from the Hackman & Oldham (1976) work design model: skill variety, feedback, autonomy, significance, and identity.

Interventions

A meta-analysis conducted by Halbesleten (2006) aimed to find the relationship between burnout and work and nonwork sources of support. Findings showed a sample-weighted mean correlation between emotional exhaustion and supervisor support (-.24), coworker support (-.20), friends (-.14), and family (-.10). In general, the author found that work-related sources of support are more strongly correlated with exhaustion because they play a direct influence on work demands (Halbesleten, 2006). Moreover, the supervisor support is important to reduce negative effects and burnout when difficulties occur at work (Abramis, 1987). When a negative mood is transformed into a positive experience, this change aids employees in perceiving job demands as reduced (Bolte, Goschke & Kuhl, 2003; Fredrickson, Tugade, Waugh & Larkin, 2003). Moreover, organizations must invest in performance appraisal criteria that consider the capacity to provide support from peers and supervisors, reducing job demands and consequently burnout. Because the avoidance of negative emotions and suppression have been considered in the literature as ineffective strategies (Gross & Johns, 2003) in order to avoid undesirable long-term

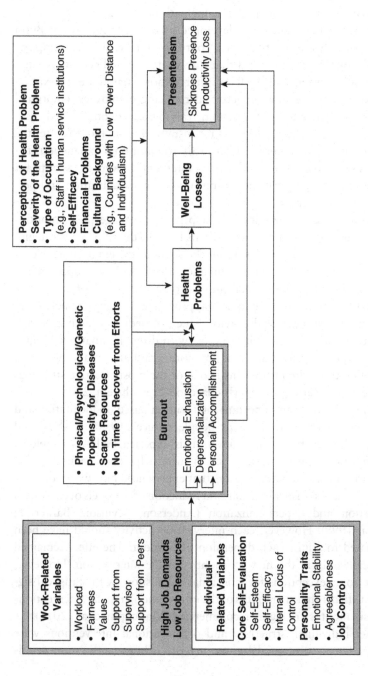

Figure 1 Integrated model of burnout explaining health and presenteeism

consequences, managers should provide employees with skills/compe-tences to increase the capacity to cope with burnout.

Another meta-analysis was developed by Maricuțoiu, Sava & Butta (2016) to study the effectiveness of controlled interventions on employ-ees' burnout. Results showed that intervention-based cognitive beha-vioral interventions, as well as interventions based on relaxation techniques, are the most effective in reducing employees' emotional exhaustion. The authors found that training effects on reduced emo-tional exhaustion tended to remain constant even six months after the last day of the intervention. Contrarily to emotional exhaustion, the authors showed that the results of the intervention were not significant for the remaining dimensions of burnout: depersonalization and per-sonal accomplishment.

Cognitive-based therapies also help people manage their emotions and cognitions. Essentially, individuals learn to develop new strategies to perceive their own reality about the self and the environment (e.g., family and work) (Kushnir & Milbauer, 1994). With this approach in mind, individuals receive instructions to restructure their cognitions (i.e., to identify and change some inappropriate thinking), to help them find more appropriate behaviors (i.e., scheduling activities less demanding) and the capacity to cope with difficult situations by gra-dually exposing the individual to more gradual demanding tasks. According to the literature, this is one of the most effective strategies to reduce occupational stress (Richardson & Rothstein, 2008).

Therapy-based is an important intervention based on meditation and reflection, which basically helps people reduce physiological arousal through the benefits of meditation. This experience allows people to stay in a deep state of rest, which in turn, helps them reduce fatigue and burnout. Studies with teachers that experienced nine weeks of med-itation found a statistically significant reduction of the levels of emotional exhaustion and depersonalization (Anderson, Levinson, Barker & Kiewra, 1999). However, each intervention activity should have been designated to adjust each dimension of burnout. The effect remained significant only in the first six months of the intervention. However, despite some exceptions for emotional exhaustion (with statistical sig-nificant effects after six months of the intervention), regular interventions every six months are highly recommended (Maricuțoiu et al., 2016).

Other individual, structural and organizational interventions were found to have a substantial decrease in terms of burnout (for more details see West, Dyrbye, Erwin & Shanafelt, 2016). For example, as we can see in Table 1, strategies that involved mindfulness, stress management and small group discussion (e.g., self-care training and communication skills training) were effective approaches to reduce burnout (West et al., 2016). The authors developed a meta-analysis with 37 cohort studies and found empirical evidence revealing that burnout decreased from 54 percent to 44 percent (difference 10 percent [95% CI 4–14]) and that structural and organizational interventions were more effective than individual-focused approaches to reduce burnout.

Another way to minimize stress is to provide extended orientation and training programs, observation of more senior workers and intensive supervision (Richardsen & Burke, 1995). As mentioned before, it is important to develop a climate with supportive and people-oriented supervision. Other initiatives might include problem sensing, data collection with subsequent confrontation and feedback. It is also important to relocate job tasks, promoting more variety and designing ways to decrease interpersonal conflicts. Managers that supervise teams should formally establish explicit rules regarding attendance norms when employees are sick and hence, create a healthy environment culture for all (Luksyte, Avery & Yeo, 2015). It is also important to develop training programs to promote diversity and to provide cultural tools that help managers work with demographical diversity (Luksyte et al., 2015).

Improved affect regulation should contribute to both employee well-being and performance. Alleviating and managing health problems should improve productivity significantly, not only through lower absenteeism, but also by decreasing the negative consequences of presenteeism (Koopman et al., 2002). Disease and disability management, optimal pharmaceutical utilization and health promotion programs lead to less medical costs and productivity loss (Loeppke, Hymel, Lofland, et al., 2003). For Hemp (2004), employees should feel that the organization cares about their health state. From the literature, we know that leisure, social and physical activities promote psychological relaxation, increasing the employees' level of engagement and well-being (Ten Brummelhuis & Bakker, 2012). Fortunately, employers are increasingly concerned about the impact of illness in the workforce, creating conditions to promote employees' well-being (Loeppke et al., 2003) and the development of positive organizational behavior (Peterson & Luthans, 2002).

Table 1 *Summary of the proposed interventions for burnout reduction and health improvement.*

Interventions	Outcomes
Support from supervisor, coworkers, friends and family.	Reduced emotional exhaustion and lower levels of negative effects.
Cognitive/behavioral interventions.	Reduced emotional exhaustion and capacity to manage emotions and cognitions.
Relaxation techniques.	Reduced emotional exhaustion; improved well-being.
Meditation and reflection.	Reduced physiological arousal; fatigue and burnout removal.
Training: mindfulness, stress management, small group discussions.	Reduced burnout.
Health promotion programs.	Higher job engagement and well-being. Lower frequencies of sickness presence.

Conclusion

According to Demerouti et al. (2009), presenteeism is a risk-taking organizational behavior that should be prevented or at least managed. Employees who have positive emotions, manage burnout at work, or are highly engaged, are the types of workers that most HR managers desire. Accordingly, managers may want to align HR practices in order to increase work engagement and, consequently, decrease the levels of emotional exhaustion and loss of well-being at work.

In the current chapter, a comprehensive model supported by the existing literature, reinforces the need to focus on the work and individual variables that promote burnout symptoms. At the same time, managers should pay attention to reducing job demands, as well as provide incentives that increase job resources, decreasing the levels of burnout and increasing job engagement (Bakker & Demerouti, 2007). As we can see in Figure 1, job burnout might lead to serious health problems which, in turn, decrease the quality of life/well-being (Maslach et al., 2001; Melamed et al., 2006; Nahrgan et al., 2011). Following the same reasoning, previous studies showed that the lack of well-being has a negative impact on organizational outcomes (Cooper

& Dewe, 2008). Derived from previous studies (e.g., Neto et al., 2017), the current model shows that loss of well-being reflects lower levels of productivity associated with sickness presence. However, the findings from the literature shed some light and optimism with empirical evidence, suggesting that different interventions may reduce burnout and increase employees' productivity.

References

Abramis, D. J. (1987). Fun at work: Does it matter? Paper presented at the 95th Annual Convention of the American Psychological Association. (August–September), New York, NY.

Adler, D. A., McLaughlin, T. J., Rogers, W. H., Chang, H., Lapitsky, L. & Lerner, D. (2006). Job performance deficits due to depression. *The American Journal of Psychiatry*, 163, 1569–1576.

Admasachew, L. & Dawson, J. (2011). The association between presenteeism and engagement of National Health Service staff. *Journal of Health Services Research & Policy*, 16 (Supplement 1), 29–33.

Alarcon, G., Eschleman, K. J. & Bowling, N. A. (2009). Relationships between personality variables and burnout: A meta-analysis. *Work & Stress*, 23(3), 244–263.

Anderson, V. L., Levinson, E. M., Barker, W. & Kiewra, K. R. (1999). The effects of meditation on teacher perceived occupational stress, state and trait anxiety, and burnout. *School Psychology Quarterly*, 14, 3–25.

Aronsson, G. & Gustafsson, K. (2005). Sickness presenteeism: Prevalence, attendance-pressure factors, and an outline of a model for research. *Journal of Occupational and Environmental Medicine*, 47, 958–966.

Aronsson, G., Gustafsson, K. & Dallner, M. (2000). Sick but yet at work: An empirical study of sickness presenteeism. *Journal of Epidemiology and Community Health*, 54, 502–509.

Bakker, A. B. & Demerouti, E. (2007). The Job Demands–Resources model: State of the art. *Journal of Managerial Psychology*, 22, 309–328.

Bakker, A. B., Demerouti, E. & Verbeke, W. (2004). Using the Job Demands–Resources model to predict burnout and performance. *Human Resource Management*, 43(1), 83–104.

Bakker, A. B., Schaufeli, W. B., Leiter, M. P. & Taris, T. W. (2008). Work engagement: an emerging concept in occupational health psychology. *Work & Stress*, 22, 187–200.

Böckerman, P. & Laukkanen, E. (2010). What makes you work while you are sick? Evidence from a survey of workers. *The European Journal of Public Health*, 20(1), 43–46.

Boles, M., Pelletier, B. & Lynch, W. (2004). The relationship between health risks and work productivity. *Journal of Occupational and Environment Medicine*, 46, 737–745.

Bolte, A., Goschke, T. & Kuhl, J. (2003). Emotion and intuition: Effects of positive and negative mood on implicit judgments of semantic coherence. *Psychological Science*, 14(5), 416–421.

Brown, S. & Sessions, J. G. (2004). Absenteeism, presenteeism, and shirking. *Economic Issues*, 9(1), 15–21.

Burton, W. N., Pransky, G., Conti, D. J., Chen, C. Y. & Edington, D. W. (2004). The association of medical conditions and presenteeism. *Journal of Occupational Environment Medicine*, 46(6), 38–45.

Cooper, C. L. (1996). Editorial: Working hours and health. *Work & Stress*, X, 1–4.

Cooper, C. & Dewe, P. (2008). Well-being – absenteeism, presenteeism, costs and challenges. *Occupational Medicine*, 58, 522–524.

Cordes, C. L., Dougherty, T. W. & Blum, M. (1997). Patterns of burnout among managers and professionals: a comparison of models. *Journal of Organizational Behavior*, 18(6), 685–701.

D'Abate, C. P. & Eddy, E. R. (2007). Engaging in personal business on the job: extending the presenteeism cqonstruct. *Human Resource Development Quarterly*, 18(3), 361–383.

Darr, W. & Johns, G. (2008). Work strain, health, and absenteeism: A meta-analysis. *Journal of Occupational Health Psychology*, 13, 293–318.

Demerouti, E., Le Blanc, P. M., Bakker, A. B., Schaufelli, W. B. & Hox, J. (2009). Present but sick: A three-wave study on job demands, presenteeism and burnout. *Career Development International*, 14, 50–68.

Econtech (2011). Economic modelling of the cost of presenteeism in Australia. Retrieved from www.medibank.com.au/client/documents/pdf s/sick_at_work.pdf

Elovainio, M., Raaska, H., Sinkkonen, J., Makipaa, S. & Lapinleimu, H. (2015). Associations between attachment-related symptoms and later psychological problems among international adoptees: results from the FinAdo study. *Scandinavian Journal of Psychology*, 56(1), 53–61.

Ferreira, A. I. & Martinez, L. F. (2012). Presenteeism and burnout among teachers in public and private Portuguese elementary schools. *The International Journal of Human Resource Management*, 23, 4380–4390.

Fila, M. J., Purl, J. & Griffeth, R. W. (2017). Job demands, control and support: Meta-analyzing moderator effects of gender, nationality, and occupation. *Human Resource Management Review*, 27(1), 39–60.

Fredrickson, B. L., Tugade, M. M., Waugh, C. E. & Larkin, G. (2003). What good are positive emotions in crises? A prospective study of resilience and emotions following the terrorist attacks on the United States on 11 September 2001. *Journal of Personality and Social Psychology*, 84, 365–376.

Golembiewski, R. T. (1986). The epidemiology of progressive burnout: A primer. *Journal of Health and Human Resources Administration*, 9, 16–37.

Gross, J. J. & John, O. P. (2003). Individual differences in two emotion regulation processes: implications for affect, relationships and well-being. *Journal of Personality and Social Psychology*, 85(2), 348–362.

Gucer, P. W., Oliver, M., Parrish, J. M. & McDiarmid, M. (2009). Work productivity impairment from musculoskeletal disorder pain in long-term caregivers. *Journal of Occupational and Environmental Medicine*, 51, 672–681.

Hackman, J. R. & Oldham, G. R. (1976). Motivation through the design of work: Test of a theory. *Organizational Behavior and Human Performance*, 16(2), 250–279.

Hagberg, M., Vilhemsson, R., Tornqvist, E. W. & Toomingas, A. (2007). Incidence of self-reported reduced productivity owing to musculoskeletal symptoms: Association with workplace and individual factors among computer users. *Ergonomics*, 50, 1820–1834.

Hakanen, J. J., Schaufeli, W. B. & Ahola, K. (2008). The Job Demands–Resources model: A three-year cross-lagged study of burnout, depression, commitment, and work engagement. *Work & Stress*, 22(3), 224–241.

Halbesleben, J. B. (2006). Sources of social support and burnout: A meta-analytic test of the conservation of resources model. *Journal of Applied Psychology*, 91(5), 1134–1145.

Hemp, P. (2004). Presenteeism: At work – But out of it. *Harvard Business Review*, 82, 49–58.

Hobfoll, S. E. (1988). *The Ecology of Stress*. New York, NY: Hemisphere.

Hobfoll, S. E. (2001). The influence of culture, community, and the nested self in the stress process: Advancing conservation of resources theory. *Applied Psychology: An International Review*, 50, 337–370.

Hobfoll, S. E. & Freedy, J. (1993). Conservation of resources: A general stress theory applied to burnout, in W. B. Schaufeli, C. Maslach & T. Marek (Eds.), *Professional Burnout: Recent Developments in Theory and Research*. Washington, DC: Taylor & Francis.

Johns, G. (2010). Presenteeism in the Workplace: A Review and Research Agenda. *Journal of Organizational Behavior*, 31, 519–542.

Kahn, J., Schneider, K. T., Jenkins-Henkelman, T. M. & Moybe, L. L. (2006). Emotional social support and job burnout among high school teachers: is it all due to dispositional affectivity? *Journal of Organizational Behavior*, 27, 793–807.

Koopman, C., Pelletier, K. R., Murray, J. F. et al. (2002). Stanford presenteeism scale: health status and Employee Productivity. *Journal of Occupational and Environmental Medicine*, 44, 14–20.

Krohne, K. & Magnussen, L. H. (2011). Go to work or report sick? A focus group study on decisions of sickness presence among offshore caring section workers. *BMC Research Notes*, 4, 1–7.

Kühnel, J., Sonnentag, S. & Bledow, R. (2012). Resources and time pressure as day-level antecedents of work rngagement. *Journal of Occupational and Organizational Psychology*, 85, 181–198.

Kushnir, T. & Milbauer, V. (1994). Managing stress and burnout at work: A cognitive group intervention program for directors of day-care centers. *Pediatrics*, 94, 1074–1077.

Lee, C. & Ashforth, B. E. (1996). A meta-analytic examination of the correlates of three dimensions of job burnout. *Journal of Applied Psychology*, 81, 123–133.

Loeppke, R., Hymel, P. A., Lofland, J. H. et al. (2003). Health-related workplace productivity measurement: General and migraine specific recommendations From the ACOEM Expert Panel. *Journal of Occupational and Environmental Medicine*, 45(4), 249–359.

Lu, L., Lin, H. Y. & Cooper, C. L. (2013). Unhealthy and present: motives and consequences of the act of presenteeism among Taiwanese employees. *Journal of Occupational Health Psychology*, 18, 404–416.

Lu, L., Peng, S., Lin, H. Y. & Cooper, C. L. (2014). Presenteeism and health over time among Chinese employees: The moderating role of self-efficacy. *Work & Stress*, 28(2), 165–178.

Luksyte, A., Avery, D. R. & Yeo, G. (2015). It is worse when you do it: Examining the interactive effects of coworker presenteeism and demographic similarity. *Journal of Applied Psychology*, 100(4), 1107–1123.

Maricuțoiu, L. P., Sava, F. A. & Butta, O. (2016). The effectiveness of controlled interventions on employees' burnout: A meta-analysis. *Journal of Occupational & Organizational Psychology*, 89(1), 1–27.

Maroco, J. & Tecedeiro, M. (2009). Inventário de Burnout de Maslach Para Estudantes Portugueses Maslach burnout inventory-student survey: Portuguese version. *Psicologia, Saúde e Doenças*, 10(2), 227–235.

Maslach, C. (1982). *Burnout: The Cost of Caring.* Englewood Cliffs, NJ: Prentice Hall.

Maslach, C. (1998). A multidimensional theory of burnout, in C. L. Cooper (Ed.), *Theories of Organizational Stress* (pp. 68–85). New York, NY: Oxford University Press.

Maslach, C. & Leiter, M. P. (2008). Early predictors of job burnout. *Journal of Applied Psychology*, 93(3), 498–512.

Maslach, C., Schaufeli, W. B. & Leiter, M. P. (2001). Job burnout. *Annual Review of Psychology*, 52, 397–422.

Meijman, T. F. & Mulder, G. (1998). Psychological aspects of workload, in P. J. Drenth, H. Thierry & C. J. de Wolff (Eds.), *Handbook of Work and Organizational Psychology* (2nd ed., pp. 5–33). Hove: Taylor & Francis.

Melamed, S., Shirom, A., Toker, S., Berliner, S. & Shapira, I. (2006). Burnout and risk of cardiovascular disease: Evidence, possible causal paths, and promising research directions. *Psychological Bulletin*, 132, 327–353.

Miraglia, M. & Johns, G. (2016). Going to work ill: A meta-analysis of the correlates of presenteeism and a dual-path model. *Journal of Occupational Health Psychology*, 21(3), 261–283.

Nahrgang, J. D., Morgeson, F. P. & Hofmann, D. A. (2011). Safety at work: A meta-analytic investigation of the link between job demands, job resources, burnout, engagement and safety outcomes. *Journal of Applied Psychology*, 96, 71–94.

Neto, M., Ferreira, A. I., Martinez, L. F. & Ferreira, P. C. (2017). Workplace bullying and presenteeism: The path through emotional exhaustion and psychological wellbeing. *Annals of Work Exposures and Health*, 61(5), 528–538.

Park, H. I., Jacob, A. C., Wagner, S. H. & Baiden, M. (2014). Job control and burnout: A meta-analytic test of the Conservation of resources model. *Applied Psychology: An International Review*, 63(4), 607–642.

Peterson, S. & Luthans, F. (2002). Does the manager's level of hope matter? Preliminary research evidence of a positive impact. Proceedings of the Midwest Academy of Management. Indianapolis, IN.

Pohling, R., Buruck, G., Jungbauer, K. & Leiter, M. P. (2016). Work-related factors of presenteeism: The mediating role of mental and physical health. *Journal of Occupational Health Psychology*, 21(2), 220–234.

Pransky, G. S. & Dempsey, P. G. (2004). Practical aspects of functional capacity evaluations. *Journal of Occupational Rehabilitation*, 14, 217–229.

Ragsdale, J. M. & Beehr, T. A. (2016). A rigorous test of a model of employees' resource recovery mechanisms during a weekend. *Journal of Organizational Behavior*, 37(6), 911–932.

Richardsen, A. & Burke, R. (1995). Models of burnout: Implications for interventions. *International Journal of Stress Management*, 2(1), 31–43.

Richardson, K. M. & Rothstein, H. R. (2008). Effects of occupational stress management intervention programs: A meta-analysis. *Journal of Occupational Health Psychology*, 13, 69–93.

Rössler, W. (2012). Stress, burnout and job dissatisfaction in mental health workers. *European Archives of Psychiatry & Clinical Neuroscience*, 262, 65–69.

Schaufeli, W. & Bakker, A. (2004). Job demands, job resources, and their relationship with burnout and engagement: a multi-sample study. *Journal of Organizational Behavior*, 25, 293–315.

Schaufeli, W., Leiter, M. P., Maslach, C. & Jackson, S. E. (1996). The Maslach Burnout Inventory-General Survey, in C. Maslach, S. E. Jackson & M. P. Leiter (Eds.), *Maslach Burnout Inventory Manual* (3rd ed). Palo Alto, CA: Consulting Psychologists Press.

Shirom, A. (2005). Reflections on the study of burnout. *Work & Stress*, 19 (3), 263–270.

Simpson, R. (1998). Presenteeism, power and organizational change: long hours as a career barrier and the impact on the working lives of women managers. *British Journal of Management*, 9, 37–50.

Stambor, Z. (2006). Employees: A company's best asset. *Monitor on Psychology*, 37(3), 28–30.

Taris, T. W. (2006). Is there a relationship between burnout and objective performance? A critical review of 16 studies. *Work & Stress*, 20, 316–334.

Ten Brummelhuis, L. L. & Bakker, A. B. (2012). Staying engaged during the week: The effect of off-job activities on next day work engagement. *Journal of Occupational Health Psychology*, 17, 445–455.

Wan, H. C., Downey, L. A. & Stough, C. (2014). Understanding non-work presenteeism: Relationships between emotional intelligence, boredom, procrastination and job stress. *Personality and Individual Differences*, 65, 86–90.

West, C. P., Dyrbye, L. N., Erwin, P. J. & Shanafelt, T. D. (2016). Interventions to prevent and reduce physician burnout: a systematic review and meta-analysis. *Lancet*, 388(10057), 2272–2281.

10 | Presenteeism and Innovative Behavior

HSUEH-LIANG FAN

Introduction

Employee presenteeism, which is as common a phenomenon as absenteeism in organizational settings, has received much theoretical and empirical attention in organizational behavior studies for two decades. The most recent scholarly conceptualization of presenteeism involves "showing up for work when one is ill" (Johns, 2012). In other words, presenteeism occurs when employees are physically present although they actually feel they should be taking sick leave (Lu, Peng, Lin & Cooper, 2014). Managers and scholars consider presenteeism as a negative construct, because it reduces the productivity of a job due to real health problems and distractions. Moreover, the cost and loss of productivity attributable to presenteeism may actually be higher than that caused by absenteeism (Halbesleben, Whitman & Crawford, 2014).

Prior literature has also suggested that presenteeism is harmful to individual work outcomes. When employees come to work when they are ill, they often demonstrate many negative work outcomes, such as lower levels of performance, reduced job satisfaction, and physical and mental health (Cooper & Lu, 2016; Lu, Lin & Cooper, 2013). Unfortunately, although the innovative behavior of employees is seen as a type of work performance (Yuan & Woodman, 2010), no study has yet been conducted to explore the relationship between presenteeism and employees' innovative behavior.

Innovative behavior involves both the generation of ideas and the subsequent stages of internal promotion and implementation of such new ideas (Anderson, Potocnik & Zhou, 2014; De Clercq, Dimov & Belausteguigoitia, 2016). In spite of there being no direct empirical evidence to verify the role of presenteeism on employees' innovative behavior, nonetheless, there is growing awareness that presenteeism is

241

negatively associated with many factors, and such factors are also harmful to employee creativity and to innovative behavior. These factors include mood and anxiety disorders (Esposito, Wang, Williams & Patten, 2007), and brain functions, such as the loss of energy, concentration levels, and the quantity/quality of work produced (Hargrave, Hiatt, Alexander & Shaffer, 2008).

Although previous studies (e.g., Cooper & Lu, 2016; Johns, 2010) have attempted to propose integrated models to explain the antecedents and consequences of presenteeism, according to their literature reviews, most of the consequences of presenteeism are centered on productivity or mental health, and their studies did not discuss individuals' innovative behavior. Furthermore, most antecedents of the studies of presenteeism have focused on the effect of contextual and personal factors on presenteeism-related decision-making in individuals, while no studies have examined the motivation behind presenteeism. Johns (2010) indicated that the effect of presenteeism on productivity may be influenced by various types of motivation and, thus, it is inappropriate to simply discuss the negative relationship between presenteeism and productivity. Rather, the types of motivation that support employee behavior should be explored in detail to determine how different types of motivation are associated with behavior and behavioral consequences. In other words, presenteeism behavior cannot be explained based solely on the behavior itself; it is necessary to understand the presenteeism behavior of employees, to comprehend the motivation behind such presenteeism.

Based on a review of the gap in the literature, to help creativity and innovation researchers to better understand the phenomenon of presenteeism, this chapter develops an extended componential model of creativity to presenteeism based on Amabile's (1996) componential theory of creativity.

Extending the Componential Model of Creativity to Presenteeism

In a rapidly changing competitive market, organizations need to become innovative to gain and maintain a competitive advantage in the market, and the starting point of any organizational innovation is the willingness of employees to demonstrate innovative behavior at work (Amabile, Conti, Coon, Lazenby & Herron, 1996; Scott & Bruce, 1994). Creativity refers to the generation of novel and useful ideas, while innovative behavior involves both the idea generation and the subsequent stages of employees' intentional introduction, promotion, and implementation of any such new ideas in their work roles (Scott & Bruce, 1994; Yuan & Woodman, 2010). Examples of innovative behavior include generating creative ideas, promoting and championing ideas to others, and investigating and securing the funds required to implement new ideas (Scott & Bruce, 1994).

Innovation refers to a type of high-risk activity that has a complex and volatile nature. When employees are engaged in creative thinking, problem-solving, trial and error, or innovative activities that put creativity to work, their level of innovative behavior is determined by whether their organization supports innovation; this is reflected by the work situation as well as the various management practices of the organization (Amabile, 1996; Scott & Bruce, 1994). As a result, when examining factors influencing employees' innovative behavior, researchers have begun with theories of motivation, of which Amabile's (1996) componential theory of creativity is one of the most frequently cited (Anderson et al., 2014). The componential theory of creativity emphasizes that an individual's creativity consists of intrinsic task motivation, domain-relevant skills, and creativity-relevant skills. More specifically, the work environment of an organization affects its members' innovative motivation through the perceived organizational climate of innovation (Amabile, 1996). For example, a talented R&D employee may perform relatively favorably in terms of domain-relevant and creativity-relevant skills, but such an employee is subject to organizational reality and must seek support from their organization or from their colleagues before promoting innovation. Once this employee has recognized that their organization supports innovation, he or she will be more willing to put effort into innovation-related tasks and into sustaining their level of concentration at work. This example illustrates the role of perceived work environment factors on employee motivation. In organization innovation research, "work environment factors" refers to the organizational innovation climate.

In the following sections, this chapter discusses the possible roles of presenteeism on innovative behaviors by integrating prior literature on creativity, innovation, and presenteeism. The discussion is specifically focused on the theoretical elaborations of motivation and the organizational innovation climate, which are two of the most important constructs in creativity and innovation literature. The discussion also covers the effects of creative self-efficacy, which is one of the types of

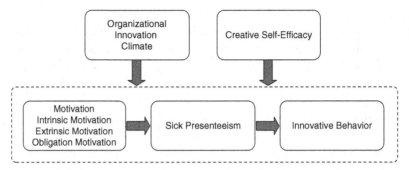

Figure 1 Extending the componential model of creativity to presenteeism

creativity-relevant skills frequently discussed by researchers and also deemed a crucial variable of presenteeism in existing literature. The proposed conceptual model is shown in Figure 1.

The Motivation Assumption of Innovative Behavior

Three types of motivation are discussed in this paper: intrinsic motivation, extrinsic motivation, and obligation motivation. Most researchers have explained the innovative behavior of individuals based on intrinsic and extrinsic motivations. Intrinsic motivation refers to the specific behavior of an individual that is elicited when the individual is enjoying or is curious about an activity. In this case, the individual is more motivated and more willing to put in additional effort and accept challenges. An employee with intrinsic motivation is more likely to take on an innovation task, express innovative behavior, enjoy their work, and gain intrinsic satisfaction (Amabile, 1996; Deci & Ryan, 2008). From the perspective of intrinsic motivation, this paper proposes that employees go to work when they are sick probably because they are interested in their work and gain satisfaction from it. In this type of situation where the employee is sick, they still work hard, remain focused, and exhibit innovative behavior.

Proposition 1: *The act of presenteeism is positively related to employees' innovative behavior where employees are intrinsically motivated.*

Conversely, the second type of motivation is extrinsic motivation, which refers to factors driving the expression of certain behavior because of anticipated outcomes of reward or fear of punishment (Deci & Ryan, 2008). Cooper (1996) examined presenteeism based on the effects of economic and industrial development on organizations. He suggested that when employees are confronted with external effects, such as a bad economy, they are afraid to take sick leave because of job insecurity. Therefore, Cooper (1996) defined presenteeism in terms of the resultant lack of productivity, or lower productivity, resulting from employees coming to work when they feel sick, or when they are fatigued because of extended working hours. From the perspective of extrinsic motivation, if an employee's presenteeism is extrinsically driven, the employee will regard these extrinsic factors as a means adopted by the company to control its employees. Consequently, such employees coming to work despite sickness, neither become involved in the work nor demonstrate any innovative behavior.

Proposition 2: *The act of presenteeism is negatively related to employees' innovative behavior where employees are extrinsically motivated.*

Aside from intrinsic and extrinsic motivation, there is a third and critical type of motivation known as the obligation motivation. In contrast to the aforementioned types of motivation, obligation motivation highlights the moral fortitude of an individual, and it prompts the individual to behave according to the norms of a specific value system. When obligation motivation is satisfied, no violation of the norm of reciprocity will be made and, therefore, no social stigma will be generated within the organization (Cooper & Jayatilaka, 2006). To explore the connotations of obligation motivation, the author interviewed two managers, one of whom is a senior manager of a post office. He maintained that the following sentiments are associated with, and help to explain, the concept of obligation motivation: "causing trouble to other people," "feeling obligated to chair a meeting," and "being afraid of asking for leave."

For certain occupations, such as [working in the] public services, presenteeism has nothing to do with a fear of losing one's job, making a negative impression on managers, or disturbing the progress of work; it is more concerned with a sense of responsibility. This is because public organizations are more conservative workplaces. For example, post office employees work interdependently, and anyone taking leave will cause trouble to other employees. Managers are perhaps reluctant to take leave because they feel they are obligated to chair a meeting. Recently, a senior mail carrier fainted in his car; he always does his job without complaint because he is afraid of asking for leave.

Another manager working for a public relations company stated that she goes to work when sick to maintain the company's operation:

If I think my work performance is not affected by my illness, or if my presence makes a customer or colleagues feel more comfortable even though my work performance is compromised, I still go to work and I share my workload with others.

This chapter asserts that intrinsic motivation is the primary factor driving employees' innovative behavior. Behaviors associated with the perspective that going to work is an obligation may be disadvantageous to the creative potential of employees. If an employee's act of presenteeism is driven by obligation motivation, the employee may not actively search for new problems at work and constantly be involved in the problem-solving processes.

Proposition 3: *The act of presenteeism is negatively related to employees' innovative behavior where employees are driven by obligation motivation.*

Contextual Influence of the Organizational Innovation Climate

An organizational innovation climate refers to employees' subjective perceptions of their work environment. When the innovation climate of a work environment is optimal, employees feel that innovative behavior is supported and encouraged, and they are more likely to participate in constructive debates with colleagues rather than criticizing others. They will also express their viewpoints without worrying about punishment, they will develop an interest in their work, and they will feel secure if they take on a challenge. Employees will also be motivated to become involved in innovative activities. For these reasons, such employees are more likely to demonstrate favorable innovative performance if the climate is welcoming (Amabile et al., 1996). Hunter et al. (2007) indicated that according to creativity and innovation researchers, among the various organizational factors, an organizational innovation climate has been identified to be the most crucial.

Some studies have already demonstrated that organizational contextual factors have a critical effect on employees' decision-making regarding presenteeism. Factors that result in employees presenting for work when sick include personal attributes, perceptions of pressure from supervisors or coworkers, fear of disciplinary action or risking the loss of promotion opportunities, and job insecurity (Halbesleben et al., 2014; Johns, 2010). For example, Johns (2010) demonstrated the importance of contextual factors, which comprise work-related factors (such as work requirements, teamwork, work substitutability, and the level of autonomy for work adjustment) and organizational factors (such as organizational attendance culture, the reward and appraisal system, and organizational work safety welfare). For example, when the work requirements are stringent, employees will limit their absence even if they are ill. Similarly, the level of absenteeism is low for individuals involved in teamwork or who work with little or no autonomy, even if some employees have health concerns, whereas the level of presenteeism is high. Demerouti et al. (2009) investigated nurses in the Netherlands and found that work requirements are a significant predictor of presenteeism. In other words, organizational environmental factors affect employees' decision-making about whether to go to work when sick.

In the context of organizational innovation, this chapter suggests that a positive organizational innovation climate both directly increases employees' work motivation and functions as a critical resource in assisting employees to work effectively. Firstly, the organizational innovation climate affects employees' presenteeism motivation, and employees express corresponding innovative behavior. From the social information processing perspective, the behavioral norms and messages of the social environment context affect an individual's cognition and behavioral pattern through the individual's perception, experience and assessment. When employees identify themselves with their social environment, their motivation, attitude, and behavior inclines them toward meeting the norms and expectations of that environment (Salancik & Pfeffer, 1978). If employees recognize that their organization's management practices (such as organization and management encouragement, group support, work autonomy and challenges, and resource adequacy) encourage innovation, then more innovative behavior will occur because of elicited intrinsic motivation (Amabile et al., 1996). Thus, even if employees come to work when they are sick, they will still have high intrinsic motivation and display innovative behavior. Conversely, those working in an environment that does not support innovation, or that may even discourage innovation by presenting hindrances such as time pressure or too many work requirements, would expect the receipt of less support from their organizations. This would be accompanied by a larger increase in the cognitive cost of performing innovatively and decrease employee desire to propose novel and useful ideas and to implement them subsequently.

Secondly, an organizational innovation climate is a resource that contributes to employees' work efficiency. This can be explained by the theory of conservation of resources (COR). COR theory proposes that people are driven to acquire, protect, and retain resources (i.e., time, physical energy, emotional energy, and attention) for themselves and keep away from situations that may cause the loss of any valued resources (Morrison, 2011). According to COR theory, presenteeism means individuals are losing at least two key resources (Baeriswyl, Krause, Elfering & Berset, 2017). First, individuals will lose physical and mental health related resources, and secondly, individuals are alerting the threats of resources losses in economic-related resources, such as the fear of losing one's job. These two key resources may decrease the capacity for flexible thinking and the energy of employees (Roskes, De Dreu & Nijstad, 2012). In such circumstances, individuals may tend to overcome the loss of resources by constantly changing their cognitive and behavioral efforts. If employees feel that their organization supports innovation, the organization is perceived as being likely to provide employees with the support required to perform innovative tasks. For example, an organization, managers, or colleagues can offer the required mental, social, or work support, can assist employees in turning disadvantages into advantages, and can make employees willing to put in additional effort and to exhibit innovative behavior.

Proposition 4: *The organizational innovation climate will moderate the relationship between sick presenteeism and innovative behavior.*

Inevitably, organizational innovation is linked to organizational demand and risk-taking, so that employees may perceive their work environment as negative and will demonstrate negative attitudes and behaviors, such as employees who perceive job demands that are not conducive to creativity and innovation. Job demands refer to physical, social, or organizational aspects of a job that require sustained physical or mental effort, and are thus linked with certain physiological and psychological costs (Demerouti, Bakker, Nachreiner & Schaufeli, 2001). Job demands are typically operationalized as workload pressure (e.g., "employees are often required to work very quickly," and "employees often have a great deal of work to do"; Spector & Jex, 1998), and long working hours. Prior literature has suggested that workload pressure is an obstacle to employee innovation. For example, Amabile, Hadley and Kramer (2002) found that professionals who perceive excessive workloads and time pressures report fewer creative ideas over time.

If employees detect high job demands, they may judge that they are losing key energy resources for creative cognitive thinking and execution. They may tend to overcome the loss of resources by constantly changing their cognitive and behavioral efforts. When they further perceive additional job demands, they may conclude that they are receiving less support from their organizations. This would be accompanied by a larger increase in the cognitive cost of performing innovatively, and a decrease in employees' desire to propose novel and useful ideas and to implement them subsequently. Job demands will thus exacerbate the negative role of presenteeism in the development of employees' innovative behavior. Consequently, this study has formulated the following proposition:

Proposition 5: *Jobs demands may exacerbate the negative influence of presenteeism on innovative behavior.*

Creative Self-Efficacy

According to flow theory (Csikszentmihalyi, 1996), creativity-eliciting flow experience is both related to an individual's intrinsic motivation and to the individual's capability. Only when the level of skills possessed by an individual matches the challenge perceived by the individual can selfless concentration occur. This type of concentration can in turn elicit creativity in individuals and have positive effects on both the organization and society. According to the componential theory of creativity, if an individual working in an organization with a favorable innovation climate also has more confidence regarding the completion of innovative work, this individual will be more motivated to be creative and will exhibit innovative behavior. Creativity and innovation studies also suggest that the effect of innovative efficacy is the effect most closely associated with an individual's capability. Creative self-efficacy is a concept derived from the self-efficacy theory of Bandura (1986), which defined self-efficacy as an individual's confidence, in a specific context, that they will complete an innovation task. The higher an individual's creative self-efficacy, the more confident the individual will be in performing the innovation task, and the more likely it will be that the individual will succeed (Tierney & Farmer, 2002, 2011). While a supportive organizational climate promotes innovative activities among employees, it is self-motivation induced by innovative efficacy that prompts employees to pursue innovation opportunities. Nonetheless, few empirical studies have examined the association between personality traits (such as self-efficacy and performance-based self-esteem) and presenteeism (Löve et al., 2010). This chapter proposes that innovative efficacy may be a critical factor for inducing positive motivation in employees to the degree that employees insist on going to work while sick and will continue to exhibit innovative behavior.

Proposition 6:   *Creative self-efficacy will moderate the relationship between sick presenteeism and innovative behavior.*

Conclusion and Discussion

Employee presenteeism involves complex motivation factors, and presenteeism behavior cannot easily be eradicated in the workplace. To stimulate innovative behavior in employees, organizations must use multiple methods concurrently. First, they should create an appropriate environment and climate that is perceived by their employees as both positive and innovative. Such an environment is crucial for eliciting employees' intrinsic motivation and expression of innovative behavior. An organizational innovation climate is also a critical resource for employees, because it can reduce the negative effects of employees' extrinsic-motivation- or obligation-motivation-driven presenteeism on innovative behavior. Amabile and Kramer (2011) suggested that the optimal method of encouraging employees and inducing their motivation is to allow them to achieve small successes from meaningful work. The more frequent the experience of small successes, the more likely the employees are to express innovative behavior. This paper thus suggests that both employees and managers should adopt this strategy of small successes to cope with presenteeism. If presenteeism occurs, any tasks assigned to the individual should be made easier and less complicated to enable small successes. Managers should handle employee presenteeism by designing employee tasks that will give them small successes, such as flexibility in the design of the work content, to provide the necessary resources and assistance.

Selecting the right employees is also crucial. Companies should make adequate use of on-the-job training and work experience to increase employees' innovative efficacy. As for employees, they must be interested and confident in the activity or task in which they are involved if they are to dedicate themselves to the work and perform favorably, thereby eliminating difficulties and confronting challenges head on. Consequently, an organization should select appropriate personnel, take leadership behavior into consideration, and provide relevant training and consultation to maintain or enhance the innovative efficacy of its staff. Taking personnel selection as an example, an organization should choose individuals with self-efficacy traits, such as emotional stability, openness to learning, friendliness, a strong work ethic, earnestness, and a good sense of responsibility (Thoms, Moore & Scott, 1996). With regard to employee training, the holding of innovative activities or contests, managers providing timely assistance or suggestions, and the offering of professional and technical training will help employees to improve their professional capacity and to obtain successful innovation experience. Most critically, organizations should arrange for employees to complete challenging new tasks systematically to improve their innovative efficacy over time (Kelley & Kelley, 2012). In summary, pluralistic training is indispensable for both the development of expertise and the improvement of self-efficacy.

References

Amabile, T. M. (1996). *Creativity in Context*. Boulder, CO: Westview Press.

Amabile, T. M. & Kramer, S. J. (2011). The power of small wins. *Harvard Business Review*, 89(5), 70–80.

Amabile, T. M., Conti, R., Coon, H., Lazenby, J. & Herron, M. (1996). Assessing the work environment for creativity. *Academy of Management Journal*, 39(5), 1154–1184.

Amabile, T. M., Hadley, C. N. & Kramer, S. J. (2002). Creativity under the gun. *Harvard Business Review*, 80(8): 52–61.

Anderson, N., Potocnik, K. & Zhou, J. (2014). Innovation and creativity in organizations: a state of the science review, prospective commentary, and guiding framework. *Journal of Management*, 40(5), 1297–1333.

Baeriswyl, S., Krause, A., Elfering, A. & Berset, M. (2017). How workload and coworker support relate to emotional exhaustion: the mediating role of sickness presenteeism. *International Journal of Stress Management*, 24, 52–73. doi: 10.1037/str0000018

Bandura, A. (1986). *Social Foundations of Thought and Action: A Social Cognitive Theory*. Englewood Cliffs, NJ: Prentice-Hall.

Cooper, C. L. & Lu, L. (2016). Presenteeism as a global phenomenon: unraveling the psychosocial mechanisms from the perspective of social cognitive theory. *Cross Cultural & Strategic Management*, 23(2), 216–231.

Cooper, R. B. & Jayatilaka, B. (2006). Group creativity: the effects of extrinsic, intrinsic, and obligation motivations. *Creativity Research Journal*, 18(2), 153–172.

Cooper, C. (1996). Hot under the collar. *Times Higher Education Supplement*, 21, 15.

Csikszentmihalyi, M. (1996). *Flow and the Psychology of Discovery and Invention*. New York, NY: Harper Collins.

De Clercq, D., Dimov, D. & Belausteguigoitia, I. (2016). Perceptions of adverse work conditions and innovative behavior: the buffering roles of relational resources. *Entrepreneurship Theory and Practice*, 40(3), 515–542.

Deci, E. L. & Ryan, R. M. (2008). Self-determination theory: a macrotheory of human motivation, development, and health. *Canadian Psychology*, 49 (3), 182–185.

Demerouti, E., Bakker, A. B., Nachreiner, F. & Schaufeli, W. B. (2001). The job demands–resources model of burnout. *Journal of Applied Psychology*, 86(3), 499–512.

Demerouti, E., Le Blanc, P. M., Bakker, A. B., Schaufeli, W. B. & Hox, J. (2009). Present but sick: a three-wave study on job demands, presenteeism and burnout. *Career Development International*, 14(1), 50–68.

DeVellis, R. F. (2012). *Scale Development: Theory and Applications* (3rd ed.). Thousand Oaks, CA: SAGE.

Esposito, E., Wang, J. L., Williams, J. V. A. & Patten, S. B. (2007). Mood and anxiety disorders, the association with presenteeism in employed members of a general population sample. *Epidemiologia E Psichiatria Sociale—An International Journal for Epidemiology and Psychiatric Sciences*, 16(3), 231–237.

Gorgievski, M. J. & Hobfoll, S. E. (2008). Work can burn us out or fire us up: conservation of resources in burnout and engagement, in Halbesleben J. R. B. (Ed.) *Handbook of Stress and Burnout in Health Care*, Hauppauge, NY: Nova Science, pp. 7–22.

Halbesleben, J. R. B., Whitman, M. V. & Crawford, W. S. (2014). A dialectical theory of the decision to go to work: bringing together absenteeism and presenteeism. *Human Resource Management Review*, 24(2), 177–192.

Hargrave, G. E., Hiatt, D., Alexander, R. & Shaffer, I. A. (2008). EAP treatment impact on presenteeism and absenteeism: implications for return on investment. *Journal of Workplace Behavioral Health*, 23(3), 283–293.

Hunter, S. T., Bedell, K. E. & Mumford, M. D. (2007). Climate for creativity: a quantitative review. *Creativity Research Journal*, 19(1), 69–90.

Johns, G. (2010). Presenteeism in the workplace: a review and research agenda. *Journal of Organizational Behavior*, 31(4), 519–542.

Johns, G. (2012). Presenteeism: a short history and a cautionary tale, in J. Houdmont, S. Leka & R. Sinclair (Eds.), *Contemporary Occupational Health Psychology: Global Perspectives on Research and Practice*: vol. 2: 204–220. Malden, MA: John Wiley & Sons.

Kelley, T. & Kelley, D. (2012). Reclaim your creative confidence. *Harvard Business Review*, 90(12), 115–118.

Löve, J., Grimby-Ekman, A., Eklöf, M., Hagberg, M. & Dellve, L. (2010). Pushing oneself too hard: performance-based self-esteem as a predictor of sickness presenteeism among young adult women and men—a cohort study. *Journal of Occupational and Environmental Medicine*, 52(6), 603–609.

Lu, L., Lin, H. Y. & Cooper, C. L. (2013). Unhealthy and present: motives and consequences of the act of presenteeism among Taiwanese employees. *Journal of Occupational Health Psychology*, 18(4), 406–416.

Lu, L., Peng, S. Q., Lin, H. Y. & Cooper, C. L. (2014). Presenteeism and health over time among Chinese employees: the moderating role of self-efficacy. *Work and Stress*, 28(2), 165–178.

Morrison, E. W. (2011). Employee voice behavior: integration and directions for future research. *Academy of Management Annals*, 5, 373–412.

Roskes, M., De Dreu, C. K. W. & Nijstad, B. A. (2012). Necessity is the mother of invention: avoidance motivation stimulates creativity through cognitive effort. *Journal of Personality and Social Psychology*, 103(2), 242–256.

Salancik, G. R. & Pfeffer, J. (1978). A social information, processing approach to job attitudes and task design. *Administrative Science Quarterly*, 23(2), 224–253.

Scott, S. G. & Bruce, R. A. (1994). Determinants of innovative behavior: a path model of individual innovation in the workplace. *Academy of Management Journal*, 37(3), 580–607.

Spector, P. E. & Jex, S.M. (1998). Development of four self-report measures of job stressors and strain: interpersonal conflict at work scale, organizational constraints scale, quantitative workload inventory, and physical symptoms inventory. *Journal of Occupational Health Psychology*, 3, 356–367.

Thoms, P., Moore, K. S. & Scott, K. S. (1996). The relationship between self-efficacy for participating in self-managed work groups and the big five personality dimensions. *Journal of Organizational Behavior*, 17(4), 349–362.

Tierney, P. & Farmer, S. M. (2002). Creative self-efficacy: its potential antecedents and relationship to creative performance. *Academy of Management Journal*, 45(6), 1137–1148.

Tierney, P. & Farmer, S. M. (2011). Creative self-efficacy development and creative performance over time. *Journal of Applied Psychology*, 96(2), 277–293.

Yuan, F. R. & Woodman, R. W. (2010). Innovative Behavior in the workplace: the role of performance and image outcome expectations. *Academy of Management Journal*, 53(2), 323–342.

PART IV

Understanding Presenteeism in a Cross-Cultural Context

11 | *Presenteeism and Work–Family/Family–Work Conflict: A Cross-Cultural Approach with Two Latin Countries*

LUIS F. MARTINEZ, ARISTIDES I.
FERREIRA, AND TÂNIA A. M. NUNES

Introduction

Structural changes in society have led to an increasing participation of women in the labor market. Accordingly, marriage and maternity occurs at an older age, women's qualifications levels have systematically increased, flexible jobs are on the rise, and there is a social pressure for equal opportunities between men and women. Consequently, there is a greater recognition of male participation in the upbringing of children, as male parents are increasingly involved in their children's education (Clark, 2000). All these factors play a role in explaining the work–family conflict (WFC) and family–work conflict (FWC) (Kodz, Harper & Dench, 2002; Worral, Cooper & Campbell, 2000) making it a hot topic for research.

While in the mid-nineties the concern to achieve a balance between work and personal life was mainly an organizational issue, nowadays there are more factors that encourage the study of this topic, as people's lives are increasingly crammed with obligations and interdependencies. Organizational change (e.g., advances in technology, innovation, globalization, strategic alliances, organizational restructuring and downsizing) is the basis of such a paradigm shift. Also, due to the still-recent economic crisis, important challenges arise, and many organizations have been either downsizing their employees, or going out of business. In this challenging labor context, presenteeism tends to increase due to job insecurity and reduced resources (Lu, Lin & Cooper, 2013a). Employees are forced to go to work despite being ill, as the culture of presenteeism forces employees to stay extra hours at work (Simpson, 1998). This extra time devoted to work introduces notorious problems for individuals' lives – thus posing serious consequences in the balance between family and work.

Stevens (2004) suggested presenteeism as a vital construct to be studied, as companies continue to seek ways of reducing costs, improving productivity, and promoting employees' health and well-being. Thus, recognizing presenteeism as an inevitable and either tolerable or toxic behavior within the workforce and the balance between family and work spheres, should be the milestone into getting organizations to deal actively with this problem. Furthermore, it is important to diagnose its' nature and incidence, as well as develop organizational policies to reduce this phenomenon and promote both physical and mental health at work (Gosselin & Lauzier, 2011) as well balance between work and family. Moreover, it urges to explore the way in which presenteeism is related to economic and social constraints and workplace cultures (Dew, Keefe & Small, 2005). The first step for research might be to accurately measure the impact of this phenomenon in terms of how it affects productivity and how it affects the borders and spheres between family and work.

Sickness presence – presenteeism – involves working when sick (Johns, 2010). This could result in diminished productivity, burnout, cynicism, amongst many other detrimental consequences for workers, organizations and families. Protracted presenteeism may eventually worsen workers' health in the long term (Bergström, Bodin, Hagberg et al., 2009). The reasons people work while sick range from feeling indispensable to their employer, or wanting to prevent losing pace with their workload, to fearing sick days statistics will be incorporated into layoff decisions, or losing income from additional days missed (Loeppke, Taitel, Haufle, Parry, Kessler & Jinnett, 2009).

Also, the role conflicts that employees have to manage are expected to lead to a decrease in productivity associated with presenteeism, essentially due to the absence of psychological well-being – e.g., lack of optimism, initiative, and dedication to work (Schaufeli, Salanova, González-Romá & Bakker, 2002). Engagement appears to be associated with the explanation of this phenomenon, as it was found to be a predictor of organizational success (Harter, Schmidt & Hayes, 2002; Richman, 2006). As few studies have addressed the role of engagement in relation to presenteeism, we sought to examine its mediating role in the relationship between WFC/FWC and productivity associated with presenteeism.

According to De Beer (2014), employees with higher levels of engagement will experience less discomfort and distraction, thus reporting less health problems related to presenteeism. When employees are psychologically present, they recognize the importance of their involvement and contribution to the organization, and strive to perform their tasks while they are present at work.

Recent research on presenteeism has mainly focused in regions such as North America and Scandinavia (Böckerman & Laukkanen, 2010; Johns, 2010). Thus, a further exploration of presenteeism based on a cross-cultural approach is definitely needed (Lu, Cooper & Lin, 2013b). Moreover, as we mentioned before, our society is rapidly changing and organizations are facing new (and more demanding) challenges. Advances – and occasional setbacks – in globalization and internationalization processes influence – and are influenced by – the dynamics and conflicts between work and family. This allegedly introduces new challenges for managers regarding cross-cultural concerns. In order to shed some light into this phenomenon, we posit the following research question: *"Is the relationship between WFC, FWC and productivity despite sickness presence conditioned by the cultural inner aspects of each country"?*

The cross-cultural literature shows that employees from countries with high masculine cultures tend to devote more time to work, and receive more incentives to stay long hours at work in high competitive environments (Hofstede, 1994; Simpson, 1998). Additionally, a higher investment in the work sphere tends to increase conflicts and interfere with other domains of life (e.g., family, friends). On the contrary, employees from countries with low masculine values are expected to value other domains of life apart from work, such as family and the importance of recovering from job demands. Hence, cultures that value other activities out of work allow employees to switch off from their jobs' routines, which results in more time to recover from potential stressful events (Meijman & Mulder, 1998) and thus depicting less problems related with conflicts at home due to job demands. Despite the pertinence of this topic, to our knowledge, these assumptions were never empirically tested. In order to address this issue, the current research focused in two countries that share the same cultural roots (i.e., the Latin cluster; see Javidan, House, Dorfman, Hanges & Luque,

2006; Javidan, Stahl, Brodbeck & Wilderom, 2005), but have different characteristics in terms of masculine culture (Portugal, MAS score of 31; Ecuador, MAS score of 63). Particularly, we sought to examine if the relationship between WFC/FWC has a different contribution on presenteeism and productivity losses due to sickness presence, by comparing the two countries.

In the next subsections, we extend literature insights on presenteeism, WFC/FWC, the mediator role of job engagement, and cross-cultural issues (specially focused on Latin countries), as well as presenting the rationale that leads to our research hypotheses.

Presenteeism

Over the last twenty years, plenty of research on presenteeism has been conducted by authors from a wide range of scientific backgrounds. Accordingly, two stems of research on the topic emerged in the literature. The first originated from the United States and studied the impact of presenteeism on workplace productivity, whereas the second emerged from Europe and focused on presenteeism as a reaction by workers to a lack of job security, due to fear of contract termination (Böckerman & Laukkanen, 2010; Johns, 2010). Johns (2010) also presented a framework illustrating how a health condition could – depending on the context (job demands, job security, reward system, absence policy, absence culture, and ease of replacement) and the person (work attitudes, personality, perceived justice, stress, perceived absence legitimacy) – result in presenteeism, absenteeism, or both, leading to detrimental future consequences in productivity and/or health. In essence, Johns (2010) made an attempt to bridge the two bodies of literature into one unified theory and equate presenteeism to absenteeism.

The illnesses most associated with presenteeism in the literature are allergies, arthritis, acid reflux disease, asthma, diabetes, migraines, and irritable bowel syndrome (Koopman et al., 2002). Mental illness such as depression and anxiety are also featured in the literature as well as contagious diseases like gastroenteritis. A response among firms is to make medications and treatments cheaper (by lowering the required copayment) and making employee counseling and screening available. Another reaction is providing ergonomic chairs, tables, and computer peripherals to make workers suffering from conditions such as arthritis more comfortable and relatively pain free. All these solutions increase costs, therefore monitoring for an increase in productivity, and decrease in absenteeism and presenteeism is necessary in order to prevent overinvestment in health care.

In a rare study carried out in Portugal with high school teachers, Ferreira & Martinez (2012) found that public sector teachers experienced higher presenteeism levels than their private sector colleagues. On the contrary, a paper by Bergström et al. (2009), which also compared presenteeism between public and private organizations, found that private organizations are more prone to presenteeism. Bergtröm et al. (2009) adjusted for individual characteristics, but the two groups are extremely different. Considering gender issues in illness, female employees are more prone to presenteeism (Aronsson & Gustafsson, 2005; Simpson, 1998) and absenteeism (Coté & Haccoun, 1991) than males. Aronsson & Gustafsson (2005) also found that females tend to take jobs that entail high levels of presenteeism, like school teachers and nurses. In a sample of Portuguese nurses, Martinez & Ferreira (2012) found that although females revealed higher prevalence levels for most of the presenteeism causes, no gender differences were found regarding the number of hours people were affected by presenteeism. They also found a negative correlation between perceived health status and presenteeism. Additionally, more experienced and highly paid nurses tended to be less affected by presenteeism. However, despite the importance of gender in the presenteeism literature, the structural changes in society and the social pressure for equal gender opportunities (Clark, 2000), WFC and FWC impact on presenteeism has become an inescapable topic of analysis in the existing literature.

Work–Family Conflict (WFC)/Family–Work Conflict (FWC)

As employees typically spend extended periods of time working in their companies, this has a severe impact on the conflict between work and family. WFC is a "specific form of inter-role conflict in which work and family roles are mutually discordant in some respect" (Allen, Cho & Meier, 2014: 101). This phenomenon is more prevalent in companies with high presenteeism climate where both the coworkers and supervisors may pressure employees to continue working beyond the time necessary for efficient performance at work. A presenteeism climate results from beliefs and values about the sector, department or organization and also the society (Nicholson & Johns, 1985) that compel employees to attend work despite being ill. Attributes such as competitiveness, extra-time valuation, difficulty of replacement and lack of supervisor support (Ferreira, Martinez, Cooper & Gui, 2015; Zhou, Martinez, Ferreira & Rodrigues, 2016) all contribute to WFC. Also, prior research has established that working time arrangements are important determinants of presenteeism in organizations (Böckerman & Laukkanen, 2010).

As with presenteeism, most studies in WFC have been conducted with US samples (Casper, Allen & Poelmans, 2014). There is a lack of research on the work–family interface outside North America, as cultural differences might play a significant role in this domain. Prior studies reported differences in WFC in countries with higher levels of gender equality (Behan, Drobnič & Präg, 2014). In addition, meta-analytic results have shown that work characteristics, role stressors, social support, and personality are WFC antecedents (Michel, Kotrba, Mitchelson, Clark & Baltes, 2011). Specifically, performing hard at work might reduce the energy and personal resources for other life domains such as the family (Michel et al., 2011). According to the equity theory (Adams, 1965), these effects may be mediated by any feelings of injustice due to perceptions of unequal treatment at work.

Variables such as the employees' individual characteristics (e.g., perception of the legitimacy of presenteeism/absenteeism), job characteristics (e.g., responsibilities and task interdependence) and contextual characteristics (e.g., competition among workers and pressure from supervisors) all contribute to foster a presenteeism climate (Ferreira et al., 2015; Nicholson & Johns, 1985; Zhou et al., 2016). WFC has significant correlations not only with presenteeism, but also with organizational justice and stress (Judge & Colquitt, 2004). The organizational justice construct concerns the degree to which people feel that they have been treated fairly by their organizations and those in their immediate surroundings (e.g., customers or patients) (Smith, Bond & Kağitçibaşi, 2006).

Moreover, the increasing interest in nontraditional gender roles, working hours and dual-income households has also been the subject of WFC research (Clark & Weismantle, 2003). Meta-analytic results have shown that work schedules, work characteristics, work role stressors, work social support, and personality are antecedents to WFC

(Michel et al., 2011). Exhausting physical or emotional commitment at work could also reduce the resources available for other life domains such as family (Michel et al., 2011). All these variables work as vital antecedents to WFC.

The Mediating Role of Work Engagement

Throughout the process of globalization, engagement has been one of the most discussed topics in the areas of Organizational Psychology and Human Resource Management. In this sense, the first scholar to study the concept of engagement was Kahn (1990: 694) characterizing it as "being fully physically, cognitively, and emotionally connected with their work roles." This author introduced the concept of psychological presence and mental state, which is related to both individual (e.g., personal growth and development) and organizational (e.g., quality of work performance) results. Later, engagement was defined as the ability to solve problems, connect with people, and develop innovative services (Bakker & Leiter, 2010). Engagement is a positive mental state related to work, including the dimensions of vigor (energy and mental resilience at work), dedication (level of involvement in work and feelings of pride and inspiration), and absorption (feeling of absolute concentration, as if "time is flying").

Prior research has shown that engagement is a strong predictor of organizational results, such as satisfaction, productivity, employee retention, extra-function performance, and health levels (Bakker & Leiter, 2010; Buckingham & Coffman, 1999). Accordingly, engagement is expected to facilitate role conflict and time-based tensions and, consequently, promote productivity despite the prevalence of health problems (Schaufeli et al., 2002). Employees who are "psychologically present at work" recognize the importance of their involvement and contribution to the organization, and strive to work hard even when suffering with health conditions. On the other hand, the absence of peer and organizational support to help coping with family and work tensions might facilitate a decrease in the engagement levels (Bakker & Leiter, 2010).

Individuals who experience conflicts in many dimensions of their lives might be prevented from enjoying work and other life aspirations and responsibilities, largely due to stress (Karanika-Murray, Duncan, Bridges & Griffiths, 2015). This is a psychological health condition with a major influence on presenteeism and productivity (Gosselin, Lemyre & Corneil, 2013). In short, conflicts and tensions between personal and professional life are expected to decrease the productivity associated with presenteeism, as employees tend to experience less engagement, mainly due to increased stress and reduced psychological well-being. However, we expect other mediating variables in this process, such as emotional exhaustion (Neto, Ferreira, Martinez & Ferreira, 2017). The latter variable might help explaining – along with engagement – the relationship between WFC/FWC and productivity loss due to presenteeism. Thus, we expect a partial mediation, hypothesizing that:

H1a.   *The relation between work–life conflict and productivity associated with presenteeism is partially mediated by work engagement.*

H1b.   *The relation between life–work conflict and productivity associated with presenteeism is partially mediated by work engagement.*

Cultural Values in Presenteeism and WFC/FWC

Cultural values can be summarized as commonly-held standards of what is acceptable, important, right, or workable in any community or society (Rokeach, 1973). One of the most used models of cross-cultural comparison is the GLOBE (Global Leadership and Organizational Behavior Effectiveness Research) project. This project has its roots in previous cross-cultural research findings (Hofstede, 1980) but it specifically identifies different cultural competencies and groups countries into societal clusters (House, Hanges, Javidan, Dorfman & Gupta, 2004).

Specifically, country characteristics play a significant role in the loss of productivity due to presenteeism (Knies, Candel, Boonen et al., 2012). Other studies have found cross-cultural differences for mental and physical presenteeism between Indian and US employees (Garczynski, Waldrop, Rupprecht & Grawitch, 2013) and also between British and Chinese workers (Lu et al., 2013a). Latin countries tend to have a high performance orientation, representing the need to seek high standards in decision-making and innovation (Kogut & Singh, 1988). This is a charismatic value-based dimension where people are inspired and their passion act as the engine which leads to performance.

The collective dimension plays a key role in encouraging and rewarding group members to perform well (House et al., 2004). Collectivism and leaders' charisma ensure employee's confidence and stability and also influence worker perceptions of organizational justice.

Accordingly, a presenteeism climate is contingent on values or beliefs embedded in the society, thus further suggesting the importance of research into how cultural differences affect the influence of presenteeism climate on employees' behavior. Also, there is evidence that indicates that family is a more extensive and pervasive aspect in Latin countries (House et al., 2004).

Moreover, the way people organize their daily lives and allocate time to family and work varies across cultures. Thus, WFC has distinct manifestations in different countries due to the material and psychological interdependence of the differing family models. Material interdependence appears stronger in collectivistic societies, whereas psychological interdependence has no cultural specificity (Smith et al., 2006). Collectivist societies are those cultures oriented to groups (e.g., Eastern Asian and Latin countries). In fact, most studies comparing individualist and collectivist cultures involve comparisons between the USA and Eastern Asian countries rather than Latin countries (Torres, 2009).

In this study, we will contrast two countries belonging to the Latin cluster (Javidan et al., 2005) – but with strong differentiation considering the high scores of masculine culture for Ecuador (MAS score of 63) and feminine culture for Portugal (MAS score of 31). These two countries despite being Latin integrate a different culture pattern that might affect the relationship between work and family as well between family and work (Hofstede, 1994). Countries with low masculine culture (such as Portugal) are more oriented toward relationships, quality of life and relationships are important aspects of life. Employees from these countries have preference for fewer working hours and have flexible family structures. According to the Hofstede Center, the key word is consensus, cooperation and concession are important aspects of life and decisions are made by participation. Contrarily, countries with high scores on masculine culture, such as Ecuador, tend to be more ego oriented and money/career are important aspects in life. Masculine societies tend to be driven by competition, career achievement and success throughout life. Employees from countries with high masculine culture seek membership in power and influenced groups, which allow them to achieve status and a successful career. Consequently, leisure and family are commonly sacrificed against work (Hofstede, 1994).

Taking into account that employees working in feminine cultures value the family and relationships, we expect that employees from Portugal (a feminine country) develop less acts of presenteeism. Countries with feminine cultures tend to be less competitive and the pressure to go to work despite being ill is less prominent, also because supervisors allow people to stay at home while ill. In turns, we expect a low correlation between work–family conflict and concentration and non-completed work. According to the Effort–Recovery (E–R) model (Meijman & Mulder, 1998), due to the extra time devoted to family, employees could switch off from work recovering from stressful events. Off-work activities with family are important recovery experiences that help employees to detach from work. The lower career investment as compared to the investment devoted to the family allows people from low masculine cultures to invest much more time in family issues, which will in turn affect their performance at work. In the opposite, employees from countries such as Ecuador, with high score in masculine values, tend to develop cultures of presenteeism (Ferreira et al., 2015) where supervisors and coworkers compel employees to attend work despite being ill. In general, employees tend to perceive high levels of competitiveness, pressure to work overtime and receive lack of supervisor support (Zhou et al., 2016).

Thus, we propose the following hypotheses:

H2.   *Countries with high masculine cultural values (Ecuador) tend to develop more acts of presenteeism than countries with low masculine (i.e., feminine) cultural values (Portugal).*

H3a.   *Due to the extra time devoted to work in countries with high masculine cultural values (Ecuador), work–family conflicts reveal a higher correlation with productivity losses due to presenteeism than in countries with low masculine (feminine) cultural values (Portugal).*

H3b.   *Due to the extra time devoted to family in countries with low masculine (i.e., feminine) cultural values (Portugal), family–work conflicts reveal a higher correlation with productivity losses due to presenteeism than in countries with high masculine cultural values (Ecuador).*

Method

Methodological Strategy

We conducted two separate studies to test our predictions. In Study 1, we sought to examine the mediating role of engagement in the relationship between WFC/FWC and productivity losses (SPS-6). To test our hypotheses, we used the PROCESS macro for IBM SPSS (Hayes, 2013) and linear regressions were conducted following the procedure by Baron and Kenny (1986). These authors recommend three steps to examine the relation between variables. First (Model 1), we regressed the independent variables (WFC/FWC) on the dependent variable (productivity loss – SPS-6), yielding a significant correlation coefficient. Second (Model 2), we regressed the independent variables (WFC/FWC) in the mediator variable (engagement), also yielding a significant correlation coefficient. Third (Model 3), we regressed both the independent variables (WFC/FWC) and mediator variable (engagement) in the dependent variable (productivity loss – SPS-6). Next, we assessed if there was a partial or a total mediation (i.e., a partial mediation occurs when the importance of the predictor variable in the model decreases but remains significant, whereas a total mediation exists when the regression coeficient of the predictor variable is no longer significant). All the linear regression assumptions were verified (Field, 2004).

In Study 2, we conducted our research in the health sector, as it ranks high in terms of emotional costs, employee turnover, and pressure to attend work while ill (Aronsson, Gustafsson & Dallner, 2000; Martinez & Ferreira, 2012). In order to choose the countries for comparison, we referred to the GLOBE model, which accounts for countries' clusters, such as the Latin countries (House et al., 2004). The identification of a general Latin cluster (considering Latin European and Latin American countries) is widespread in the cultural literature and appears as a typical outcome of colonialism (Kogut & Singh, 1988; Laurent, 1983). Taking into account that there are countries from Europe and America that share the same roots and language, we opted to choose Portugal (Europe) and Ecuador (America) – as both countries share the same cultural roots.

Participants and Procedure for Study 1

In Study 1, data were collected from a convenience sample totalizing 130 employees from a multinational company operating in the tech industry. All employees working in the company (n = 323) were invited to participate (40.2 percent response rate). Respondents received an email message from the HR Director and were asked to fill in an online questionnaire (Qualtrics platform) and were free to participate or decline. The research project was approved by the company's HR Department. Respondents were assured of complete confidentiality. Regarding sample characterization, 67.7 percent of participants were males. Participants were on average 35 years old (SD = 6.98), ranging from 22 to 60 years old. The majority of participants (57 percent) reported having children – specifically, 32 percent mentioned one child while 25 percent stated two or more children. Additionally, 45 percent of participants reported seniority of one year or less.

Participants and Procedure for Study 2

In Study 2, our total sample consisted of 225 health professionals from the health sector (nurses, doctors, physicians, laboratory analysts, and administrative staff), working at two large public hospitals in two different Latin countries: Portugal (n = 135) and Ecuador (n = 90). Respondents were asked to fill in a questionnaire (online or paper-and-pencil format) and were free to participate or decline. The research project was approved by the two hospitals' Institutional Review Boards. Respondents were assured of complete confidentiality. Regarding sample characterization, 53.3 percent and 50 percent of participants from Portugal and Ecuador (respectively) were female. Participants were on average 39.32 years old (SD = 10.04) in Portugal and 28.09 years (SD = 11.07) in Ecuador. Additionally, Portuguese participants reported 14.05 years of work experience (SD = 10.10) whereas Ecuadorians reported 7.03 years (SD = 7.15). Reported seniority levels (in years) were 12.82 (Portugal) and 4.67 (Ecuador). About 20.7 percent (Portugal) and 36.7 percent (Ecuador) of participants exerted supervision functions.

Measures

Work–Family Conflict/Family–Work Conflict (Netemeyer, Boles & McMurrian, 1996). WFC and FWC assess how work affects family life and how family affects work (respectively). Both constructs were assessed with five items each from the original scale (Netemeyer et al., 1996). All items were scored on a seven-point Likert-type, with higher scores representing a higher conflict. Example of items were: *"The amount of time my job takes up makes it difficult to fulfil family responsibilities"* and *"Due to work-related duties, I have to make changes to my plans for family activities."* WFC presented Cronbach alphas of .91 (Portugal) and .88 (Ecuador), and FWC presented Cronbach alphas of .94 (Portugal) and .91 (Ecuador). Construct validity was measured through Principal Components Analysis (PCA) with varimax rotation. The final rotated structure took into account the test allowed and two factors were obtained with 78.66 percent of the total explained variance for the Portuguese sample and 71.84 percent of the explained variance for the Ecuadorian sample.

Utrecht Work and Well-being Survey (UWES-9; Schaufeli, Bakker & Salanova, 2006). This nine-item scale measures the employees' work engagement. The scale's three dimensions include: vigor, dedication, and absorption. All items were scored on a seven-point Likert-type scale ranging from 0 (never) to 6 (always). Examples of items were: *"At my work, I feel bursting with energy,"* *"My job inspires me,"* and *"I am proud of the work that I do."* The scale presented a Cronbach alpha of .96.

Acts of Presenteeism. Previous studies (e.g., Johns, 2011) had adopted a single item question to measure the frequency of presenteeism (i.e., presenteeism behavior). Accordingly, participants were asked the following question: *"How many days did you go to work in the past six months even though you were sick or not feeling well?"*

Stanford Presenteeism Scale (SPS-6) (Koopman et al., 2002). In order to measure productivity losses due to sickness presence, we included the SPS-6 – specifically, the validated Portuguese version (Ferreira, Martinez, Sousa & Cunha, 2010), which includes two constructs of productivity losses: Avoiding Distraction and Non-Completing Work. Both dimensions were measured with three items. In line with previous studies (e.g., Neto, Ferreira, Martinez & Ferreira,

2017), in Study 2 we simplified the reading by replacing "Avoiding Distraction" with "Concentration." The items were answered on a five-point rating scale that ranged from "if you strongly disagree with the statement" (1) to "if you strongly agree with the statement" (5). Non-Completing Work items were reverse scored. Concentration presented Cronbach alphas of .81 (Portugal) and .66 (Ecuador) and Non-Completed Work presented Cronbach alphas of .87 (Portugal) and .71 (Ecuador). We also conducted a PCA (with Varimax orthogonal rotation) and Kaiser–Guttman scree test/Velicer to determine the number of factors to be retained. Results showed a bi-factorial structure (Concentration and Non-Completed Work) that explained 77.60 percent of the total variance for the Portuguese sample and 63.93 percent of the total variance for the Ecuadorian sample. In Study 1, we considered the composite score of SPS-6 – productivity loss, which is the mean score between Concentration and Non-Completed Work dimensions.

Structural Invariance (Only for Study 2)

We developed a Multi-Group Confirmatory Factor Analysis (MGCFA) to test structural invariance for the SPS-6 and WFC/FWC scales considering the invariance across samples from different countries (Portugal and Ecuador). We studied the measurement invariance by testing fitted models with incremental invariance properties. We adopted the methodology proposed by Cheung & Rensvold (2002) to test changes in CFI (ΔCFI) values and to compare nested models. In this sense, as the models became more restrictive, the difference of CFI between models should be equal or below to 0.01, meaning that the fit of the data did not change considerably. Accordingly, we found that – for the studied instruments – when constraining the measurement weights variance to be equal in both groups, a reduced decrease in fit for the studied samples did not change significantly the CFI value (ΔCFI < 0.01; p = .371). However, subsequent restrictive models suggested significant structural variance changes for measurement intercepts, structural covariances and measurement residuals. Taking into account that the measurement weights remained invariant across countries, we considered our instruments in the current study.

Table 1 *Means, standard deviations, and correlations among the measures (Study 1)*

Variables	M	SD	1	2	3
1. WFC	3.52	.93			
2. FWC	2.11	.82	.24*		
3. Engagement	5.43	1.16	−.25*	−.32**	
4. SPS-6 – Productivity losses	2.58	.63	.25*	.26**	−.29**

Notes. M = Mean; SD = Standard Deviation; WFC = Work–Family Conflict; FWC = Family–Work Conflict

**$p < .001$, *$p < .01$

Results

Study 1

In Study 1, we aimed to test if there was a significant positive relation between WFC and productivity loss as well as between FWC and productivity loss. We expected the former relations to be mediated by work engagement. Table 1 presents the means, standard deviations, and correlations among the measures. All variables presented significant correlations.

Table 2 shows the multiple linear regression analyses explaining the mediator role of job engagement in the relation between WFC/FWC and productivity losses (SPS-6). Accordingly, in Model 1, WFC and FWC are significantly and positively related with productivity losses (β = .17, $t(127)$ = 2.86, $p < .01$; β = .20. $t(127)$ = 3.09, $p < .01$, respectively). Next, in Model 2, both WFC and FWC were found to be negatively related with the mediator variable work engagement. Lastly, the independent variables WFC and FWC were tested with the mediator variable. Thus, in Model 3, engagement revealed a negative relation with productivity losses (β = −.13, $p < .01$), reducing the relation between both WFC (β = .12, $t(127)$ = 2.12, $p < .05$) and FWC (β = .14, $t(127)$ = 2.16, $p < .05$) with productivity losses due to presenteeism (SPS-6). Overall, data suggested a partial mediation (which confirmed both H1a and H1b). The indirect effect of WFC and FWC was then confirmed to be significant (Sobel Z = 1.99, $p < .05$; Sobel Z = 2.12, $p < .05$, respectively).

Table 2 *Multiple linear regressions explaining the mediator role of job engagement (Study 1)*

	Model 1	Model 2	Model 3
	SPS-6 – Productivity Losses	*Engagement*	SPS-6 – Productivity Losses
	β	β	β
WFC	.17**	–.32**	.12*
Engagement	-	-	–.13**
R_{square}	.06	.06	.12
FWC	.20**	–.45***	.14*
Engagement	-	-	–.13**
R_{square}	.07	.10	.12

Notes. Values are standardized regression coefficients; WFC = Work–Family Conflict; FWC = Family–Work Conflict
$***p < .001$, $**p < .01$, $*p < .05$

Study 2

Taking into account that there is a relationship between WFC/FWC and productivity losses, in Study 2 we aimed to test if this relationship was invariant across two different countries with the same Latin roots (Portugal and Ecuador). Moreover, Study 1 integrated a sample with employees from a multinational technological company. Thus, we aimed to see in Study 2 if the established relationships remained the same, considering a sample with employees from the health sector.

Table 3 shows means, standard deviations and correlations among WFC/FWC and the two SPS-6 dimensions as well the variable acts of presenteeism. Correlations results for the general sample showed that both WFC ($r = -.32$, $p < .01$) and FWC ($r = -.26$, $p < .01$) were significantly and negatively correlated with concentration. Results also showed that having higher WFC was significantly related to FWC ($r = -.50$, $p < .01$). Moreover, findings showed that the significant negative correlation between FWC and concentration appeared only in the Portuguese sample. In the Ecuadorian sample, the correlation between WFC and concentration was higher ($r = -.34$, $p < .01$) than in the Portuguese sample ($r = -.25$, $p < .01$).

Table 3 *Means, standard deviations and correlations among the measures for the total sample and for the Portuguese and Ecuadorian samples (Study 2)*

Total Sample (*n* = 225)						
	Mean	*SD*	1	2	3	4
1. Acts of presenteeism	18.71	47.72	-			
2. Concentration	3.52	.98	–.10	-		
3. Completed Work	3.77	1.06	.12	–.09	-	
4. WFC	4.00	2.00	.02	–.32**	.09	-
5. FWC	2.95	1.51	.01	–.26**	.01	.50**
Portuguese sample (*n* = 135)						
1. Acts of presenteeism	[1]10.87***	39.27	-			
2. Concentration	[2]3.78	.95	–.08	-		
3. Completed Work	[3]3.73**	1.16	.10	–.12	-	
4. WFC	[4]3.76***	1.66	–.10	–.25**	.13	
5. FWC	[5]2.67**	1.42	–.11	–.24**	.00	.42**
Ecuadorian Sample (*n* = 90)						
1. Acts of presenteeism	30.39	56.33	-			
2. Concentration	3.13	.89	.01	-		
3. Completed Work	3.82	.88	.15	.02	-	
4. WFC	4.36	1.44	.06	–.34**	–.02	-
5. FWC	3.39	1.54	.02	–.13	.01	.59**

Notes. T-test comparisons between Portuguese and Ecuadorian samples [1]t = –5.154***, [2]t =.653, [3]t = 2.786**, [4]t = 3.594***, [5]t = 3.056**; SD = Standard Deviation; WFC = Work–Family Conflict; FWC = Family–Work Conflict
***p < .001, **p < .01

Inferential analyses allowed us to compare the mean differences between the two studied countries. Results showed significant differences for the variables acts of presenteeism and concentration, with Ecuador presenting a higher frequency of acts of presenteeism (p < .01). This evidence supported hypothesis 2. On the contrary, the Portuguese sample presented a higher level of SPS-6 Concentration (p < .001). Moreover, results showed that employees from the Ecuadorian sample presented higher mean scores of WFC and FWC (p < .01).

We also used linear regression analysis (enter method) to estimate the impact of WFC/FWC (predictors) on the presenteeism measures (criterion). The three presenteeism measures (i.e., the SPS-6 constructs of concentration and non-completed work as well the acts of presenteeism) were used as dependent variables. As our data included participants from two countries (Portugal and Ecuador), we conducted both separate and combined analyses of results. Previously, we had tested regression assumptions with the use of collinearity statistics. All of the variance inflation factor scores were below 5.0, which revealed that these variables did not contain redundant information (Field, 2004). In the first set of regression analyses, we examined the impact of WFC/FWC dimensions on the SPS-6 – concentration measure for the Portuguese sample. The regression results are presented in Table 4 and showed that both WFC and FWC predict SPS-6 – concentration ($\beta = -.186$, $p < .05$, $\beta = -.161$, $p < .05$, respectively), whereas WFC positively predicts non-completed work ($\beta = .158$, $p < .10$). We found no significant correlations between WFC/FWC and acts of presenteeism. Overall, WFC/FWC dimensions accounted for 8.6 percent of the variance of the SPS-6 – concentration, and 2.1 percent of the explained variance for SPS-6 – non-completed work. Second, we analyzed the sample from Ecuador. In this case, only WFC was negatively related to SPS-6 – concentration ($\beta = -.186$, $p < .05$). In the Ecuadorian sample, WFC/FWC accounted for 12 percent of the variance of SPS-6 – concentration. We also found that WFC/FWC did not significantly contribute to the explanation of non-completed work and acts of presenteeism.

In general, and considering the two WFC/FWC antecedents, we found that WFC had the highest correlation with SPS-6 – concentration with employees from the Ecuador. Moreover, we found FWC only related with SPS-6 – concentration of employees from the Portuguese sample. Overall, the negative relationship was stronger for the WFC and the SPS-6 – concentration measures. These results partially supported hypotheses 3a and 3b. Against our expectations, the higher correlation between WFC and productivity in Ecuador (high masculine values) was only significant for the SPS-6 – concentration variable. As for hypothesis 3b, the expected higher correlation with productivity and FWC in countries with low masculine values was, again, significant only for the SPS-6 – concentration dimension (and non-significant for non-completed work).

Table 4 *Results of the regression analysis for WFC/FWC variables predicting presenteeism variables for the Portuguese and Ecuadorian samples (Study 2)*

	Portugal (n = 135)			Ecuador (n = 90)		
	Concentration	Non-Completed Work	Acts of Presenteeism	Concentration	Non-Completed Work	Acts of Presenteeism
	β	β	β	β	β	β
WFC	-.186*	.158†	-.065	-.397**	.081	.079
FWC	-.161*	-.066	-.025	.105	.076	-.025
F	6.192**	1.391	1.078	5.856**	.029	.194
R_{square}	.086	.021	.016	.120	.001	.004

Notes. Values are standardized regression coefficients; WFC = Work–Family Conflict; FWC = Family–Work Conflict
** $p < .01$, * $p < .05$, † $p < .10$

Discussion

In line with the findings from Janssens, Clays, de Clercq et al. (2016), this study verified that psychosocial characteristics, namely the conflict between work and family, plays an pivotal role on the concept of productivity associated with presenteeism. Moreover, not just the conflict between work and family, but also the conflict between all the dimensions of employees' lives, has a decisive impact in their productivity due to presenteeism. The results of the present study were also in line with the results of Opie & Henn (2013), who verified in a study conducted among mothers that the conflict between work and family has a negative impact on work engagement. This conclusion once again suggests that the family exerts a major influence in the engagement levels, thus human resource management should adopt a more integrative (and comprehensive) view of the individuals' lives. The Resource Conservation Model (Hobfoll, 1989) assumes that unfavorable situations experienced at work undermine the individuals' resources, such as well-being, health, and domains of personal life. The tension between work and personal life and vice versa (WFC/FWC) hinders employees' cognitive functioning, namely through insomnia, stress, burnout, concentration problems, and nervous system diseases (Neto et al., 2017; Sparks, Cooper, Fried & Shirom, 1997; Stankiewickz, Bortnowska & Lychmus, 2014). However, employees with higher levels of engagement reported less discomfort and distraction (De Beer, 2014), as well as fewer headaches, cardiovascular problems and stomach pains (Schaufeli & Bakker, 2004). In addition, workers experiencing engagement increased their professional performance, as they begin to manifest their positive emotions, as well as having better levels of physical and psychological health, and managing their professional and personal resources (Bakker, 2009). Thus, this study reveals that WFC/FWC increased productivity losses associated with presenteeism, and that engagement is important to explain this relationship.

Overall, there is ample evidence that each of the issues related to presenteeism is influenced by national cultural values (Lu et al., 2013a). Casper et al. (2014) summarized studies of the work–family domain and called for further research on the context of cultural influence. Other studies have reported differences in WFC/FWC in countries with higher levels of gender equality (Behan et al., 2014) and differences related to the individualism-collectivism and power distance cultural dimensions (Billing et al., 2014; Stock et al., 2016). Gender equality, individualism and power distance issues have a substantial impact in Latin countries, which tend to have high uncertainty avoidance, focusing on planning and creating stability as a way of dealing with life's uncertainties (Smith & Bond, 1999).

In Study 2, we developed a cross-cultural approach, with the aim to extend previous findings by comparing two Latin with distinct orientations toward the masculinity dimension (Hofstede, 1994). We found that employees with high masculine cultural values (Ecuador) tend to develop more acts of presenteeism than employees with low masculine (feminine) cultural values (Portugal). This is inline with the fact that presenteeism culture is highly prevalent in masculine and more competitive cultures (Ferreira et al., 2015; Hoftede, 1994; Simpson, 1998).

Also, due to the extra time devoted to work, in a country with high masculine cultural values (Ecuador), WFC reveals a higher correlation with productivity losses due to presenteeism than in countries with low masculine (feminine) cultural values (Portugal). Following the same line of reasoning, due to the extra time devoted to family, in a country with low masculine cultural values (Portugal), FWC reveals a higher correlation with productivity losses due to presenteeism than in countries with high masculine cultural values (Ecuador). Surprisingly, these effects only occurred for the concentration dimension of productivity loss due to presenteeism (and not for the non-completed work dimension). In our view, concentration might reveal to be a highly "psychological" variable, which is more prone to be affected by conflict and other cross-cultural discrepancies, whereas non-completed work relies much more on organizational variables such as technology and processes. From the literature (e.g., Sparks et al., 1997; Stankiewickz et al., 2014), we know that WFC/FWC may increase the propensity for psychological diseases such as depression and burnout, which in turn affects the employees' capacity to concentrate while performing their tasks. On the contrary, non-completed work is a more complex phenomenon, as it is more dependent from organizational support (i.e., supervisors and peers), task characteristics and other work environmental variables.

This research is not without limitations. First, we used self-reported descriptive measures in a technological sector (Study 1) and in two hospitals from two different countries (Study 2), rendering the generalizability of results problematic, especially outside the technological and health sectors. Second, data was essentially cross sectional, with measures focusing on a single moment in time. Because fear of being fired is much more a concern for private sector workers, it would be a good addition to the literature if future research could study cross-cultural presenteeism and WFC/FWC in both public and private companies (e.g., Ferreira & Martinez, 2012). Third, further research could study if presenteeism and WFC/FWC is pro-cyclical with macroeconomic trends. For instance, we anticipate that the occurrence of presenteeism would be likely to increase during recessions. Fourth, unemployment rates could play a role, as the fear of losing job might promote presenteeism. As of 2016 – due to the Euro zone economic crisis – Portugal has an employment rate of over 10 percent, which is significantly higher than in Ecuador – more than double (OECD, 2017). So, future studies could seek to compare Latin countries with similar levels of unemployment. Finally, company size (e.g., small vs. large firms) and industry type (apart from the health sector) could play a role in shaping presenteeism and WFC/FWC relations in Latin countries. On the other hand, given the large inter-individual variance (McCartney, 2003), it would be imperative to study which specific family resources workers might lose when they go to work while sick, thus triggering WFC. Also, it would be pertinent to recognize which resources are invested in the family (FWC) that might influence productivity losses when people are sick.

Concluding Remarks

In the modern economy, absenteeism continues to be a challenge for human resource management, but a new and growing body of literature has recognized that there can be other drains on workplace productivity that are not accounted for in a conventional attendance statistic. Workers could come to work every day, but still have their work and family suffer. In the case of presenteeism, they could – intentionally or unintentionally – have the quality of their work decline, requiring tasks to be redone or addressed by other workers, as well as engaging in WFC/FWC issues.

This study concluded that WFC/FWC decreases productivity associated with presenteeism, and that this relationship is mediated by the effect of engagement. Individuals seek to conserve their existing resources both at work and within the family. The energy spent in preserving these resources ends up affecting the productivity of employees when they are sick (presenteeism). However, WFC is higher in countries with more masculine cultures (Ecuador), essentially because culturally they emphasize the maintenance of work resources in detriment of family resources. On the other hand, in countries with a more feminine culture (Portugal), the conservation of resources is highlighted in the family, thus verifying a significant relationship between FWC and concentration. Overall, this need to preserve the resources of work and family reduces the levels of engagement (vigor, dedication and absorption), leading to a decrease in productivity levels.

In sum, for organizations to remain competitive in their markets, an effective management of presenteeism is essential (Hemp, 2004). To achieve this outcome, it is crucial that individuals feel synchronization between the various dimensions of their lives, such as family, health, social activity, hobbies, among others. Organizations and human resources professionals should adopt effective policies and practices which promote a work–life balance – such as mindfulness – thus emphasizing the need for both psychological well-being and physical health of employees (Kiburz, Allen & French, 2017). More studies are definitely needed in order to better understand the mechanisms behind these health at work and family issues, particularly in Latin countries.

Note

We thank Andrea Naranjo for her help with data collection in Equador for study 2.

References

Adams, J. S. (1965). Inequity in social exchange. in L. Berkowits (Ed.), *Advances in Experimental Social Psychology* (pp. 267–300). New York, NY: Academic Press.

Allen, T. D., Cho, E. & Meier, L. L. (2014). Work–family boundary dynamics. *Annual Review of Organizational Psychology and Organizational Behavior*, 1, 99–121.

Aronsson, G. & Gustafsson, K. (2005). Sickness presenteeism: Prevalence, attendance-pressure factors, and an outline of a model for research. *Journal of Occupational and Environmental Medicine*, 47, 958–966.

Aronsson, G., Gustafsson, K. & Dallner, M. (2000). Sick but yet at work. An empirical study of sickness presenteeism. *Journal of Epidemiology and Community Health*, 54, 502–509.

Bakker, A. B. (2009). Building engagement in the workplace, in R. J. Burke & C. L. Cooper (Eds.), *The Peak Performing Organization*, 50–72, Oxford, UK: Routledge.

Bakker, A. B. & Leiter, M. P. (2010). *Work Engagement: A Handbook of Essential Theory and Research*. New York, NY: Psychology Press.

Baron, R. M. & Kenny, D. A. (1986). The moderator-mediator variable distinction in social psychological research: conceptual, strategic and statistical considerations. *Journal of Personality and Social Psychology*, (51), 1173–1182.

Behan, B., Drobnič, S. & Präg, P. (2014). The work–family interface of service sector workers: a comparison of work resources and professional status across five European countries. *Applied Psychology: An International Review*, 63(1), 29–61.

Bergström, G., Bodin, L., Hagberg, J. et al. (2009). Does sickness presenteeism have an impact on future general health? *International Archives Environmental Health*, 82, 1179–1190.

Billing, T. K., Bhagat, R. S., Babakus, E. et al. (2014). Work–family conflict and organizationally valued outcomes: the moderating role of decision latitude in five national contexts. *Applied Psychology: An International Review*, 63(1), 62–95.

Böckerman, P. & Laukkanen, E. (2010). Predictors of sickness absence and presenteeism: Does the pattern differ by a respondent's health? *Journal of Occupational and Environmental Medicine*, 52(3), 332–335.

Buckingham, M. & Coffman, C. (1999). *First, Break all the Rules: What the World's Greatest Managers do Differently*. New York, NY: Simon & Shuster.

Casper, W. J., Allen, T. D. & Poelmans, S. A. Y. (2014). International perspectives on work and family: an introduction to the special section. *Applied Psychology: An International Review*, 63(1), 1–4.

Cheung, G. W. & Rensvold, R. B. (2002). Evaluating goodness-of-fit indexes for testing measurement invariance. *Structural Equation Modeling*, 9(2), 233–255.

Clark, S. C. (2000). Work-family border theory: A new theory of work/family balance, *Human Relations*, 53(6), 747–770.

Clark, S. L. & Weismantle, M. (2003). *Employment Status: 2000*. Census Brief Series.

Coté, D. & Haccoun, R. R. (1991). L'absentéisme des femmes et des hommes: Une meta analyse. *Canadian Journal of Administrative Sciences*, 8, 130–139.

De Beer, L. T. (2014). The effect of presenteeism-related health conditions on employee work engagement levels: A comparison between groups. *SA Journal of Human Resource Management*, 12(1), 1–8.

Dew, K., Keefe, V. & Small, K. (2005). "Choosing" to work when sick: Workplace presenteeism. *Social Science & Medicine*, 60, 2273–2282.

Ferreira, A. I. & Martinez, L. F. (2012). Presenteeism and burnout among teachers in public and private Portuguese elementary schools. *The International Journal of Human Resource Management*, 23(20), 4380–4390.

Ferreira, A. I., Martinez, L. F., Cooper, C. L. & Gui, D. M. (2015). LMX as a negative predictor of presenteeism climate: A cross-cultural study in the financial and health sectors. *Journal of Organizational Effectiveness: People and Performance*, 2(3), 282–302.

Ferreira, A. I., Martinez, L. F., Sousa, L. M. & Cunha, J. V. (2010). Tradução e validação para a língua portuguesa das escalas de presentismo WLQ-8 e SPS-6 [Validation into Portuguese language of presenteeism scales WLQ-8 and SPS-6]. *Avaliação Psicológica*, 9, 253–266.

Field, A. (2004). *Discovering Statistics using SPSS*. Sage: London.

Garczynski, A. M., Waldrop, J. S., Rupprecht, E. A. & Grawitch, M. J. (2013). Differentiation between work and nonwork self-aspects as a predictor of presenteeism and engagement: Cross-cultural differences. *Journal of Occupational Health Psychology*, 18(4), 417–429.

Gosselin, E. & Lauzier, M. (2011). Le Présentéisme. *Revue Française de Gestion*, 211, 15–26.

Gosselin, E., Lemyre, L. & Corneil, W. (2013). Presenteeism and absenteeism: Differentiated understanding of related phenomena. *Journal of Occupational Health Psychology*, 18(1), 75–86.

Harter, J. K., Schmidt, F. L. & Hayes, T. L. (2002). Business-unit – level relationship between employee satisfaction, employee engagement, and business outcomes: A meta-analysis. *Journal of Applied Psychology*, 87, 268–279.

Hayes, A. F. (2013). *Introduction to Mediation, Moderation, and Conditional Process Analysis: A Regression-Based Approach*. New York, NY: The Guilford Press.

Hemp, P. (2004). Presenteeism – At work: But out of it. *Harvard Business Review*, 82, 49–58.

Hobfoll, S. E. (1989). Conservation of resources: A new attempt at conceptualizing stress. *American Psychologist*, 44, 513–524.

Hofstede, G. (1980). *Culture's Consequences: International Differences in Work-Related Values*. Beverly Hills, CA: Sage Publications.

Hofstede, G. (1994). *Cultures and Organizations: Software of the Mind*. London: Harper Collins Publishers.

House, R. J., Hanges, P. J., Javidan, M., Dorfman, P. & Gupta, V. (2004). *Culture, Leadership, and Organizations: The GLOBE Study of 62 Societies*. Thousand Oaks, CA: Sage Publications.

Janssens, H., Clays, E., de Clercq, B. et al. (2016). Association between psychosocial characteristics of work and presenteeism: a cross-sectional study. *International Journal of Occupational Medicine and Environmental Health*, 29(2), 331–344.

Javidan, M., House, R., Dorfman, P., Hanges, P. & Luque, M. S. (2006). Conceptualizing and measuring cultures and their consequences: A comparative review of GLOBE's and Hofstede's approaches. *Journal of International Business Studies*, 37, 897–914.

Javidan, M., Stahl, G. K., Brodbeck, F. & Wilderom, C. P. M. (2005). Cross-border transfer of knowledge: Cultural lessons from Project GLOBE. *Academy of Management Executive*, 19(2), 59–76.

Johns, G. (2010). Presenteeism in the workplace: A review and research agenda. *Journal of Organizational Behavior*, 31, 519–542.

Johns, G. (2011). Attendance dynamics at work: The antecedents and correlates of presenteeism, absenteeism and productivity loss. *Journal of Occupational Health Psychology*, 16(4), 483–500.

Judge, T. A. & Colquitt, J. A. (2004). Organizational justice and stress: The mediating role of work-family conflict. *Journal of Applied Psychology*, 89(3), 395–404.

Kahn, W. A. (1990). Psychological conditions of personal engagement and disengagement at work. *Academy of Management Journal*, 33, 692–724.

Karanika-Murray, M., Pontes, H. M. & Griffiths, M. D. (2015). Sickness presenteeism determines job satisfaction via affective-motivational states. *Social Science and Medicine*, 139, 100–106.

Kiburz, K. M., Allen, T. D. & French, K. A. (2017). Work–family conflict and mindfulness: Investigating the effectiveness of a brief training intervention. *Journal of Organizational Behavior*, forthcoming.

Knies, S., Candel, M. M., Boonen, A. et al. (2012). Lost productivity in four European countries among patients with rheumatic disorders are absenteeism and presenteeism transferable? *Pharmacoeconomics*, 30(9), 795–807.

Kodz, J., Harper, H. & Dench, S. (2002). *Work–Life Balance: Beyond the Rhetoric. Institute for Employment Studies Report,* 384. London: IES.

Kogut, B. & Singh, H. (1988). The effect of national culture on the choice of entry mode. *Journal of International Business Studies,* 19 (3), 411–432.

Koopman, C., Pelletier, K. R., Murray, J. F. et al. (2002). Stanford Presenteeism Scale: Health status and employee productivity. *Journal of Epidemiology and Community Health,* 44, 14–20.

Laurent, A. (1983). The cultural diversity of Western conceptions of management. *International Studies of Management & Organization,* 13(1/2), 75–96.

Loeppke, R., Taitel, M., Haufle, V., Parry, T., Kessler, R. C. & Jinnett, K. (2009). Health and productivity as a business strategy: A multi-employer study. *Journal of Occupational Environmental Medicine,* 51(4), 411–428.

Lu, L., Cooper, C. L. & Lin, H. Y. (2013a). A cross-cultural examination of presenteeism and supervisory support. *Career Development International,* 18(5), 440–456.

Lu, L., Lin, H. Y. & Cooper, C. L. (2013b). Unhealthy and present: motives and consequences of the act of presenteeism among Taiwanese employees. *Journal of Occupational Health Psychology,* 18(4), 406–416.

Martinez, L. F. & Ferreira, A. I. (2012). Sick at work: Presenteeism among nurses in a Portuguese public hospital. *Stress and Health,* 28(4), 297–304.

McCartney, C. (2003). *Work–Life Balance: A Guide for Organisations.* West Sussex, UK: Roffey Park Institute.

Meijman, T. F. & Mulder, G. (1998). Psychological aspects of workload, in P. J. D. Drenth & H. Thierry (Eds.), *Handbook of Work and Organizational Psychology (vol. 2). Work Psychology* (pp. 5–33). Hove, England: Psychology Press.

Michel, J. S., Kotrba, L. M., Mitchelson, J. K., Clark, M. A. & Baltes, B. B. (2011). Antecedents of work–family conflict: A meta-analytic review. *Journal of Organizational Behavior,* 32(5), 689–725.

Netemeyer, R. G., Boles, J. S. & McMurrian, R. (1996). Development and validation of work–family conflict and family–work conflict scales. *Journal of Applied Psychology,* 81(4), 400–410.

Neto, M., Ferreira, A. I., Martinez, L. F. & Ferreira, P. C. (2017). Workplace bullying and presenteeism: The path through emotional exhaustion and psychological wellbeing. *Annals of Work Exposures and Health,* 61(5), 528–538.

Nicholson, N. & Johns, G. (1985). The absence culture and the psychological contract: Who's in control of absence? *Academy of Management Review*, 10, 397–407.

OECD (2017). Unemployment rate (indicator). doi:10.1787/997c8750-en. Retrieved February 15, 2017 from https://data.oecd.org/unemp/unemploy ment-rate.htm.

Opie, T. J. & Henn, C. M. (2013). Work–family conflict and work engagement among mothers: Conscientiousness and neuroticism as moderators. *South African Journal of Industrial Psychology*, 39(1), 1–12.

Richman, A. (2006). Everyone wants an engaged workforce: how can you create it? *Workspan*, 49, 36–39.

Rokeach, M. (1973). *The Nature of Human Values*. New York. NY: The Free Press.

Schaufeli, W. B. & Bakker, A. B. (2004). Job demands, Job resources and their relationship with burnout and engagement: A multi-sample study. *Journal of Organizational Behavior*, 25, 293–315.

Schaufeli, W. B., Bakker, A. B. & Salanova, M. (2006). The measurement of work engagement with a short questionnaire: A cross-national study. *Educational and Psychological Measurement*, 66(4), 701–716.

Schaufeli, W. B., Salanova, M., González-Romá, V. & Bakker, A. B. (2002). The measurement of engagement and burnout: A two sample confirmatory factor analytic approach. *Journal of Happiness Studies*, 3, 71–92.

Simpson, R. (1998). Presenteeism, power and organizational change: long hours as a career barrier and the impact on the working lives of women managers. *British Journal of Management*, 9, S37–S50.

Smith, P. B. & Bond, M. H. (1999). *Social Psychology Across Cultures* (2nd ed). Massachusetts: Allyn and Bacon.

Smith, P. B., Bond, M. H. & Kağitçibaşi, Ç. (2006). *Understanding Social Psychology Across Cultures: Living and Working in a Changing World*. London: Sage.

Sparks, K., Cooper, C., Fried, Y. & Shirom, A. (1997). The effects of hours of work on health: a meta-analytic review. *Journal of Occupational and Organizational Psychology*, 70, 391–408.

Stankiewickz, J., Bortnowska, H. & Lychmus, P. (2014). Conditions necessary to maintain work-life balance of employees – in the light of the research results. *Management: The Journal of University of Zielona Góra*, 18, 326–340.

Stevens, M. (2004). Present dangers: Presenteeism is the next area of focus as companies seek to maximize their investment in human capital by improving productivity and promoting employee health and wellness – disability. *Risk & Insurance*, online content retrieved December 15, 2016 from www.injurynet.com.au/resource/Pr esent_Dangers.pdf.

Stock, R. M., Strecker, M. M. & Bieling, G. I. (2016). Organizational work–family support as universal remedy? A cross-cultural comparison of China, India and the USA. *The International Journal of Human Resource Management*, 27(11), 1192–1216.

Torres, C. V. (2009). *Do Social Norms Have an Influence in Leadership Style Preference? Assessing Leadership Style Differences Between Americans and Brazilians*. London: VDM.

Worrall, L., Cooper, C. & Campbell, F. (2000). The new reality for UK managers: Perpetual change and employment instability. *Work, Employment & Society*, 14, 647–668.

Zhou, Q., Martinez, L. F., Ferreira, A. I. & Rodrigues, P. (2016). Supervisor support, role ambiguity and productivity associated with presenteeism: A longitudinal study. *Journal of Business Research*, 69(9), 3380–3387.

12 | Presenteeism in the Chinese Work Context

YANXIA WANG, CHIH-CHIEH CHEN, AND
PATRICIA FOSH

Introduction

Rapid economic development in China provides both opportunities
and challenges for employees. The report by the International
Institute for Management and Development (IMD), *Competitiveness
and the Global Trends Roadmap: 2015–2050*, states that "despite the
slowing growth rates, the USA and China will lead the way to global
economic recovery with more than half of global growth coming from
these countries." Thus, on the one hand, individuals are able to pursue
a better life with convenient and comfortable experiences. On the other
side, however, individuals employed by organizations are faced with
increasing work demands. This leads employees being compelled to
work harder and harder. For example, Lu & Chou (in press) state that
17.6 percent of Taiwanese employees work more than 50 hours per
week (Lu & Chou, in press).[1] Such increased pressure on employees
can lead to presenteeism, defined in this chapter as employees coming
to work although they are ill.[2] Displays of presenteeism can lead,
however, to mental and physical health problems for employees that,
in turn can affect organizational profitability.

Presenteeism is recognized worldwide as a workplace phenomenon,
usually conceived of as employees' reaction to job insecurity when
faced with the difficulty of managing their sickness and productivity.
Presenteeism has two components: presenteeism motivation and presenteeism behavior. Below, we refer, in short, to presenteeism behavior
as presenteeism, except where it is necessary to distinguish between the
two components.

Presenteeism is costly for organizations: a number of studies in
Western countries, such as the USA, the UK, and Australia, have
estimated the losses caused by presenteeism and have found

presenteeism costs much more than absenteeism does (Centre for Mental Health, 2011; Hemp, 2004; Medibank, 2011[3]). The considerable costs attributed to presenteeism have led in a number of countries to considerable scholarly interest in establishing the reasons for presenteeism, explaining its mechanisms and understanding its consequences (Johns, 2010). Most research on, and scale development for, presenteeism has been conducted in Western countries. British and other European scholars in the fields of management, epidemiology, and occupational health have focused on the effect of job insecurity on presenteeism, while American and Australian scholars have focused on the effect of presenteeism on work productivity (Johns, 2010; Garrow, 2016).

There is a compelling need to examine presenteeism in non-Western countries such as China, given that scholars agree that employees' presenteeism is strongly affected by their cultural background (Lu, Cooper & Lin, 2013a). In China, employees' perceptions, motivations and priorities in balancing their work and life are strongly influenced by their upbringing and we need to understand how this affects presenteeism.

Over a long period, Chinese society has established a value system that differs considerably from that of Western countries. The main philosophical tenets in Confucianism, Taoism, and other Chinese doctrines emphasize values such as harmony, balance, and reciprocity (Fan, 2000; Redding, 1990). These values are deeply rooted in social rules, families and organizations in China and continue to influence Chinese employees today to a significant degree (Ralston, Gustafson, Elsass, Cheung & Terpstra, 1992; Vertinsky Tse, Wehrung & Lee, 1990; Whitcomb, Erdener & Li 1998).

In this chapter, we discuss how current research on presenteeism behavior and motivation and assess its relevance for understanding presenteeism in the Chinese context. First, we review the limited research and data available on the prevalence and consequences of presenteeism behavior in China and its effects on organizations and employees' well-being. Second, we combine the limited available research on presenteeism motivation in China and other Asian countries in order to explore the reasons why Chinese employees may attend work even when they are ill. These reasons reflect the influence of national culture, laws and regulations, organizational actors and features, and employees' personality and experiences. Finally, we make suggestions for tackling presenteeism in the workplace – both short-term and long-term. We offer practical advice for managers for reducing the negative effects of presenteeism, advice that takes account of national culture. We also, however, emphasize the importance of legislation and organizational policies in reducing presenteeism.

How Prevalent is Presenteeism in China and What are its Consequences?

The issue of presenteeism has caught the attention of those in many Western countries. Both in consultants' reports and in academic research there is general agreement that presenteeism is an ongoing workplace problem. The severity of the problem in Western countries is illustrated by the following examples. The Centre for Mental Health, in a UK study, compared the costs of presenteeism and absenteeism due to mental ill health problems and concluded that presenteeism cost about £15.1 billion per year, whereas absenteeism cost only £4.8 billion.[4] Medibank issued a series of reports that demonstrated that presenteeism cost the Australian economy $34.1 billion in 2010, a figure which amounted to a reduction of 2.7 percent in GDP.

So far, there is limited statistical information on the prevalence of presenteeism and its consequences available in China. In terms of prevalence, we note the study by Lu et al. (2013a), who demonstrate that, compared to their Western counterparts, Chinese workers report a higher rate of presenteeism. We note the work of the Human Resource Research Center in Qianchengwuyou[5] that gives, for 2016, the proportion in China of employees displaying presenteeism. In its report, *The organizational cost of absence leave*, the Center examined a sample of 362 employees and 392 organizations; these organizations were drawn from various industries, the top three being informational technology, consumer goods, and manufacture. Its report showed that, in 2016, 73.5 percent of employees sampled reported presenteeism. We note that one of the biggest online recruiting platforms (ZhilianZhaopin)[6] in a 2015 report, *Survey on the quality of life in the workplace: Eight hours among white-collar workers*, found that more than 67 percent of office clerks were required to work at least five hours overtime per week. Finally, we note Lu, Lin & Cooper's (2013b) view that the negative influences of presenteeism on physical health, mental health, and job satisfaction among Chinese employees are becoming more prominent in studies of Chinese organizations.

In terms of the consequences of presenteeism, there is again limited information for China. Authorities in China are beginning to pay attention to the consequences of presenteeism. For example, in 2014 the Seventh Chinese Mental Health Academic Conference was held in Beijing, in which the Association of Mental Health in China released a report entitled *Depression in the Chinese workplace*. It was the first survey of depression that included both employers and employees in China. The results demonstrated that depression is very damaging in Chinese workplace: nearly 70 percent of patients took sick leave in order to obtain medical treatment, and more than half were forced to quit their jobs due to inattention, distraction, and low productivity.

The Japanese expression, *karoshi*, refers to death by overwork and was first used in 1978 (Iwasaki, Takahashi & Nakata, 2006). *Karoshi* has attracted a great deal of attention in China as well as in other Asian countries and regions such as South Korea and Taiwan (Yang, Yang & Li, 2015). *Karoshi* has been found to be more prevalent in certain occupations such as IT and the education industry and to have more effect on knowledge-based workers than on manual workers, and more effect on younger workers than on older ones. Karoshi has relevance for Chinese workplaces. ZhilianZhaopin in its 2015 report *Survey on the quality of life in the workplace: Eight hours among white-collar workers* states that 92 Chinese employees died from working overtime in 2015 and that the average age of people suffering *karoshi* was 44 years. Those subjects who worked in public security, journalism, informational technology, and education died even younger.

For other effects on employees short of death by overwork, ZhilianZhaopin, in its reports referred to above, states that more than 70 percent of office clerks in its study experienced one or more of 15 medical conditions, including constipation, migraine/headache, and back, neck, and spinal pain.

The Chinese research so far fits well with Western research such as that reported by The Centre for Mental Health, in a discussion paper on managing presenteeism behavior, where it concluded that mental health issues, such as depression and anxiety, are more likely to lead to presenteeism (Centre for Mental Health, 2011). It also fits with a study, conducted by KPMG Econtech on behalf of Medibank, which reported that 12 medical conditions led to presenteeism, of which depression was the most significant (21 percent).

To help our review, we consider below evidence from other countries that we can use to understand the consequences of presenteeism more systematically. The consequences of presenteeism can be roughly categorized as health-related or pecuniary-related (Collins et al., 2005; Lu et al., 2013b).

In terms of health consequences, recovery theory suggests that individuals need time and energy to recover from sickness (Meijman & Mulder, 1998). Presenteeism, however, deprives sick employees of recovery time, thereby causing their physical and mental health to deteriorate in the long run (Gosselin, Lemyre & Corneil, 2013; Lu et al., 2013b). Further Chinese research is needed in this area.

In terms of pecuniary consequences, cost associated with presenteeism is usually caused by reduced work output, errors on the job and failure to meet performance standards (Schultz, Chen & Edinton, 2009). While absenteeism is easy to observe and count number of employees who do not turn up for work and consequent productivity loss, presenteeism is not. Employers are less able to identify employees' various medical conditions and consider how they impact on productivity (Hemp, 2004); further, they do not have sight of their employees' medical receipts and pharmacy bills. Thus organizations lack the data necessary to assess the extent of their employees' presenteeism (Schultz et al., 2009). In practice, different methodologies and measurement scales are used to evaluate and estimate productivity losses: for example, Stanford Presenteeism Scale (SPS-6), Work and Health Interview (WHI), and Work Limitations Questionnaire (WLQ). Some Chinese researchers have investigated the psychometric properties of those measurement scales by using Chinese samples because there are not Chinese-specific calculation tools yet. WLQ and SPS-6 have, however, been shown to have reliability and validity for Chinese employees (Dong, Liu, Wang & Peng, 2013; Zhao, Dai, Yan, Yang & Fu, 2010).

Schultz et al. (2009) in their literature review, proposes a three-step method for converting productivity loss into a so-called dollar value. The first step is to convert the percentage decrease in productivity due to presenteeism into the number of hours per week is to multiply the percentage by the required working hours per week for one employee. The second step is to multiply the reduced working hours due to presenteeism by the average hourly wage and benefits for one employee, which gives the monetary loss for an individual employee for one week. The last step is to multiply that figure by the number of employees with the same situation within the organization in order to compute the total financial cost attributed to presenteeism per week. Schultz et al. (2009) also argue, however, that researchers need to be prudent when interpreting the dollar value of those losses (Garrow, 2016; Schultz et al., 2009). With the development of information technology, online evaluation tools have emerged for use in estimating and calculating the productivity loss of presenteeism, such as the Integrated Benefits Institute platform (Hou & Zhan, 2016)[7]. These tools are, however, designed to fit organizations in the USA. As we saw above, there are, so far, no specific calculator or measurement scales designed to suit the Chinese context. Further research is needed to develop measurement and calculation tools suited to the Chinese context, enabling more precise calculations for presenteeism monetary loss in China.

Why Do Chinese Employees Attend Work While Ill?

There is also limited research on presenteeism motivation in mainland China. There have been, however, several studies undertaken in Taiwan (Lu et al., 2013b; Lin & Lu, 2013). Due to the increasing concern in China over the effects of presenteeism on organizations' profitability and employees' well-being, there is an urgent need to understand why Chinese employees attend work even though they are ill. Given this lack of research, we set out in this section some suggestions for presenteeism motivation for Chinese employees; we base these on extant Western findings but we also include a consideration of the effect of the Chinese context.

A substantial number of Western scholars have investigated employee motivation for presenteeism: for example, Johns (2010), Baker-McClearn et al. (2010), and so on. These scholars usually focus on the role of organizational, work-related, and personal-related factors. Scholars are now, however, beginning to consider the influence of culture on presenteeism motivation and to understand how cultural values and social trends affect employees' presenteeism.

We begin by considering the effect of national culture and legislation on presenteeism motivation. We then illustrate the effect of organizational culture and policies on this phenomenon, followed by an explanation of the effect of employees' social experiences, organizational experiences, and psychological characteristics. We finish by discussing how presenteeism is affected by economic fluctuations, by industry, and by individual demographics.

The Effect of National Culture and Legislation on Presenteeism

China is an ancient nation with a longstanding and uninterrupted history, and its culture has been passed down for thousands of years. The major indigenous cultural values of Confucianism dominate the Chinese people's view of their responsibilities, their expected roles, and their behaviors (Fung, 1997: 45).

Confucius gave his disciples a set of propositions that he believed to benefit society (Fung, 1997, chapter 4). The core tenets of these propositions are heartedness and righteousness *(Ren and Yi)*: these two tenets regulate individuals' both internal and external behavior. They establish individuals' general societal expectations and impose consequential obligations. In the Analects, heartedness *(Ren)* is described as all virtues combined, rather than denoting a special kind of virtue. *Ren* involves loving others (Analects, XII, 2.2.). Righteousness *(Yi)* means the "oughtness" in society, based on the premise that everyone has certain things that he ought to do in society (Fung, 1997: 58). The five cardinal dyadic relationships *(Wu Lun)* express both *Ren* and *Yi*, showing how individuals are obliged to behave towards others: sovereign/subject, father/son, husband/wife, elder/younger brother, friend/friend; thus, the subject must always obey his sovereign and a wife must obey her husband. Given these relationships, Chinese employees have a strong disposition to ignore their own needs in order to meet those of their employers (Lin & Lu, 2013).

There are a number of aphorisms in China that show how Confucian tenets are enshrined in popular culture: considering these can help us to understand how Chinese employees may attend work despite sickness. Examples include "bend one's body and exhaust one's energy until the last moment" *(ju gong jin cui)*, and "do not leave the battlefield due to a minor wound" *(qing shang bu xia huo xian)*. These aphorisms, common across Chinese industries and organizational levels, support the moral expectation that one goes to work if ill.

Work values stemming from Confucianism positively correlate with work attitudes and behavior amongst Chinese employees (Yang &

Cheng, 1987). In order to sustain a harmonious relationship with their supervisor and colleagues, Chinese employees, when faced by work–life conflict, tend to satisfy organizational needs first and their life needs second. Their personal health is often the last factor they consider. The relationship between presenteeism and Chinese national cultural values works two ways. On the one hand, ill employees display presenteeism as a way of saving "face" *(mianzi)*, to show that they can accomplish their tasks. Fear of informing their supervisors or colleagues of their health problems discourages employees from asking for sick leave. On the other hand, Chinese employees have imbibed the cultural values of persistence and endurance with the result that they fail to perceive absenteeism as legitimate and are, thereby, reluctant to ask for permission to take sick leave. Hansen & Anderson (2008), in their Danish study, found that, when employees had a conservative attitude towards sick leave and absenteeism, they displayed greater presenteeism. This suggests that Chinese employees may have a higher potential for presenteeism as they are more tolerant of strict sick leave regulations. Note also Lu and Chou's (in press) point that the presenteeism in Chinese organizations may be an extreme response to long working hours, to overwhelming work demands; thus, presenteeism may be seen as a response to tough working conditions that fits well with the strong Chinese work ethic.

In addition to the influence of national cultural values, the lack of legislation and poor implementation of extant legislation increases the presenteeism in Chinese workplaces. In China, although Labor Law (No. 36 in the subsection of Working hours and holidays) states that an employee's working hours should not exceed eight hours per weekday and 44 hours per week on average, the implementation of this law is not monitored and, in general, violators are not punished.

A further legislative factor affecting presenteeism in China is the provision of sickness benefit. According to Chinese regulations, employees off work are paid only part of their normal wage, although this should not be lower than 80 percent of the minimum wage.[8] Thus, for financial reasons, employees are motivated to display presenteeism. Furthermore, the Regulations on Work Injury Insurance cover only industrial injury or occupational disease; this limits employees' receipt of medical subsidies, again motivating employees to work while ill.[9] Research by Hansen & Andersen (2008), in Denmark, also demonstrates how national provision of sick pay may affect presenteeism.

These authors found that blue-collar and unskilled workers were covered by different sick-pay systems and displayed different rates of presenteeism. Although employees had the right to receive pay from their first day of the illness when they took sick leave, only white-collar workers were paid their full daily salary; many blue-collar and unskilled workers were entitled only to 90 percent of the minimum wage in their trade.

The Effect of Organizational Culture and Policies on Presenteeism

Organizational culture has an important effect on presenteeism (Johns, 2010). Dew and colleagues (2005) conducted research on a number of organizations in New Zealand in order to investigate the relationship between organizational culture and presenteeism. Using interviews and focus groups, they found that working culture and climate were significantly related to employees' presenteeism. In a small private hospital in their study, employees described their workplace as a "sanctuary" and they came to work when ill because they wanted to keep pace with their team members and to be loyal to their colleagues. In a large public hospital in their study, employees used the metaphor of a "battleground" in order to describe their workplace; they came to work when ill due to their strong sense of responsibility and moral obligation. In a small manufacturing site in their study, employees compared their organization to a "ghetto" where they experienced little security and a lack of care, with the result that they felt they had no choice but to come to work when ill due to management pressure (Dew, Keefe & Small, 2005).

Turning to China, although the so-called "iron rice bowl" in state-owned firms has been broken, there still remain some differences between Chinese and Western organizations – for example, the much greater emphasis in Chinese organizations on harmony and performance orientation (Cheng, 1990; Liu, 2003). Thus, Chinese employees' greater willingness to pursue harmonious relationship with their supervisors and colleagues, and their greater motivation to work hard for extra rewards and benefits, encourage them to display presenteeism more frequently than their Western counterparts (Lu et al., 2013a).

We also need to consider how the intense business competition and abundant labor supply in China result in higher levels of job insecurity that, in turn, lead to long work hours. Research has shown that long working hours are much more prevalent in East Asian countries than in Western countries. Lausanne's IMD publishes data on yearly working hours across the world; its data showed that, on average, Korean employees worked 2,312 hours per year, Taiwanese employees worked 2,074 hours per year, and Japanese employees worked 1,997 hours per year (IMD 2010; Cheng, Park, Kim & Kawakami, 2012; Lu & Chou, in press); in contrast, the data showed that most employees in Western countries worked in the range of 1,600–1,900 hours per year. We suggest that the number of hours worked by Chinese employees would be similar to those worked in these Asian countries. Given the demand to work long hours in China, employees are encouraged to display presenteeism as a consequence of their bicultural self (Lu, Kao, Chang, Wu & Jin, 2008). On the one hand, the individual-oriented self urges employees to display presenteeism in order to obtain extra benefits or rewards: this can be described as constructive motivation. On the other hand, in order to comply with societal role expectations, the social-oriented self-pressurizes employees to perform in line with others, and thereby weakens their uniqueness; this be described as compulsive motivation (Lu & Chou, in press; Porter, 2004).

In terms of the effect of organizational policies, organizational sick pay provision has an important effect on presenteeism. Harsh restrictions on sick leave can increase presenteeism: employees either feel guilty about letting down their team members or, if their organization limits the number of occasions on which staff may take sick leave, regard the sick absence as risky (Grinyer & Singleton, 2000).[10] The common practice in China of rewarding employees for full attendance (Lin & Lu, 2013) also increases employees' propensity to display presenteeism. More generally, Garrow (2016) suggests that positive managerial treatment can reduce absenteeism and, thereby, increase the possibility of employees displaying presenteeism (Garrow, 2016).

Additionally, managerial introduction and implementation of advanced Western management practices, such as flexible working time, have had an unexpected influence on presenteeism in Chinese workplaces. The primary aim of a flexible working time is to reduce employees' tensions at work by providing them with more freedom in handling their work tasks. Due to its outcome-orientation, flexible working creates difficulties, however, in measuring and supervising work hours. This increases the possibility of employees working while ill, even when employees are not required to present at the work-place (Lu & Chou, in press).

The Effect of Employees' Organizational Experiences, Social Experiences, and Psychological Characteristics on Presenteeism

Beginning with organizational experiences, we noted before how the tendency to work overtime increases the probability of displaying presenteeism. Lu et al. (2013b) identified two distinct dimensions in Chinese employees' motivation for presenteeism behavior: the avoid-ance and approach dimensions. The avoidance dimension attributes presenteeism to the fear of losing one's jobs or of making a poor impression on one's supervisor and colleagues. The approach dimen-sion attributes presenteeism to one's responsibility and loyalty to the organizations. Thus, in terms of the avoidance dimension, when indi-viduals are confronted by pressure to engage in extended work hours, they may display presenteeism because they are afraid of punishment and they feel guilty for not meeting social expectations. In terms of the approach dimension, when employees feel a sense of pleasure and enjoyment in their job, they display presenteeism because their work helps them to achieve their life goals and makes them feel worthy and inspired. To some extent, the approach dimension of presenteeism motivation can be seen as a by-product of economic development. Rapid development creates a variety of interesting and meaningful jobs for people. This also stimulates employees to take advantage of their potential and energy to achieve success, which can, in turn, result in employees ignoring their health and their leisure time and persist in coming to work, even when feeling unwell. Further, the importance to Chinese employees of maintaining *mianzi* in front of their family members, peers or friends prompts them to spare no effort in pursuing career success, even at the cost of their health or family time.

Turning to social experiences, we note how many studies have demonstrated that the work domain interferes with the family domain; there has been comprehensive research on the interaction of the two (see, for example, Michel et al., 2011). Some presenteeism studies demonstrate that the conflicting demands of work and family increase the possibility of working while sick (Hansen & Andersen, 2008; Johns, 2011). Chinese employees perceive the role of family and work in their lives in a different way from their Western counterparts. The Chinese perception, however, appears contradictory. On the one hand, in China, as a so-called "family-centered" country, family is the key tie connecting individuals with society, and work is seen as an instrument to accomplish the family goals. This reality results in employees putting family interests above individual needs: Lau (1982) labels this *utilitarianistic familialism*. On the other hand, the family normally yields to work demands when these conflict with family demands (Zhang, Li, Wei & Yang, 2011). The Chinese traditional family pattern of "4–2–1" (two pairs of grandparents, one pair of parents, and one child) plays a role in this: this family pattern provides a great deal of family support for employees, with the result that they can focus on their work without distraction from family needs (Jin, Xu & Wang, 2014).[11] Thus, this seeming paradox may stimulate Chinese employees to display presenteeism because their values lead them to rank work above their individual needs.

Turning to psychological characteristics, we note that, growing up in a Confucian society, Chinese people are taught to perceive their identity as a member of a team, a group, a community, a society and their country, instead of perceiving themselves to be a lone individual. In 1980, Hofstede identified, based on his research on the differences in values between different countries, four dimensions for individuals' tendencies for perceiving and dealing with situations: collectivism/individualism, masculinity/femininity, power distance, and uncertainty avoidance. Collectivism and high power distance are the dimensions most relevant for understanding presenteeism in China. Collectivism refers to the extent that the individual identifies himself (or herself) as a member of group. High power distance refers individuals having a high tolerance towards authority and being more open to accepting an unequal distribution of power (Hofstede, 1980).

Hofstede's research demonstrated that China was a classic case of high collectivism and high level of power distance (Hofstede, 1980). Thus, Chinese employees tend to focus more on how to sustain harmonious interrelationships *(guanxi)* within their organizations, rather than to fulfill their own desires. *Guanxi* is an important feature of Chinese society and a major resource in achieving career success: see, for example, Wei, Liu, Chen & Wu (2010). The Conservation of Resources Theory suggests that individuals are prone to sustain and protect resources that are important to their career and to utilize them to achieve further success (Hobfoll, 1989). Thus, in order to maintain *guanxi* with supervisors and colleagues, employees are likely to display presenteeism in order to accomplish their work tasks on their own, without burdening their colleagues and, thereby, to impress their supervisors with their perseverance.

Also useful to consider in our discussion of presenteeism motivation for Chinese employees is the concept of traditionality developed by Farh (Farh, Early & Lin, 1997). Farh drew, in developing his concept, on the work of Yang and colleagues who based on their research into how people live in contemporary Chinese society. Yang and colleagues argue that there are five interrelated aspects of thinking: submission to authority; filial piety and ancestor worship; conservatism and endurance; fatalism and defensiveness; and male dominance (Yang, Yu & Yeh, 1989). Thus, a predisposition to submit to organizational authority leads to employees displaying presenteeism.

Farh's concept of traditionality focuses on the individual level and therefore contrasts with Hofstede's concern with societal level values such as collectivism. Farh applied his indigenous construct of traditionality to organizational research in China, defining it as follows (Farh, Hackett & Liang, 2007: 717).

The extent to which an individual endorses the traditional hierarchical role relationships prescribed by Confucian social ethics.

Farh argues that employees with a higher level of traditionality have more tolerance towards authority; thus, it is difficult for them to refuse organizational requests (Farh et al., 1997; Farh et al., 2007). Employees' reluctance to refuse organizational requests leads them to display presenteeism. Research has shown the concept of traditionality to be the most effective indicator of Chinese employees' personality and value orientation, possibly due to Farh and his colleagues' explicit Chinese focus in his construct (Farh et al., 1997; Hui, Lee & Rousseau, 2004).

Also useful in understanding presenteeism motivation is Aronsson & Gustafsson's (2005) concept of "boundarylessness"; this refers to the individuals' inability to set boundaries and to refuse demands. This construct has been shown to be an effective indicator of presenteeism behavior (Aronsson & Gustafsson, 2005; Hansen & Anderson, 2008).

The Variable Effects of Economic Fluctuation, Industry and Individual Demographic Characteristics on Presenteeism

In terms of economic fluctuations, it is clear that patterns of presenteeism vary with different levels of job insecurity, in line with economic fluctuation at the national and global levels. Thus, the UK Office of National Statistics revealed that the incidence of sickness absence decreased during the global financial crisis, but increased when the crisis was over, suggesting that the presenteeism may increase during crisis.[12] Similarly, in Taiwan, Lin & Lu (2013) found that, during the global financial crisis of 2009, Taiwanese employees experienced an increased fear of unemployment. Job insecurity spread among Taiwanese employees, prompting them to work while sick. In contemporary Chinese society, we suggest, however, that attention be paid to the effects of economic development. With a flourishing economy, employees are likely to be encouraged to work longer hours due to self-interest, self-accomplishment, and reward expectation. Thus, we suggest that the effect of economic fluctuations on employees' presenteeism behavior may be U-shaped.

In terms of industrial and occupational variations, research in Western countries has demonstrated that employees working in the high prestige occupations of medicine and education report a higher frequency of presenteeism due to their strong feelings of responsibility (Elstad & Vabø, 2008; McKevitt, Morgan, Dundas & Holland, 1997). We suggest that employees in high prestige occupations in China display a similar pattern of presenteeism. For teachers in China, competition in the nationwide college entrance examination is fierce; thus, teachers are likely to feel a heavy responsibility towards their students and experience considerable work stress, leading them to display presenteeism. Similarly for medical staff in China, we suggest that they, as in the West, feel a heavy responsibility towards their patients, leading them to experience work stress and to display presenteeism.

A further important occupational variation is the degree of job replaceability. Aronsson, Gustafsson & Dallner (2000), in their Swedish study, found that in the care and welfare and education sectors employees had a substantially increased risk of being at work when sick. They argue that the link between these occupations and a high degree of presenteeism was difficulties in finding replacement or stand-ins during their absence.

Research in Western countries demonstrates that educational level is negatively related to presenteeism (Johansen, 2013). The reason is that educational background is usually related to the level of job position, and the level of job position is related to flexibility and replaceability. Higher job position and lower replaceability lead to higher presenteeism (Johns, 2011).

In terms of demographic variations, Bierla, Huver & Richard (2011), in a study based in France, found age and gender to affect employees' presenteeism. Johansen (2013), in a study based in Norway and Sweden, found that lower educational levels correlated with higher presenteeism.

In China, we suggest that demographic characteristics moderate presenteeism in three ways.

(i) We suggest that, in China, older employees are more likely to adhere to traditional cultural values than younger ones. Thus, older employees express loyalty to their organization by adopting conservative attitudes toward absence leave: this means they are more likely to display presenteeism.

(ii) We suggest that, in China, male employees are more likely to display presenteeism than female ones. Our view is based on the traditional view of men's and women's roles in China: for example, consider the Chinese cultural expression *Nan zhu wai, nv zhu nei* (the husband is responsible for earning money to support the family while the wife is responsible for taking care of the household chores and the children).

(iii) We suggest that, in China, employees with lower job replaceability are more likely to display presenteeism than those with higher job replaceability as the abundant labor supply makes them fearful of taking long sick leave.

Suggestions for the Reduction of Presenteeism in China

Global Corporate Challenge (GCC) found, in their study of presenteeism, that employees reported being unproductive on the job on an average of 57.5 days per year, the equivalent of almost three working months.[13] Studies such as this suggest that effective managerial interventions for the control of presenteeism can offer competitive advantage for organizations and greater well-being for employees.

As there is a lack of empirical data on presenteeism in China, we are only in the initial stages of understanding the phenomenon of presenteeism and of making suggestions for reducing its negative effects. In this section, we offer suggestions for reducing presenteeism's negative effects based on Western countries' findings and advice but, when doing so, we also discuss how Chinese national culture might affect such advice. Studies have shown that organizations consider that their attempts to control presenteeism may offer opportunities for improving company performance through increasing organizational emphasis on employees' health (see, for example, Medibank, 2011). Given presenteeism's invisibility and its potentially lasting negative effects (Bergström et al., 2009), our suggestions are divided into two groups: ones mitigating the influence of presenteeism in the short term and ones promoting a health work improvement in the long term.

Reducing Presenteeism in the Short Term

Organizations seek to reduce presenteeism as much as possible. Hemp (2004) advises employers to take three steps in order to reduce presenteeism: (i) be aware (ii) identify and (iii) educate. Thus, employers should be aware of the problem of presenteeism; they should be equipped with the relevant knowledge to identify its causes and they should provide employees with health information and training. Just as the causes of presenteeism depend on culture, prevention should, however, also be tailored to different contexts.

The establishment in China of laws and regulations to address presenteeism has a long way to go and the shape of future legislation is beyond the scope of our discussion. We offer some advice, however, to Chinese employers on practical ways of reducing presenteeism.

(i) We suggest managers are provided with appropriate measurement scales in order to be able to track regularly employees' health status, as suggested in the literature review by Schultz et al. (2009), and with the tools they need to support employees in a confident and effective way, as suggested in the literature review by Garrow (2016).

(ii) We suggest that managers help employees to understand their health, to acknowledge their health problems, and to search for treatment as soon as possible, as suggested in the West by Smith (2016a), and to identify health conditions that could cause them future health problems, as suggested in the West by Medibank (2011).

(iii) We suggest that managers should not themselves display presenteeism but, instead, set an example to employees by understanding their own health and not working while ill.

(iv) We suggest employers establish organizational policies that go beyond national legal requirements – such introducing a pharmacy benefit plan in order to make it easier for employees to access medication, as suggested by Schultz et al. (2009).

(v) We suggest employers provide employees with return to work programs or support for employees so that they can regain competency by catching up with work they miss while ill, as suggested in the West by Munir, Yarker & Haslam (2008).

Promoting a Healthy Work Atmosphere in the Long Term

Presenteeism does not only lead to less productivity; it also triggers a high probability of absence in the future (Bergström et al., 2009). From a long-term standpoint, it is important to note that managerial interventions for improving employees' health can benefit both employers and employees. According to a recent White Paper issued by Underwriters Laboratories Workplace Health & Safety (2016),[14] organizations can address presenteeism through integrating worker health and workplace safety.[15] The White Paper reports that some organizations have separate specialized EHS professionals (environment, health, and safety) and administrative healthcare planners in independent but interrelated departments, so that employers may more easily regain lost productivity due to employees taking sick leave and can, therefore, more easily control the cost of healthcare insurance and sickness compensation.

As we saw above, a country's laws and regulations influence employee presenteeism; thus, the means of reducing presenteeism vary by country and culture. Currently, in China, there are no specific labor laws and regulations addressing presenteeism: there are no legal definitions, measurements and means of protecting employees' physical and mental health. Yang et al. (2015) studied the history of worker compensation in mainland China, and found that only *Regulations on Work Injury Insurance* regulate work-related deaths. Even so, this categorization applies only to sudden death within 48 hours, which to a large extent excludes most cases of *karoshi*. We note also that the failure in China to comply with the Labor Law requirements for maximum working hours. Although the Labor Law stipulates that an employee's weekly maximum of work should not exceed 44 hours, enforcement is not mandatory. In contrast, in Japan, South Korea, and Taiwan, countries that have long hours' cultures as does China, there is official recognition for work-related cardiovascular diseases, diseases which can lead to *karoshi*. Thus, we suggest that a primary and fundamental step needed in China is to establish a reasonable and strict compensation system: such a system should ensure that legal requirements for working hours are enforced and that penalties for illegal actions are imposed and enforced.

Turning to the organizational level, we strongly support the propositions that, as presenteeism reflect the symptoms of employees' underlying health problems (Centre for Mental Health, 2011), this critical breakthrough point for employers should be developing a health and well-being strategy that manages and solves health problems, instead of simply addressing symptoms (Centre for Mental Health, 2011). We make the following practical suggestions for Chinese organizations.

(i) We suggest providing continuous training, for both managers and employees, on the importance of occupational health so that they can better understand how to accomplish their tasks without endangering their health, as suggested in the literature review by Garrow (2016).

(ii) We suggest implementing advanced managerial practices, such as flexible working, so that employees are not encouraged to work beyond the maximum 44 hours per week. Also, we suggest that managers should be shown how to transform current strict sick leave systems and rewards for attendance as suggested by Garrow (2016).

(iii) We suggest that it is important to pay attention to employees' mental health. Managers should be trained to identify the early warning signs of mental illness and to help employees confront their problems as early as possible (Centre for Mental Health,

2011). Traditional Chinese culture and societal misunderstanding can lead employees to conceal their mental health difficulties and this may exacerbate presenteeism.

(iv) We suggest that organizations introduce programs with future-oriented perspectives; for example, organizations can set up in-house fitness centers, or provide employees with fitness cards for local centers, as a means of enabling employees to stay healthy (Schultz et al., 2009). Managers can monitor employees' health on a day-to-day basis in order to detect presenteeism as suggested by the Centre for Mental Health (2011). Organizations can implement programs developed from the findings of Western research. For example, Work Health Promotions (WHP) has proved effective at reducing presenteeism.[16] WHP focuses on four aspects: organizational leadership, health risk screening, individually tailored programs, and a supportive workplace culture (Cancelliere, Cassidy, Ammendolia & Côté, 2011; Garrow, 2016).

Suggestions for Future Research on Presenteeism in China

Given the discussion above, our recommendations for future research in China emphasize the importance of the effect of Chinese culture on presenteeism. We suggest the following research.

(i) Researchers studying the effect of national culture, organizational policy and individual perceptions on presenteeism in Chinese workplaces should go further than merely comparing the influences of these factors on presenteeism between China and Western countries (Lu et al., 2013a). Although such a research focus is valuable, we suggest that researchers need to expand their interests and investigate how presenteeism in China compares and contrasts with that in other countries. It is important to take into account in such wider research that, while presenteeism behavior appears similar across the world, presenteeism motivations may vary widely between countries. Thus, while presenteeism in China is linked to Confucian values and Chinese personality traits (Lin & Lu, 2013), these factors are unlikely to be pertinent for understanding presenteeism in a Western country. Researchers need to analyze which factors affect presenteeism generally and which factors affect presenteeism in particular contexts.

(ii) A difficulty with controlling presenteeism in Chinese organizations is the entrenched cultural belief, held by both managers and employees, that displaying presenteeism equates with displaying organizational citizenship behavior (OCB) (Taylor, 2016). Thus, we suggest that organizations should seek to persuade their members at all levels that they will not be rewarded for presenteeism as this is dysfunctional citizen behavior.

(iii) We suggest that scholars with an interest of presenteeism should integrate their research with that undertaken in other fields, such as the welfare of vulnerable groups in society and the representation of women in the labor force (Lin & Lu, 2013). This grouping of related fields could lead to valuable cross-fertilization of theories and concepts that could play a significant role in increasing our understanding of how to combat the negative effects of presenteeism on employees' well-being and organizations' profits.

Notes

1. Lu & Chou (in press) drew this percentage form the Executive Yuan of the Directorate-General of Budget, Accounting and Statistics (DGBAS).
2. Presenteeism can also include other behavior such as staying at work after the formal finishing time.
3. KPMG-Econtech conducted this research on behalf of Medibank.
4. Centre for Mental Health, a UK mental health charity, was founded by the Gatsby Charitable Foundation. It began life in March 1985, as the National Unit for Psychiatric Research and Development (NUPRD). Since July 2010 it has been known as Centre for Mental Health. As an entirely independent charity, it focuses on the two key areas: employment and criminal justice. See www.centreformentalhealth.org.uk.
5. QianChengWuYou, also known as 51job, is an influential human resource service supplier in China and is listed on the NASDAQ in the United States as JOBS. Using Internet media and advanced information technology, the company employs experienced consultants with diverse specialties to provide organizations with comprehensive professional HR services such as recruitment, training, evaluation, and outsourcing. One of the leading HR service institutions, QianChengWuYou has established 25 offices across China.
6. ZhilianZhaopin started in 1994 and has been listed on the New York Stock Exchange as ZPIN since 2014. Its strategic goal is to establish a platform for both organizations and job hunters. It aims to offer

professional career development services to job hunters such as self-evaluation, online recruitment, and career training so as to create a closed loop for the Chinese labor market.

7. See https://ibiweb.org/.

8. *Regulations on the medical treatment period of sickness and non-industrial injury among employees* was issued by the Department of Labor of China in 1995 with the authorization number of 479, in accordance with the requirements of the Labor Law. It focuses on medical treatment periods.

9. *Regulations on work injury insurance* was issued by the State Department of China, and it came into force in 2004.

10. According to Grinyer & Singleton (2000), organizations use "trigger points" to limit the number of occasions on which staff take sick leave.

11. These traditional family patter will change to a new tendency of "4–2–2" because China began to relax the one-child policy in 2014.

12. See the reference: UK Office of National Statistics, available at www.statistics.gov.uk.

13. Smith (2016a). The GCC report and data were quoted by Smith, and he published this article on the EHS today website.
Here is the reference link: http://ehstoday.com/safety-leadership/presenteeism-costs-business-10-times-more-absenteeism.

14. The white paper "Phoning It In: The Dilemma of Employee Presenteeism" was issued by UL Workplace Health & Safety in 2016. Please find it at the web link: http://cdn2.hubspot.net/hubfs/356480/Worker_Presenteeism_White_Paper.pdf.

15. This paper was quoted by Smith (2016b).
Here is the reference link: http://ehstoday.com/health/phoning-it-do-you-know-how-much-presenteeism-costs-your-business

16. Work Health Promotions was defined by European Network for Workplace Health Promotion as "the combined efforts of employers, employees and society to improve the mental and physical health and well-being of people at work." Reference: Luxembourg Declaration on workplace health promotion in the European Union, 1997.

References

Aronsson, G. & Gustafsson, K. (2005). Sickness presenteeism: prevalence, attendance-pressure factors, and an outline of a model for research. *Journal of Occupational and Environmental Medicine*, 47(9), 958–966.

Aronsson, G., Gustafsson, K. & Dallner, M. (2000). Sick but yet at work. An empirical study of sickness presenteeism. *Journal of Epidemiology and Community Health*, 54(7), 502–509.

Baker-McClearn, D., Greasley, K., Dale, J. & Griffith, F. (2010). Absence management and presenteeism: The pressures on employees to attend work and the impact of attendance on performance. *Human Resource Management Journal*, 20(3), 311–328.

Bergström, G., Bodin, L., Hagberg, J., Lindh, T., Aronsson, G. & Josephson, M. (2009). Does sickness presenteeism have an impact on future general health?. *International Archives of Occupational and Environmental Health*, 82(10), 1179–1190.

Bierla, I., Huver, B. & Richard, S. (2011). Presenteeism at work: the influence of managers. *International Journal of Business and Management Studies*, 3(2), 97–107.

Cancelliere, C., Cassidy, J. D., Ammendolia, C. & Côté, P. (2011). Are workplace health promotion programs effective at improving presenteeism in workers? A systematic review and best evidence synthesis of the literature. *BMC Public Health*, 11(1), 395.

Centre for Mental Health (2011). Managing presenteeism: a discussion paper. Retrieved www.centreformentalhealth.org.uk/managing-presenteeism.

Cheng, B. S. (1990). Quantitative testing of organizational cultural values. *Journal of Chinese Psychology*, 33, 31–49.

Cheng, Y., Park, J., Kim, Y. & Kawakami, N. (2012). The recognition of occupational diseases attributed to heavy workloads: experiences in Japan, Korea, and Taiwan. *International Archives of Occupational and Environmental Health*, 85(7), 791–799.

Collins, J. J., Baase, C. M., Sharda, C. E. et al. (2005). The assessment of chronic health conditions on work performance, absence, and total economic impact for employers. *Journal of Occupational and Environmental Medicine*, 47(6), 547–557.

Dew, K., Keefe, V. & Small, K. (2005). "Choosing" to work when sick: workplace presenteeism. *Social Science & Medicine*, 60(10), 2273–2282.

Dong, X. F., Liu, Y. J., Wang, J. X. & Peng, Z. M. (2013). Development of the Work Limitations Questionnaire Chinese version (WLQ-C). *Chinese Journal of Practical Nursing*, 29(12), 54–57.

Elstad, J. I. & Vabø, M. (2008). Job stress, sickness absence and sickness presenteeism in Nordic elderly care. *Scandinavian Journal of Public Health*, 36(5), 467–474.

Fan, Y. (2000). A classification of Chinese culture. *Cross Cultural Management: An International Journal*, 7(2), 3–10.

Farh, J. L., Earley, P. C. & Lin, S. C. (1997). Impetus for action: A cultural analysis of justice and organizational citizenship behavior in Chinese society. *Administrative Science Quarterly*, 42, 421–444.

Farh, J. L., Hackett, R. D. & Liang, J. (2007). Individual-level cultural values as moderators of perceived organizational support–employee outcome relationships in China: Comparing the effects of power distance and traditionality. *Academy of Management Journal*, 50(3), 715–729.

Fung, Y. L. (1997). *A Short History of Chinese Philosophy*. Simon and Schuster.

Garrow, V. (2016). Presenteeism: a review of current thinking. *Institute for Employment Studies Report*, 507.

Gosselin, E., Lemyre, L. & Corneil, W. (2013). Presenteeism and absenteeism: Differentiated understanding of related phenomena. *Journal of Occupational Health Psychology*, 18(1), 75–86.

Grinyer, A. & Singleton, V. (2000). Sickness absence as risk-taking behaviour: a study of organisational and cultural factors in the public sector. *Health, Risk & Society*, 2(1), 7–21.

Hansen, C. D. & Andersen, J. H. (2008). Going ill to work–What personal circumstances, attitudes and work-related factors are associated with sickness presenteeism? *Social Science & Medicine*, 67(6), 956–964.

Hemp, P. (2004). Presenteeism: At work-but out of it. *Harvard Business Review*, 82(10), 49–58.

Hobfoll, S. E. (1989). Conservation of resources: A new attempt at conceptualizing stress. *American Psychologist*, 44(3), 513–524.

Hofstede, G. (1980). Motivation, leadership, and organization: do American theories apply abroad? *Organizational Dynamics*, 9(1), 42–63.

Hou, W. J. & Zhan, J. (2016). Measuring productivity loss ascribed to presenteeism in the workplace. *Human Resource Development of China*, 13, 48–54. (In Chinese.)

Hui, C., Lee, C. & Rousseau, D. M. (2004). Psychological contract and organizational citizenship behavior in china: Investigating generalizability and instrumentality. *Journal of Applied Psychology*, 89, 311–321.

International Institute for Management Development (IMD). (2010). *The World Competitiveness Yearbook*. IMD, Lausanne.

Iwasaki, K., Takahashi, M. & Nakata, A. (2006). Health problems due to long working hours in Japan: working hours, workers' compensation (Karoshi), and preventive measures. *Industrial Health*, 44(4), 537–540.

Jin, J. F., Xu, S. & Wang, Y. X. (2014). A Comparison Study of Role Overload, Work-Family Conflict and Depression between China and North America: The Moderation Effect of Social Support. *Acta Psychologica Sinica*, 8, 010. (In Chinese.)

Johansen, V. (2013). Sickness presenteeism in Norway and Sweden. *Nordic Journal of Social Research*, 3, 88–102.

Johns, G. (2010). Presenteeism in the workplace: A review and research agenda. *Journal of Organizational Behavior*, 31(4), 519–542.

Johns, G. (2011). Attendance dynamics at work: the antecedents and correlates of presenteeism, absenteeism, and productivity loss. *Journal of Occupational Health Psychology*, 16(4), 483.

Labor Law of People's Republic of China. 1995.

Lau, S. K. 1982. *Society and Politics in Hong Kong*. Hong Kong: Chinese University Press.

Lin, H. Y. & Lu, L. (2013). Presenteeism in workplace: Constructing a cross-cultural framework. *Journal of Human Resource Management (Taiwan)*, 13(3), 29–55. (In Chinese.)

Liu, S. (2003). Cultures within culture: Unity and diversity of two generations of employees in state-owned enterprises. *Human Relations*, 56(4), 387–417.

Lu, L. & Chou, C. Y. (in press). To be published in C. L. Cooper & M. Leiter (Eds.), *Routledge Companion to Wellbeing at Work*. London, UK: Routledge.

Lu, L., Kao, S. F., Chang, T. T., Wu, H. P. & Jin, Z. (2008). The individual-and social-oriented Chinese bicultural self: A subcultural analysis contrasting mainland Chinese and Taiwanese. *Social Behavior and Personality: an International Journal*, 36(3), 337–346.

Lu, L., Cooper, C. & Yen Lin, H. (2013a). A cross-cultural examination of presenteeism and supervisory support. *Career Development International*, 18(5), 440–456.

Lu, L., Lin, H. Y. & Cooper, C. L. (2013b). Unhealthy and present: Motives and consequences of the act of presenteeism among Taiwanese employees. *Journal of Occupational Health Psychology*, 18(4), 406–416.

McKevitt, C., Morgan, M., Dundas, R. & Holland, W. W. (1997). Sickness absence and "working through" illness: A comparison of two professional groups. *Journal of Public Health Medicine*, 19, 295–300.

Medibank (2011). Sick at work: The cost of presenteeism to your business and the economy. Research paper draws on the results from Economic Modelling of the Cost of Presenteeism in Australia: 2011 Update (Medibank, KPMG Econtech) published in July 2011.

Meijman, T.F. & Mulder, G. (1998), Psychological aspects of workload, in Drenth, P. J., Thierry, H. & de Wolff, C. J. (Eds.), *Handbook of Work and Organizational Psychology*, 2nd ed., Taylor & Francis, Hove, pp. 5–33.

Michel, J. S., Kotrba, L. M., Mitchelson, J. K., Clark, M. A. & Baltes, B. B. (2011). Antecedents of work–family conflict: A meta-analytic review. *Journal of Organizational Behavior*, 32(5), 689–725.

Munir, F., Yarker, J. & Haslam, C. (2008). Sickness absence management: encouraging attendance or "risk-taking" presenteeism in employees with chronic illness? *Disability and Rehabilitation*, 30(19), 1461–1472.

Porter, G. (2004). Work, work ethic, work excess. *Journal of Organizational Change Management*, 17(5), 424–439.

Ralston, D. A., Gustafson, D. J., Elsass, P. M., Cheung, F. & Terpstra, R. H. (1992). Eastern values: A comparison of managers in the United States, Hong Kong, and the People's Republic of China. *Journal of Applied Psychology*, 77(5), 664–671.

Redding, G. (1990). *The Spirit of Chinese Capitalism (Vol. 22)*. Walter de Gruyter.

Schultz, A. B., Chen, C. Y. & Edington, D. W. (2009). The cost and impact of health conditions on presenteeism to employers. *Pharmacoeconomics*, 27 (5), 365–378.

Smith. S. (2016a). Presenteeism Cost Business 10 Times More than Absenteeism. *EHS Today*.

Smith. S. (2016b). Phoning it in: do you know how much presenteeism costs your business? *EHS Today*.

Taylor, J. (2016). Working extra hours in the Australian public service: Organizational drivers and consequences. *Review of Public Personnel Administration*, 0734371X16658335.

Vertinsky, I., Tse, D. K., Wehrung, D. A. & Lee, K. H. (1990). Organizational design and management norms: A comparative study of managers' perceptions in the People's Republic of China, Hong Kong, and Canada. *Journal of Management*, 16(4), 853–867.

Wei, L. Q., Liu, J., Chen, Y. Y. & Wu, L. Z. (2010). Political skill, supervisor–subordinate guanxi and career prospects in Chinese firms. *Journal of Management Studies*, 47(3), 437–454.

Whitcomb, L. L., Erdener, C. B. & Li, C. (1998). Business ethical values in China and the US. *Journal of Business Ethics*, 17(8), 839–852.

Yang, K. S., Yu, A. B. & Yeh, M. H. (1989). Chinese individual modernity and traditionality: Construct definition and measurement. *Proceedings of the Interdisciplinary Conference on Chinese Psychology and Behavior* (Vol. 2870354) (In Chinese.)

Yang, K. S. & Cheng, B. S. (1987). Traditional value, modernity and organizational behavior: amicro-examination of post-Confucian hypotheses. *The Central Research Institute of Ethnology*, 64, 1–49.

Yang, Z., Yang, B. & Li, J. (2015). Perspectives on compensation and legislation of death due to work overload: Karoshi. *An International Journal of Medicine*, 108(4), 349–350.

Zhang, M., Li, H., Wei, J. & Yang, B. Y. (2011). Cross-over effects or direct effects? The mechanism linking work–family conflict with outcomes. *Acta Psychological Sinica*, 43, 573–588. (In Chinese.)

Zhao, F., Dai, J. M., Yan, S. Y., Yang, P. D. & Fu, H. (2010). Reliability and validity of Stanford Presenteeism Scale Chinese version. *Chinese Journal of Industrial Hygiene and Occupational Disease*, 28(9), 679–682. (In Chinese.)

Index

Printed in the United States
by Baker & Taylor Publisher Services